B+T
19.50
14 Jan'80

*The Economic Consequences
of Slowing Population Growth*

STUDIES IN POPULATION

Under the Editorship of: H. H. WINSBOROUGH
Department of Sociology
University of Wisconsin
Madison, Wisconsin

Samuel H. Preston, Nathan Keyfitz, and Robert Schoen. Causes of Death: **Life Tables for National Populations.**

Otis Dudley Duncan, David L. Featherman, and Beverly Duncan. Socioeconomic Background and Achievement.

James A. Sweet. Women in the Labor Force.

Tertius Chandler and Gerald Fox. 3000 Years of Urban Growth.

William H. Sewell and Robert M. Hauser. Education, Occupation, and Earnings: Achievement in the Early Career.

Otis Dudley Duncan. Introduction to Structural Equation Models.

William H. Sewell, Robert M. Hauser, and David L. Featherman (Eds.). Schooling and Achievement in American Society.

Henry Shryock, Jacob S. Siegel, and Associates. The Methods and Materials of Demography. *Condensed Edition by Edward Stockwell.*

Samuel H. Preston. Mortality Patterns in National Populations: **With Special Reference to Recorded Causes of Death.**

Robert M. Hauser and David L. Featherman. The Process of Stratification: Trends and Analyses.

Ronald R. Rindfuss and James A. Sweet. Postwar Fertility Trends and Differentials in the United States.

David L. Featherman and Robert M. Hauser. Opportunity and Change.

Karl E. Taeuber, Larry L. Bumpass, and James A. Sweet (Eds.). Social Demography.

Thomas J. Espenshade and William J. Serow (Eds.). The Economic Consequences of Slowing Population Growth.

In preparation

Frank D. Bean and W. Parker Frisbie (Eds.). The Demography of Racial and Ethnic Groups.

Maris A. Vinovskis (Ed.). Studies in American Historical Demography.

The Economic Consequences of Slowing Population Growth

Edited by

Thomas J. Espenshade
Department of Economics and Center for the Study of Population
Florida State University

William J. Serow
Tayloe Murphy Institute
University of Virginia

ACADEMIC PRESS   New York   San Francisco   London   1978
A Subsidiary of Harcourt Brace Jovanovich, Publishers

The conference out of which the papers included in this volume were generated was sponsored by the Center for Population Research and its parent organization, the National Institute of Child Health and Human Development (a subdivision of the National Institutes of Health) and was held in May 1977 in Washington.

COPYRIGHT © 1978, BY ACADEMIC PRESS, INC.
ALL RIGHTS RESERVED.
NO PART OF THIS PUBLICATION MAY BE REPRODUCED OR
TRANSMITTED IN ANY FORM OR BY ANY MEANS ELECTRONIC
OR MECHANICAL, INCLUDING PHOTOCOPY, RECORDING, OR ANY
INFORMATION STORAGE AND RETRIEVAL SYSTEM, WITHOUT
PERMISSION IN WRITING FROM THE PUBLISHER.

ACADEMIC PRESS, INC.
111 Fifth Avenue, New York, New York 10003

United Kingdom Edition published by
ACADEMIC PRESS, INC. (LONDON) LTD.
24/28 Oval Road, London NW1 7DX

Library of Congress Cataloging in Publication Data
Main entry under title:

The Economic consequences of slowing population growth.

Bibliography: p.
Includes index.
1. United States--Population--Economic aspects
--Addresses, essays, lectures.   I.   Espenshade, Thomas J.
II.   Serow, William J.
HB3505.E35   330.9'73'092   78-3334
ISBN 0-12-242450-6

PRINTED IN THE UNITED STATES OF AMERICA

Contents

List of Contributors	ix
Foreword	xi
Preface	xiii
List of Tables	xvii
List of Illustrations	xix

1
The Demographic Dimensions of Slowing Population Growth in the United States — 1
V. JEFFERY EVANS AND SIGNE I. WETROGAN

Trends and Prospects in U.S. Population Growth	2
Changes in Age Composition	5
Spatial Redistribution of the Population	8
Conclusion	10

2
The Economics of Declining Population Growth: An Assessment of the Current Literature — 13
WILLIAM J. SEROW AND THOMAS J. ESPENSHADE

Demographic Aspects	15
Theoretical Developments	16

Empirical Studies	22
Policy Implications and Additional Suggestions for Further Research	37

3
Zero Population Growth Now: The Lessons from Europe   41
HILDE WANDER

Zero Population Growth: Theory and Reality	41
Social and Economic Implications during the Transition to Zero Population Growth	51
Future Implications of Zero Population Growth or Progressive Decline	59

4
The Fiscal Policy Dilemma: Cyclical Swings Dominated by Supply-Side Constraints   71
MICHAEL L. WACHTER AND SUSAN M. WACHTER

Amendments to the Secular Stagnation and Kuznets Cycle Models	74
A Simplified Model of Supply-Side Imbalances	76
Estimating the Nonaccelerating-Inflation Rate of Unemployment	80
The Capital Stock Bottleneck	85
The Potential Impact of the Fertility Twist and Slowing Population Growth	91
The Role of Fiscal Policy	95

5
Is Secular Stagnation Just around the Corner? A Survey of the Influences of Slowing Population Growth upon Investment Demand   101
LARRY NEAL

Introduction, Summary, and Outline of Conclusions	101
Population and Investment Demand in the Short Run	104

Contents vii

Population and Investment Demand in the Long Run	108
Slower Population Growth and Investment Demand during Trend Transitions:	
The Long-Swing Hypothesis Revisited	111
Emerging Characteristics	
of the New Economic–Demographic Era	120

6
The Effects of Slowing Population Growth on Long-Run Economic Growth in the United States during the Next Half Century   127
RONALD G. RIDKER

Determinants of Economic Growth	128
Results	142
Conclusions and Qualifications	153

7
Social Security and Aging Populations   157
ALFRED M. PITTS

Slowing Population Growth and the Social Security System	159
Slowing Population Growth and Pay-As-You-Go	183
Alternative Financing Approaches	187
The Case for Reform and the Objectives of Social Security	190

8
The Impact of Demographic Change on the Distribution of Earned Income and the AFDC Program: 1975–1985   197
RICHARD F. WERTHEIMER II AND SHEILA R. ZEDLEWSKI

Introduction	197
Critical Features of DYNASIM	198
Key Assumptions and Mechanics of the Simulations	202
Simulation Results	207

9
*Emerging Public Concerns
over U.S. Population Movements
in an Era of Slowing Growth*   225

PETER A. MORRISON

Introduction	225
The Contrasting Growth Trends in Population and Households	228
New Migration Trends	230
Population Decline in Individual Metropolitan Areas	236
Emerging Concerns	245

10
Policy Implications and Future Research Needs   247

ROBERT L. CLARK

Introduction	247
Summary Findings	250
Policy Implications	258
Further Research Needs	259

References	*263*
Index	*281*

List of Contributors

Numbers in parentheses indicate the pages on which the authors' contributions begin.

ROBERT L. CLARK (247), Department of Economics and Business, North Carolina State University, Raleigh, North Carolina 27650

THOMAS J. ESPENSHADE (13), Department of Economics and Center for the Study of Population, Florida State University, Tallahassee, Florida 32306

V. JEFFERY EVANS (1), Center for Population Research, National Institute of Child Health and Human Development, Bethesda, Maryland 20014

PETER A. MORRISON (225), The Rand Corporation, Santa Monica, California 90406

LARRY NEAL (101), Department of Economics, University of Illinois at Urbana–Champaign, Urbana, Illinois 61801

ALFRED M. PITTS (157), Department of Economics and Center for Demographic Studies, Duke University, Durham, North Carolina 27706

RONALD G. RIDKER (127), Resources for the Future, 1755 Massachusetts Avenue, N.W., Washington, D.C. 20036

WILLIAM J. SEROW (13), Population Studies Center, Tayloe Murphy Institute, University of Virginia, Charlottesville, Virginia 22906

MICHAEL L. WACHTER (71), Department of Economics, University of Pennsylvania, Philadelphia, Pennsylvania 19174

SUSAN M. WACHTER (71), Department of Finance, Wharton School, University of Pennsylvania, Philadelphia, Pennsylvania 19174

HILDE WANDER (41), Kiel Institute of World Economics, 23 Kiel 1, Düsternbrooker Weg 120/122, Federal Republic of Germany
RICHARD F. WERTHEIMER II (197), The Urban Institute, 2100 M Street, N.W., Washington, D.C. 20037
SIGNE I. WETROGAN (1), Population Division, U.S. Bureau of the Census, Suitland, Maryland 20023
SHEILA RAFFERTY ZEDLEWSKI (197), The Urban Institute, 2100 M Street, N.W., Washington, D.C. 20037

Foreword

The Center for Population Research has a continuing interest in the causes and consequences of population change. The Center has a particular interest in delineating the possible consequences of the falling rate of population growth in the United States. It is likely that this rate will remain low or possibly fall even further in the near future and that this phenomenon could necessitate important adjustments in the economy and in the social structure of our country. Only by exploring the relationships between population and socioeconomic change can we know whether our society is adjusting optimally in response to changed demographic conditions.

This book examines a number of relationships between the rate of population growth and the economy. Its chapters were, for the most part, prepared for a conference entitled "The Economic Consequences of Slowing Population Growth," sponsored by the Center and held at NIH May 26-27, 1977. The conference was designed to assess what is known about the relationship of slowing population growth to the economy and to bring together social scientists who are engaged in empirical research in order to extend the frontiers of knowledge in this area. Another objective of the conference was to identify the important policy and research questions that demand to be answered by future research. This book reflects all three aspects of that conference, and the reader can expect to encounter a wide variety of topics and research styles.

It is hoped that the chapters in this book will be useful to demographers, economists, and public policymakers and that they will stimulate more social scientists to become involved in population research in general and in the economic consequences of slowing population growth in particular.

V. Jeffery Evans
Center for Population Research
National Institute of Child Health and Human Development
National Institutes of Health

Preface

A book appearing 15 or 20 years ago with this title would very probably have addressed itself to population and economic issues in the Third World. It is only in the past decade, as fertility levels in industrialized countries began to approach and then dip even further down than those experienced during the depression era of the 1930s, that concern has been renewed over the long-run ramifications—economic, social, and political, as well as demographic—of an epoch of sustained low fertility.

Interest in the economic consequences of declining population growth dates back at least to the 1930s, when it was believed, especially in Europe, that the falling birth rate was partly responsible for the adverse economic trends. Because of a shorter-lived baby boom and, hence, a more rapid return to slower growth after World War II, concern with the implications of low fertility resumed more quickly in Europe than in North America or Oceania. In 1965, for example, Joseph Stassart published *Les avantages et les inconvénients économique d'une population stationnaire* (The Hague: Martinus Nijhoff). Interest in the demographic possibilities for the United States developed shortly thereafter, as witnessed by Tomas Frejka's article in the November 1968 issue of *Population Studies* ("Reflections on the Demographic Conditions Needed to Establish a U.S. Stationary Population Growth"). This was followed by a session at the 1970 annual meeting of the Population Association of America for which Frank Notestein prepared a paper dealing with the broader consequences of zero population growth (Notestein's paper and the comments by Philip Hauser, Judith Blake, and Paul Demeny are published in the October–December 1970 issue of *Population Index*). The first specifically economic analysis was published in 1971 by Joseph Spengler under the title *Declining Population Growth Revisited* (Chapel Hill: Carolina Population Center). In 1972, the research reports of the Commission on Population Growth and the American Future appeared, and many of these, particularly those in Volume 2 edited by Elliott R. Morss and Ritchie H. Reed (*Economic Aspects of Population Change*), dealt especially with the economic consequences of declining fertility. Later, in 1975, Joseph Spengler edited a volume of papers entitled *Zero Population Growth: Implications* (Chapel Hill: Carolina Population Center), many of which examined economic implications of a stationary population.

Yet these and the many pieces of research output that have appeared subsequently do not encompass all the ramifications that sustained low fertility will have in an industrialized economy. This book is designed to meet an additional part of this need.

The present volume is grouped into three parts. The first of these includes the chapters by Evans and Wetrogan, Serow and Espenshade, and Wander. The purpose of these is to inform the reader of the background to the present situation, including the demographic trends and prospects for the United States; of those economic consequences that we know, those of which we are uncertain, and those of which we are ignorant; and of what the actual consequences of low fertility have been in that region of the world where low fertility has been the norm for the past two generations. These papers, taken together, present a review and critique of the current state of the art and underscore the importance of the findings in the subsequent sections.

The second section, which includes the chapters by Wachter and Wachter, Neal, and Ridker, is intended as a study of the main economic consequences of declining population growth rates. Wachter and Wachter analyze the relationship between economic policy, unemployment, and inflation and prescribe policy measures aimed at reducing levels of unemployment without touching off accelerating inflation. The demographic component is crucial in determining the rate of unemployment that can be attained without accelerating inflation. The entry of the baby boom cohorts into the labor market substantially increased this rate, and the passage of these cohorts into more stable employment ages should have the opposite effect.

Neal's contribution deals with the second major determinant of output levels, that is, capital formation and investment. Neal suggests the possibility of a new era in economic–demographic interactions. In the past, population growth responded positively (in the form of immigration and fertility) to economic change, creating an additional demand for investment. This process continued until deferred household formation and immigration were exhausted, touching off the downward part of the cycle. Neal's analysis suggests that the cycle has been reversed in the postwar period, with increases in output being associated with a decrease in births, and vice versa. The long-run effects of this new relationship, if unchecked, can be adverse, since future investment booms can be choked off by labor shortages. The easing of present immigration laws and encouragement of American investment abroad (if it creates demand for U.S. exports) are suggested by Neal as possible means of avoiding this outcome.

Ridker's chapter is somewhat more broadly based than the two preceding in that it presents the results of a large-scale economic simulation model employing three alternative population projections. The nature of the demographic assumptions is such that one may contrast the short-, medium-, and long-term effects of fertility rates leading to moderate population increase, population stabilization, and population decline. Even though the range of final population increase by the end of the projection period (the year 2025) is over 100 million persons, relative economic differences turn out to be fairly insignificant. Perhaps more important is the nature of changes in the future vis-à-vis present circumstances. Ridker's projections of components of the Gross National Product (GNP), of distribution of consumption, and of demand for and production of energy are crucial inputs into adequate planning to cope with slower rates of population growth.

The third section of the book includes chapters by Pitts, Wertheimer and Zedlewski, and Morrison and stresses the implications for public programs in an era of slowing population growth. Pitts's analysis of social security examines the need for restructuring the present system to avoid both depletion of the fund and excessive burden on the working population. In addition to the possibility of full reserve funding, Pitts calls for a rethinking of the basic nature of the system so that the government would act as an insurer of the last resort for the benefit of those whose retirement savings have been adversely affected by economic uncertainty.

The Wertheimer–Zedlewski chapter presents short-run simulations (1975–1985) showing the effects of varying fertility, marriage, and divorce rates on the size distribution of family income and on the size and cost of the Aid to Families with Dependent Children (AFDC) program. Although the results may not be sufficient to answer questions on the long-run economic consequences of slowing population growth, the approach of Wertheimer and Zedlewski serves as a model for those concerned with specific program areas.

Morrison's chapter is more broadly concerned with the consequences of declining fertility and population redistribution at the subnational level. With reductions in the level of fertility, population change at the local level is becoming more and more the consequence of internal migration. In planning for the provision of public services, especially those that are age-related (such as education), it becomes increasingly important for local governments to cope with local migration trends. Aid to local governments is often population dependent, yet areas whose population (and tax base) declines stand to lose federal and state largesse even though their needs may actually be greater. On the other side of the coin, some local areas are attempting to limit population growth through exclusionary zoning and the like, thus raising the constitutional issue of the freedom to travel.

In the final chapter, Clark transcends the tripartite division we have suggested. His paper summarizes the findings of the previous chapters and tells us what we have learned that we did not know before; it stresses the implications for demographic and economic policy that are inherent in the results; and it indicates what additional research is still needed in this newly emerging area.

List of Tables

Table 1.1	Estimates and Projections of the Population of the United States in Selected Age Groups: 1900-2050	6-7
Table 1.2	Estimates of the Population of the United States by Census Region: 1900-1976	9
Table 3.1	Net Reproduction Rates in Selected Western European Countries: 1960, 1964, 1970, and Latest Available Year	42
Table 3.2	Natural Increase in Selected Western European Countries: 1960, 1964, 1970, 1975, 1976 (per 1,000 of mean population)	43
Table 3.3	Patterns of Variation in Age Composition of West German Native Females after Stabilization of Assumed Cycles of Fertility Change	48
Table 4.1	U_{NI}^t: Normalized Rate of Unemployment, 1955, 1965, and 1975, 14 Age-Sex Groups	83
Table 4.2	U_{NI}: Normalized Unemployment Rate Series, 1948-1976	84
Table 4.3	Growth Rates in Labor and Capital, 1948-1976	86
Table 4.4	Estimated Unemployment Rate Equations, 1954:1-1977:2	88
Table 4.5	Unemployment Rate Associated with Capacity Utilization at 93%	89
Table 5.1	Summary of U.S. Statistics: Testing Equality of Means and Variances: 1890-1929 and 1930-1968	118
Table 5.2	Low-Frequency Coherence Statistics between Economic and Demographic Variables, 1890-1929 Compared with 1930-1968	119
Table 6.1	Population by Age Groupings and Median Age, Alternative Projections, 1972-2025	130
Table 6.2	Labor Force and Dependency Ratios, Alternative Projections, 1972-2025	132
Table 6.3	GNP and Principal Components, Alternative Population Projections, 1975-2025	144
Table 6.4	Educational and Health Expenditures, Public plus Private, Alternative Population Projections, 1975-2025	146
Table 6.5	Composition of Consumption Expenditures, Alternative Population Projections, 1975-2025	147

Table 6.6	Energy Production and Use, Alternative Population Projections, 1975–2025	149
Table 6.7	Environmental Indexes, Alternative Population Projections, 1975–2025	151–152
Table 7.1	Federal Outlays for Selected Old-Age Assistance Programs, Fiscal 1974	160
Table 7.2	Long-Run OASDI Current Cost Projections, 1975–2050 (Present Overindexed System)	164
Table 7.3	Projections of the Old-Age Dependency Ratio under Various Fertility Assumptions	170
Table 7.4	Long-Run OASDI Cost Estimates under Various Fertility Assumptions Using Present Overindexed System and "Decoupled" System	173
Table 7.5	Sensitivity of OASDI Cost Projections to Changes in Selected Assumptions ("Decoupled System")	175
Table 8.1	Births, Deaths, Marriages, and Divorces in the Base Run, 1975–1985 (numbers in 1000s)	205
Table 8.2	Specifications of the Base Run and the Eight Experiments	208
Table 8.3	Percentage Change in the Number of Families, Number of Persons, and Average Family Size, 1974–1985	209
Table 8.4	Persons by Age and Marital Status in 1985 in the High and Low Stability Simulations (numbers in 1000s)	211
Table 8.5	The Effect of Demographic Change on the Distribution of Total Family Income in 1985	213
Table 8.6	AFDC Program Projections: Base Run Assumptions	215
Table 8.7	Percentage Change in AFDC Caseload from the Base Run	217
Table 8.8	AFDC Caseload Elasticities	218
Table 8.9	Impact of High and Low Family Stability on the AFDC Caseload	220
Table 8.10	AFDC Caseload Regression	???
Table 9.1	Population Change by Component for Each Region: 5-Year Periods, 1950–1975 (in millions. Periods begin July 1.)	233
Table 9.2	Net Migration for Selected Areas: 5-Year Periods, 1950–1975	235
Table 9.3	Components of Population Change for Groups of Metropolitan and Nonmetropolitan Counties: 1960–1970 and 1970–1975	237
Table 9.4	Components of Population Change for 36 SMSAs with Declining Population, 1970–1975	239

List of Illustrations

Figure 1.1 Estimates and projections of the population of the United States: 1900–2050.   3
Figure 1.2 Estimates and projections of the annual growth rate of the United States population: 1900–2050.   4
Figure 3.1 Net reproduction rates (N) of selected West European countries, 1920–1976.   44
Figure 3.2 The age composition in Germany (1933 and 1975) and in Sweden (1930 and 1973) compared with respective stationary models (females only).   45
Figure 3.3 Actual and projected variations in the number of females of German nationality in the FRG, 1925–1975 and 120 years ahead assuming constant mortality and changing fertility leading (1) to ZPG and (2) to progressive decline.   46
Figure 3.4 Actual and projected variations in youth, old age, and total dependency ratios of females of German nationality in the FRG, 1925–1975 and 120 years ahead, assuming constant mortality and changing fertility leading (1) to ZPG and (2) to progressive decline.   56
Figure 4.1 Alternative levels of full-employment U and U_{CAP} compatible with nonaccelerating inflation.   90
Figure 5.1 U.S. Gross Private Domestic Investment (GPDI) and marriages, 1889–1968.   115
Figure 5.2 Annual growth rates in Gross Private Domestic Investment, 1890–1968.   116
Figure 5.3 Annual growth rates in marriages, 1890–1968.   116
Figure 5.4 Annual changes in the level of real output (Y), births (B; inverted), capital stock (K), labor force (L), and female labor force (L_f), 1952–1976.   121
Figure 6.1 Changes as a percentage of total consumption.   148
Figure 8.1 The number of families receiving AFDC in three simulations (1974–1985).   221

Figure 9.1 Annual growth rates in population and number of households, 1940–1974, and projections to 1990. 229
Figure 9.2 Population change for 5-year periods by region: 1950 to 1975. 232
Figure 9.3 Components of change for SMSAs with moderate (quartiles 2 and 3) growth rates, 1970–1975. 241
Figure 9.4 Components of change for SMSAs with low or negative (bottom quartile) growth rates, 1970–1975. 243
Figure 9.5 Components of change for SMSAs with high (top quartile) growth rates, 1970–1975. 244

1

The Demographic Dimensions of Slowing Population Growth in the United States

V. JEFFERY EVANS and SIGNE I. WETROGAN

There is hardly a societal institution that is not touched in some way by population changes. During the 1950s the children of the baby boom swelled our nation's classrooms and caused elementary schools to operate on half-day sessions. Beginning in the mid-1960s and continuing until today, a growing number of job seekers has placed great burdens on the economy to expand. Regional shifts of population have transformed political alliances and created corresponding implications for the sharing of federal revenues. And the marked decline in the birth rate has been accompanied by an unprecedented increase in the labor force participation of married women. The examples are practically endless. This book is about how demographic changes affect our economy and, in particular, about the economic implications of the slowdown in population growth in the United States. As a first step toward understanding these influences, Chapter 1 describes the major demographic changes that have occurred in the United States since 1900 and outlines a number of plausible alternatives for the future. We begin with a discussion of population size and growth and then consider the age composition and spatial distribution of our population.

Trends and Prospects in U.S. Population Growth

Figure 1.1 traces the growth of the U.S. population from 1900 to 1976. Starting from a total of 3.9 million persons at the time of the first census in 1790, the population grew to 76 million by 1900. By the end of World War II it had reached 140 million, and it stood at 215 million in 1976.

The apparent smoothness in the trajectory of population exhibited in Figure 1.1 largely conceals the fact that this growth was accompanied by major ups and downs in the *rate* of change. Annual rates of population growth are illustrated in Figure 1.2. For most years prior to World War I annual growth rates exceeded 1.5% and were generally closer to 2%. Following the passage of several important immigration acts in the early 1920s, the rate of growth slowed noticeably, and this reduction was accentuated by the Great Depression, which brought growth rates to the lowest levels ever recorded.[1] Growth rates rebounded with the end of World War II and were consistently above 1.5% between 1946 and 1962. Beginning in the late 1950s, however, the rate underwent another steep decline. From a value of 1.81 in 1956–1957, it fell to .74 in 1975–1976, a drop of almost 60% in less than two decades.

Changes in these population growth rates have been dominated mainly by variations in the rate of childbearing. Measured in period terms, the total fertility rate fluctuated between 3000 and 3600 during the first quarter of this century.[2] It fell to replacement level during the depression and was near, at, or below 2200 throughout most of the 1930s.[3] Since then, fertility rates have undergone a pronounced swing, first rising to a postwar maximum of nearly 3700 in the late 1950s and then falling to an estimated value of 1739 by 1976.[4]

On the other hand, changes in mortality and immigration (less emigration)—the other two components of population gain or loss—

---

[1]The smallest gain of .59% was registered between 1932 and 1933.

[2]The period total fertility rate is the average number of births 1000 women would have by the end of their childbearing years if they were subject at each age to the birth rates observed among women of different ages in a given year.

[3]Replacement level is the value of the total fertility rate which, if sustained and if there were no emigration or immigration or change in mortality, would ultimately cause the population to reach and maintain a constant size. Currently, that value is approximately 2100. During the depression, when death rates were somewhat higher, it was slightly larger.

[4]Data for 1900–1916 are for the white population only and are contained in Coale and Zelnick (1963, p. 36). Data on total fertility rates between 1917 and 1970 are from National Center for Health Statistics (1976), Table 1A, and since 1970 from U.S. Bureau of the Census (1977c), Table A-5. The rate for 1976 has been estimated from provisional data on total births and 1972–1974 trends by age.

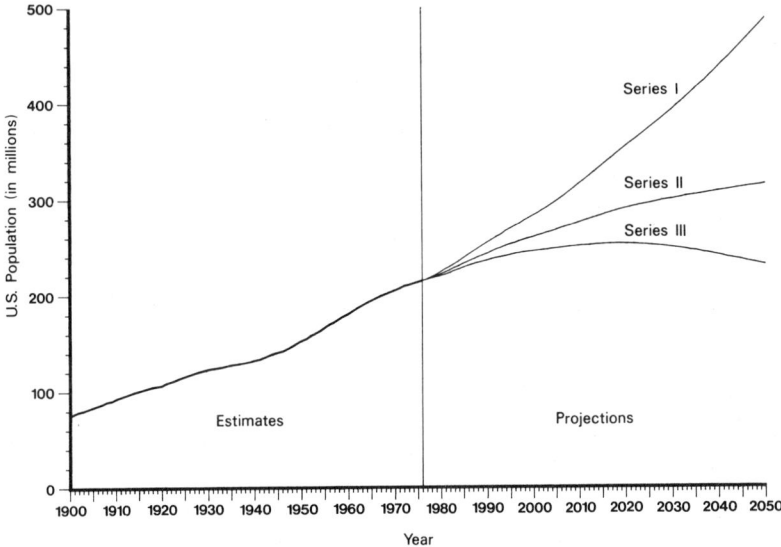

Figure 1.1. Estimates and projections of the population of the United States: 1900–2050.

were less extreme. Survival rates have shown consistent improvement throughout this century. In 1900 life expectancy at birth for males and females was 46.3 and 48.3 years, respectively. By 1976 these values had increased to 69.1 for males and 77.0 for females. And since the early 1920s, with the exception of the depression years, the annual number of immigrants to the United States has averaged between 300,000 and 400,000.

What do these trends portend for the future? Projections of the U.S. population to the year 2050 made by the U.S. Bureau of the Census (1977c) permit us to give some tentative answers to this question. The Census Bureau has prepared three alternative projections, each being distinguished by what it assumes about the future course of fertility. In Series I, it is postulated that fertility will move gradually from a total fertility rate in 1975 of 1771 to an average number of lifetime births per woman of 2.7. A value of 2.1 is assumed for Series II and 1.7 for Series III.[5] Taken together, these assumptions are believed to provide a range that will embrace subsequent U.S. fertility.

[5] Period total fertility rates in each series do not approximate their ultimate levels until about 2000. In the short run, the fertility assumptions have been lowered slightly to reflect trends in annual fertility and in the birth expectations of young married women. In Series II, for example, the period total fertility rate falls to 1727 in 1976 before turning up toward 2100. And in Series III, a low of 1558 is reached in 1979.

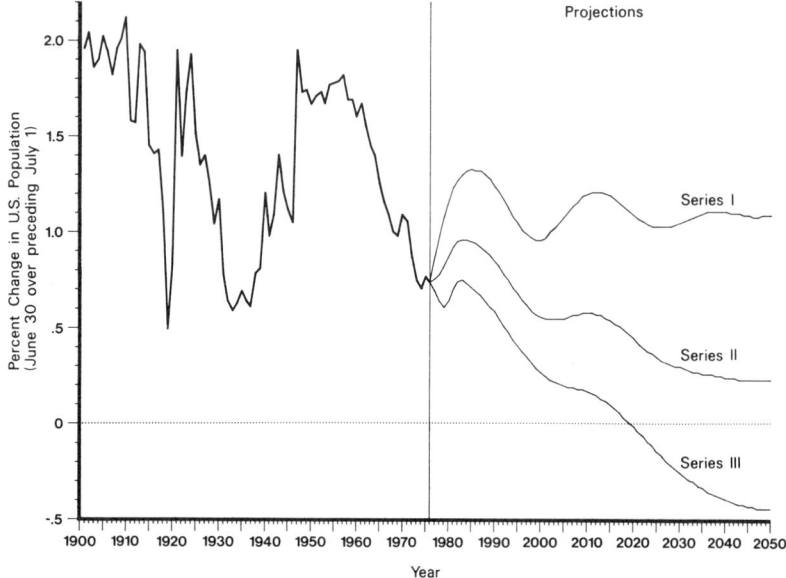

Figure 1.2. Estimates and projections of the annual growth rate of the United States population: 1900–2050.

The assumptions about future mortality take into account the decline in age-specific death rates in the middle and older adult ages. In all three series, life expectancy at birth is projected to increase by the year 2050 to 71.8 years for males and to 81.0 years for females. The assumption of 400,000 net immigrants per year maintains the postulate in previous Census Bureau reports and reflects the recorded level of legal immigration in past years.[6]

The implications of these alternative sets of assumptions for the future size and growth rate of the U.S. population are illustrated in Figures 1.1 and 1.2. All three populations exhibit continued growth through the year 2000 by which time total population size is expected to fall between

[6]Until recently this appeared to be a fairly realistic assumption. However, according to unpublished Census Bureau data, during 1976 the total number of immigrants was approximately 300,000. More troublesome perhaps is the fact that the figure of 400,000 does not reflect the volume of illegal immigration to the United States nor does it make any allowance for emigration. Estimates of these magnitudes vary widely because of the lack of reliable data. In an article in the *Washington Post,* Rowen (1977) reported figures on the number of illegal aliens in the United States that ranged from 4 to 12 million, although a study by Lancaster and Scheuren (1977) puts the number much closer to 4 million. Estimates of the annual volume of illegal immigration made by the Immigration and Naturalization Service range from 800,000 to 2 million. An INS press release dated December 8,

246 million (Series III) and 283 million (Series I). Despite its assumption of subreplacement fertility, the Series III population continues to grow well into the twenty-first century because of the relatively large proportion of the population in the childbearing ages and because of the 400,000 net immigrants that are added to the population each year. This series reaches a maximum size of 253 million about 2020 and thereafter declines. On the other hand, the Series I and Series II populations will grow forever; by the year 2050 they will have reached 488 million and 316 million, respectively.

The rate of population growth implied by the lowest fertility projection more or less extends beyond 1976 the decline in the U.S. rate of population growth begun in the late 1950s (Figure 1.2). All three series experience some increase in growth rates during the 1980s as the baby boom cohorts move into the prime childbearing ages. Because fertility rates are increasing fastest in Series I, the rise in the growth rate is most salient there. Although Series II incorporates fertility that tends ultimately to the replacement level, the growth rate approaches zero, but never quite reaches it due to persistent immigration. The growth rate in Series I undergoes damped oscillations and ultimately settles on a value of approximately 1.1% annually.

Changes in Age Composition

Changes in the growth rate of the U.S. population have inevitably produced changes in its age structure. As shown in Table 1.1, the United States experienced a progressive aging of its population over the first three quarters of this century as fertility rates were more than halved.[7]

1975, for example, claimed that the volume of illegal immigration was 750,000 in 1975 and growing. Cornelius (1977) reports that the volume of both legal and illegal migration from Mexico to the United States has been increasing.

Information on total emigration from the United States appears to be no more precise. Finifter (1976) argues that emigration is on the rise, claiming that the rate more than doubled between 1960 and 1970 (from 12.5 per 100,000 to 29.6) and that emigration was one-seventh as large as immigration by 1969. To corroborate this finding, she cites Gallup Poll data indicating that the proportion of people interviewed who said they would like to go and settle in another country if they were free to do so increased from 6% in January 1960 to 12% in February 1971. Warren and Peck (1975) estimate that the emigration from the United States of *foreign-born* persons was 1,065,000 between 1960 and 1970. Total emigration would be even more because these estimates exclude the movement of native and naturalized citizens. What this brief discussion suggests is that to assume 400,000 net immigrants to the United States each year may not even be a good first approximation and that more research on this topic is needed.

[7] According to the sources cited in Footnote 4 the period total fertility rate was 3560 for whites in 1900 and an estimated 1739 for the total population in 1976.

TABLE 1.1.
Estimates and Projections of the Population of the United States in Selected Age Groups: 1900–2050[a] (in thousands)

	All ages	Under 5	5–13	14–17	18–24	25–44	45–64	65 and over	Median age	Dependency ratio[b]
Estimates										
1900	76,094	9,181	15,402	6,132	10,383	21,434	10,463	3,099	22.9	.572
1930	123,077	11,372	22,266	9,370	15,482	36,309	21,573	6,705	26.5	.488
1976	215,118	15,339	32,955	16,897	28,166	55,120	43,707	22,934	29.0	.495
Projections										
1985										
Series I	238,878	22,887	31,012	14,392	27,853	71,235	44,194	27,305	30.7	.515
Series II	232,880	18,803	29,098	14,392	27,853	71,235	44,194	27,305	31.5	.477
Series III	228,879	16,235	27,665	14,392	27,853	71,235	44,194	27,305	32.0	.452
2000										
Series I	282,837	23,638	44,725	19,698	28,029	75,794	59,132	31,822	32.5	.548
Series II	260,378	17,852	35,080	16,045	24,653	75,794	59,132	31,822	35.5	.483
Series III	245,876	14,158	28,915	13,831	22,225	75,794	59,132	31,822	37.3	.438
2025										
Series I	373,053	32,931	58,767	24,976	38,336	97,609	69,516	50,920	31.5	.619
Series II	295,742	19,495	36,639	16,356	26,978	77,669	67,686	50,920	37.6	.567
Series III	251,915	12,700	25,016	11,669	20,348	64,956	66,306	50,920	42.4	.543
2050										
Series I	488,230	44,378	77,006	32,372	51,587	127,555	95,096	60,235	30.9	.592
Series II	315,622	20,917	38,486	17,128	29,123	81,379	73,096	55,494	37.8	.572
Series III	230,998	11,404	22,074	10,314	18,474	57,078	59,342	52,312	43.7	.591

Percentage Distribution

	Total									
Estimates										
1900	100.0	12.1	20.2	8.1	13.6	28.2	13.8	4.1	—	—
1930	100.0	9.2	18.1	7.6	12.6	29.5	17.5	5.4	—	—
1976	100.0	7.1	15.3	7.9	13.1	25.6	20.3	10.7	—	—
Projections										
1985										
Series I	100.0	9.6	13.0	6.0	11.7	29.8	18.5	11.4	—	—
Series II	100.0	8.1	12.5	6.2	12.0	30.6	18.9	11.7	—	—
Series III	100.0	7.1	12.1	6.3	12.2	31.1	19.3	11.9	—	—
2000										
Series I	100.0	8.4	15.8	7.0	9.9	26.8	20.9	11.3	—	—
Series II	100.0	6.9	13.5	6.2	9.5	29.1	22.7	12.2	—	—
Series III	100.0	5.8	11.8	5.6	9.0	30.8	24.1	12.9	—	—
2025										
Series I	100.0	8.8	15.8	6.7	10.3	26.2	18.1	13.6	—	—
Series II	100.0	6.6	12.4	5.5	9.1	26.3	22.9	17.2	—	—
Series III	100.0	5.0	9.9	4.6	8.1	25.8	26.3	20.2	—	—
2050										
Series I	100.0	9.1	15.8	6.6	10.6	26.1	19.5	12.3	—	—
Series II	100.0	6.6	12.2	5.4	9.2	25.8	23.2	17.6	—	—
Series III	100.0	4.9	9.6	4.5	8.0	24.7	25.7	22.7	—	—

[a] For 1900 and 1930, U.S. Bureau of the Census, *Current Population Reports*, Series P-25, No. 311, "Estimates of the Population of the United States by Single Years of Age, Race, and Sex, 1900 to 1959," July 1965; and for 1976–2050, U.S. Bureau of the Census, *Current Population Reports*, Series P-25, No. 704, "Projections of the Population of the United States: 1977 to 2050," July 1977.

[b] The number of persons under 14 years of age and 65 years and over per number of persons aged 14–64.

The median age, for example, rose by 6 years from 22.9 in 1900 to 29.0 in 1976. For the future, continued aging over 1976 levels is expected although the high fertility assumption (Series I) causes the population to become somewhat younger after the year 2000. On the other hand, if Series III prevails the median age is projected to reach 43.7 years by 2050 when almost one out of every four people will be 65 or over.

Attention to the growth of the total population disguises what is happening to selected age groups. In the mid- to late 1960s and into the early 1970s, college and university enrollments in the United States were inflated by increasing proportions of high school seniors electing to go to college and by the movement of the baby boom cohorts into the 18-24 age group. However, depending on the appeal that college has for tomorrow's youth, postsecondary enrollments could begin to fall as the smaller birth cohorts of the 1960s and 1970s reach college age. Even the high fertility projection suggests that universities collectively will constitute a no-growth industry throughout the remainder of this century. Under the most pessimistic assumptions (Series III), the pool of "eligibles" (those aged 18-24) will peak at 29,512,000 in 1981 and then decline to 22,225,000 by the year 2000. It is small wonder that university officials are looking to older age groups to service through their continuing education programs.

Especially noteworthy is the behavior of the population 65 years of age and older. Between 2005 and 2030 this group is projected to grow from 32 million to 55 million as the baby boom children of the 1940s and 1950s reach age 65. This projected increase of 23 million in a 25-year span is equal to the 1976 population 65 years and over.

Spatial Redistribution of the Population

Focusing attention on the national population obscures what is happening at the subnational level. At the same time that the U.S. population was undergoing great changes in size, growth rate, and age structure, it also was experiencing substantial internal migration of its people. Table 1.2 illustrates the regional realignments of population that have taken place since 1900. The share of the total population in the South has remained almost constant since 1900. The Northeast and North Central sections of the country have both lost in proportion to other regions, while the West has been the biggest gainer.

This westward movement of the population also is reflected in the geographic center of population. At the time of the first census in 1790 this center was located several miles east of Baltimore, Maryland. Since

TABLE 1.2.
Estimates of the Population of the United States by Census Region: 1900–1976[a] (in thousands)

Year	Total U.S.	Northeast		North Central		South		West	
		Number	Percentage	Number	Percentage	Number	Percentage	Number	Percentage
1976	214,659	49,503	23.1	57,739	26.9	68,855	32.1	38,562	18.0
1970	203,212	49,041	24.1	56,572	27.8	62,795	30.9	34,804	17.1
1960	179,323	44,678	24.9	51,619	28.8	54,973	30.7	28,053	15.6
1950	151,326	39,478	26.1	44,461	29.4	47,197	31.2	20,190	13.3
1940	132,165	35,977	27.2	40,143	30.4	41,666	31.5	14,379	10.9
1930	123,203	34,427	27.9	38,594	31.3	37,858	30.7	12,324	10.0
1920	106,022	29,662	28.0	34,020	32.1	33,126	31.2	9,214	8.7
1910	92,228	25,869	28.0	29,889	32.4	29,389	31.9	7,082	7.7
1900	76,212	21,047	27.6	26,333	34.6	24,524	32.2	4,309	5.7

[a] For 1900 to 1970, U.S. Bureau of the Census, *Census of Population: 1970*, Vol. 1, Characteristics of the Population, Part 1, United States Summary, Section 1, Table 8, U.S. Government Printing Office, 1973; for 1976, U.S. Bureau of the Census, *Current Population Reports*, Series P-25, No. 642, "Revised 1975 and Provisional 1976 Estimates of the Population of States, and Components of Change, 1970 to 1976," December 1976.

then it has moved steadily westward generally following the path cut by U.S. Interstate 40 through central West Virginia, southern Ohio, Indiana, and Illinois. By 1970 this demographic center of gravity was in southwestern Illinois about 20 miles southeast of East St. Louis. Between 1970 and 1975 it continued to move west and south; put on a decade basis it traveled approximately 26 miles west and 17 miles south. The westward movement is roughly typical of previous intercensal shifts, but the southerly change is the largest ever recorded.[8]

Conclusion

The past 20 years in American demographic history have seen a major decline in the rate of population growth. Will this decline continue or will fertility rates rise again as they did following the depression and cause a resurgence in the growth rate? Answers to this question are important since they enable policymakers to plan for the expected consequences of emerging population trends. Historically, however, demographers have not been adept at forecasting the future. The magnitude as well as the duration of the postwar baby boom came as a surprise as has much of the recent rapid decline in birth rates.

Faced with uncertainty, demographers have resorted to preparing alternative population projections predicated upon alternative sets of assumptions about how fertility, mortality, and migration will behave. If the Series III postulates materialize, for example, then the demographic implications for the size, growth rate, and age composition of the population can be foretold with complete accuracy. On the other hand, Series II assumptions might ultimately turn out to be more correct, or even Series I. The problem in predicting the future is in judging which underlying set of assumptions is most likely to hold true.

The variable subject to the greatest fluctuations and, hence, uncertainty, is fertility, and it is the alternative assumptions about fertility that distinguish the three population projections discussed in this chapter. In this concluding section we briefly review the evidence on how U.S. fertility is likely to behave in the future.

The estimated U.S. total fertility rates for 1976 and 1977 were 1739 and 1816, respectively.[9] These rates are slightly above the Series II assumptions for those years. Current fertility, however, is an unreliable guide to

---

[8]Data on the estimated center of population for 1975 have been supplied by John Long, U.S. Bureau of the Census.

[9]These rates were estimated from provisional data on total births and 1972–1974 trends by age.

tomorrow, and data on the birth expectations of young women may be more useful. According to the U.S. Bureau of the Census (1977d), survey data for the period 1974–1977 indicate that young wives of all races aged 18–24 expect to bear about 2.1 children per woman. If these expectations are valid, then much of the decline in fertility rates can be attributed to changes in the timing of births, that is, to a delay on the part of many women in beginning their childbearing, and a small upturn in birth rates should appear in the near future.[10] This would suggest a preference for the Series II fertility assumption. However, early expectations do not always coincide with later performance. Whereas in the 1950s females underestimated their future childbearing (Whelpton et al., 1966), it has been shown that more recent female expectations of future births have surpassed their performance (Westoff & Ryder, 1977; Wetrogan, 1973).

Sklar and Berkov (1975) predicted that the decline in the U.S. birth rate was coming to an end and that we were about to witness a turnaround in fertility. Their argument, based mainly on data for California, was that increasing proportions of married young American women were childless, yet there was data to suggest they did not intend to remain that way. The pent-up demand for children, when and if satisfied, was likely to cause a rise in rates of childbearing.[11] Moreover, despite the availability of legal abortion in California, the rate of out-of-wedlock births (especially to teenagers) has resumed its upward trend. But Gibson (1977) has countered that neither a large nor a sudden increase in fertility would be needed to enable young couples to adjust their present family size to stated goals. In addition, Gibson doubts whether California trends are suitable indicators for the rest of the nation, and he argues that the unfavorable economic conditions in 1974–1975 were not readily conducive to an upturn in fertility.

Economists' theories do not yield unambiguous answers either. Easterlin (1973) hypothesizes that U.S. fertility is low because today's young couples were raised with expectations of a high standard of living. At the same time, these desires are difficult to realize because, among other things, income-earning prospects have deteriorated as the labor market has been strained to find work for the large baby boom cohorts. Having fewer births is one way of coping with a standard of living that is lower than the one desired. On the other hand, children born during the fertility decline of the 1960s and 1970s will encounter a relatively uncongested labor market, which suggests that fertility might begin to rise

[10] As already noted, some increase was detected between 1976 and 1977.
[11] This position has also been taken by Campbell (1978).

during the 1980s. Empirical support for this position has been provided by Lee (1977), who concludes that U.S. fertility is only temporarily low and that it should turn up again after 5 or 10 years to perhaps as much as a total fertility rate of over three children per woman by the year 2000.

A different view is held by Butz and Ward (1977). Their analysis of the fertility swing from 1948 to 1974 does not deny a role for the Easterlin relative income variables, but it does question whether they were very important. Instead, Butz and Ward distinguish between male income and female wage effects. Increases in husband's income should raise the demand for children. An increase in female earnings also increases family income and thereby contributes to larger family size desires. But a rise in female wages also increases the opportunity cost of children, which operates to reduce family size. This effect should be especially important if large proportions of women are in the labor force. Butz and Ward argue that the impressive postwar growth in the employment of women of childbearing age has intensified the strength of this negative price effect and has contributed significantly to the falloff in birth rates. They summarize their findings as follows: "Predictions for the more distant future must account for a potential bottoming out of the secular decline in fertility. Certainly these rates will not reach zero. However, we look for a continuing secular fertility decline toward the asymptote punctuated by countercyclical fertility movements [p. 33]."

We cannot predict confidently what our demographic future will be. This brief review of the evidence suggests that any number of alternatives is possible; fertility may rise, it may stay relatively constant perhaps fluctuating near replacement, or it may fall even further.[12] Despite this uncertainty, we do know that the slowing growth of the U.S. population over the past 20 years has left an indelible imprint on the age composition of the population that will not wane until well into the twenty-first century. These past trends will have implications for our economy independent of the future course of fertility.

---

[12]Westoff (1974) adopts a position that is intermediate between that espoused by Easterlin and Lee on the one hand and by Butz and Ward on the other. In a cautious appraisal, Westoff says, "My guess is that we can expect swings in fertility rates of five to 10 years' duration, ranging perhaps from as low as 1.5 births per woman to as high as 2.5 as fertility responds to short-term economic changes and to various other changes in ideology and fashion. There is no reason in principle that fertility could not rise above or fall below this range in some countries, but it seems unlikely that the developed world as a whole will experience such wide swings [pp. 114–115]."

2

The Economics of Declining Population Growth: An Assessment of the Current Literature

WILLIAM J. SEROW[1] and THOMAS J. ESPENSHADE

The decline in fertility rates in the United States and other Western nations that has been evident for the past several years has had the effect of rekindling interest among economists and other social scientists in the long-run effects of a diminution or even cessation of population growth. It is, of course, true that similar concerns were expressed during the period of low fertility that took place some 40 years ago (Foust, 1974; Serow, 1975; Sweezy, 1975), but theoretical, technological, and methodological advances that have taken place during the intervening years have given rise to more broadly based and comprehensive analyses that permit investigation of the complex interactions that determine the economic and social consequences of population change. Additionally, the world economy is much more complex at present, and many national economies are very susceptible to fluctuations in world markets (Wander, 1976).

[1] Serow's contributions to this chapter were supported, in part, by funds from Administration on Aging Grant 90-A-978.

It is the purpose of Chapter 2 to examine the recent literature that addresses itself to the topic of the consequences of low rates of population growth. It is, perhaps, most convenient to do so by dividing the literature into two categories, theoretical and empirical. The overall thrust of the chapter will be to summarize and evaluate the recent contributions to the theoretical underpinnings, to summarize and evaluate the empirical studies in light of these underpinnings, and finally to indicate the apparent gaps in the research to date, particularly in view of the importance of this knowledge for the formulation of population policy. This chapter, then, does not aim to forecast future population or to examine the determinants of the low fertility (Rückert, 1977; Simons, 1976) that have led to the population projections that underlie the analyses to be discussed.

It is perhaps appropriate to make two comments about the contents of this chapter that are not obvious from its title. As will be readily apparent, our effort primarily deals with analyses of population stationarity within the context of the United States. The interest in this question in other parts of the developed world is probably at least equal to that found in this country. A synthesis of the writings on the economic consequences of population stationarity stemming from scholars in Europe and Oceania would be a profitable extension of the present undertaking. For an indication of the extent of these research efforts, one need only look, for example, at the works of Stassart (1965), Bourgeois-Pichat and Taleb (1970), Sauvy (1973), Schubnell (1974a; 1974b), and O'Neill (1977).

Many nations have established analogs to the Commission on Population Growth and the American Future; many of these commissions have issued reports on the implications of varying rates of future population growth in their own national context. A listing of these study commissions may be found in the introduction and summary section of Berelson (1974). Furthermore, the content of the initial report of the Australian National Population Inquiry is analyzed in papers by Jupp (1976) and McNicoll (1976). Additionally, in September of 1976 the Council of Europe conducted a seminar dealing with the implications of a stationary or declining population in Europe.

A second point to consider is that the principal focus of this chapter is economic implications. While we have attempted to view economics in a broad sense, it should be recognized that both authors are economists, as well as demographers, by training and may be subject to some narrowness of vision. There are certainly implications of stationary populations that are either ignored or treated summarily here and which traditionally fall into the purview of social sciences other than economics.

Many of these issues are treated in papers contained in the volumes edited by Westoff and Parke (1972) and by Mazie (1972). The student of the family may also find contributions by Blake (1972), by Matthiessen (1977), by Jürgens (1977), by Pool and Bracher (1974), and by Winger (1976) to be of interest. Furthermore, there has been an interest in the consequences of declining population growth for the environment (Friedman, 1977), for regional planning (zu Castell *et al.*, 1977; Eversley *et al.*, 1977; Schwarz, 1977), and for crime rates (Markides and Tracy, 1976). Finally, several of the issues here have been raised in a slightly different context by social gerontologists. Much of the research in this area is summarized in pages 289-292 of the United Nations's *The Determinants and Consequences of Population Trends* (1973).

Demographic Aspects

The demographic consequences of a diminution in the rate of population growth have been studied extensively, particularly in the context of the United States and Europe (Coale, 1972; Frejka, 1968; Guilmot and Renaerts, 1976; Ryder, 1972, 1975; U.S. Bureau of the Census, 1972a). Notestein (1975) has gone one step further and demonstrated the demographic effects of a program aimed at reducing the size of the U.S. population by 50%. The basic result of a lessening of growth is a marked change in the age composition of the population. To a very great extent, many of the social and economic consequences that have been hypothesized or evaluated are based, either directly or indirectly, on this change. The differences between the absolute cessation of population growth or its continuance at an absolutely low level are, in this context, relatively insignificant.

Although most of the recent literature on the demography of stationary populations has concerned the United States, Frejka (1973) and the Bureau of the Census (1971) extended the analysis to a large number of countries that represent almost the entire spectrum of the demographic transition. An important contribution to the demographic literature was made by Keyfitz (1971), who demonstrated that the time required for growth of population to cease in any closed demographic system once replacement-level fertility is permanently attained depends on the degree to which the present age structure of the system differs from that of the ultimate stable-stationary system. Rogers and Willekens (1976) extended this work to permit analysis of internal population redistribution. Thus, a country with a recent history of high fertility rates will require a longer period of time, ceteris paribus, to reach a true state of zero population growth (ZPG) than will a country whose recent demographic past has been characterized by low or moderate fertility, since the age composition of the rapidly growing nation will be young in relationship to its ultimate stable–stationary population as well as to the that of the second country.

Theoretical Developments

For the purpose of this review, many works of a general nature have been excluded, not because of any deficiencies on their part, but rather because the conclusions reached by these writers (Enke, 1973; Hogan, 1972; Mayer, 1974; Miller, 1971; Notestein, 1970) have been reached by others who presented their analyses in a more rigorous and systematic fashion. Furthermore, theoretical growth models of the type developed by Solow, Swan, Niehans, and others, which allow for the existence of the stationary state, are neglected here, since we are concerned with the implications of population stationarity in a definite context. The views of Hieser (1973), which are discussed in what follows, are generally reflective of the conclusions of these models. An excellent summary of this class of model is found in Chapter 4 of Pitchford (1974).

Perhaps the most basic or underlying question that can be raised regarding the probable economic consequences of lower rates of population growth is the impact on per capita income (or output or consumption). Leibenstein (1972) in his analysis of the problem seeks to answer the following: Would the economic welfare of the average family be lowered to any significant extent by the year 2000 if the average annual rate of population growth in the United States were .5–1.0% instead of 0? Perhaps the most widely sweeping statement in support of the argument that economic welfare could be affected adversely by the continuation of population growth is found in many works of Spengler (1971, 1972a, 1975a,b). Although Spengler (1976) has suggested that a stationary population contains many facets that may present difficulties to the economic well-being of older persons, the thrust of his basic argument is that under conditions consistent with the attainment of a stationary population the changes in the age composition will be such as to increase the ratio of the labor force to the entire population. In other words, the decrease (absolutely or relatively) in the number of young dependents will more than offset the increase in the number of older dependents, although, as Spengler points out, the cost of maintaining an old dependent is substantially higher than that of maintaining a young dependent (see also Kreps, 1976). Furthermore, a decline in fertility will release a relatively large number of women from childrearing-related chores for entry into the labor force. There is, according to Spengler, no reason for employment levels to be affected adversely in the long run, and output per worker should rise since capital formerly required to equip new entrants to the labor force can be utilized to increase the capital–labor ratio. This line of reasoning closely parallels that of Coale and Hoover (1958) in their seminal study of the economic effects of demographic change in developing countries.

The problems that Spengler foresees in this context are primarily institutional. One is that the aggregate mobility of labor (both occupational and geographic) may be affected adversely due to aging and the relative depletion of what Spengler calls the "mobile labor reserve" (younger workers). This also implies the possibility of higher structural unemployment if the composition of consumer demand is altered to any significant degree. The solutions to this problem as well as to related problems such as barriers to the employment of older workers and the potential difficulties for promotion within a hierarchical structure are, again, felt to be institutional rather than economic in nature.

Similar lines of reasoning are to be found in the works of other students of the question. Wander (1972) agrees with the potentiality of mobility-related problems and adds that the relative shortage of younger workers can act to diminish wage differentials between younger and older workers (or less and more experienced workers) and, hence, impair incentives for younger workers to upgrade their occupational skills.

Phelps (1972) agrees with Spengler that declining population growth enhances the opportunity for increases in per capita consumption (at any given level of capital intensity) and that if the current level of capital intensity can be maintained, there will be definite increases in the level of per capita consumption relative to that which would result from an initially similar population growing at a greater rate over time. However, Phelps feels that the rate of increase in per capita consumption in a stationary population will eventually come into equality with the rate of technical progress and that this rate will be lower than it would otherwise have been due to the relative decline in the number of younger workers.

The current literature may be summarized as holding the view that the problem of the cessation of population growth is basically one of adjustment to a new economic environment. At the crux of the question of economic well-being is the question of the level of per capita output. This can, in turn, be subdivided into productivity of labor and capital accumulation. While Spengler argues that declining population growth enhances the opportunity to save, Phelps notes that it is likely that the

Federal Reserve System will have to take action to force down rates of interest, lest the problems of capital surplus and deficiency of aggregate demand that are associated with Keynes (but see Sweezy, 1975 on the general misconception of Keynes's position) arise. Wander (1972) also emphasizes the need for investment opportunity to avoid a decline in economic growth and notes that "under a stationary population there would be more scope for renewal of the old capital supply per worker... [p. 24]." In brief, the problem is, according to Wander, the replacement of the broadening of production by the intensification of production.

The literature contains more ambiguity than the foregoing discussion might suggest. Leibenstein, for example, finds it difficult to analyze the effects of population change on the economy without knowing the nature and magnitude of concomitant change in other elements of the system. It is difficult to determine how innovation is affected by population growth (Kelley, 1972) and, furthermore, what guarantee exists that this innovation necessarily will be labor augmenting (Dorfman, 1972). If economic growth does continue into the future, can we expect that resources will continue to be equally productive, or will diminishing returns in the Ricardian sense set in?

Another question that is relevant here is the implications of an older work force on labor productivity, disregarding for the moment the possible variation in the capital–labor ratio. While one might theorize that, in general, the greater experience of older workers will offset their relative lack of mobility or physical strength, Leibenstein notes that what he calls the replacement effect of the skill level of the labor force might come into play. He argues that relatively large numbers of new entrants to the labor force at one time have the effect of increasing the overall level of human capital per worker. Hence, as the number of new entrants diminishes relative to the existing work force, so too does the rate of increase in human capital embodied in the labor force.

Despite this, the overall consensus of opinion thus far would appear to be that the net impact of a decline in population growth would be positive, in terms of a per capita measure of economic well-being. As Leibenstein puts it, even if the effect of diminished population growth is negative in terms of marginal per capita output, this influence should be smaller than that which would result from a continuation of higher rates of population growth.

An important exception to the overall optimistic outlook is to be found in Hieser (1973), who reiterated the point made by Phelps that the rate of economic growth must eventually converge with the rate of technical progress, since the latter will be the only means of absorbing net investment. However, Hieser states that if the most common assumption, neutral technical progress, is accepted, then all required investment could be financed by amortization funds and net investment (and net profits) will fall to zero. The only way out is "in the direction of strongly and consistently labor-saving innovations... [p. 260]," as this creates "artificial" population growth. However, even this effect can be nullified if workers shift preferences toward leisure and away from goods. Clark and Spengler (1977) point to an additional reason why slower population growth might inhibit the growth of real per capita income. While both the youngest and the oldest segments of the population may be economically dependent, not only may the per capita costs of older dependents be greater, but also a large proportion of the dependency costs of the young are for education, which creates human capital and influences future earnings and productivity. Expenditures on the aged are, however, primarily maintenance costs and do not add to the productive potential of the economy.

A similar line of reasoning is found in Barber (1975). Barber notes that as the natural rate of growth falls in conjunction with that of the labor force and population, an increase of about two-thirds will be necessary in the capital–output ratio to bring the warranted rate of growth in line with the natural rate. This change will likely produce a sharp reduction in the marginal product of capital, and, hence, in the return to capital. As the rate of growth of output falls, both the ratio of capital consumption to gross fixed investment and the ratio of replacement capital to capital consumption will increase. This reduction in the level of net investment will be particularly severe in the residential construction sector, due to the low income elasticity of housing. All in all, Barber suggests that as the rate of growth of output falls from 4 to 2.5%, the annual level of net investment would fall from approximately 10 to about 6% of net national product.

The reasons for the disagreement between scholars on the probable consequences of a stationary population upon economic well-being are doubtless complex. It may be noted that those who approach the problem from a theoretical perspective tend to be pessimistic, while those who approach the problem from an empirical perspective tend to be rather more optimistic. To understand the causes of this disparity, consider the features of the Harrod–Domar and neoclassical growth models, which underlie much of the theoretical reasoning.

In the former case, the rate of growth of an economy's total output is equivalent to the product of the capital coefficient (output–capital ratio) and the marginal propensity to save. Changes in either of these will affect the observed growth rate of total output. When equivalence occurs ex ante, this growth rate is termed the "warranted" rate of growth, and is an equilibrium value. There is, in this formulation, another rate of growth, called the "natural" rate of growth, which is that allowed by increases in population and technical progress. In the long run, the actual growth rate cannot exceed this natural growth rate. In the absence of population (labor force) growth, therefore, increases in per capita output, and, hence, in economic well-being, are determined solely by technical progress.

The same conclusion is reached by application of neoclassical growth theory. In its simplest form (using a Cobb–Douglas production function of first-degree homogeneity, with neutral technical progress and diminishing returns), the growth rate of output is a function of the rate of technical progress and the growth rates of capital and labor. But in the long run, the growth rates of output and capital must be identical, if equilibrium is to be attained. If labor force growth is zero, then per capita output can grow only with technical progress. If one believes, as does Hieser, that potential technical progress will be channeled into directions other than production, then the long-run prognosis for increased economic well-being under a regime of population stationarity is bleak.

The empirical perspective is couched primarily in terms of the ratio of members of the labor force to nonmembers. From the viewpoint of labor supply, an overall population growth rate of about zero is one that maximizes the ratio of persons of working age to others. Hence, under reasonable schedules of labor force participation and employment, the labor force–population ratio is at a maximum, and the share of labor income devoted to the support of the economically dependent is approximately minimized (depending upon the level of costs per dependent as a function of the age of the dependent population).

Ambiguity regarding economic well-being remains no matter which perspective one chooses to follow. From a theoretical perspective, the unanswered question is the effects of declining population growth on the rate of technical progress and on the neutrality of this progress. From an empirical perspective, the critical unanswered questions are the demand for labor under conditions of declining population growth and the response of individual labor force participation to changes in the demand for labor (and corresponding changes in wage levels).

Perhaps the best summary of the state of analysis regarding the influence of a cessation of population growth on economic well-being is expressed by Kelley (1972) who suggests that given the current state of theory and empirical analysis, a population policy based on a hypothesized significant increase in per capita consumption (as a result of the attainment of a stationary population) is unwarranted. While there seems to be little doubt that increasing growth of population leads to diminishing returns to fixed factors and a dampening of the aggregate capital–labor ratio, there are a variety of interactions about which we know comparatively little. These include the impact of population growth on the rate of technical progress; the role of population growth where the pool of investable resources depends not only on the level of income, but also on its source; the intermediate-run effects of population growth where technological change is partially embodied in new capital; and the influence of population growth on the level of human capital and productivity of the labor force. Despite the large volume and high quality of the empirical studies that will be discussed subsequently, Kelley's remarks provide an excellent agenda for further theoretical and empirical investigation into the economic and social consequences of a cessation of population growth.

While most theoretical investigation has dealt with the influence of slow or no population growth on the level of economic activity, there have been some theoretical investigations into somewhat different topics. Denton and Spencer (1973) have constructed a model designed to test the cyclic effects on the economy of what they term demographic shocks. If, for example, the attainment of the replacement level of fertility were initially accomplished by a sharp reduction in the level of period fertility, a demographic shock would occur that, after an initial lag, would lead to relatively long swings in economic variables. While any shock produces disequilibrating effects, the greater the relative shock, the greater the degree of disequilibration. Hence, in evaluating the economic influence of a cessation of population growth, the time path followed by fertility can be of paramount importance.

One additional theoretical development that should not be neglected is Spengler's (1972b) argument that a cessation of population growth is likely to increase upward pressure on the level of prices. The growth rate of the labor force will eventually approximate that of the entire population (allowing for adjustment of labor force participation rates). This labor force also will be relatively immobile as a result of aging. Spengler argues that unemployment rates will eventually reach the level on the Phillips curve where wages must inexorably rise. Labor will be in relatively short supply, and those industries requiring additional labor will be forced either to bid them away from other industries or to attract nonparticipants into the work force. The first instance will require a premium for overcoming immobility, whereas the second requires meeting the reservation price of nonworkers. In neither case is there any reason to anticipate increases in the level of labor productivity. Additionally, Spengler sees that much of the increase in demand for labor will occur in the service industries, where the level of productivity has historically been low vis-à-vis that of goods-producing industries. Finally, Spengler feels that governmental decision makers will recognize the increased political power of older persons and seek to redress their losses through inflation by supplemental payments that are likely to give further impetus to the forces of inflation.

Empirical Studies

In addition to the theoretical developments outlined previously, the past few years have also seen the publication of a considerable number of studies dealing with particular economic or social areas that appear to be most susceptible to demographic variation. The variety of topics covered by these analyses is perhaps surprisingly limited. The primary areas that have been the subject of analysis include:

1. Social security and pensions.
2. Education.
3. Spatial considerations.
4. Labor force.
5. Consumption.

Each of these will be treated in turn.

Social Security and Pensions

The influence of diminished rates of population growth in the funding of social security and pensions rests on the institutional arrangements of the Old Age, Survivors, Disability, and Health Insurance (OASDHI) program (and many private pension plans). Basically, of course, contributions by workers to the system are utilized to pay benefits to retired persons and other beneficiaries. The basic argument is that as a population ages (a necessary consequence of reduced population growth), the ratio of workers to retired persons will decline, and consequently the burden of support will be heavier on the shoulders of future generations of workers. The continuation of the pay-as-you-go system, without any alteration, seems to be an impossibility, according to the findings of Rejda and Shepler (1973), Hogan (1974, 1976), Turchi (1975), and R. Clark (1976b, 1977). The first two studies deal exclusively with the OASDHI system; Turchi expands the analysis to include private pension plans as well; and Clark goes still further and includes discussion of other government transfer systems.

The conclusions of all investigators clearly indicate that the publicly financed system is unlikely to continue in its present format under conditions of population stationarity. As Clark (1977) put it: "All of our projections indicate that the movement toward zero population growth will require even greater transfers of income to support the elderly, with the Social Security System being forced to bear much of the burden [p. 53]." Denton and Spencer's (1975a) analysis of the Canadian case yields similar conclusions.

Rejda and Shepler point to the possibility of general revenue financing as does Hogan, who indicates that increased demand for public funds to pay social security retirement benefits and medicare would be offset by the decreasing demand for what he terms "youth-related" (OASDHI dependent and survivor benefits, aid to dependent children, and elementary and secondary education) expenditures, so that the share of net national product devoted to these five categories would be slightly less under conditions of population stationarity than they were in 1970. Similar findings are presented by Van Gorkom (1976). This approach, as well as that of Rejda and Shepler, clearly requires substantial change in the existing legislation. A more sweeping proposal has been made by Browning (1973), who suggests that workers be compelled to purchase bonds that the government will redeem when they retire.

A portion of Turchi's research explicitly deals with those private pension plans that are actuarially funded. Turchi suggests that, under conditions of no growth of either population or per capita income, net dissaving is likely to characterize the aggregate behavior of all participants in the plan. Of course, the possibility of sustained economic growth would mitigate this conclusion. Turchi also makes the point that, via its implicit control over the retirement age, the social security system can contribute to the inflationary pressures suggested by Spengler. This presumably would result from an increase in the level of real benefits and/or a reduction in the age at which an individual would be entitled to receive the full monthly pension.

On balance, we may accept the findings of Rejda and Shepler, Hogan, Turchi, and Clark in that the cessation of population growth will make it extremely inequitable to continue the present mechanism for funding OASDHI retirement benefits. Given the time period that will elapse before real pressures are placed on the system, there should not be any difficulty in changing this institutional mechanism to permit either general revenue financing or something akin to Browning's retirement bond proposal. Munnell (1976) underscores this conclusion by stating that if the cost increases in the program become excessive, the financial requirements can be reduced by either allowing the replacement rate (that is, the ratio of benefits to prior earnings) to decline or by extending the retirement age (or both).

Perhaps the more important issue is that of savings, touched upon by Turchi and also by Schulz (1973). A great deal needs to be done, from both a theoretical and from an empirical standpoint, on the relationship between prospective population change and the level of savings. Winger (1976) suggests that, if only the household sector is considered (and it should be recognized that the importance of this sector in terms of share of savings generated is diminishing), with a stationary population the number of families whose ability to save is reduced due to increased family size will be smaller, and that periods favorable to saving over the family life cycle are lengthened. Eversley (1976) points out that, due to declining fertility, compression of the reproductive period, and greater labor force participation of married women, there exists only a short period (less than 10 years) over the family life cycle when the typical family would be characterized by the one-earner, multidependent model that had been typical until quite recently. Furthermore, the number of dependents even during this short span would be less than in the past.

As Kelley (1976b) notes, there is some doubt regarding the veracity of widely applied generalizations concerning the allegedly negative impact of children on household savings rates. Maillat (1976) suggests that this hypothesis does not hold up "if it is accepted that a reduction in family size is the result of a choice (substitution) made by the parents between the number of children and the acquisition of other consumer durables as and when family income rises [p. 16]."

Even if the supply of savings is assured, there is still the issue raised by Phelps and Hieser regarding the profitability of these savings in traditional modes of investment. Maillat (1976), however, notes that changes in the dynamics of the labor force will require industry to seek more capital-intensive methods of production. The future, to Maillat, must "be envisaged in terms of adaptability to new needs. The problem that then arises is whether... society will be capable of making the necessary changes to satisfy the various new needs [p. 19]."

Education

The impact of a decline in the rate of population growth on the educational system of the United States is, on the surface, fairly obvious. At the elementary and secondary level, where attendance is mandatory, rates of school enrollment will be 95% or higher, so enrollment or demand for education at this level will closely parallel future trends in the population aged 6–17. At higher levels of education, however, demand is perhaps more sensitive to economic and social conditions, and one cannot be nearly as sanguine in estimating the effects of population change in enrollment levels.

Due, perhaps, to these basic differences between elementary and secondary education, on one hand, and higher education, on the other, there has been somewhat more attention paid to the latter type than the former. A comprehensive study of the future of elementary and secondary school enrollment from 1970 to 2000 under the Census Bureau's Series B and Series E population projections is found in Appleman et al. (1972). Their basic finding is that under either demographic scenario, the quality of education can rise (quality as measured by constant dollars expended per student), but that if population growth can be held to a minimum, the United States can provide a much higher quality of schooling for its young people while spending a lower fraction of gross national product on education. Additionally, the rate of increase of expenditures (constant dollar) was found to be much slower in the future, no matter what the course of fertility, than has been the case in the past two decades. Morrison (1976b) adds to these findings by providing an analysis of prospective changes on enrollment and the future demand for instructional personnel. Maillat (1976) notes that while the proportion of school age children in the population will surely decline by the end of the century, school needs will not necessarily be reduced. Economic, institutional, and cultural variables may be as important as demographic trends in determining the financial requirements of the educational and training system. Among these variables Maillat includes general economic well-being, the broadening of preschool programs, the duration of compulsory education, the scale of vocational training, and the pupil–teacher ratio.

The question of the impact of slower population growth on higher education has been addressed by Dresch (1975), Evans (1975), and McMahon (1975). It should be apparent that education at this level is more clearly an example of voluntary human capital formation than is true at lower levels of education, and indeed, as Dresch points out, is subject to modification with changes in the level of economic activity and technology. However, as Evans notes, education can be an item of consumption as well as an investment good. In this sense, persons can demand additional education for its own sake or as a form of leisure, rather than acting in response to market forces pertaining to the demand for labor. In this sense, then, educational attainment can be not only a factor associated with the secular rise in the level of real income, but also a result of this increase.

An important point worthy of additional study has been raised by Evans in that future enrollment in educational institutions is likely to consist of more older persons and more part-time students. A great deal of this may well be related to the question of labor mobility, which Spengler touches upon and will be covered more thoroughly in following paragraphs. Simply, as persons become displaced due to technological change, it will be advantageous for them to learn new skills or to upgrade the quality of their present skills. The system of higher education may be able to meet a considerable portion of these needs, but again, institutional flexibility will be required in an institution that, on the whole, generally is not thought of as being particularly responsive to change. Furthermore, if this situation does come about, many of the concerns expressed by Leibenstein regarding the replacement effects of new entrants to the labor force, and the consequent upgrading of the human capital stock embodied in the labor force, will be mitigated. In any event, the potential demand for higher education for consumption and for job retraining purposes in response to technological change is an area that requires considerable further investigation.

Spatial Considerations

The research that is considered under this heading concerns the extent to which a decline in the rate of population growth in the United States will affect the spatial distribution of economic activity (Brinkman, 1972), the spatial distribution of population (Morrison, 1972), and the economic and social problems of the central city (Hoover, 1972). Although these studies are included under the overall heading of empirical research, it should be noted that they are somewhat more speculative in nature than many of the other studies reported here.

Brinkman's and Morrison's studies yield more or less parallel results in that they anticipate continued redistribution of economic activity and population to medium-sized metropolitan areas located in the faster growing regions (South and West) of the nation. To this extent, then, they anticipate a continuation of trends that have become more and more apparent. Morrison, however, expects the tempo and volume of migration to be lowered due to the aging of the population. It is well known that migration tends to be highly selective of age, and, as the total population ages, the relative number of events that promote migration (completion of school, first job, marriage, military service, higher education) will decline relative to the population. Morrison anticipates that the trend toward increasing suburbanization will be moderated, but not eliminated.

According to Brinkman, the areas that would be most favorably impacted by a cessation of population growth would be nonmetropolitan areas, particularly those heavily dependent upon agriculture. On the theory that a stationary population would lead in relatively short order to a stationary demand for agricultural products, coupled with increasing mechanization of American agriculture, this might appear to be an appealing hypothesis. There are, however, a variety of mitigating circumstances that suggest that this hypothesis should be subjected to more careful scrutiny prior to complete acceptance. The agricultural population per se is but a small portion of the entire rural population. While an older population may be less mobile, it is also conceivable that more of these persons might choose to remigrate to the area of their birth or to an area far removed from the disamenities of large metropolitan areas. For example, areas of long-time population decline such as Northern Michigan, the Ozarks, and Central Appalachia have seen a turnaround in the rate of population growth.

Perhaps the real question is which outcome is most preferable. There are costs and benefits associated with every pattern of population redistribution and, as Spengler (1975a) notes: "Heterogeneity of tastes and expectations thus adds to the difficulty of arriving at a single overriding and conduct-determining conception of what is 'preferable,' in light of which urban size and structure, as well as population distribution, can be optimized [p. 140]."

According to Brinkman, many large cities are at a point on their average cost curve that is supraoptimal (i.e., average costs are increasing), and "In the absence of zero population growth, additional people... would increase those costs even further and more rapidly than in smaller cities [p. 968]." Additionally, according to Hoover, these cities could move one step beyond and improve the efficiency of the delivery of their services. For example, the greater incidence of smaller families should promote more high-density housing, thus increasing the efficiency of urban transportation systems. There will be less need to construct new service facilities; thus, the annual level of investment can be reduced while maintaining the status quo, or can be maintained and lead to a more rapid replacement of outmoded and inadequate facilities.

A caution is added by Alonso (1973), who notes that even with a national stationary population "vast cross-movements of the population will continue, as will structural changes with society and the economy. Many of today's problems will continue to exist, and some new ones will arise [p. 206]."

In general, there would appear to be a great deal of additional research, primarily empirical in nature, that needs to be done in the area of spatial relationships and the potential consequences of a cessation of population growth. The implications for the present hierarchy of urban areas and the implications for the future would presumably lead the list. One area that could be particularly critical is that of transportation; the requirements for the movement both of individuals and of goods need to be considered. For example, one might ask whether the travel demands of individuals would be lessened due to aging, be increased due to greater discretionary time and income, or unaffected as these factors cancel each other out. Will demand for goods be of such variety that the locus of production will shift more toward the supply of raw materials or the ultimate market? Will this shift, if any, require substantive changes in the present transportation network?

The Labor Force

Questions regarding the labor force are at the very heart of the theoretical discussions we have already considered: Spengler on problems of mobility and advancement, Kelley and Leibenstein on questions of labor productivity, Hieser on the role of leisure, and the general question of whether the substitution effect (of leisure for income) would grow in relative importance under a regimen of population stationarity. Such questions are at the heart of the determination of such crucial variables as the level of per capita output and the composition of final demand.

A variety of approaches has been taken to yield answers to some of these questions. Johnston (1972) has provided an invaluable service by projecting the probable characteristics of the labor force of the future. These include, inter alia, an older, more predominately female, and decidedly more heavily white-collar, orientation. The first of these is merely a reflection of the aging of the population and, consequently, of the labor force. The second is a recognition of recent trends of relatively rapid increases in rates of labor force participation among women of all ages, coupled with the realization that sustained fertility decline can release many women from the traditional family-making role, if they so desire (Zollinger, 1977). The third consequence seems likely in light of the economic history of the United States and other developed countries, although there exists a considerable need to expand the scope of Johnston's projections to include a wider occupational–industry breakdown. To do so, of course, requires a concomitant effort in projection of all sectors of final demand, with recognition of patterns of occupational demand by industry, as well as likely change in patterns in the future. Johnston, indeed, recognizes this problem in observing that while the demand for jobs requiring little education will decrease in the future, the supply of poorly educated persons will diminish even more rapidly (thus, a rapid educational upgrading is likely). However, Johnston goes on to note that the matching of the labor supply (with varying amounts of formal education) to changing relative proportions and skill requirements of particular occupations will be problematic. Johnston also suggests that this problem will be more serious under conditions of relatively high population growth; this, too, is a hypothesis that is worthy of considerable further investigation.

In addition to these considerations two other points regarding the labor force have been made in the literature. These concern productivity and mobility. One might be tempted to reason that growth of the labor force enhances the level of aggregate productivity, on the notion that productivity bears an inverse relationship to age after some point. Sweezy and Owens (1974) demonstrate that for countries in Western Europe there appears to be little relationship between the level of productivity and labor force growth. Additionally, Ryder (1975) notes that: "Organizations that are successful tend to have higher growth rates and, therefore, relatively young age distributions. This may lead us to associate youth with success, without asking whether the former is a cause or a consequence of the latter [p. 19]." Ryder goes on to suggest that often the tendency is to equate productivity (or, at least potential productivity) with recency of education (and hence age). But, he notes, "The assumption underlying this argument is that training ceases upon entry into the labor force. But such is not an institutional imperative [p. 19]." Ryder goes on to reiterate the notion expressed earlier that education of the future labor force may become more of a lifelong, continuous process, rather than follow the abrupt break between formal education and labor force participation that is generally characteristic of the present system.

A corollary to the foregoing discussion is the notion that the older labor force will be less responsive to change and less creative. What exactly constitutes creativity is, of course, somewhat of a moot point; however, both Day (1972) and Sweezy and Owens (1974) agree that this is somewhat of a false issue in general. Actually, Sweezy and Owens's use of Nobel prize winners suggest that the age group of maximum creativity is more or less the pivotal age group in the transition from population growth to population stabilization, in that the share of population in the 35–44 group is relatively constant under any reasonable assessment of the future age composition of the American population. Day goes one step further in suggesting that the older age composition may actually stimulate productivity in that the problem of promotion (to be discussed shortly) may prevent an excessive number of creative individuals from being placed into administrative positions for which they have no talent; in other words, the deleterious effects of the Peter principle will be somewhat weakened.

A major need that appears to be unmet thus far is a study of the effects of declining population growth on the aggregate level of labor productivity. Ideally, such a study will take into account demographic influences on the formation of new capital as well as analyze age, sex, and educational characteristics of the labor force. Additionally, this study also might incorporate the suggestion raised by Dorfman (1972) regarding the concept of effective workers; this may be taken as the actual number of workers adjusted (upward, presumably) for a technical improvement factor and lessened by a factor incorporating the increasing difficulty of production as a result of the potential onset of diminishing returns and the inclusion of social costs of production (such as pollution) in the value of output.

Serow (1976) has provided one attempt to measure the influence of the changing age composition of the labor force on labor productivity as a function of age of the labor force and capital endowments. Serow compares the male labor force consistent with census projections Series D and E for the period 1970–2020. The Series E projection yields a higher level of productivity as a result of a more favorable age composition and a higher capital–labor ratio, although the margin of difference is relatively slight in each instance. This effort, however, must be regarded as a somewhat uncertain first step, due to the exclusion of the female labor force and the failure to take into account prospective changes in the occupational and industrial composition of the labor force.

The question of labor mobility may be approached from a number of perspectives. One might be concerned with the movement of persons between occupations, between geographical areas, and within hierarchical structure (Spengler, 1977). As we have noted previously, Spengler and Johnston have expressed concern with "stickiness" in terms of mobility between occupations, although Ryder's and Evans's notion of education becoming more of a continuous process might ameliorate such considerations. Geographical mobility does, indeed, decline with age, and the alleged role of migration as an equalizer of interregional labor supply and demand imbalances may be hampered by this fact; indeed, a projection of interregional economic growth differentials under conditions of a stationary national population would be extremely helpful in assessing the volume of net interregional migration that would be necessary within this framework. The migration: chicken or egg discussion is relevant here, of course; see Muth (1971, 1972) and Mazek and Chang (1972). The stimulation of labor migration by market and nonmarket mechanisms is an approach that might be utilized to cope with these problems (Browning, 1975).

An interesting question that has potential significance for the question of productivity is the role played by declining population growth in the probability of individual advancement. Keyfitz (1973) flatly and unequivocally notes: "An increasing population facilitates individual mobility. One of the consequences of moving toward the inevitable stationary population is that mobility will become more difficult [p. 335]." It seems at least plausible that such a situation, if left uncorrected, will enhance worker disgruntlement and have adverse consequences for labor productivity. Both Keyfitz (1973) and Spengler (1972a) suggest replacing the steplike process of economic and social advancement with a process more analogous to a ramp, although Keyfitz suggests that individuals are not likely to be stimulated by newly contrived, finely cut divisions of alleged points of status, and that "people may become more concerned with pay and the goods they can buy than with rank and title. Our increasing command over goods may compensate for diminishing command over people [p. 348]." Wander (1976) adds that many of these difficulties may be attributable to temporary or structural shortage of work, rather than to an abundance of older workers blocking career paths.

Another possibility for dealing with the problem of individual mobility is the manipulation of ages at entry to and exit from the labor force (Browning, 1975; Ryder, 1975). Browning notes that early departure should have greater impact due to the obvious linkage of age and seniority. One possible drawback of this suggestion concerns the intensification of the problems associated with social security retirement funding and inflationary pressures that already have been discussed. Again, the interaction of earlier retirement with these variables is a topic worthy of additional research. On the other hand, there exists considerable sentiment among social gerontologists for lengthening working life, or at least for providing greater flexibility in the customary retirement age (Schulz, 1973). Clark (1976c) also points out that a rise in the normal retirement age would also relieve much of the economic burden discussed previously. His projections suggest that in such a situation the proportion of total income needed to support the elderly would approximate that experienced in 1975.

Consumption

There seems to be a myth that there exists within the private sector of the economy widespread support for continued population growth because a cessation of this growth would also spell the end to economic growth (Enke, 1973). While the only support that we could find for this conclusion came from Sinclair Lewis's novel *Babbitt*, there does exist the justifiable question of how a decline in population growth will affect:

1. The absolute volume of consumption
2. The volume of consumption relative to savings
3. The distribution of consumption to competing industries

All of these questions have been addressed by various studies.

In the long run, of course, the absolute volume of consumption will be less under conditions of population stationarity than under population growth, due to the sheer weight of numbers. Such a statement is, of course, essentially gratuitous, because there is some point at which the efficiency of production is maximized, and, beyond that range, diminishing returns and increasing costs set in. While there is little doubt that the rapid population growth of nineteenth-century America provided the basic impetus for the transformation of the nation from the agrarian society of 1800 to the industrial society of 1900, one is compelled rather strongly to agree with Kelley (1972) in his assertion that the impetus provided by population growth to the realization of economies of scale has probably diminished in quantitative importance over time, possibly to the point of insignificance. The real question is the relationship between rates of population growth and levels of per capita consumption.

Resek and Siegel (1974) have examined consumer expenditure patterns under a variety of demographic conditions. They suggest that the rate of population growth affects consumption via an influence on the age composition of the population and on the level of per capita income. Their findings suggest that slower population growth enhances the level of per capita income and hence per capita consumption. Similar findings were reported previously by Serow (1972) and in the projections prepared by the Bureau of Economic Analysis for use in the research reports of the Commission on Population Growth and the American Future (Appleman *et al.*, 1972; Howard & Lehmann, 1972; Jones, 1972). Furthermore, Resek and Siegel's empirical findings support the contention of Spengler (1972a) that the savings rate will increase under conditions of slow population growth.

Most of the studies in this area have dealt with the changing shares among industries of the total volume of consumption (Eilenstine and Cunningham, 1972; Espenshade, 1978; Howard and Lehmann, 1972; Resek and Siegel, 1974), or with particular industries; for example, agricultural commodities (Serow, 1972), health and welfare (Appleman *et al.*, 1972; Denton and Spencer, 1975b), and housing (Jones, 1972; Marcin, 1974). We have treated education as a separate area for our purposes, but to some extent it could have easily been included under the heading of consumption.

The degree to which prospective changes in the rate of population growth will affect the composition of consumer demand seems to be determined by the degree of aggregation utilized in the analysis. Looking at the rather broad categories utilized by the Consumer Expenditure Survey of 1960–1961, Eilenstine and Cunningham summarize their findings as follows: "The consumption patterns of a stationary population are sufficiently like those associated with a growing population, so that there is no real reason to fear economic disorder from this source with the cessation of population growth [p. 230]." Similar findings are reported by Resek and Siegel, but they noted that, with lower population growth, there is "a change in the distribution of the sectors toward durables at the expense of services, with little effect in the relative share of nondurables [p. 290]."

Using a somewhat different analytical technique, Espenshade (1978) arrives at results parallel to those just mentioned. The basic data set utilized are actual consumption expenditures by category in the United States from 1929 to 1941 and from 1946 to 1970. These data are analyzed in a multiple regression framework that uses relative prices, previous levels of consumption (by category), and measures of age composition and household size as independent variables. The net differences in the composition of consumption between a continuously growing population and one approaching the stationary state are negligible. Espenshade notes that, "In general, the changes in consumption spending occasioned by . . . a stationary population are counteracted by the increase in total consumption per head accompanying the reduction in fertility [p. 157]."

The degree of aggregation in this study, like those of Eilenstine and Cunningham and Resek and Siegel, is rather great. Espenshade suggests that a greater degree of disaggregation of expenditure categories "might show demographic influences hidden in the aggregations that were used [p. 158]." The findings of Denton and Spencer (1976) also address themselves to this point. By utilizing time series analysis of Canadian data and cross-sectional analysis of international data, they find that "aggregate consumption is not affected directly by variations in average household size or in the age distribution of the population.... Of course, this does not imply an absence of direct household and age effects on particular *categories* of consumption, but only on the aggregate [p. 93, emphasis in the original]." The sorts of changes that might be expected with a greater degree of disaggregation have been outlined by Wander (1976). Three points are made:

1. Demand for such goods and services as food and clothing for children, toys, sporting facilities, and nurseries will decline unless new domestic or foreign markets are found.
2. Due to a greater number of small, adult-only households, demand for higher priced consumer durables, personal effects, recreation, entertainment, adult education, and the like will rise.
3. Increases in per capita income will shift demand from short- to long-lasting goods, from poorer to higher quality goods, from essentials to luxuries, and from the conventional to the new [p. 10].

Similar findings were reported by Howard and Lehmann, although the analysis was done in terms of specific industries rather than segments of final demand. Generally speaking, their findings show that industries that cater to those segments of the economy most directly benefited by increasing amounts of discretionary time and income will be the best off. While they note that many individual business concerns will have to adjust their market strategies or product mixes or both, the well-being of industry as a whole will not be much affected by population change.

The influences of differential rates of population growth in the demand of welfare and health services have been studied by Appleman *et al.* (1972). It should first be noted that "welfare" in this context refers only to public assistance payments of various forms. Their results are somewhat tentative, but suggest that the dollar volume of welfare required to lift all persons above the poverty guideline will at best slowly decline and may even increase. Generally, the findings suggest that the aggregate needs of the poor are relatively insensitive to differential population growth, and may even be adversely affected by slow growth if that situation does, in fact, lead to a higher level of per capita income. Eversley (1976) suggests that it is possible that poverty and welfare problems might increase, since a portion of the population most at risk (i.e., the elderly) will increase and they will have, on the average, fewer children to look after them.

This raises the important issue of the implications of population stationarity for income distribution. The only contribution to this area to date has been that of Heeren (1976). The preliminary conclusion that

Heeren reaches is that while the evidence suggests that there is not likely to be

> a significant increase in income inequality, this stability may conceal a possible shift in the composition of the poverty population. In particular, the proportion of the poor who are aged 65 and over may become larger in the decades ahead. *Whether these results will occur depends on the validity of the assumptions traditionally made by students of income distribution theory* [p. 51, emphasis added].

It is clear that there are important theoretical and empirical issues that need to be resolved in this area. Given that income redistribution is at least nominally a goal of governmental policy, it is crucial that research be conducted to ascertain how prospective population changes will affect the levels of income of different subpopulations and the extent and nature of differential effects. One is reminded of Phelps's (1972) contention that an increase in real wages is beneficial to those relatively well endowed with human capital, while a decline in real profits harms those relatively well endowed with nonhuman capital. Since under conditions of a stationary population, labor will be a relatively scarce resource, then it would seem reasonable to conclude that wages will rise in relative importance as a source of total income while income from profits on capital will fall, in a relative sense. Because wage and salary income represents a larger proportion of total income in low- and middle-income groups, the relative increase in wages might be anticipated to enhance the overall distribution of income. Furthermore, because the aged are less likely to be active members of the labor force, their relative economic position will be weakened, as Heeren suggested. These are contentions that can and should be subjected to empirical testing in order to establish whether a trend toward slower population growth will create more or less income inequality.

The work of Appleman *et al.* regarding the demand for health services (defined in their analysis only as visits to physicians and dentists, as well as utilization of hospitals) shows that relatively rapid growth between 1970 and 2000 would require substantially higher total outlays than would slower population growth. Given that the difference in total population size between the Series B and Series E projections is about 50 million persons by 2000, this is not a surprising result. The authors suggest that future demand for health services will be primarily a function of economic conditions and the availability of health insurance, rather than of population growth (on the individual level). While this is, in itself, a subject of additional research, one is also curious to know whether the differing age structure of the stationary population would have any quantitative importance. A longer period analysis of Canadian data (Denton and Spencer, 1975b) suggests that population change is likely to have considerable impact on the cost of health care, due to fertility variation and its influence on age structure.

The area of demand for housing is clearly one that is highly responsive to changes in economic and demographic conditions. One need only look at the fluctuations in the number of new housing starts, for example, to see the veracity of this in the short run. Of interest here, of course, is the longer-run situation, particularly as a response to demographic change. Studies of this effect have been undertaken by Jones (1972), Marcin (1974), and Morrison (1977a). Jones's effort is somewhat hampered by the fact that his time horizon ends with the present century. Although the Series B and E projections differ considerably in terms of total population size and age composition by 2000, the number of households does not vary greatly, since only a small fraction of households are headed by persons under age 30 (i.e., those born during the projection period). Marcin's results are somewhat more comprehensive in that his time horizon extends to the middle of the next century, when economic and demographic factors have been allowed to interact for a considerable period of time. While Marcin's results are useful in terms of illustrating the prospective nature of change in the demand for housing (in terms of size and composition of demand), it would seem that further work in this area could usefully be coupled with the analysis of population and income redistribution that has been suggested previously. Morrison's analysis is more general than these, but includes discussion of differential mortality and changing household status as well as age composition and population and income redistribution.

The final consumption-related topic to be included is Serow's (1972) study of demand for agricultural commodities. This study allows for economic–demographic interaction over an extended period of time, but is hampered, as are many of the aforementioned studies, by the assumption of constancy in marginal propensities to consume over time. It would appear that useful additional work could be undertaken in the determination of changes in these propensities in light of the demographic–economic change implicit in the attainment of stationary population.

The discussion thus far has focused entirely on the role of the household sector and its demand for goods and services. Similar questions can be raised regarding the industrial and governmental sectors, as well. In the former case, analysis might well take an input–output approach, allowing variation in consumer demand to affect, both directly and indirectly, the demand for the output of industry components. Although the governmental sector is implicitly represented in many of the analyses suggested previously (social security, education, health, transportation), there exists considerable need for additional work on the demands of this sector in light of prospective changes in the composition of the population and its rate of increase.

Policy Implications and Additional Suggestions for Further Research

The policy questions pertaining to the attainment of a stationary population are not of the variety that ask "whether," but rather concern "when." As Coale (1968) has noted, "In the long run, an average rate of increase of zero is not only desirable but inevitable [p. 469]." Thus, the questions to be asked are

1. When should population growth cease (or what is the appropriate population optimum) (Ryder, 1972)?
2. What time horizon should be employed to achieve this goal (that is, what is the appropriate time path to follow to minimize social and economic disruption)?
3. What instruments should be employed to attain the desired result?

The first question is really the old optimum population issue, one which has never been resolved satisfactorily (see Zinam, 1974). Are we better off with the higher ultimate stationary population achieved by allowing population to grow for additional periods, or should growth cease at once? As Coale notes, "the choice is inevitably not only for ourselves but also for future generations [p. 471]," and a decision to end growth at once or relatively quickly may do our descendants "a favor that they will never appreciate [p. 472]." More research is needed into the question of the differential effects of size differences in this ultimate population.

The second question is in many ways the same as the first. The crucial point is that in this case we need to know much more about the economic and social implications of alternative paths to the stationary population. It is probable that a very abrupt attainment of stationarity would have a severely disequilibrating effect in the short and intermediate run, but the population would be of a smaller size than the ultimate stationary–stable population achieved by a more gradual transition. Thus, we need to know more not only about the costs and benefits of alternative ultimate population sizes, but also about the costs and benefits of alternative paths to population stationarity as well.

In this connection, it is important to realize that as population growth rates settle down to approximate zero, current (period) rates of fertility are likely to fluctuate rather than to remain perfectly constant (Wander, 1977). The measurement of costs and benefits should also include some provision for differences in the period and amplitude of these oscillations. Studies for the Belgian economy by Wijewickrema et al. (n.d.) suggest that the period of oscillation is more important than the amplitude, and that economic disruption is relatively less severe with a short (13 years) or long (52 years) cycle, than with a medium term (26-year) one.

Finally, what means should be employed to meet whatever goal is chosen? Davis (1973) notes that the technology is simple and on hand. The motivational and educational aspects are of compelling importance. Davis adds: "They (people) do not want runaway population growth either, but they want it painlessly. They want a solution that leaves them their freedom to have five children if they wish. In short they want a miracle [pp. 28–29]."

Ryder (1973) lists a variety of policies available to governments to reduce the course of population growth: education and exhortation; economic incentives and disincentives; and, compulsion. Further research is needed to establish the consequences, costs, and benefits of these alternative approaches (and combination of approaches, where feasible). In choosing among these alternatives, and in evaluating them, it is also imperative to bear in mind Heeren's (1974) comment that "every kind of population policy must link up with existing demographic developments and trends, rather than try to run counter to these trends [p. 252]."

There remains one more policy-related issue to raise, and this is the question of international effects of population stationarity. The answer would appear to lie in the entire demographic context in which the stationarity occurs. If stationarity characterizes the population of one or a few countries while in the remainder population growth persists, then questions of the international distribution of goods and raw materials come into play. Certainly, the foreign-trade sector can be affected in somewhat different ways under different assumptions of worldwide demographic trends. Furthermore, since the importance of foreign trade differs among national economies, the results are apt to differ substantially. Hence, cross-national analysis of this question is another area in which fruitful research could be initiated.

Barber (1975) has made some assessment of the relative economic effects of a stationary population on developed countries. He argues that the effect of a cessation of population growth on capital spending would be somewhat different for countries in North America or Oceania than would be the case in Western Europe or Japan. This conclusion is based on the fact that most of the output increases in the former group are attributable to increases in employment, while in the latter group most of these increases are attributable to increased productivity. Furthermore, Western Europe and Japan have, according to Barber, greater remaining potential for shifting resources into spheres of industrial activity that is more productive. The degree of productivity in North America and Oceania is already quite high, and the extent to which further reorganization of industrial activity will enhance productivity is quite limited.

With large-scale warfare of the future likely to be conducted more and more by mechanical devices, it is possible that the economic and military aims of the state might best be fostered by smaller rather than larger population vis-à-vis those of competing states. In other words, if one chooses to adopt a neomercantilist perspective of the appropriate aims of the state, the appropriate policy regarding population in the current context might be the precise opposite of mercantilist population policy. Kelly (1976) suggests that there is a range of population between the smallest and largest that will yield output sufficient for both subsistence and defense needs. Within this range, a country might apply policies to increase or decrease population or to alter the age composition, but presumably would try not to move its population out of this range. While Organski and Organski (1961) state that population size is one determinant of national power, the level of economic development and the efficiency of the national government are also of critical importance. In view of the relationship, discussed previously, between population growth and income, it is far from apparent that population growth implies a concomitant increase in national power (for a different view, in the context of developing countries, see Hendershot, 1973).

The interest in the size and growth rate of the population of one country vis-à-vis another has had a long history in Western Europe, especially in France. Calot and Hecht (1976) reviewed pronatalist policies actually adopted in Europe. In reviewing such measures as economic incentives, disincentives, and changes in the availability of contraception and abortion, they conclude that "the ways to encourage fertility are to make further provision in the traditional field of family benefits, with a greater effort in favour of the 3rd child and subsequent children, and to try to make it easier for mothers to combine family responsibilities with a job [p. 18]." Even this, in their view, is unlikely to make much difference in light of past reactions of the public to such experiments. Government policy, in the view of Calot and Hecht, would be better advised "to try to control the consequences of unfavorable fertility trends than to count on being able to correct such developments if and when they occur [p. 19]."

Van de Kaa (1976) came to a similar conclusion in remarking that levels of fertility "reflect to a very large extent the choice of the population in the matter as to how an optimum quality of life can best be achieved under the circumstances currently prevailing in Western Europe [p. 12]." Governments, therefore, concludes van de Kaa, should be slow to ask the citizenry to subordinate their individual interest to the perceived collective interest unless the collective interest (in this case, a higher rate of population growth) can be clearly shown to exist.

In addition to attempts to stimulate fertility, another proposal that has been advanced for stimulating population growth, where government policy had determined that such was advisable, is immigration. Sica (1976) raises the question: "What are the long-term chances of maintaining the population by means of immigration [p. 2]?" He concludes that these chances depend upon two fundamental conditions: First, the host country must be able to rely on immigrant pools sheltered from political, economic, and social vicissitudes; second, the host country must agree to become polycultural. Sica suggests that both conditions are unlikely, the first due to political reasons, the second due to the historic aversion of European nations to polyculturalism ("but nearly all the countries of Europe cherish the idea of the single-culture nation state [p. 3]"). The degree to which immigration as a means of sustaining economic growth will be successful is questioned by Barber (1975), who notes that in the case of exporting nations such as Canada and Australia the rate of growth in their markets (particularly the United States, Western Europe, and Japan) may well be the decisive factor.

In closing, a variety of research topics has been suggested in the present and foregoing sections. The proper approach to some of these requires a microperspective, whereas that of others requires a macroperspective. What is of overriding importance is that these undertakings be carried out in a manner that will allow the result to be compiled and evaluated as a body of knowledge rather than as isolated studies operating in the abstract (de Sandre, 1976). A careful selection of models (see Arthur & McNicoll, 1975) and assumptions is needed to ensure comparability.

3

Zero Population Growth Now: The Lessons from Europe

HILDE WANDER

Zero Population Growth: Theory and Reality

Conformity and Disconformity with Stable Models

According to stable population theory, any closed demographic system will eventually attain a stable-stationary state once replacement level fertility is reached and permanently continued. Under such conditions birth rates and death rates will ultimately stabilize at identical levels, and population will cease to grow and will attain a constant sex-age composition. It is often assumed that the demographic transition from high to low fertility and mortality levels will finally lead to such a state. Indeed, much of the ongoing discussion concerning the implications of zero population growth (ZPG) is based on the properties of models simulating perfect stationarity.

In most parts of Western Europe—with the main exceptions of Ireland, Portugal, and Spain—fertility has reached or even fallen below replacement level (see Table 3.1). While there is still a moderate excess of births over deaths in many of these countries, there are several others where natural increase has practically ceased or turned negative[1] (see

---

[1] In the German Democratic Republic, too, death rates have come to surpass birth rates, but Eastern Europe will not be dealt with in this chapter.

Table 3.2). We do not know how fertility will develop in the future; nevertheless, the incidence of zero growth or decline as such suggests the beginning of a new secular stage of demographic development. Never before in the long history of demographic transition did population ever stop growing, in normal times, because of deficient fertility. The few incidents of nongrowth or decline on record were always associated with wars or other hardships forcing death rates up and bringing birth rates down for a short period. Even in the 1930s, when fertility fell much below replacement level in many Western European countries, none—except for France—experienced absolute population decline. At that time the number of fertile women born before the secular fall in fertility set in was still large enough to produce an excess of births over deaths in spite of very low fertility. Today this potential is much smaller, so that any drop in fertility now tends to depress population growth much more immediately than ever before.

Unlike stationary models, which assume a complete standstill of population, the state reached in several Western European countries and swiftly approached in others can at best be termed as "pseudo-

TABLE 3.1.
Net Reproduction Rates in Selected Western European Countries: 1960, 1964, 1970, and Latest Available Year[a]

Country	1960	1964	1970	Latest available year
Austria	1.19	1.30	1.07	.91 (1975)
Belgium	1.19	1.27	1.06	.88 (1975)
Denmark	1.20	1.23	.93	.91 (1973)
England and Wales	1.25	1.36	1.13	.96 (1973)
France	1.29	1.37	1.17	.91 (1975)
Federal Republic of Germany	1.11	1.18	.94	.65 (1975)
Greece	.99	1.01	1.12	1.09 (1974)
Ireland	1.70	1.87	1.79	1.79 (1972)
Italy	1.07	1.23	1.11	1.07 (1973)
Netherlands	1.46	1.50	1.22	.84 (1975)
Portugal	1.33	1.32	1.20	1.33 (1972)
Spain	1.24	NA	1.35	1.32 (1973)
Sweden	1.02	1.18	.92	.90 (1975)
Switzerland	1.08	1.26	.98	.82 (1975)

[a] UN, Demographic Yearbook, New York, 17th Issue (1965), p. 611 ff.; 21st Issue (1969), p. 475 ff.; 27th Issue (1975), p. 524 ff.—Population Index, Princeton, N.J., Vol. 42 (1976), No. 2 (April), p. 367 ff.—Various sources of individual countries.

TABLE 3.2.
Natural Increase in Selected Western European Countries: 1960, 1964, 1970, 1975, and 1976 (per 1,000 of mean population)[a]

Country	1960	1964	1970	1975	1976
Austria	5.1	6.2	1.9	−.3	−1.0
Belgium	4.0	5.0	2.3	.0	.2
Denmark	7.0	7.7	4.6	4.2	2.2
England and Wales	5.7	7.1	4.3	.4	−.3
France	6.5	7.5	6.1	3.5	3.2
FRG	6.3	7.2	1.7	−2.4	−2.1
Greece	11.6	9.8	8.1	6.8	7.5
Ireland	9.9	11.1	10.3	10.9	10.3[b]
Italy	8.8	10.4	7.1	4.9	4.3
Netherlands	13.2	13.0	10.0	4.7	4.6
Portugal	13.4	13.2	9.2	8.6	9.0[b]
Spain	13.0	13.5	11.1	9.9	9.7
Sweden	3.6	6.0	3.7	1.8	.9
Switzerland	8.0	9.6	6.9	3.8	3.2

[a]UN, Demographic Yearbook, op. cit., various issues.
—UN, Monthly Bulletin of Statistics, New York, Vol. 31 (1977), No. 6, p. 6 ff; Vol. 32 (1978), No. 5, p. 6 ff.
[b]Preliminary.

stationary."[2] It has evolved from fertility rates fluctuating around replacement level for about six decades rather than always keeping constant at this level. Figure 3.1 shows the changes in net reproduction rates (N) in five Western European countries since 1920, that is, over a period during which roughly 80% of today's population were born. Except for the Netherlands, which has been included to indicate the specific conditions in countries where fertility has remained fairly high until the early 1970s, in the other countries (those shown in Figure 3.1 and several others, too) periods of subreplacement fertility interchanged with periods of surplus fertility, thus keeping N close to 1.0, on an average.

Obviously, fluctuating fertility cannot bring about a regular and invariant age structure, but rather leads to distinct deviations from the respective stationary model such as exemplified in Figure 3.2 for the Federal Republic of Germany (FRG) and Sweden. Contrary to the situation in the 1930s, the age composition of both populations has assumed some marked features of a pseudostationary state. It resembles its stationary

[2]This term was first used by DeKerpel et al. (1976). I consider it superior to the term "quasi-stationary" which I used in some of my previous works.

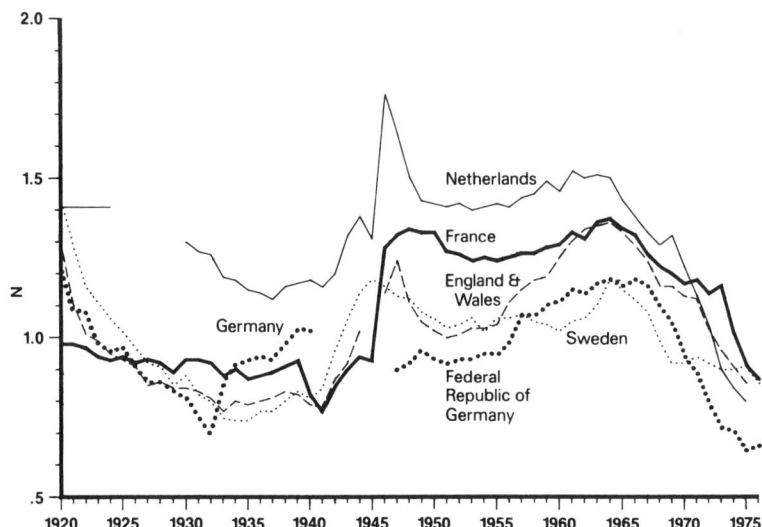

Figure 3.1 Net reproduction rates (N) of selected West European countries, 1920–1976. German Reich in varying boundaries. Rate partly estimated.

equivalent only for broad age groups, whereas individual age groups vary to either side of the model.

There is nothing to suggest that birth rates eventually will stop fluctuating, nor is it certain that they will swing around replacement level in a way to restore permanently the stock of population. Zero population growth as presently experienced in parts of Western Europe may as well make up only a short interlude on the way toward progressive decline through natural decrease. Discussions concerning the social and economic consequences of the downturn in births should therefore also consider the possibility of long-term population decline. In the Federal Republic of Germany, which has experienced the sharpest fall in births, the stage is already set for such a development, unless fertility should climb immediately and keep well above replacement level for at least one to two decades. Immigration aside, the lower fertility drops and the longer it remains deficient, the greater is the danger that the process of shrinking cannot be stopped again.

At any rate, neither ZPG nor progressive population decline can be expected to follow a smooth course. In both cases the actual path is due to oscillate around a horizontal or sloping trend line, respectively. Zero growth can thus be described as a succession of alternating short- or medium-term variations in population increase and decrease that compensate each other over time, thus keeping population size "constant," on balance. Similarly, a shrinking (or growing) population of the "pseudostable" sort may be defined as the outcome of changing growth paths that leave a negative (or positive) balance in the long run. Moreover, as birth rates always affect only one age cohort at the time, resulting swings in growth trends are bound to be much more pronounced in individual age groups than in the total population. Thus, a population keeping nearly constant or experiencing an almost constant decline in total numbers may nevertheless undergo remarkable variation in age structure.

Indeed, such shifts have been observed in many Western European countries, although total population did not change very much, at least not from natural causes. This fact is exemplified in Figure 3.3 by West

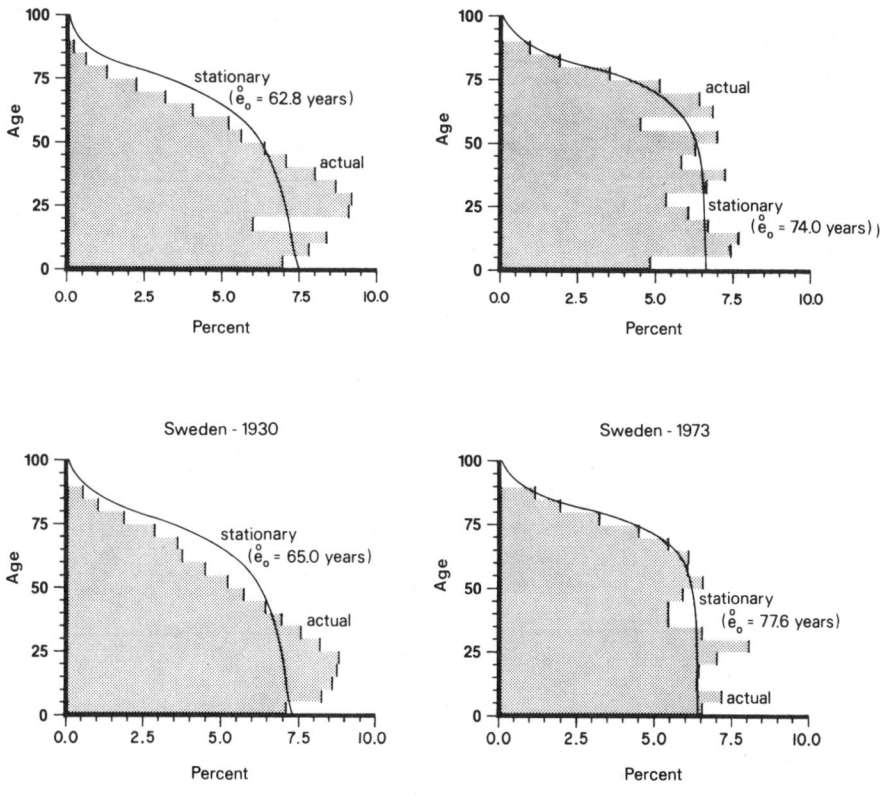

Figure 3.2. The age composition in Germany (1933 and 1975) and in Sweden (1930 and 1973) compared with respective stationary models (females only).

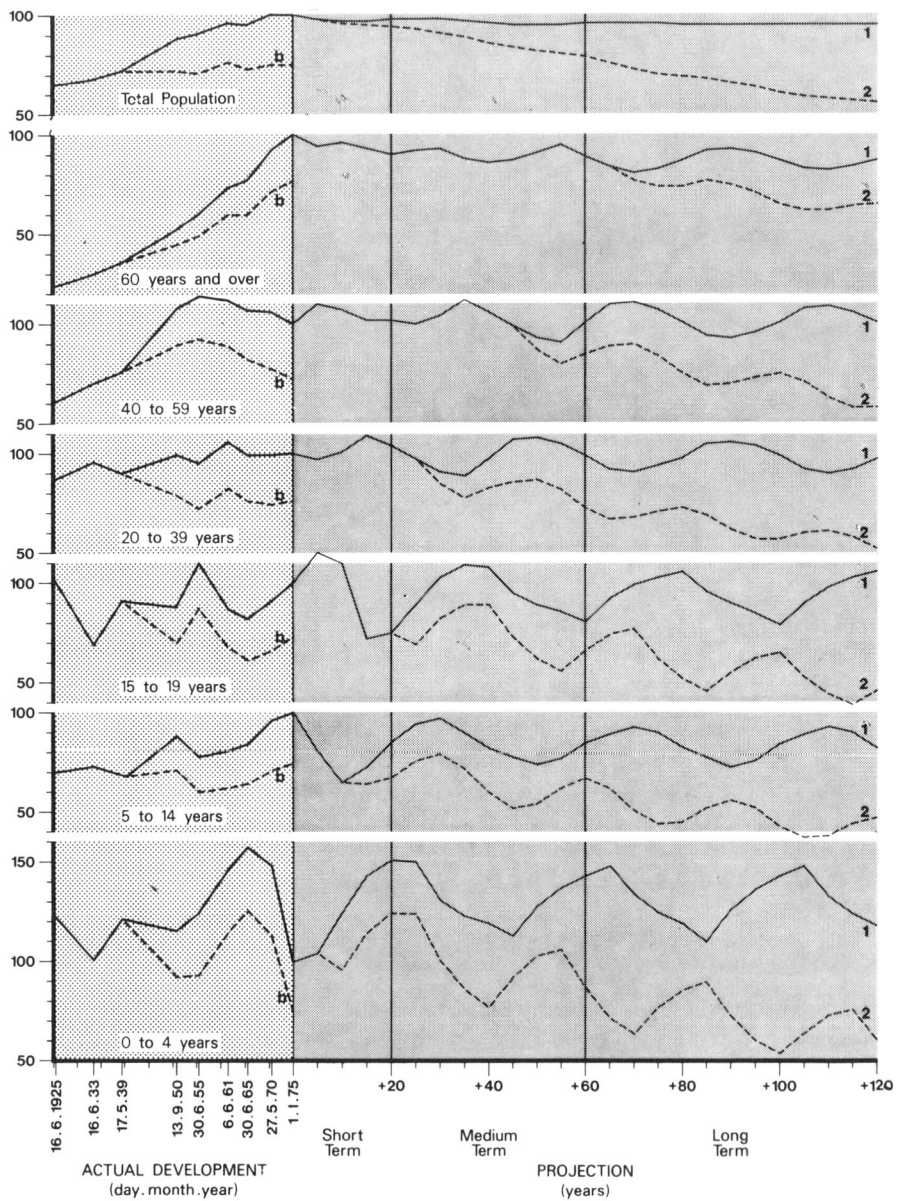

Figure 3.3. Actual and projected variations in the number of females of German nationality in the FRG, 1925–1975 and 120 years ahead assuming constant mortality and changing fertility leading (1) to ZPG and (2) to progressive decline. Projections are based on assumptions shown in the text. Curve b is for natives, excluding German refugees.

German native females.[3] It reveals both actual variations in the size of some important age groups between 1925 and 1975 as well as future changes projected to occur if mortality would always keep constant at the 1975 level ($\mathring{e}_0$ = 74 years) and if N would fluctuate (1) between .8 and 1.2 or (2) between .7 and 1.0 in a specific regular time sequence.[4] The first projection, which involves a 40-year cycle of change, leads to approximate zero growth, whereas the second one, which has a cycle of 30 years, implies progressive decline. It is interesting to note that without the influx of refugees after World War II the West German female population virtually would have stopped growing as early as the 1930s. Moreover, in the course of time, all age groups, except for the older ones, were successively subjected to cyclical swings. This general pattern of alternating gains and losses in the number of people in the various age groups will continue and also include the upper strata, disregarding whether further development will turn to zero growth or to long-lasting decline. The variations that the young groups below 20 years have been following are indeed quite similar to the succeeding swings indicated by the projections.

With given assumptions, age composition in both projections will ultimately attain some sort of "moving stability." It will constantly change according to a fixed pattern as determined by the amplitude and periodicity of the fertility variations, but it will never match the respective stationary ($N = 1.0$) or stable ($N = .86$) age structures. The latter represent only the average of all age compositions to be attained successively within each periodic cycle (see Table 3.3).

This finding is very important. It suggests that the conventional stationary or stable models are not well suited to analyze the implications of ZPG or of continuous population decline. Rather than total population, it is the individual age groups or age-related groups that are most crucial in economic and social respects. Since some of these groups tend to expand while others shrink in consequence of fluctuating fertility, the social and economic implications of ZPG or continuous population decline, too, are always a corollary of both falling and rising birth trends but never of constant fertility. At any rate, changes in volume and struc-

---

[3]There was a heavy influx of refugees after World War II, but the age composition of the migrants was very much the same as that of the indigenous population. Females have been used rather than total population, since their age structure was not much affected by casualties of war.

[4]Both projections start with $N = .8$. In projection (1), N increases to .9 in the following 5-year period, to 1.0 in the next, etc., until the upper limit of 1.2 is reached. Then N declines in regular steps (of .1 in every 5 years) until the lower limit of .8 is reached, etc. In projection (2), N decreases to .7 over the first 5 years, before it climbs up in regular steps (of .1 in every 5-year period) to 1.0. From there it turns down again in regular steps to .7, etc.

TABLE 3.3.
Patterns of Variation in Age Composition of West German Native Females after Stabilization of Assumed Cycles of Fertility Change

Age group (years)	Length of cycle (years)	Percentage of persons in age group		Coefficient of variance (%)
		Lower and upper limits	Average[a]	
(1) Zero growth [$\mathring{e}_0 = 74$ years; $N = .8$–1.2]				
0–19	40	24.4–28.1	26.4	4.8
20–39	40	23.9–28.3	26.1	5.6
40–59	40	23.2–26.9	25.0	4.5
60+	40	21.1–24.1	22.5	4.0
(2) Progressive decline [$\mathring{e}_0 = 74$ years; $N = .7$–1.0]				
0–19	30	20.4–23.7	22.1	4.7
20–39	30	22.3–26.8	24.6	6.0
40–59	30	23.9–28.8	26.4	6.1
60+	30	25.9–28.0	26.9	3.0

[a] Corresponds to stationary population ($N = 1.0$) in respect of assumption (1) and to a stable declining population with $N = .86$ in respect of assumption (2).

ture of important groups, especially working-age population and population beyond working age, have been predetermined for several decades ahead by previous fluctuations in births such as indicated in Figure 3.1.

Clearly, birth fluctuations are not peculiar to ZPG or population decline, but they are of special relevance in such settings. As long as fertility is high enough to insure continuous population growth, temporary fertility decline is less likely to lead to sharp reductions in the number of births, and age groups are consequently less liable to pronounced periodic swings. However, within the rigid framework of ZPG or progressive decline, there is less scope for dampening the effects of fertility fluctuations, and age groups are therefore subject to more pronounced gains and losses in absolute size. This fact implies certain difficulties for the economy and the social system to adjust to the various age-specific needs that tend to expand and contract. On the other hand, some demographic instability of this sort may well stimulate special investment activities and counteract certain tendencies toward a downturn in business cycles that many observers expect to arise from nongrowth or decline in total population.

Apart from these general features that distinguish stagnant or shrinking populations from growing ones, neither ZPG nor progressive population decline of given speed signify unequivocal conditions in demographic and other respects. Both paths of demographic development are consistent with innumerable patterns of fertility change and of resulting variations in age structure. This, in turn, implies many different sorts of age-related social and economic consequences depending, at any time, on the specific phase attained in the fertility cycle and on the amplitude and periodicity of the cycle.[5] Several Western European countries that have reached ZPG suffer from shortages of training and employment capacity to absorb properly the young generation now entering the labor market in large numbers, whereas in 10 to 15 years the respective age groups will probably be too small to fill available training and working places. In contrast, school population, which is presently decreasing, may then increase again and likely meet with insufficient supply of staff and teaching facilities.

The Role of the Social and Economic Setting

Apart from the structural and cyclical peculiarities just described, the social and economic framework has an important bearing on the present and prospective implications of ZPG in Western Europe. Demographic processes affect the economy through the consumption needs and the productive activities of the people, and it is clear that these needs and activities are determined largely by economic circumstances, social opportunities, institutional norms, productive skills, and many other conditions guiding working and spending behavior, and not just by population size. The impact of a given population trend is therefore never fixed. It always depends on the interplay of all relevant factors, which tend to vary constantly in combination and relative importance. The more developed and differentiated the social and economic setting is, the more will the demographic effects intermingle with others.[6]

Over the last few decades and especially after World War II, industrial structure, production techniques, market organization skill requirements, and, last but not least, international economic integration, have very much advanced in Western Europe and have accordingly altered the relation between population and economic growth. Due to more intensive international trade relations, Western European economies have become less dependent than before on an ever expanding volume of national consumers in order to secure sufficient outlets for investment

[5] The different impact on GNP exerted by different fertility cycles is clearly reflected in the models devised by DeKerpel *et al*. (1976).

[6] It is, of course, impossible to disentangle sufficiently the complicated interplay of demographic and other variables by either models or empirical research. All the more so is it necessary to consider this limitation when interpreting the findings of such studies.

and employment, but instead are more susceptible to disturbances from the world market. Due to rapidly advancing technical progress, there is a much greater need for flexible and highly qualified workers rather than for a steadily growing labor force. Moreover, with the increasing role of the welfare state and its tighter control over the factors affecting production, employment, and income distribution, there is a better chance to counteract any undesirable consequences of demographic stagnation or decline—for example, on consumption, saving, or labor mobility—by means of economic and social policy.[7] At any rate, the implications of ZPG or shrinking population in Western Europe and, in particular, the tendency toward more pronounced variations in age structure must be seen in relation to the economic and social setting and to prospective changes in this setting. Experiences or theories based upon previous economic and social conditions may be misleading when indiscriminately applied today or to future periods.

A further point to be considered concerns the time interval over which the different social and economic implications of fertility change will materialize. It is obvious that fertility change affects immediately only the group of infant consumers and that any future consequences may be modified in various ways depending on the social and economic conditions that will then exist (e.g., whether or not the decline in births in Western Europe will eventually lead to labor shortage is largely a matter of labor demand and working habits prevailing two or three decades hence). In general, the longer the time period, the less chance of distinguishing between the effects of fertility change and those of other factors. Moreover, as we shall see later, the way in which the more immediate problems of fertility change (especially in the field of education) are being tackled has an important bearing on the strength of any later problems and on the possibilities to solve them.

This is not to minimize the social and economic relevance of the steep downturn in births observed in Western Europe, but rather to stress the complexity of the problems and to warn against any rigorous conclusions. What can be brought to light in the following analysis are general tendencies that may be subject to severe modification under the influence of social and economic change. Nevertheless, since fertility trends as well as economic and social development have been very similar in the past in many Western European countries, one may expect much conformity in future trends as well. With this assumption, the model shown in Figure 3.3 seems suitable to reveal certain possible implica-

---

[7]The importance of adaptive policies has been stressed by Reddaway (1977) and Wander (1971).

tions of ZPG or continuous decline that concern many of the highly developed market economies of Europe. It is true that fertility in the Federal Republic of Germany—on which the model is based—has fallen much more than elsewhere, but this fact allows one to indicate the path that other countries soon may follow or should preferably avoid. The model can disclose the intricate task of safeguarding ZPG and preventing long-lasting decline after fertility has reached extremely low levels. Since it embraces a period of 170 years, it permits the illustration of the transition to ZPG and also the comparison of short-, medium-, and long-term implications of ZPG with those arising from progressive shrinking.

Social and Economic Implications during the Transition to Zero Population Growth

Fertility Change and Business Cycles

The six to seven decades of this century that preceded ZPG in the Federal Republic of Germany and some other Western European countries include several phases of decreasing fertility that mostly coincided with economic or political crises, and several phases of increasing fertility, which mostly coincided with economic and social improvement. This fact should, however, not be taken as evidence for the existence of any fixed association between birth decline, slowing population growth, and economic deterioration, or between rising birth rates, expanding population, and economic prosperity, as suggested by some critics.[8] There was certainly a tendency among couples to postpone births in times of hardships and to replace them later in times of economic recovery. This type of response caused short-term fluctuations in births and, in turn, varying age composition, but it did not involve any major change in completed fertility. Indeed, in spite of the heavy slump in births during both world wars and during the economic depression of the 1930s, completed fertility of most cohorts born between the late 1890s and the early 1940s kept fairly close to two children per woman in the Federal Republic of Germany; and similar steadiness around a somewhat higher or lower level respectively has been observed in France, Sweden, and England and Wales over quite extensive periods.[9]

---

[8]Such a simplistic view has been rejected convincingly for earlier periods by Lösch (1936).
[9]See INED (1977), p. 336 ff.

More important, as experienced today, fertility also may decline under conditions of economic prosperity. Never before have living standards been so high and birth rates so low as today in Western Europe. It may be that the rise in unemployment after 1973 has somewhat accelerated the ongoing fall in fertility, but this does not remove the fact that the downward trend started and advanced during a period of full employment and economic expansion.

Thus, if fertility decline may be associated with both economic boom and depression, it is hard to see why it should affect business cycles in any determinate manner. The numerical loss of some infant consumers, which is the most immediate consequence of any decrease in births, can of itself not bring about a downturn in effective demand, investment activities, and employment chances. The relationship that exists between demographic and economic processes is much more complicated and highly influenced by such imponderable issues as norms, life-styles, tastes, chances, and aspirations that motivate both the generative and the economic behavior of the population.

Economic and reproductive behavior patterns emerge from the same set of values. They are brought into balance within this framework and through a complicated institutional system of social restraints and impulses rather than through direct response. Economic goals and activities associated with a decline (or a rise) in births can therefore vary fundamentally among individuals and social groups as well as over time. Couples may want fewer children because they cannot afford to raise more at acceptable income and living standards (which was largely the case in the early 1930s), or because they wish to improve further their social and economic well-being (which agrees more with the present-day situation), and in pursuing such goals they have various options. They may consume more (or less) and save less (or more), they may invest more (less) time and money in education and training, or they may reduce (increase) leisure in favor of longer (shorter) working hours.

It is clear that any possible behavior pattern—as soon as it is accepted by sufficiently large population groups—has a different bearing on the economy. Moreover, it is important to realize that from the viewpoint of economic growth and stabilization none can simply be labeled as "good" or "bad." In the short run, supply and demand for goods and services as well as savings and investments are not always consistent. Increased savings may cause the economy to develop more rapidly or to slow down, depending on the demand for capital. Likewise, increased demand for goods and services may relieve economic depression or cause inflation, depending on the utilization of labor, skills, and installed production capacity.

Thus, while it might have been economically more advantageous in the 1930s if the downward trend in births had coincided with rising propensity to consume, such conditions contributed to strain the economy in the early 1970s. Yet, in fact, the causal links between fertility and business flows worked primarily the other way round: In the 1930s, it was the economic crisis and the resultant shortage of purchasing power that was responsible for the sluggish demand for goods as well as for the postponement of births, whereas in the late 1960s and early 1970s economic prosperity, growing income, and expanding social chances for all population groups and especially for women favored both rising consumption and declining fertility. However, there is much to suggest that at high levels of living and social security, as are now common in wide parts of Western Europe, economic considerations tend to lose importance over other (e.g., psychological and political) aspects in the decision of parents for or against another child, and that, for this reason, the association between fertility and business cycles is noticeably weaker today than it was in the 1930s.

These considerations lead us to two general conclusions:

1. The implications of fertility change on business cycles depend heavily on the circumstances under which it takes place, that is, on the prevalent social and economic behavior pattern, the general social and economic conditions, and the attained standards of living and social security.
2. As these circumstances are governed largely by social and economic policy, the implications of fertility change over the transition period, too, were highly related to the quality of policy action (e.g., in the fields of training, employment, income distribution, and social welfare) and not just to the varying numbers of people. They are therefore indeterminate, hard to identify, and unfit for easy generalizations, especially with regard to the future.

Birth Fluctuation and Utilization of Infrastructure

The aforementioned conclusions do not, of course, rule out the fact that fertility change had—and always has—some clear and direct impact on certain essential economic elements, especially on potential labor resources and on the demand for many indispensable goods and services. In this respect the provision of social and economic infrastructure, such as schools, hospitals, roads, means of transportation, housing, and working places, is of particular importance. These facilities bear a close relation to the level of economic performance and to social standards as well as to the quality of the population and labor force in terms of health and skills. Most kinds of social and economic infrastructure are meant for long-term use and require expensive investments. It is therefore hard to keep them in balance with needs that are frequently changing in consequence of fluctuating fertility and resultant swings in the size of age groups. Such basic difficulties arose and tended to grow in the course of the transition to ZPG. They deserve much more attention than the highly indeterminate implications of the general slowdown of population growth on overall economic activity.

It is true that fertility fluctuations affect the individual age groups only successively and with fairly long delays. Changes in the number of applicants for most kinds of public services and in the demand for respective facilities could therefore be identified much in advance. However, the precautions that could be and actually were taken to adjust infrastructure to the foreseeable swings in demand were rather limited, so that expensive capacity was temporarily idle and temporarily overused. These adjustment problems were most pronounced with respect to schools, training facilities, and other infrastructure catering to small population groups such as infants, school-age children, and juveniles, as compared to houses, roads, hospitals, and other infrastructure serving the total population or large parts of it.

The needs of the young generation in terms of education, training, and employment are very diversified and highly related to age. They are therefore particularly liable to disturbances from the demographic side. This situation was further aggravated by increasing specialization in education and skill requirements. A most flexible use of teaching staff as well as of training and employment facilities would have been necessary, but such reforms were hard to accomplish given the rigid structure of the conventional school and career systems. Serious mismatch between demand for and supply of educational and training services as well as of first jobs has been experienced repeatedly over the transition period in many parts of Western Europe. In the Federal Republic of Germany, large cohorts of school leavers pushed up youth employment in the 1930s, the 1950s, and the 1970s due to the failure to provide enough training and working places. At the same time, school population declined and caused unemployment of teachers and training facilities or led to less investment in new capacity. In other periods, increases in infant or school population gave rise to severe shortage of nurseries, classrooms, teachers, etc. and, in turn, to a delay in the needed improvement of educational standards.

After World War II the Federal Republic of Germany (and to some lesser extent France, Switzerland, Great Britain, and Sweden) experienced heavy immigration that makes it difficult to determine the impact of natural increase. Figure 3.3 shows separately German nationals and those born in the Federal Republic of Germany.[10] It becomes evident that without the influx of refugees the population of the Federal Republic of Germany would have remained almost constant over the last few decades. However, the intensity of the swings in age composition was not much altered by the migrants, since their age structure was very similar to that of the West German natives. Thus, while without migration ZPG might have started somewhat earlier and with a smaller population, the implications on infrastructure attributable to fertility fluctuations would have been essentially the same as actually experienced in the Federal Republic of Germany.

The Impact of Aging

Contrary to all other age groups, which temporarily expanded or contracted in size, population beyond working age (60 years and over) has constantly gained in absolute and relative terms throughout the whole period of transition to ZPG.[11] In the Federal Republic of Germany this population quadrupled between 1925 and 1975 (see Figure 3.3).[12] At the same time, the ratio of this group to persons of working age (20-59 years)—the so-called old-age dependency ratio—trebled (see Figure 3.4). Since youth dependency dropped only moderately (about 15%) over this period, total dependency ratios largely followed the trend of old-age dependency. It is no wonder that this development gave rise to particular concern.

It is important to realize that accelerating aging is a normal and unavoidable by-product of the transition to ZPG and that it has never led to an economic setback or a breakdown of pension systems, as was prophesied by many observers whenever birth rates turned down. Of course, rising shares of national income had to be devoted to the main-

[10]This excludes the offspring of refugees as far as they were granted refugee status and were accordingly registered. A clear-cut division between descendants of West German natives and descendants of refugees is not possible.

[11]Legal retirement age is still mostly around 65 years in Western Europe, but there is a growing tendency for workers to retire earlier.

[12]Without the influx of refugees it still would have almost trebled.

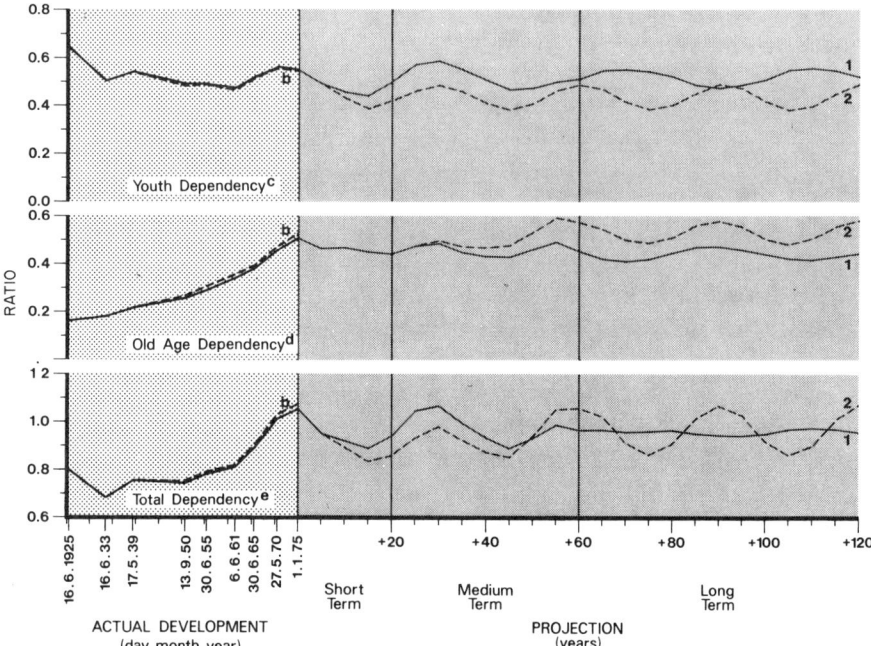

Figure 3.4. Actual and projected variations in youth, old age, and total dependency ratios of females of German nationality in the FRG, 1925-1975 and 120 years ahead, assuming constant mortality and changing fertility leading (1) to ZPG and (2) to progressive decline. Curve b shows natives excluding German refugees. Youth dependency is defined as the ratio of persons below 20 to those between 20 and 60. Old age dependency is defined as the ratio of persons 60 and older to persons between 20 and 60. Total dependency is defined as the ratio of persons below 20 and of 60 years of age and over to persons between 20 and 60.

tenance of old people. In the Federal Republic of Germany, pension payments proper by the three most important funds[13] equaled 1.2% of Gross Domestic Product (GDP) in 1925, but made up as much as 7.8% in 1975. However, this increase was only partly attributable to aging. In fact, the number of those entitled to social security allowance and the average amount of money paid to them increased much more than the number of old people. In 1925 important groups, for example, self-employed persons, were not yet covered by the social security system,

[13]Pension funds of wage workers, salaried employees, and miners. Total expenditures of these funds equaled 1.4% of GDP in 1925 and 11.1% in 1975, indicating the rapid expansion of other services rendered by these funds (e.g., in the field of health) along with pension payments.

while today almost everybody is included, and many hold claims against more than one fund. While the demographic old-age dependency ratio trebled between 1925 and 1975, the ratio of pensioners to persons in the labor force quadrupled, and real monthly rents per pensioner (in prices of 1970) rose almost 10 times over the same period.[14] It is true that workers had to divert increasing shares of their income to pension funds, but under conditions of rapid economic expansion this did not reduce their living standards. In fact, the average monthly wage bill per employed person (in 1970 prices) after deduction of taxes and social contributions (which also include sickness and unemployment insurance as well as various kinds of supplementary insurances) was also about four times higher in 1975 than in 1925.[15]

Clearly, the care for a rapidly rising proportion of old people created many more problems apart from pension payments, especially in the fields of health and housing. On the other hand, expenditure on many social services catering to population groups other than pensioners also grew very much in the course of time. Between 1960 and 1975, social security payments increased by 67% in real terms, but all other social expenditures (such as family allowances, housing allowances, and health care) rose by more than 100% and now make up almost ⅔ of the total West German social services budget.[16] Yet, in spite of this fact, it is the payment for old people that is most experienced as a burden, not the least because the respective individual contributions are clearly identified on the wage bill.

It is seldom realized that a child absorbs more resources than an old person, on the average. At current mortality and current standards of consumption, educational performance, and social security in the Federal Republic of Germany, it costs society about one-fourth to one-third

[14]These estimates are based on pensions rather than on pensioners and thus include persons who receive more than one pension. Moreover, many of the claimants—insured persons and their dependents—are still below normal retirement age. On the other hand, large groups, for example, government officials, are disregarded. Nevertheless the extraordinary expansion of old-age security services in comparison to demographic aging is reflected clearly by the preceding estimates. The wage workers' fund made about 8 million pension payments in 1975—65% to insured persons (48% to those beyond retirement age) and the rest to widows and orphans. Average allowance per widow was about 81% and per orphan 36% of the pension paid to an insured person on an average (Germany, Federal Republic, 1976, p. 390f).

[15]Concerning the United Kingdom, Reddaway (1977) comes to the following conclusion: "On the whole, therefore, one should dismiss the increased pensions' bogey as quantitatively negligible, so far as it rests on demographic factors: its real basis is the general desire to improve the provision made for the elderly by raising the real value of the pension [p. 29]."

[16]Germany, Federal Republic (1977), p. 43 and Germany, Federal Republic (1976), p. 526.

more to bring up an average child from birth to the age of 20 than to support an average person of 60 years over the rest of his or her life. This estimate is based on national accounts statistics of the Federal Republic of Germany of 1973 and refers to final private and public consumption expenditure as well to fixed capital formation for internal use. It rests on the assumption that all of these expenses serve the population in one way or another and hold certain relationships to age. As joint expenditures (e.g., on traffic, defense, and security) are included, the estimate gives some idea of the comparative social costs imputable to the young and the old generations rather than of the comparative amount of money directly spent on their maintenance (e.g., on food, education, or health).[17] It is likely that the comparative cost ratio has largely kept within the estimated range over the last few decades, since (private and public) outlays per child and per old person have increased.

Therefore, the secular decline to near replacement fertility and the continuation of this level over several decades, although provoking rapid aging of the population, was a basic condition for the release of funds necessary to raise educational standards, skills, and labor productivity and, in turn, to support larger proportions of old people. Moreover, the concentration of the labor force within the most active age groups (due to prolonged education and earlier retirement) has contributed greatly to raising the average skill level of the work force and to improving output and productivity in turn. Despite the declining proportions of active workers and shorter working hours, per capita income has risen sharply, on balance. One must also take into account the fact that the rising share of income absorbed by the older population segment did not just imply an increase in actual burden. In some respects and under certain conditions it may well have contributed to economic stability. The more conservative demand pattern of older people has

---

[17]Twenty-one expenditure groups (several of them broken further down by subgroups) have been subdivided to fit the specific needs of the population by 5-year age groups. While all joint expenditure was distributed proportionally to age, special scales were used in respect to most direct expenditure. It is clear that much subjective judgment is involved in this procedure. Therefore, in all important cases—especially public expenditure on health and social services—two different scales have been applied. Total expenditure in respect to individual age groups (expressed in income units rather than in actual currency) divided by persons in the age group supplied the age-specific rates of annual per capita expenditure needed to work out the required life-span rates. In the latter procedure, the 1972–1974 life table of the Federal Republic of Germany was used. By applying rather contrasting alternative scales, average costs spent on a child over the first 20 years of life came out to be 21% higher in one and 39% higher in the other estimate than the respective average costs spent on a 60-year-old person over the rest of the person's life. The true ratio of comparative costs may likely lie in the middle.

tended to support the production of essential consumption goods and services and to counteract the pressure toward excessive change in demand, production structure, skill requirements, and labor turnover that was evident especially after World War II due to heavy immigration and rapidly rising per capita income.

Future Implications of Zero Population Growth or Progressive Decline

Short-Term Implications

The following analysis of future implications of ZPG in Western Europe will be based on the model described on page 47 and in Footnote 4. For reasons already explained, it represents only one out of a great variety of cases that meet the conditions of ZPG or continuous population decline. In the Federal Republic of Germany, which serves as the basis of the model, the downturn to an extremely low fertility level suggests some early revival rather than further speedy decline. Therefore and due to the fact that relatively large groups of females are about to enter childbearing age, birth rates and the number of infants are likely to rise soon, regardless of whether fertility will follow path (1) or path (2) of our model or any path between. Since all other age groups will for some shorter or longer time take a course set by earlier birth trends, the model gives a quite realistic example of the shifts in total population and its most important subgroups during the earlier phases of ZPG (see Figure 3.3).

If we take a period of 20 years as "short run," it is clear that the population in and above working age (i.e., of 20 years and more) will not yet be affected by the assumed course of fertility and that neither income growth nor the burden of old-age dependency will be already directly influenced. Consequently, the prospective variations in the potential of young consumers will have no immediate impact on the volume of purchasing power and, in turn, on aggregate demand. It is true that changes in demographic behavior are normally accompanied by changing propensity to spend, save, or work but, as was explained before, there is nothing to suggest any definite association. The common assertion that lower fertility implies higher labor force participation, more savings because of smaller families and, in turn, higher income denotes possible but not certain consequences. Such indirect effects depend on the prevailing social and economic setting and on behavior patterns that are subject to change (e.g., through policy action). The direct consequences that are considered in this analysis result solely from changes in demographic quantities and are, therefore, comparatively "fixed." By isolating them and indicating their "latent" force, the scope and need for intervening social and economic policy is more easily understood.

In our model, the ratio of young dependents to persons of working age is sharply declining over the short run period, especially with the lower fertility assumption, (2). This is the result of both a decrease in the number of persons under 20 years and an increase in the number of persons of working age.[18] Old-age dependency also will fall slightly and support a rather appreciable downturn in total dependency (see Figure 3.4).[19] As the ratio of economically active persons to working-age population will change only a little, income per head is bound to rise, provided all other factors determining income formation and saving behavior keep constant.

Both trends, a shrinking volume of young consumers and a rising amount of spending power per capita, tend to modify demand patterns in the following ways:

1. In consequence of a declining number of young dependents, products with low income elasticity such as basic food and clothing or those specifically directed toward the needs of young people may suffer from contracting markets, unless new demand is being created through frequent shifts in style and taste.
2. Due to the rising share of small households consisting only or mainly of adults, demand is likely to turn more than otherwise toward consumer durables, personal effects, and various kinds of private and public services offering entertainment, recreation, education, and the like.
3. Increasing per capita income will work in favor of both tendencies. It will contribute particularly to the diversification of demand and will direct it to more sophisticated modern goods and services, especially those with high inputs of capital and skills.

Such demographically induced modifications in the structure of demand are, in essence, the same as those provoked by economic growth and rising living standards, but they are normally only weak. The changes in age composition and the attributable increase in per capita

---

[18]This disregards the fact that the individual age groups follow diversive courses (see Figure 3.3).

[19]If ZPG were to start at a phase of the fertility cycle other than that in our case, dependency ratios would go up and affect demand in the opposite way as described here.

income are much too slow and too small to have any immediate strong effect of the aforementioned kind. A decline in youth dependency may merely support an already existing tendency toward such shifts in demand, whereas a rise in youth dependency may somewhat hamper it. This is true even more in respect of ensuing changes in investment and employment patterns. The final outcome of these interrelated processes depends, in the first instance, on the flexibility of the economy. Whether changing demand will promote inflationary pressure or structural shifts in production and employment is largely a matter of the supply of mobile labor and capital. These conditions bear no immediate relation to short-term population change, but previous demographic trends may be relevant. In our model, increasing numbers of young persons, born in the 1950s and 1960s, are about to enter the labor force. They could alleviate the needed restructuring of the economy if they were properly skilled and placed.

The most important problems associated with ZPG are related to human investment. As can be seen from Figure 3.3, the age groups below 20 years that make up the young generation will develop in a rather contrasting manner. Infants in demand of special health care, nurseries, kindergartens, playgrounds, etc. are likely to increase in numbers during the whole short-term period, whereas the school-age population will shrink over the first 10 years and expand over the next 10. Young persons in need of secondary education, vocational training, or first jobs, on the other hand, will initially gain and then heavily lose in numbers.

It should be remembered that these remarkable shifts (which will be even more pronounced in smaller age groups than those shown in the figure) will take place with comparatively little change in total population and total labor force. Moreover, it must be realized that the capability of the society to respond properly to the respectively varying needs for educational and other relevant services is very much influenced by demographic and related conditions originating far back in the past. In this respect, the high share of old people and their extended security rights deserve special mention as antipode to the young generation in the demand for and allocation of public funds.[20] Since the old population is generally in a politically stronger position, a shortage of funds (a rather chronic feature of public finance) tends to disfavor the young generation first, and to aggravate the problems of inadequate provision

---

[20]It is true that pensions are mostly paid out of special funds, but government decides about increases in pension payments and also guarantees these payments.

of educational and other relevant services. There is sufficient evidence that authorities often are inclined to reduce standards if cohorts are large and staff and equipment short, and to cut down new investments immediately whenever birth rates fall and signal some "relief" in the future.

Such response to fluctuating needs of the young generation clearly disregards the negative consequences of insufficient human investment on the quality of the future work force. A proper approach to these problems would include basic reorganization and coordination of the various educational and training systems in order to facilitate the transfer of resources from one service to another according to varying numbers of applicants. Such efforts must be geared to the needs of all population groups in respect of training, retraining, vocational guidance, job information, etc. Since total population and total labor force tend to keep rather constant under conditions of ZPG, flexible, multipurpose services are required that can be adapted to the divergent internal shifts of a demand which, in total, will also remain relatively stable, as far as demographic determinants are concerned. Such new comprehensive systems have still to be devised. They make necessary, inter alia, a change in mental attitudes toward a more equitable social recognition of the different lines of education and careers, of life-long learning, and of repeated change of occupation, which clearly cannot be enforced. Nevertheless, it is in this direction that a logical answer to the most prominent problems of ZPG is to be found.

In the short run, progressive population decline (projection 2) may seem to be more favorable in social and economic terms than ZPG (projection 1). The comparatively smaller number of children implies—ceteris paribus—more spending power per private consumer, more tax revenue for the public sector (as a consequence of fewer tax exemptions for children), and less public expenditure on family allowances, health care, and education. However, apart from current expenditures, the raising of the young generation largely involves investments that pay dividends in the future, and, in this sense, continuous depletion of the young stock means continuous depletion of future labor resources. This suggests that more investment per child is needed if the prospective losses in labor potential are to be compensated for by better quality in terms of productive skills and behavior. While such substitution of quality also will be necessary during the low fertility phases of ZPG, it is obvious that it cannot be carried on incessantly as would be required under conditions of progressive shrinking. Therefore, the short-run advantages that a declining population may hold over a (pseudo) stationary one will turn into disadvantages as soon as investments in skills and physical capital

Medium-Term Implications

It follows from the previous discussion that the implications of ZPG or continuous population decline pertaining to the working-age population and its economically active components will be highly influenced by preceding policy action in favor of the young generation and in support of economic growth. These groups are affected by the assumed fertility change with a time lag of about 20 years, and it is likely that social and economic conditions will then be different, depending upon whether population stagnated or declined. There is, however, no way to determine these differences that are only partly and indirectly related to demographic trends. It is possible that the declining population will enter the medium-term period (t_{20}–t_{60} of our projections) with a larger labor force than the stagnant population, since more women would be free to work. Yet again, this is no compelling consequence of lower fertility but is subject to various other conditions including policy action.

We must keep this fact in mind when we interpret the different labor force trends in our two projections that rest on the assumption that work-force participation is the same in both instances and keeps constant over time. As before, this approach makes it possible to isolate the immediate demographic effects from the indeterminate and changeable secondary ones.

Given equal work-force participation,[21] total economically active population in our model makes up roughly 40% of total population in both projections, and this proportion tends to change very little in the course of time. However, while under conditions of ZPG (1) the work force keeps fairly constant in absolute numbers, too, in the declining population (2) it will lose more than one-fifth of its initial stock over the medium-term period. As the shrinking process starts from the lower age brackets, it is the younger work force, and especially the new entries, that will be dissipated most. At the end of the medium-term period the potential of workers below 25 years turns out to be about 30% smaller in the declining model (2) than in the ZPG model (1). Moreover, this group, which needs to be properly placed in the labor market, will follow a very irregular course in both instances. It will expand in the first half and contract in the second half of the medium-term period, with

---

[21]These are age-specific work force participation rates as observed in 1975 for the Federal Republic of Germany.

heavily fluctuating rates, which in the ZPG model largely compensate each other over time, but in the declining model leave a remarkable negative balance. Thus, without early precaution of the kind mentioned before, periods of youth unemployment are likely to interchange with periods of shortage of young workers, in both instances.

Of course, neither an increase nor a decrease in the prospective number of young people indicates in itself whether they will have good or bad chances in the labor market. The degree to which the young generation actually will be employed depends on the demand for labor at the time they start to look for a job. Apart from business fluctuations that are unpredictable, general economic trends and related changes in industrial structure as induced by technical progress and intensive international competition point toward further basic modification in the need for labor and skills. Due to rising productivity, workers will continue to be shifted from primary and secondary to tertiary industries, from labor-intensive branches to those with high inputs of capital and skills, as well as from smaller to larger firms or companies. This development suggests a rising demand for mobile and qualified workers and an increasing disparity in the labor markets, while total labor demand will rather tend to stagnate or even decline, depending on the rate of investment.

Regarding the growing need for skills that require more basic knowledge and more specialized formal and informal training in all technical, commercial, and organizational fields, the declining population (projection 2) may seem to involve smaller adjustment problems than ZPG (projection 1). Given equal conditions in both cases, it should be easier to improve the skills and employment chances of smaller cohorts as compared to larger ones. However, such simple reasoning proves wrong when viewed in wider perspective. In fact, whatever amount of labor may still be saved by further technical and organizational improvements, a progressively shrinking and aging labor force is unlikely to generate a sufficient supply of adaptable and mobile workers, even with some temporary rejuvenation of its stock, as suggested in projection (2).[22] Although future labor demand may call for a smaller work force, such a reduction should not arise from shrinking demographic potentials, but rather from shorter working hours and from further constriction of working life to the most active and productive life span. This latter process, which is intimately related with the general process of economic and social development, can proceed more smoothly with ZPG than with continuous population decline. The larger and more

---

[22] The speed of shrinking is, of course, also important.

stable work-force potential evolving from ZPG is comparatively better suited to adapt to the prospective change in both volume and structure of labor demand.

Although the number of persons beyond working age will continue to follow a course set by previous demographic trends, the burden that it will place on the economy is very much determined by the size, composition, and quality of the work force throughout all of the medium-term period. Our projections start with a very high ratio of persons beyond working age (60+) to persons of working age (20–60) (Figure 3.4), which was attained at the end of the transition period, that is, in 1975. It is important to realize that this level will not be reached again under the assumed conditions of ZPG, while it will be markedly surpassed in the second half of the medium-term period under conditions of continuous population decline. This finding opposes the widely held opinion that ZPG will lead to an increase in the burden of old dependents. Progressive aging is a phenomenon of the transition period, but not of ZPG. There is nothing to suggest that the high standards of old-age security achieved when the number and percentage of claimants was rapidly expanding could be endangered by ZPG, which implies a much more stable ratio of old dependents. With proper investment in human and physical capital and adequate precautions to meet the changing needs for education and employment, no deterioration should arise in social security standards as a consequence of ZPG.[23]

However, as shown by Figure 3.4, total dependency ratios in the ZPG model will noticeably surpass those in the declining model over most of the medium-term period due to the higher level of youth dependency. This comparative disadvantage is not only transient in the sense that it will vanish over time, but it is also much more fictitious than real, considering the better chances to promote economic growth and to support the inactive population with a constant rather than with a steadily shrinking potential labor force. When comparing the implications of ZPG with those of progressive population decline, numerical change must be taken into account together with structural variations. While a declining population may suggest a more favorable ratio of labor reserves to dependents over a substantially long period, continuous depletion in stock must eventually slow down economic development and, in turn, social standards. Serious problems of this kind are indicated in model (2) toward the end of the medium-term period, when the shrinking process

[23]Graf (1975), in contrast, sees various social and economic problems—for example, labor and capital shortage and excessive dependency burden—to arise in consequence of ZPG. He disregards the fact that such problems would instead result from failure in provident policy action.

gains full speed and dependency ratios turn up steeply. Zero population growth does not suggest such a dangerous course.

Long-Term Implications in Present-Day Perspective

Contrary to the short- and medium-term periods during which the different implications of preceding birth fluctuations evolve successively, in the long run all occur together. Of course, at any given point in time some of them will be more pressing than others, but over time all are subject to change in accordance with the swings by which the individual age groups develop. Continuous adjustment of the social and economic setting to temporary increases and decreases in the various age-related needs for infrastructure, working places, and social security as well as to changing impacts on the demand for goods will be a basic requirement to counteract any undesirable implications of ZPG in the long run. It should, however, be remembered that proper adaptation to changing circumstances is a general prerequisite for any balanced development, regardless of whether population grows, stagnates, or declines. Nevertheless, adjustment to the conditions of ZPG (and even more of population decline) calls for greater mobility of capital, labor, and skills as well as for more flexible behavior patterns than may be necessary with continuous population growth. Needless to say, rapid adjustment can be accomplished better the more the economy expands; this opposes the view that ZPG or decline would allow economic activity to take a smoother course than otherwise.[24] As ZPG (or population decline) may be associated with rapid as well as with slow variations in age composition, the pressure for adjustment to changing conditions may differ widely. No uniform judgment concerning adjustment problems arising from ZPG is therefore feasible; fertility cycles from which it evolved and the resultant pattern of swings in the size of important age groups must always be taken into account.

Our model leads eventually to a "pseudo" state of stable nongrowth or decline, with structural variations as described in Table 3.3. Obviously, such a systematic pattern of change will not evolve in reality, but it is nevertheless useful to show toward what conditions development will ultimately turn, given our fertility assumptions. While, in relative terms, both the stationary and the declining population suggest similar social and economic problems arising from continuously changing age compositions and respectively changing needs for goods, services, and jobs, progressive depletion of human stock in the declining population

[24]See Leyhausen (1973, pp. 79ff.).

system must ultimately give rise to progressive shrinking of the social and economic system as well. Under conditions of ZPG, alternating increase and decrease in the potential of young persons and in their various competing needs may perhaps induce special investment activities and organizational improvements that help to make the economy more flexible. In a declining population, however, such efforts in response to fluctuating needs may at best bring about a temporary delay in the gradual economic downturn bound to follow eventually from a continued reduction in the overall supply of consumers and workers. Obviously, the intensity of population decline is also very important. It is certainly easier for the economy to adapt to a slowly rather than to a rapidly declining population. However, in principle and under long-term aspects steady depletion of human reserves implies economic decline as well.

These considerations may appear rather academic in view of the long time span that must elapse before such a fatal development is likely to gain momentum. It must, however, be remembered that the period during which the downward trend may still be redressed is very much shorter. This critical period possibly will have passed long before any negative effects will be noticed, inasmuch as in the initial phases of decline the smaller burden of youth dependents suggests some comparative advantage over a stagnant or growing population, and this apparent advantage tends to be the more pronounced the lower the fertility level.

As soon as the potential number of fertile women starts to dwindle, that is, after 20–30 years, birth rates will turn down more steeply while death rates go up, thus accelerating population decline. Swings in fertility as assumed in our model (2) tend to mitigate the speed of decline as well as the intensity of aging, but they are not sufficient to prevent the shrinking from gaining momentum over time. The longer fertility remains below replacement level and the steeper its fall, on the average, the more difficult will be a return to fertility levels that eventually will check population decline.

The impact of time is clearly reflected in our model (2), which assumes a repeated increase of fertility to the replacement level. At this level, which will be attained every 30 years beginning at t_{20} of our projections, chances for further increase in fertility and for a return to population growth seem comparatively good. It can, however, be shown that attempts to accomplish such goals are more promising when they are made at t_{20} than 30 years later. If we assume a regular rise in fertility (a rise in N by .1 every 5 years), population would begin to grow again after 15 years and at a net reproduction rate of 1.3 if t_{20} is chosen as a starting point as compared to t_{50} when 20 years and a rise of N to over 1.4 would be needed to achieve comparable results. In the first case, total population would decline by only 2% over the intermediate period ($t_{20}-t_{35}$), which suggests a rather quick and effective halt of the shrinking, whereas in the second case population would shrink by 5% (during $t_{50}-t_{70}$) before it would grow again. In addition to the longer time and greater efforts needed to check population decline at the later phase, stronger variations in age composition and greater adjustment problems are due to arise from the steeper increase in fertility.

Yet the main obstacle lies in the fact that fertility cannot be raised at will whenever it seems politically feasible to stop population decline. Changes in generative behavior cannot be enforced, nor are they likely to adapt spontaneously to any fixed target in the presence of strong social, economic, or other disincentives. While this is a general handicap, higher old-age dependency at the later stage works clearly against an effective fertility increase. As shown in Figure 3.4, old-age dependency ratios are much lower and much less disposed to increase at t_{20} than they are at t_{50} and t_{80} of our projection (2). The burden of old dependents is largely predetermined and cannot simply be shifted off by the individual taxpayer. A rise in youth dependency, on the other hand, can be avoided more easily, since the decision for or against another child rests solely with the individual couple. Seen from this perspective, the long-term consequences of progressive population decline bear a very real relation to the present, in the sense that they must be dealt with now.

Zero population growth, on the other hand, does not imply any latent forces disposed to weaken the economy eventually, although it may cause serious adjustment problems. It therefore provides, in principle, a much better answer to the various demographic, social, and ecological problems in Western Europe than "shrinking," which some critics still advocate as a means to reduce crowding and prevent environmental decay. However, ZPG is not a development supported by some innate mechanism, as is long-term growth and even more so long-term decline. It is rather a border case between growth and decline, liable to opposing forces. Whereas, in theory, a stationary population may any time turn into a growing or a declining one, depending on the forces that take the lead, conditions characterizing the present stage of ZPG in Western Europe and particularly in the Federal Republic of Germany, that is, the low level of fertility and the top-loaded age structure, are much more prone toward further population decline than a return to steady growth. Zero population growth, although a desirable goal, may therefore be hard to maintain in view of the limited possibilities to influence fertility levels by means of population policy.

These difficulties may appear negligible considering the large potentials of population and workers in the less developed countries willing to migrate and to fill gaps in the native population of several Western European countries. However, immigration is no easy way to cope with the problems of deficient natural growth. It has to serve two largely competing purposes:

1. To respond to the shifts in labor demand
2. To raise the level of fertility

As has been shown before, the supply of young indigenous workers will tend to change markedly in the course of time, which suggests respective variations in the demand for immigrant workers and, in turn, migration policy in favor of temporary admission. Such policy tends to conflict with the rising need for qualified workers, which implies increasing selectivity in favor of skilled migrants and measures to keep the migrants permanently. The changes in immigration policy of many Western European countries during the 1970s are a clear indication of these opposing trends that may become even more pronounced in future. From a demographic point of view a rather steady inflow of young families would seem desirable. Those migrants who chose to remain permanently would soon make up sizable proportions of the total population if they had to substitute for a continuous decline in the indigenous stock. On the other hand, they should comprise a suitable selection in cultural and other respects in order to avoid undue problems of integration.

This may suffice to indicate the highly conflicting nature of immigration policies in support of ZPG under conditions of deficient natural growth, not to mention the largely contrasting interests of the sending countries. The manifold problems involved are all too well known to be outlined in detail. This is not to say that demographic trends in Western Europe are almost unavoidably set for decline. There is little prospect for such a development with rapidly expanding populations and large potential numbers of migrants elsewhere, but the inflows from outside, whether spontaneous or regulated, are likely to cause additional discrepancies in age composition and additional pressure for economic adjustment rather than alleviate such problems. What I wanted to stress is that ZPG supported by net immigration is not identical with ZPG arising from natural growth, either in demographic characteristics or in social and economic respects.

4

The Fiscal Policy Dilemma: Cyclical Swings Dominated by Supply-Side Constraints

MICHAEL L. WACHTER and SUSAN M. WACHTER[1]

Since the Keynesian revolution, fiscal policy has been perceived as the central instrument of countercyclical policy for adjusting aggregate demand to achieve full employment. Some have argued, with success, that monetary policy should be the centerpiece of demand management. For our purpose, the monetary versus fiscal policy debate is not relevant. Although we shall concentrate our attention on fiscal policy, largely because of the flexibility of fiscal programs, the issues are the same for monetary policy. Our argument is that the very success of Keynesian economics coupled with unusually sharp demographic swings has bred new problems. These problems are not centered on inadequate demand. High unemployment exists today, not because of the inability of policymakers to create the extra demand and jobs, but rather because of fears of renewed or accelerated inflation as aggregate demand bumps into a rapidly changing and imperfectly understood supply or potential output constraint.

[1]This research was supported by grants from the National Institute of Child Health and Human Development, the National Science Foundation, and the General Electric Foundation.

We argue that fiscal policy options should no longer be evaluated in terms of their impact multiplier effect on aggregate demand. Rather, in today's environment, the correct policy mix is one that increases the effective aggregate supply or potential output of the economy as it increases aggregate demand. The new fiscal policy initiatives should be aimed at the supply-side problems if they are to be effective.

At the heart of the current stabilization problem is the fact that the equilibrium or nonaccelerating-inflation rate of unemployment (U_{NI}) has increased dramatically over the past 15 years. This is largely in response to demographic developments, a relative slowdown in capital growth, and the growth of government transfer payments and minimum wages. The demographic swings are indicated by a large increase in the population of young people 16–24 years of age and the associated increase in participation rates among females. Associated with the massive influx of young workers and the decrease in the average age of the labor force has been an increase in the rate of growth of the labor force.

At the same time that the baby boom was entering the labor force, the government was engaged in a process of extending minimum wages to industries that traditionally employed new workers and of increasing the relative levels of public assistance and unemployment compensation. The effect of these policies was to reduce the supply of entry jobs and increase the reservation wage of low-wage workers. Both served to increase the supply of unemployment.

These demographic and policy developments have resulted in a large increase in the equilibrium rate of unemployment. Even if the monetary and fiscal authorities could reduce the unemployment rate to 4% in 1955 without touching off accelerating inflation, this does not mean that they could reduce the rate below approximately 5.5% in, say, 1978 and still avoid accelerating inflation. More troublesome for stabilization policy is the fact that, whereas it is known that the equilibrium unemployment rate has increased substantially (between approximately 1.0 and 1.5%), there is uncertainty over its exact value. A confidence interval of approximately .5% on both sides of the 5.5% figure translates into 1 million workers.

The increase in the labor input into the production process has been only imperfectly matched by an increase in capital accumulation. For any value of the unemployment rate the capacity utilization is higher today than in the early 1960s. Heuristically, in the 1970s we ran into bottlenecks in the physical plant and equipment capacity before we ran into similar bottlenecks in the labor market. This shifting relationship between capacity utilization and unemployment is subject to uncertainty because the capacity utilization numbers are only roughly constructed.

On the other hand, it appears that the sources of error are on the side of strengthening this adverse trend for labor.

Other pivotal bottleneck sectors also appeared in the 1970s, particularly in agriculture and fuel production. These new problem areas, which are related indirectly to U.S. demographic changes, are closely tied to the world population boom of the post-World War II period and the increasing drive for industrialization. These bottlenecks, whether in capital or food and fuel, have the effect of increasing U_{NI}.

The long demographic–economic swing created by the baby boom generation is about to be reversed. The period total fertility rate as well as the actual number of births peaked in 1957, remained at a high plateau until 1961, and then declined dramatically and continuously through 1978. In other words, the baby boom bulge in the labor force has moved from the 16–19 age group to the 20–24 age group. After 1980, these younger workers, with their traditional patterns of high job turnover and unemployment, will have entered a life cycle period of more stable job attachment. In addition, after 1980 the baby bust generation will begin to enter the labor market. Over the next decade the number of new entrants to the labor market should drop precipitously, and the rate of increase of the aggregate labor force will slow.

An important question posed for fiscal policy is whether the demographic twist will create additional difficulties for the economy or help undo the problems, especially the high level of U_{NI}, created by the baby boom. Our assessment is for mixed results. The aging of the population, ceteris paribus, should translate into a significant reduction in the nonaccelerating-inflation rate of unemployment. On the other hand, the scarcity of young workers coupled with an older baby boom cohort may cause new problems.

In analyzing the unwinding of the baby boom, of prime importance is the fact that the slowdown in population growth has not occurred in most less developed countries. The continued international population explosion may serve to counteract the effects of the domestic drop in fertility.

This chapter is developed along the following lines. The first section discusses the Kuznets intermediate business cycle model and introduces certain amendments that suggest that that cycle is now driven by supply rather than demand factors. The second section outlines a model of supply-side imbalances. The third section discusses methods for estimating U_{NI} and suggests the specific impact on U_{NI} of the demographic developments of the postwar period. The fourth section expands on the problem of estimating U_{NI} by introducing evidence on the existence of potential capacity bottlenecks resulting from the rapid growth in the labor force. The fifth section outlines the potential implications of the baby bust. The final section develops the fiscal policy impact of these demographic changes, stressing the implications for lowering U_{NI}.

Amendments to the Secular Stagnation and Kuznets Cycle Models

In the historical literature, the question of demographic shifts and their implications for fiscal policy have often been examined in the context of the secular stagnation thesis and the Kuznets "intermediate-run cycle" models. The model discussed in this chapter has important, and some contradictory, implications for these two hypotheses.

During the 1930s the early Keynesians, such as Hansen (1939), placed a great deal of stress on a lack of aggregate demand originating in the private sector. Some viewed this lack of demand as a cyclical, disequilibrium phenomenon.[2] Others argued that the problems were more fundamental. Their view, referred to as "secular stagnation," suggested that the shortfall in demand from the private sector was permanent or at least likely to be around for some time. Government expenditures to fill the private demand gap would be needed not only to reach full employment but also to maintain a high level of economic activity.

Demographic factors played an important role in the workings of the secular stagnation hypothesis. Slow population growth was viewed as a central cause of the investment shortfall, which, in the stagnation model, translated into a depression- or recession-oriented economy. The problem of the economy being lack of demand, the fewer the number of workers as a percentage of the population, the lower the unemployment rate. Consequently, low labor force participation among women, high fertility, and early retirement were valuable attributes. Nonworkers increased the demand for goods without competing for scarce jobs. The liberal policy response of the 1930s was to initiate social security to aid retirement and to argue that jobs should be allocated one per family; female breadwinners should work, but others should not be in the labor force.

[2]Once the economy was restored to full employment, demand in the private sector would be sufficient to maintain full employment. Pump priming of fiscal policy and expansionary monetary policy would lift the economy out of its short-run, low-level "equilibrium trap." Thereafter the level of government expenditure could be returned to normal levels and monetary growth could be lowered to its long-run growth path. The purpose of monetary and fiscal policies was to counter cyclical swings in private expenditure but not to fill permanently a gap in demand in the private sector.

The intermediate-run business cycle formulated by Burns (1934), Kuznets (1934), and Abramovitz (1956) was less apocalyptic than that of the secular stagnation school and viewed the demographic changes as simply one endogenous element in a concurrence of trend cycles throughout nonagricultural production. These waves in the rate of change in output were accompanied, with varying leads or lags, by swings in labor force growth, unemployment rates, and capital accumulation. New inventions, the opening of new territory, etc. were the exogenous elements that set off an extended but unmaintainable boom in aggregate demand. Changes in demand, in turn, caused fluctuations in the labor force. Prior to 1924, immigration flows were central to the labor model; that is, low rates of unemployment encouraged high rates of immigration. The slowdown in immigration altered the character of the procyclical swings in the labor force. After 1924, the endogenous labor force response depended increasingly on the discouraged worker effect and induced increases in female labor force participation rates. In these intermediate-run swings models, the induced labor force growth occurred late in the boom. Since the latecomers to the labor market tended to be lower skilled, and with the economy bumping against capacity constraints, the productivity growth of the early stages of the boom could not be maintained. As a result, the upsurge in employment and induced labor force growth were harbingers of the incipient economic bust.

In the present theoretical and empirical context, the stagnation and the intermediate-swings models are open to criticism. With appropriate use of Keynesian monetary and fiscal policies, a long-term shortfall caused by inadequate demand is unlikely. The demand for goods and services is sufficient to achieve a full-employment equilibrium over an extended period of time. That is, although the short-run business cycle continues to exist because of the inadequacies of attempts at fine-tuning the economy, demand management is able to fill in the peaks and troughs of any intermediate swings of the Kuznets variety.[3] Exogenous shocks, such as new inventions, no longer need set off an uncontrolled extended boom that must then be followed by a steep economic decline. In disequilibrium, the appropriate use of monetary and fiscal policies breaks the linkage between unemployment caused by inadequate demand and demographic swings. Regardless of the percentage of the population that is in the labor force, the economy can fluctuate around the equilibrium unemployment rate.

[3]For an excellent discussion of the debate on the role of stabilization policy, see Modigliani (1977).

Under the relatively strict regime of demand management, the unemployment rate fluctuates within a historically narrow band around its equilibrium level. That is, in this new framework, society is generally observed to be close to its supply constraint or potential output.[4] With supply and not demand as the constraining influence, some central features of the Kuznets cycle are altered. For example, the domestic fertility rate now plays the central role in determining the rate of growth of the labor force and the age structure of the population.[5] The post-World War II empirical data indicate that the baby boom of the later 1940s and 1950s has led to an increased rate of growth of the labor force in the late 1960s and 1970s. The influx of young workers and the associated increase in female participation rates, in turn, have increased dramatically the nonaccelerating-inflation rate of unemployment.[6] As a consequence, the short-run business cycles over the past two decades have been around successively higher rates of full-employment unemployment.

The result of these changes is that the intermediate-run relationship between labor force growth and unemployment has changed signs: Demand management maintains the economy relatively close to its full-employment level, so that demographic swings cause changes in the equilibrium rate of unemployment. Longer-term or averaged observations of the unemployment rate are increasingly dominated by swings in the supply side (in the equilibrium rate of unemployment) rather than by prolonged expansions and recessions. High rates of labor force growth, which cause increases in the equilibrium unemployment rate, thus become correlated with high rates of observed unemployment.[7]

A Simplified Model of Supply-Side Imbalances

The major concepts involved in the shifting role of fiscal policy can be captured in a simple macroeconomic model. The model is useful for

---

[4]For a debate on the methods of calculating potential output, see Perry (1977) and the accompanying comments.
[5]The role of fertility in the long-swings framework has been explored by Easterlin (1968).
[6]See, for example, M. Wachter (1976).
[7]In addition, during the period, the role of inflation in the intermediate-run cycle has changed. As is well known, the 5 years of 1970–1975 were characterized by high inflation, high unemployment rates, and high labor force growth rates. Here again the convergence of these factors is due in part to the rise in the equilibrium rate of unemployment caused by the population and labor force swings.

expositional purposes and is oriented towards the specific empirical factors involved in the demographic shift. To start, assume a production function that recognizes two different categories of labor—older workers who have accumulated specific training (L_A) and younger workers who lack such training (L_B). For our purposes we can view L_A as skilled workers and L_B as unskilled workers. In the long run, the production function can be written as

$$X^s = f_s(L_A^s, L_B^s, K), \tag{1}$$

where K is the capital stock, X is the level of output, and the superscript s refers to supply. In the short run, there appear to be significant lags in achieving desired absolute and relative levels of factor inputs. The lags may arise for a number of reasons including adjustment and expectational factors. The literature on investment functions indicates that long lags are especially relevant to the capital input. If the capital stock is "putty-clay," the input coefficients are fixed as part of the capital endowment. These coefficients may vary for different vintages but, to the extent that they are empirically important, they impact a difficulty in substituting against scarce factors in the short run. For expositional convenience, we assume a Leontief fixed coefficient model for the short run,[8] so that

$$X^s = \min\left\{\frac{L_A}{\phi_1}, \frac{L_B}{\phi_2}, \frac{K}{\phi_3}\right\}. \tag{1a}$$

For our purposes, aggregate demand can be viewed as being controlled by monetary (M) and fiscal (F) policies, subject to unanticipated changes in demand from the private sector (X_0):

$$X^d = f_d(M, F, X_0). \tag{2}$$

The derived demand for labor is constrained by either the level of the demand or supply for output X and by relative factor prices. For B workers, the relevant own wage is either the minimum wage (MW) or a market wage, whichever is higher.

The labor supply for both L_A and L_B is a function of the population in

---

[8]This is an extreme form of the bottlenecks model, since it allows no substitution at all among factors. Output is restricted by the single limiting factor. The economy, especially at the aggregate level, is obviously not without some potential to substitute against the scarce resource. A central thrust of our argument, however, is that the demographic changes have generated empirically important bottlenecks and that general expansionary policies—which increase aggregate demand for outputs and inputs across the board—are limited in this environment.

each cohort and the factors that determine the labor force participation rates. For A workers, we assume that the participation rate (r_A) is constant in the short run. Abstracting from influences such as school enrollment and fertility, the main forces determining participation for B workers are the market wage rates for these workers (w_B), the government transfer payments for being unemployed (T_g), the effective minimum wage (MW), and some unspecified trend factors that capture changes in life-style.[9] That is,

$$L_A^s = L_A^s(r_A, POP_A), \quad (3)$$

and

$$(L_B^s)' = L_B^{s'}(POP_B, TREND, g\{w_B, T_g, MW\}). \quad (4)$$

The relationship between the market wage and T_g determines the cost of being unemployed. The level of governmental transfers depends upon unemployment compensation and public assistance. The supply of labor relevant for the production function, denoted L_B^s, is

$$L_B^s = L_B^{s'} - g(w_B, T_g, MW). \quad (4a)$$

That is, we distinguish between an observed labor supply $L_B^{s'}$ and an effective labor supply L_B^s, which is available for employment. The discrepancy, measured by the g function, is a type of structural unemployment.[10]

Rates of price and wage inflation are determined as a distributed lag on excess demand conditions in the various goods and labor markets. For price changes,

$$\dot{p}/p = H(\Sigma\ h_j\{X_j^s - X_j^d\}, U_A, U_B, \{\dot{p}/p\}_{t-i}), \quad (5)$$

where U is the unemployment rate and $\{\dot{p}/p\}_{t-i}$ is a general lagged dependent variable(s) that operates as a distributed lag generator.

The speed with which industries respond to excess demand pressures

---

[9] The role of minimum wages in the supply function is discussed by Mincer (1976).

[10] In Eqs. (3) and (4) it is assumed that experience or skill can only be acquired with age. The result is that the number of A workers only increases with the population and participation rates of A workers. In fact, the rate of accumulation of skill can be increased by more intensive training. The cost curve for training is likely to be upward sloping and steeper in the short than in the long run. Consequently, the accumulation of human capital will be slowed as workers spread their training to avoid the higher short-run costs. (This factor of increasing short-run supply costs is also a factor in the lag of actual capital behind its optimal level.) Either the firm or the worker can pay to decrease the time needed to change B workers into A workers. In any case, it will only be paid when the wage differential is high enough to pay for the higher short-run supply costs.

is captured by their respective h_js. Differences in these response coefficients among industries make inflation a function of the distribution of excess demand as well as its level.[11] In general, empirical evidence for the United States suggests that the h_j functions are nonlinear with a greater acceleration of inflation when $X_j^s < X_j^d$ than deceleration when $X_j^s > X_j^d$.[12] Consequently, overall $X^s = X^d$ still can have inflationary pressures depending upon the distribution of excess demand among industries. Variations in h_j among industries largely reflect industry structure.

The rate of wage change for A workers can be formulated as

$$(\dot{w}/w)_A = h_A(U_A, U_B, U_{CAP}, \{\dot{w}/w\}_{t-i, A}) \qquad (6)$$

where U_{CAP} is the overall capacity utilization rate and is meant to capture the excess demand conditions in the goods market. For B workers, the wage increases depend upon transfer payment changes as well as on market conditions. Thus,

$$(\dot{w}/w)_B = h_B(U_A, U_B, U_{CAP}, \dot{T}_g/T_g, MW/MW, \{\dot{w}/w\}_{t-i, B}). \qquad (7)$$

Simply stated, the function of aggregate demand management is to attempt to set X^d equal to X^s.[13] This, however, is not an easy task. First, there are the unforeseen changes in demand in the private sector. This is the traditional Keynesian problem. Exogenous shocks in private consumption or, more likely, investment, cause shortfalls in X_0. To avoid unutilized resources, monetary and fiscal policy fill in the gap, either through government demand or by pumping up demand in the private sector. Second, because of differences in the h_j, the government must balance sector-specific demand and supply forces as well as the overall level of excess demand.

Complicating the problem of stabilization policy is that the government's perception of X^s has a large error component. This can result from the existence of short-run bottlenecks as in (1a) or from inaccurate measurement of K, L_A, and L_B (or parameters of the production func-

---

[11]For example, the evidence strongly suggests that agriculture has an unusually high h_j, so that excess demand in this sector is quickly reflected in the rate of inflation (see S. Wachter, 1976). In addition, the elasticity of supply and demand appear to be below average, so that the increase in relative prices (which sets off the inflation) does not rapidly close the $X_j^d > X_j^s$ gap in this sector.

[12]See Archibald (1970) for a discussion of some relevant evidence.

[13]This abstracts from aggregation problems and assumes a symmetric loss function for discrepancies in either direction of $X^s - X^d$.

tion).[14] Discrepancies between the observed $L_B^{S\prime}$ and the real L_B^S labor supply make this an obvious potential area of measurement error.

Independent of demand management, unemployment will vary with (a) the distribution of the labor force between A and B workers, (b) the cost of being unemployed and minimum wage effectiveness, and (c) bottlenecks of either skilled workers or capital. Over the longer run, when coefficients in production are more flexible, bottlenecks gradually lose their importance as a cause of unemployment. On the other hand, the wage equation for unskilled workers (7) indicates another source of unemployment. As bottlenecks loosen, relative wages must adjust if the surplus of B workers is to be absorbed. The evidence suggests, however, that the adjustment is very imperfect. Minimum wages prevent employers from moving down their demand curve for B workers, and unemployment compensation and public assistance maintain a high reservation wage (relative to their market wage) for the unskilled workers. These latter workers are in the labor force, but are not willing or able (due to minimum wage) to work at the market clearing wage.

Estimating the Nonaccelerating-Inflation Rate of Unemployment

Since a central goal of demand management is to lower the rate of unemployment, an obvious first goal is to estimate the nonaccelerating-inflation rate of unemployment, U_{NI}. Research on U_{NI} has centered largely on estimating wage and price equations similar to (5)–(7), setting $(\dot{w}/w)_t = (\dot{w}/w)_{t-i}$ and $(\dot{p}/p)_t = (\dot{p}/p)_{t-i}$ as the steady-state equilibrium conditions, and then solving the equations for U in terms of the fixed parameters of the system.[15] The solution value, U_{NI}, is the unemployment rate at which wage inflation is neither accelerating nor decelerating.[16]

The U_{NI} construct, however, is a statistic of the entire system. This

---

[14]The specific meaning of a short-run bottleneck in capital stock is discussed on pages 85–91.
[15]This use of the wage-price sector to calculate U_{NI} is reviewed by Tobin (1970).
[16]For example, if the wage equation is

$$(\dot{w}/w)_t = a + bU^{-1} + (\dot{w}/w)_{t-1},$$

then

$$U_{NI} = -b/a.$$

The variable U denotes an overall measure of unemployment or excess demand in general and abstracts from the disaggregated variables U_A, U_B, and U_{CAP} of Eqs. (6) and (7).

results from simultaneity and feedback effects from wages to output to unemployment, or the direct entry of other variables into the wage equation. In this framework, U_{NI} is the solution of the reduced form wage equation

$$0 = h(U, \mathbf{Z}), \tag{8}$$

where $\mathbf{Z}$ is a vector of the exogenous variables in the system. This same argument could be repeated to calculate a nonaccelerating-inflation rate of capacity utilization. Equation (8) indicates that U_{NI} is not a constant number, but a variable that changes with any of the exogenous variables in the $\mathbf{Z}$ vector. The $\mathbf{Z}$ vector includes obvious labor market variables such as the demographic composition of the population and the long-term rate of productivity growth. It also, however, may include the distribution of excess aggregate demand in the goods market and the shortfall of capacity utilization relative to labor. Although all of the exogenous variables in the economic model are determinants of U_{NI}, some are obviously more important than others. For example, the demographic variables, such as population and labor force age–sex structure, are likely to be quantitatively important factors in determining U_{NI}.

That U_{NI} is a variable does not necessarily mean that it is unstable or unpredictable. If we can forecast the variables in $\mathbf{Z}$ and if we know the functional form of h, then we can predict U_{NI} with some accuracy. However, at least some of the variables in $\mathbf{Z}$ are difficult to predict and others are even difficult to measure. Perhaps more importantly, the functional form of h, which is a transformation of the Phillips curve, has exhibited a well-publicized instability over the postwar period. If the parameters of the system are time varying, then (8) can be rewritten as

$$0 = h_\tau(U, \mathbf{Z}). \tag{8a}$$

U_{NI} now varies not only with $\mathbf{Z}$ but also as a function of the shifting parameter structure. Attempts to estimate (8) will determine some average value for U_{NI} over the estimation period. What is needed, of course, is the current value ($\tau = T$). Due to methodological problems and data limitations, time-varying parameter systems are still in their infancy.

The degree of instability in U_{NI} is a function of the environment. In a period of relative economic stability, in the sense of damped cycles, and with few new government initiatives—as was true between 1954 and 1961—U_{NI} might be reasonably stable. In the later period, with dramatic demographic swings, wide cyclical fluctuations, numerous government policy changes, and energy and food crises, the nonaccelerating-inflation rate will mirror the instability in the economy. For example, it is likely that the food price increase of the early 1970s and the Organization of Petroleum Exporting Countries increases of 1973-1974 caused an increase in U_{NI} over the short run.

The Unemployment Bottleneck

Given the difficulties of calculating U_{NI} in the wage-equation context, alternative approaches are useful. One approach that has been utilized to take into account demographic factors is to "normalize" the unemployment rate for the changing demographic composition of the labor force and the unemployment pool. By postulating certain maintained hypotheses as to the manner in which the labor market has changed, one can isolate the demographic impact on the cyclical component of the unemployment rate.[17]

The basic assumption utilized here is that the structural changes in the labor market have had the smallest impact on prime-age males. These workers show very little cyclical variation in their labor force behavior and are not significantly affected by changes in government transfer payments and minimum wage coverage. Using the prime-age male group (25-54 years of age) as a benchmark, it is possible to estimate the structural increase in unemployment of the standard age-sex categories in the labor force. The equation utilized in an earlier study is of the form

$$U_i = a_0 + a_1 U_{PM} + a_2 RP_y \qquad (9)$$

where U_i is the unemployment rate of the age-sex group, U_{PM} is the unemployment rate of prime-age males, and RP_y is the percentage of young people aged 16-24 in the population (age 16 and over).[18] The variable RP_y is an indication of demographic imbalance. It is utilized instead of the relative labor force because of the strong endogeneity of the latter. To calculate the normalized (or nonaccelerating-inflation, based on the demographic correction) unemployment rate for each age-sex group, we assume that 2.9% is the nonaccelerating-inflation level for U_{PM}. The 2.9 figure is a benchmark, and the resulting U_{NI} figures are indexed on the particular benchmark. If the 2.9 is changed, the U_{NI}s will also change in the same direction. The choice of that number is based on an examination of inflation and U_{PM} data for the postwar period. Essentially, in the postwar period, U_{PM} has been below 2.9%

---

[17] This presumably could be done for any of the variables in the Z vector; the demographic factor is chosen because it is likely to be the single most important factor causing U_{NI} to change over the past two decades.

[18] M. Wachter (1976). The equations were updated for this chapter and were estimated for the period 1948-1976.

during clear periods of excess demand, 1956:2–1957:2, 1965:2–1970:2, and 1972:4–1974:3.

Substituting into (9) the estimated values for a_0, a_1, and a_2 in each age–sex equation and 2.9% for U_{PM} leads to an estimate of the normalized unemployment rate for each age–sex group (U_{NI}^i). They are shown in Table 4.1 for 1955, 1965, and 1975. They vary over the period as RP_y changes. The demographic corrected U_{NI} figure for the economy at any point in time is then a weighted average of the U_{NI}^i for each of the 14 age–sex groups. The weights are the percentage of each group in the labor force. The aggregate U_{NI} for 1948–1976 are shown in Table 4.2.

This method for calculating the demographic adjustment to U_{NI} is designed to take account of the age–sex structure in the labor force and the skilled–unskilled bottlenecks. If only the age–sex composition were changing, RP_y in Eq. (9) would be insignificant. In this case U_{NI}^i would be stable over time so that the aggregate U_{NI} would only change as the labor force weights (i.e., the percentage of each group in the labor force) change. The RP_y variable indicates that U_{NI} is growing not only because there are more young people and females in the labor force—and these

TABLE 4.1.
U_{NI}: Normalized Rate of Unemployment, 1955, 1965, and 1975, 14 Age–Sex Groups[a]

	1955	1965	1975
Males			
16–19	10.7	13.7	15.7
20–24	6.3	7.5	8.2
25–34	3.0	3.4	3.6
35–44	2.7	2.6	2.6
45–54	3.0	2.7	2.5
55–64	3.6	3.1	2.9
65+	3.6	3.6	3.6
Females			
16–19	9.7	13.9	16.9
20–24	5.6	7.6	9.0
25–34	4.8	5.7	6.3
35–44	3.8	4.4	4.7
45–54	3.3	3.5	3.7
55–64	3.3	3.2	3.1
65+	2.4	3.5	3.5

[a]The normalization takes account of compositional shifts in the labor force.

TABLE 4.2.
U_{NI}: Normalized Unemployment Rate
Series, 1948–1976[a]

Year	U_{NI}	Year	U_{NI}
1948	4.52	1963	4.35
1949	4.42	1964	4.47
1950	4.34	1965	4.61
1951	4.18	1966	4.75
1952	4.06	1967	4.79
1953	3.96	1968	4.83
1954	3.94	1969	4.94
1955	3.95	1970	5.06
1956	3.98	1971	5.19
1957	4.00	1972	5.32
1958	4.03	1973	5.42
1959	4.10	1974	5.46
1960	4.18	1975	5.47
1961	4.22	1976	5.51
1962	4.24		

[a] The normalization takes account of compositional shifts in the labor force and relative unemployment among demographic groups.

groups have relatively high U_{NI}^is—but also because the bottleneck of prime-age male workers is causing the U_{NI}^is of the young and female groups to increase.

The preceding calculations do not specifically take into account changes in minimum wages and government transfers. Unfortunately, it is almost impossible to gain an accurate measure of the disincentive effects of the various transfer programs. The data that are available, however, indicate the MW and T_g have been increasing relative to market wages since 1962 after largely tracking market wages prior to 1962.[19] Given the time path of the baby boom, MW and T_g largely track RP_y. To this extent the RP_y variable acts as a proxy, although an imperfect one, for MW and T_g.

[19] First, although minimum wage levels have just kept pace with average wages in the economy, major extensions of coverage in the law strongly affected those areas that have traditionally been important sources of employment for younger workers and females. Second, welfare payments, especially in-kind transfers such as food stamps, have grown relative to average wages since the early 1960s. Third, unemployment compensation has also grown in coverage and in relative levels (on an after-tax basis) since the early 1960s.
Whether or not one agrees on the social desirability of these changes in transfer programs

The U_{NI} calculated in this manner only takes into account the demographic shift in the composition of the labor force. It does not include the other determinants of U_{NI}. In this sense, it is better to view the series in Tables 4.1 and 4.2 as unemployment rates normalized for demographic factors.

The Capital Stock Bottleneck

In the previous section we estimated one component of U_{NI} by normalizing the unemployment rate for adverse compositional shifts in the mixture of skilled to unskilled workers. The rapid growth of the labor force may also have contributed to what appears to be an imbalance in the rates of growth of the labor and capital inputs of the production process.

Table 4.3 shows the growth rate of the total labor force, the prime-age male labor force, and the capital stock (fixed nonresidential capital stock) on an annual basis for the period 1948–1976. Column 1 indicates that whereas the civilian labor force largely grew at a rate below 2% per year before 1969, it was well over 2% in all but 2 years between 1969 and 1976. In the face of this rapid growth in the labor force, the growth rate of the capital stock actually has slackened. The result, as indicated in Column 4, is that, over the period 1972–1976, the growth rate of the capital–labor ratio fell to its lowest level of the postwar period. Column 3 shows that, although males aged 25–54 continue to decline as a percentage of the labor force, the rapid growth rate of the labor force has spilled over into the prime-age male group as well. The vanguard of the baby boom cohort reached the age of 25 in the early 1970s. The existence of a capacity bottleneck, arising from the rapid growth in the labor force and affecting prime-age males, could mean that U_{NI}^{PM} has increased over the past few years, thus causing the calculations in Table 4.2 to understate the aggregate U_{NI}.

To study this question in more detail, it is useful to focus on trends in unemployment rates relative to capacity utilization rates. Although the capacity numbers are largely for manufacturing, there is little reason to suppose that the utilization rate is different in nonmanufacturing than in

---

is besides the point. The key fact is that there is a trade-off between market work and unemployment, particularly for those workers who can earn only low wages in the labor market. The lower the relative cost of not working, the greater the possibility that an individual will accept an additional spell of unemployment, perhaps to search for a better job, or extend the duration of a layoff in the hope of a recall.

TABLE 4.3.
Growth Rates in Labor and Capital, 1948–1976[a]

Year	Civilian labor force all workers (1)	Fixed nonresidential capital stock (2)	Civilian labor force prime-age males (3)	(2) − (1) (4)	(2) − (3) (5)
1948	2.14	NA	1.16	NA	NA
1949	1.10	3.98	.99	2.88	2.99
1950	1.50	3.51	1.06	2.01	2.45
1951	−.31	3.81	−.21	4.12	4.02
1952	.20	3.77	1.69	3.57	2.08
1953	1.41	3.64	3.07	2.23	.57
1954	1.00	3.52	.82	2.52	2.70
1955	2.17	3.49	.84	1.32	2.65
1956	2.35	3.72	.37	1.37	3.35
1957	.57	3.62	.35	3.05	3.27
1958	1.06	2.96	.60	1.90	2.36
1959	1.08	2.53	.14	1.45	2.39
1960	1.84	2.76	.36	.92	2.40
1961	1.19	2.72	.20	1.53	2.52
1962	.22	2.79	−.34	2.57	3.13
1963	1.73	2.98	.48	1.25	2.50
1964	1.75	3.24	.28	1.49	2.96
1965	1.87	4.05	.26	2.18	3.79
1966	1.77	4.85	−.12	3.08	4.97
1967	2.08	4.73	.73	2.65	4.00
1968	1.80	4.43	1.11	2.63	3.32
1969	2.54	4.54	.75	2.00	3.79
1970	2.45	4.24	1.11	1.79	3.13
1971	1.69	3.57	.75	1.88	2.82
1972	2.89	3.40	1.61	.51	1.79
1973	2.51	3.74	1.81	1.23	1.93
1974	2.59	3.82	1.81	1.23	2.01
1975	1.76	3.02	1.27	1.26	1.75
1976	2.33	2.31	1.45	−.02	.86

[a]The capital stock is the fixed nonresidential capital stock, constant dollars, excluding pollution abatement capital. It is calculated by P. Clark (1977).

manufacturing. Traditional capital stock adjustment models suggest that capital growth responds to, but tends to lag, output growth. On this basis, the rapid growth in the service sectors implies that capacity utilization is probably higher in those sectors.[20] Given the greater cyclical swings in manufacturing, this may not be true at every point in the cycle, but it is almost certainly the case over the cycle.

[20]For a method of creating capacity utilization rates which lead to this result directly, see Hickman and Coen (1976).

The results connecting unemployment and the capital stock are shown in Table 4.4. The alternative measures of labor market utilization are the total unemployment rate (U) and prime-age male unemployment (U_{PM}). The Wharton and Federal Reserve Board utilization rates are used as alternative independent variables. A third-degree polynomial time-trend is introduced to capture the changing relationship between U and U_{CAP}. In addition, a dummy variable was added that splits the sample period and allows a different constant term for each half.

In discussing Table 4.4 we concentrate on (i) and (iii). Using a benchmark capacity utilization rate of .93 for the Wharton Index, we can trace the changing relationship between capacity and unemployment between 1954 and 1977. The 93% utilization rate is chosen because it is equivalent to the nonaccelerating-inflation rate of capacity utilization in the Wharton model (denoted U_{NI}^{CAP}).[21]

When the total unemployment rate is used as the dependent variable, the time trends indicate that an unemployment rate of approximately 4% was compatible with a capacity utilization figure of .93 in the 1950s and early 1960s. The implications for U_{NI} are reasonably close to the U_{NI} measure shown in Table 4.2. After 1965, U for $U_{NI}^{CAP} = .93$ begins to increase rapidly. This is shown in Table 4.5. In 1973:1, U reaches approximately 5.25%. This again is similar to, but somewhat below, the movement in the U_{NI} series. After 1973, the trade-off becomes very unfavorable. The $U_{NI}^{CAP} = .93$ benchmark is compatible with an unemployment rate as high as 6.85% in 1977:1. If we assume, from Table 4.2, that the deterioration in U based on demographic factors is approximately 1.5% (5.5% minus 4.0% in 1957), then the additional deterioration due to the capacity utilization shortfall is an additional 1.3% (6.85% minus 5.5%). This deterioration in the relative position of the labor market appears in all of the equations and is not a function of the third-degree polynomial time-trend. However, the actual size of the increase in U, given $U_{CAP} = .93$, is dependent on the exact specification of the equation.

The results for (iii), where U_{PM} is the dependent variable, are compatible with those of (i). In this equation, the unemployment rates for prime-age males in 1954 and 1973, given $U_{NI}^{CAP} = .93$, are largely the same in the sense of being within a standard error of each other.[22] After

[21] Although the t-statistics on the time trend coefficients are insignificant in (i) and (iii), the F-statistics for all three coefficients evaluated jointly are significant. There is substantial collinearity among the three time-trend variables.

[22] The unemployment rate varies parabolically between those two dates, reaching a low of approximately 1.85%. The significance of this decline is somewhat unclear and, given the mild U-shaped time path, it may be exaggerated by the polynomial form of the time trends.

TABLE 4.4.
Estimated Unemployment Rate Equations, 1954:1–1977:2

Dependent variable[a]	Constant	Capacity utilization index	Time[b]	(Time)²	(Time)³	D_{67}[c]	$\bar{R}^2$/DW	SEE	Rho[d]
(i) U	11.8177 (.36)	−15.4930[e] (−14.47)	19.0671 (.33)	−16.7535 (−.50)	4.6521 (.72)	−.5772 (−2.23)	.9639/1.5764	.2583	.6746
(ii) U	−77.9221 (−1.33)	−15.8235[f] (−11.86)	176.6483 (1.74)	−107.3818 (−1.84)	21.6311 (1.97)	−.4343 (−1.53)	.9612/1.5295	.2672	.8289
(iii) U_{PM}	9.7645 (.39)	−15.6052[e] (−15.75)	23.0469 (.52)	−19.9803 (−.77)	5.2507 (1.05)	−.6457 (−2.66)	.9488/1.6926	.2810	.4913
(iv) U_{PM}	−54.9504 (−1.81)	−16.5135[f] (−12.92)	138.4282 (2.58)	−86.9200 (−2.77)	17.9180 (2.98)	−.8978 (−3.18)	.9448/1.7130	.2919	.6049

[a]U is the total unemployment rate; U_{PM} is the prime-age male unemployment rate; numbers in parentheses are t-statistics.
[b]Time represents a time trend beginning with a value of 1.25 in 1954:1, increasing by .01 every quarter. Alternative estimates, including (time)⁴, did not alter the results or the time path of the combined trend variables.
[c]D_{67} is a dummy variable, where $D_{67} = 1$ for 1967:1–1977:2, 0 elsewhere.
[d]Rho is the Cochrane–Orcutt adjustment coefficient for first-order autocorrelation.
[e]Wharton Capacity Utilization Index, Manufacturing.
[f]Federal Reserve Board Utilization Rate, Manufacturing.

1973, there is a sharp jump in U_{PM} associated with a capacity utilization rate of 93%. The increase is from 2.85% to 4.17%. The prime-age male unemployment rate largely abstracts from the effects of compositional changes in the labor market. The predicted increase in U_{PM} from Table 4.5, between 1973 and 1977, is approximately 1.3% and is close to the secular rise in the unemployment rate that cannot be explained by the demographic compositional shifts.

Analyzing any of these numbers is difficult because of the data problems associated with capacity utilization and the problems of interpreting a time trend. The time trends cannot represent a causal mechanism for the underlying developments and only serve to describe what has occurred in a mechanical fashion. The equations cannot be extrapolated into the future, and the results may largely reflect errors in the data.

Interpreted broadly, the results suggest that a number of developments has taken place in the inputs markets over the past several years. First, these data support the notion of a growth in the nonaccelerating-inflation rate of unemployment due to the compositional shift in the labor market. The increase in U, for U_{CAP} at .93, of 1.1 percentage points between 1954 and 1973 is only slightly below the increase in U_{NI} in Table 4.2. Second, Table 4.3 also suggests a capacity shortfall, relative to both the total and prime-age male labor force, starting around 1973. These results suggest a potential downward bias in the U_{NI} figures of Table 4.2 for the period 1973–1977.

If it is assumed that U_{NI}^{CAP} has remained at .93, then Tables 4.4 and 4.5 suggest that U_{NI} has increased above 6% between 1973 and 1977. However, another possible interpretation is that U_{NI}^{CAP} has increased over time above the .93 rate. To see this, we rewrite (8) in the general form

TABLE 4.5.
Unemployment Rate Associated with Capacity Utilization at 93%

Period	Total unemployment rate (i)	Prime-age male unemployment rate (iii)
1954:1	4.15	3.13
1959:1	4.01	2.72
1964:1	4.16	2.51
1969:1	4.22	1.85
1973:1	5.25	2.85
1977:1	6.85	4.17

$$0 = h_\tau(\{U_i\}, U_{\text{CAP}}, Z), \qquad (8b)$$

where $\{U_i\}$ is the vector of age–sex unemployment rates. A nonaccelerating rate of inflation can be achieved by "trading-off" higher unemployment for some groups in order to achieve lower unemployment for others. Similarly, as shown in Figure 4.1, higher U_{CAP} can be traded-off against lower aggregate unemployment. This diagram is drawn assuming a given (full-employment) level of aggregate demand and given structural features of the economy. It indicates, for a given level of aggregate demand, the composition of relative demand for capital and labor. Using this diagram to analyze Tables 4.2 and 4.5, assume that the economy's supply constraints were at point a in 1973. This conforms to a $U_{\text{NI}}^{\text{CAP}} = .93$ and a $U_{\text{NI}} = 5.25$ as shown in Table 4.5. The shift in U_{NI} and $U_{\text{NI}}^{\text{CAP}}$ between 1973 and 1977 could have resulted from an adverse shift in the trade-off from AA′ to BB′ and a movement to point b. This would imply an increase in U_{NI} without a corresponding increase in $U_{\text{NI}}^{\text{CAP}}$. Indeed, at any point along BB′, the economy must have a higher level of U_{NI} for any given $U_{\text{NI}}^{\text{CAP}}$. At the other extreme, the entire change in U_{NI} and $U_{\text{NI}}^{\text{CAP}}$ may be accounted for by a movement to point c along the original AA′ line. In this case, $U_{\text{NI}}^{\text{CAP}}$ could have in-

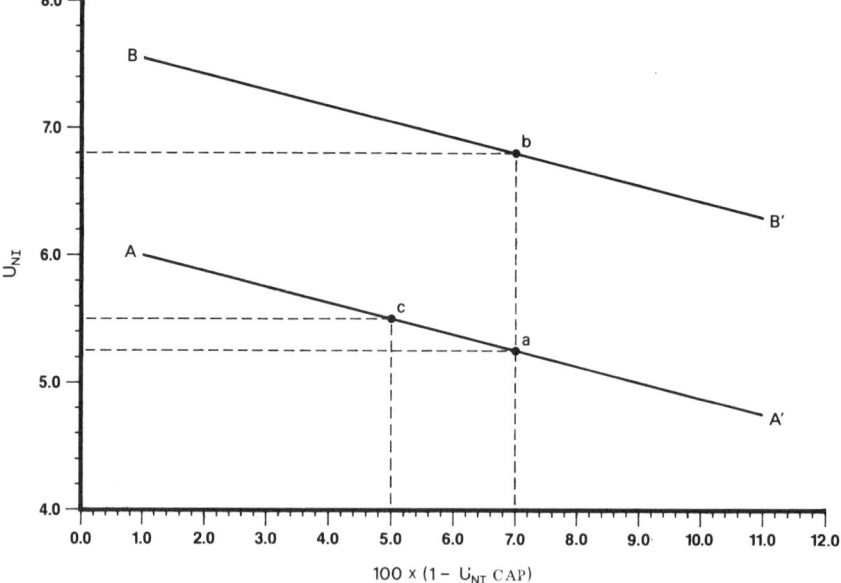

Figure 4.1. Alternative levels of full-employment U and U_{CAP} compatible with nonaccelerating inflation.

creased, for example, to 95%, and the calculations of Table 4.4, based on a constant $U_{NI}^{CAP} = .93$, would overstate the rise in U_{NI}. (Point c is chosen so that the U_{NI} is equal to the predicted value from Table 4.2.) The evidence available to date is too preliminary to suggest to what degree the 1973-1977 developments are explained by a shift in the trade-off, movement along AA', or measurement errors in the data.

In terms of the model on pages 76-80, a capacity shortfall may be due to unusual rapid growth in the labor force combined with short-run stickiness in factor substitutability [Eq. (1a)]. Vintage effects in the manipulable capital stock are particularly relevant, since the baby boom cohort is about to be replaced by the baby bust cohort. For long-lived capital there is no incentive for firms to increase the rate of capital accumulation in order to capture the peak of the labor force growth or the shifting trends in L_A/L_B caused by the baby boom cohort. The effects of lags in factor substitution are enhanced by the lags in the adjustment process of relative factor prices [for example, Eqs. (6) and (7)]. Several other major factors have also contributed to a slowdown in the capital growth rate relative to labor force growth, but a general treatment of this topic is beyond the scope of this chapter.[23]

The Potential Impact of the Fertility Twist and Slowing Population Growth

The implications of the coming slowdown in population growth can be drawn from the model on pages 76-80. To an important extent, these implications represent an unwinding of the supply-side bottlenecks caused by the baby boom. In particular, one might predict from the demographic shift that the nonaccelerating-inflation rate of unemployment would fall slightly between 1977 and 1980 and then decline more rapidly after 1980. Although a specific forecast of U_{NI} is dependent upon the particular model, the U_i Eq. (9) used to generate Table 4.2 suggests a decline in U_{NI} to 4.5% before 1985-1987. This would result from a shift in the composition of the labor force towards the older and

[23]One explanation is the unusual nature of the 1973-1977 business cycle, especially the synchronization of the cycle across the industrialized countries. This may have caused capacity utilization to increase more rapidly than the unemployment rate during this period. A second element is that the growth in the inflation rate, shifts in relative prices, and new ventures in government regulation such as OSHA and EPA have increased the risk associated with capital investment. Since rates of return to capital have certainly not increased over their historical value, and may have decreased slightly, the increased risk could be a factor in the slowdown in capital investment in the current recovery. For a discussion of the fluctuations in pretax profit rates, see Feldstein and Summers (1977).

more stable employment years.[24] In addition, the slowdown in the rate of growth of the overall labor force would give capital accumulation a chance to catch up, thereby altering the gap between unemployment and capacity utilization rates.

An important question is whether the effects of the aging of the population could be offset by changes in participation rates, especially for female groups. The evidence suggests that this will not occur. This prediction is based on the underlying trends in the age structure of the population and the U_{NI}^is of the various age-sex groups.[25]

The most likely development is that the past decade's increase in younger female participation rates should begin to spill over into higher participation rates for older females. This results from the cohort effect of younger workers aging and continuing historically above average participation rates. An important result of Table 4.1, however, is that the U_{NI}^i for older females is close to that for prime-age males and below the economywide level. For females above age 35, U_{NI}^i equals approximately 3.75%, whereas the corresponding aggregate U_{NI} is 5.51%. Hence, an increase in the participation rate of older females over the next decade should not offset the effects on U_{NI} of the aging population.

The groups with high U_{NI}^is are males 16–24 and females 16–34. For male teenage participation rates, the outlook is mixed. Participation rates have been increasing for males 16–19, but have been largely unchanged for males 20–24. These participation rate trends mirror developments in school enrollment rates. Enrollment rates for males 16–19 have been decreasing, on average, over the past 10 years. There has been little change in enrollment rates for males 20–24. Though for younger males the trade-off appears to be between school and market work, that is not true for females. Enrollment rates have been relatively flat for females 16–19 and have increased rapidly for females 20–24 over the past 10 years, whereas their participation rates have been rising. Rather, the trade-off for females appears to be between school and young children. For females aged 16–34, participation and fertility rates are closely and negatively related.

These relationships argue strongly against a continuation of at least

---

[24]For forecasting U_{NI} through the early 1990s the age structure of the population aged 16+ is largely known. The potential variables, which are assumed to be constant, are mortality and immigration. This allows one to extrapolate the RP_y variable of Eq. (9) into the future.

[25]Since U_{NI} is a function of the cost of being unemployed and of the impact of minimum wages, a potential decline in U_{NI} due to demographic factors could be offset by further changes in government policy with respect to transfer payments and minimum wages. These issues are discussed in the fiscal policy section.

the same rate of increase in participation rates for males 16–24 and females 16–34. Virtually no models that we are familiar with project a continuation of the *rate of decline* in male enrollment rates and fertility rates. This is especially true of fertility rates, which already have fallen well below the zero population growth level. In fact, some models project an increase in both enrollment rates and fertility rates.[26] Consequently, the demographics, including likely participation rate changes, are favorable for a significant decline in U_{NI} over the next decade.

An additional positive factor for a decline in U_{NI} is that, assuming that participation rates do not increase radically, the rate of labor force growth will decline significantly over the next decade, and this should allow an unwinding of the capacity utilization bottleneck discussed on pages 85–91. The degree of unwinding depends upon the extent to which the rapid growth in the labor force has been a crucial ingredient in creating the capacity bottleneck. Other explanations have been offered, including the effects of rapid changes in relative prices for food and fuel, government regulations through the Environmental Protection Agency (EPA), the Occupational Safety and Health Administration (OSHA), etc., and the unusual worldwide synchronization of the 1973–1976 business cycle. Even if these latter factors are relevant, however, a slowdown in the growth rate of the labor force should help, ceteris paribus, to alleviate the capacity shortfall.

Although the model on pages 76–80 and the discussion in the following sections can largely be put in reverse to study the slowing of population growth, this is not completely the case. In particular, as the baby bust cohort replaces the baby boom cohort in the labor market, the shortage input will be entry-level workers drawn from the dwindling supply of new entrants. A relative decline in young, less experienced or unskilled workers, however, is easier for the economy to adjust to than is a scarcity of more experienced or skilled workers. The reason, of course, is that, whereas experienced workers can be downgraded quickly to fill less skilled jobs, young inexperienced workers cannot be upgraded as rapidly to fill higher level positions.

In this new environment then, the labor market problem will shift from integrating a young population into the work force to the continual adjustment problems of the (now) older baby boom workers who are consigned to continuously competing in a relatively large cohort group. Promotion opportunities for this group should be unfavorable, and the

---

[26]This would be a prediction of the "relative income" model. See, for example, Easterlin (1969) and Wachter (1972).

less successful or lower-attachment workers may well remain in the traditional entry-level positions to compensate for the scarcity of new entrants.

Although the unemployment rate of the baby boom cohort should decline as it ages, its relative wage or income experience will likely remain relatively unfavorable. The problem for this group will switch from unemployment to low wages. In this environment, the emphasis of fiscal policy should remain on supply-side issues, such as human and physical capital accumulation, which can translate into a higher rate of growth of productivity and real wages.

The combination of an aging population, the difficulties in paying retirement benefits for a burgeoning aged 60 and over group, and the unfavorable labor market experience of the baby boom generation may result in some slowdown or even reversal in the future average retirement age. This may serve as a safety valve for some of the problems that may arise from the demographic twist. An increase in participation rates for older workers would be unlikely to offset the expected decline in U_{NI} since those groups have a low U^i_{NI} associated with their relatively low propensity for job searching and high job attachment.

In analyzing the implications of the demographic twist, it must be stressed that the second half of the twist, namely the population slowdown, has occurred largely in the United States and Europe, but not in most less developed countries. Where national economies are increasingly linked together through international trade and "temporary" immigration of workers, the impact of domestic population changes in the United States may be offset by demographic developments elsewhere. For example, although the demographic twist may contribute to a slowdown in the U.S. growth rate in demand for food and fuel, international population and development forces are likely to maintain a high international growth rate. Bottlenecks associated with food and fuel may therefore be a recurring event resulting in unanticipated (and perhaps sharp) upswings in U_{NI} and the domestic rate of inflation.

Similarly, a surfeit of young workers in less developed economies in the late 1970s and 1980s, combined with a scarcity of young American-born workers, may force a rethinking of U.S. immigration policies. After a 50-year hiatus, the immigration issue is again receiving substantial attention from policymakers. But the policy options being considered today, in an environment where there is a surplus of American-born entry-level workers, are likely to be outdated as the age structure of the native-born population increases. Over the next decade, the pressures of illegal immigration coming from abroad will continue to build. These international population factors will operate as a counterforce to the anticipated slowdown in the growth of the labor force associated with the baby bust generation.

The Role of Fiscal Policy

In terms of the model sketched out previously, there are several major problems confronting stabilization policy today. They include the uncertainties involved in determining the actual level of U_{NI}, the fact that almost any U_{NI} calculation indicates a figure that is above the stated full-employment targets of policymakers, and the need to shift fiscal policy to a supply-side approach if U_{NI} is to be reduced.

Uncertainty over the level of U_{NI} obviously makes efforts at economic stabilization more risky. Not only are policymakers uncertain about the exact magnitude and timing effects of monetary and fiscal options, but they are also unsure of the target value of U_{NI} to aim for. The demographic swing may be the single most important element causing U_{NI} to change over the past 20 years. Most researchers who attempt to control for compositional changes in the labor force calculate a U_{NI} in the range of 5.0–6.0%, with some bunching around the 5.5% figure.[27] However, once other factors in the U_{NI} calculation are introduced, such as the capacity utilization–unemployment rate trade-off, the range of uncertainty may be greater than one full percentage point on the unemployment rate.

The normative views of policymakers toward full employment have interacted with the uncertainty over its exact level to create an inflation-prone economy. For example, during the recovery of 1972–1973, it was argued by some that the economy was not overheated, so that any increase in the inflation rate was induced by exogenous forces (e.g., food and fuel). This was based on the notion that U_{NI}, if it existed as a useful construct, was at 5% or below. Our calculations, using the U_{NI} of Table 4.2, however, give different results. They indicate that the U.S. economy has been in a tight labor market ($U < U_{NI}$) for most of the decade between 1965:2 and 1974:4.[28] In addition, the recovery of the early 1970s resulted in eight quarters of $U < U_{NI}$ between 1972 and 1974. Adjusting U_{NI} further for capacity constraints would further indicate an even deeper and longer period of excess demand pressure. Consequently, a good deal of the 1978 inflation can be attributed to nearly a decade of overstimulative monetary and fiscal policies.

A relaxation of inflationary pressures arising from straight, classical

---

[27]See, for example, Hall (1974) and Modigliani and Papademos (1975).
[28]The exception is the period of U only slightly above U_{NI} between 1970:4 and 1972:4.

overheating requires the recognition that the actual, as distinct from desired, level of U_{NI} is approximately 5.5% with a large potential error. In this case, and assuming that society rules out accelerating inflation as a solution, a number of alternatives to the problem of a relatively high U_{NI} can be sketched out.

First, society could raise its unemployment target. Much of the increase in U_{NI} is due to compositional shifts in the labor force compounded by a decreasing cost of unemployment.[29] A wealthy society presumably can afford a higher relative transfer income and a higher minimum wage floor, but the cost of these policies is a higher U_{NI}. Because of this, the welfare cost of unemployment of 5.5% today may be similar to a 4% rate in 1955.[30] In any case, the acceptance of the high level of U_{NI} is made easier by the fact that a fall would be calculated to occur between 1978 and 1985 as the baby bust generation enters the labor force. And for those who do not believe that any structural supply-side policies can work, waiting for the baby bust is the only alternative.

A difficulty in accepting the level of U_{NI} is that unemployment falls unevenly among age–sex–race groups. A second solution then is to shift the incidence of unemployment or unutilized resources. This option may be useful today if U_{NI} is high because of capacity bottlenecks. In this case, fiscal policy targeted at increasing the demand for labor relative to capital could achieve a reduction in U_{NI}.[31]

Targeted fiscal policy such as public service employment also could be used to shift the structure of labor demand in favor of minorities or high U_{NI}^i groups in general. These types of policies would have the effect of increasing the U_{NI}^i of certain labor groups or capital in order to lower the U_{NI}^i of the disadvantaged groups.[32]

---

[29]If society had unemployment targets for the U_{NI}^i for each age–sex group, instead of the aggregate U_{NI}, then the perceived adverse shift in unemployment between 1955 and 1976 would have been slight. The notion of defining targets in terms of acceptable unemployment rates for each age–sex group has long been recommended by Gordon (1967).

[30]This position is stated strongly by Gordon (1977).

[31]That is, policy could be oriented toward labor-intensive projects which would circumvent the capacity problems that appear in Table 4.4. Whether or not such an approach is useful would depend upon the cause of the capacity bottleneck. If short-run labor market imbalances, resulting from the demographic twist, are the problem, then targeted policies could be successful in lowering U_{NI} until the baby bust cohort arrives. If the slowdown in capital expenditures is due to increased uncertainty, then targeting demand away from capital could be counterproductive.

[32]The aggregate U_{NI} could be lowered by decreasing the U_{NI}^i of the disadvantaged groups if those groups were operating along a flatter point on their Phillips curve than the advantaged workers with low U_{NI}^i. This point is derived formally by Baily and Tobin (1977).

The Fiscal Policy Dilemma: Cyclical Swings and Supply-Side Constraints 97

The third solution is to utilize the fiscal policy mix to lower U_{NI} by improving the economy's overall supply constraint.[33] Policies to achieve an improved supply-side posture must be oriented toward capital accumulation—both physical and human—rather than toward consumption or simple job creation. In particular, supply policies should be aimed at altering the input mix and alleviating bottleneck problems by upgrading the productivity of workers. This increases the *supply* of inputs with relatively *low* $U_{NI}{}^i$. Only the supply policy has the potential of significantly lowering the nonaccelerating-inflation rate of unemployment. Given the likelihood of capacity bottlenecks, priority could be given to increasing the supply of fixed plant and equipment. Investment tax credits and accelerated depreciation can be used to reduce the price of capital goods and thereby increase the rate of growth of the capital stock. This is not recommended here as a cyclical measure; rather our concern is the intermediate-run issue of reducing U_{NI}.

Fiscal policy measures could also be aimed at increasing the supply of semiskilled and skilled workers while reducing the supply of unskilled workers. This can be done through training programs that upgrade the unskilled workers. Skill training programs, contrary to popular belief, receive little attention today (e.g., federal funding); the emphasis, rather, is on direct job creation. Although skill training programs are difficult to construct compared with direct job creation, the evidence strongly suggests that the latter approach can be successful, especially if combined with a positive capital accumulation program.[34]

The approaching changeover from rapid to slow labor force growth in the United States and the resulting decline in U_{NI} will ease the overall policy problems facing the fiscal authorities, although some difficulties

---

[33] In terms of Figure 4.1, this would translate into a leftward shift of the trade-off.

[34] The literature on this topic is extensive. For the most comprehensive treatment of manpower programs beginning with the 1960s, see Perry *et al.* (1975).

Even in a recessionary environment, the supply approach will have a positive effect on aggregate demand. Indeed, training programs may be more successful in targeting on the disadvantaged workers. The experience of public service employment under the Emergency Employment Act and the Comprehensive Employment and Training Act has indicated that the newly created public jobs generally do not favor the disadvantaged workers. These programs are focused in theory better than in practice. Since the disadvantaged are more likely to enroll in training programs than higher-skilled workers who are temporarily unemployed, the supply-side approach will first increase the relative demand for low-skilled workers and thus, if successful, upgrade them into semiskilled workers. The limitation is that since training costs money, a given level of expenditure can hire fewer workers on a training than on a direct employment program. That is, the short-run cosmetic reduction in the unemployment rate is lower—or there is less "bang for the buck." This, of course, can be offset by simply increasing the funding level.

will remain.[35] First, uncertainty over the level of U_{NI} is generated by instability in the economic environment, and the demographic factors are obviously in a state of transition. The demographic shifts associated with the changeover from a baby boom to a baby bust generation are likely to create new problems in measuring the "normalized" unemployment rate.

Second, the baby bulge will continue to move through the age structure, and it will create problems wherever it is located. Although the older baby bulge group will have lower unemployment rates in the future, it will still suffer from low relative wage levels and promotion opportunities. To improve the economic environment facing this group will require ongoing supply-side investments in physical and human capital. The extent to which society chooses to invest in this group will have to be determined by noneconomic considerations in the sense that rates of return on investment in older workers fall dramatically with age.

Third, fiscal policy with respect to minimum wages and transfers will continue to generate problems in terms of their coordination with stabilization policies and as an alternative approach to training in dealing with the problems of low-wage workers. As discussed previously, any anticipated decline in U_{NI} due to demographic factors can be offset by sufficiently large decreases in the cost of being unemployed or increases in minimum wages. In fact, even if benefit levels are constant in relative terms, changes in the rule governing eligibility for welfare can generate important changes in U_{NI}. For example, requiring many welfare recipients to be available for work, as has been suggested in the debate over welfare reform, may generate a significant increase in U_{NI} by increasing the labor force of structurally unemployed workers. This type of increase in U_{NI} is very difficult to measure accurately and hence generates uncertainties in the proper conduct of stabilization policy.

Young workers, as a result of low skills and low job attachment, tend to be the demographic group most affected by public assistance transfers and minimum wages. The aging of the population should make these policies less important in the aggregate. At the same time, transfer payments with respect to retirement payments bulk larger and become much more burdensome in the aggregate. As the population age struc-

---

[35]We assume that the slow population growth will not generate any problems of secular stagnation. As discussed earlier, Keynesian policies should be able to fill in the peaks and troughs of any tendency towards longer-run cyclical swings in demand. In addition, important investment areas, including energy, food, and the environment, as well as the capacity shortfall, make it unlikely that public investment would be a problem area in the 1980s. For a detailed discussion of the investment issue, see Chapter 5 of this volume by Larry Neal.

ture changes radically, the parameters governing the fiscal transfer system will have to be reset in a fundamental fashion.

Finally, as just mentioned, world population pressures may well operate to lessen the predicted slowdown in the growth rate of the U.S. labor force. It is possible that, as the baby bust cohort enters the labor force, immigration restrictions or the enforcement of the rules will be loosened, and the United States would become a significant importer of workers from the less developed countries.

5

Is Secular Stagnation Just around the Corner? A Survey of the Influences of Slowing Population Growth upon Investment Demand

LARRY NEAL

Introduction, Summary, and Outline of Conclusions

As the decade of the 1970s draws to a close, an increasing number of analogies with the decade of the 1930s become apparent. Not the least is the contrast of actual economic performance with that anticipated at the end of the previous decade. In 1972, the Organization for Economic Cooperation and Development projected an average annual rate of growth of 4.9% in U.S. real Gross National Product (GNP) for the period 1970–1975. The actual rate of growth was only 2.1%. Much of the shortfall can be attributed to the failure of business investment to maintain the share of GNP it had achieved during the 1960s. Instead of being over 17% of GNP as projected, gross capital formation in plant and equipment and construction was only 14%; instead of growing at a projected rate of 6.3% annually, total investment in real terms remained nearly constant.[1] On the other hand, the slackening of population growth in the 1970s was foreseen in the late 1960s, just as demographers of the 1920s foresaw the slowdown that occurred in the 1930s. But the reduction in births, which is primarily responsible for the current slowdown, is proving to be much more serious than first predicted. The Commission on Population Growth and the American Future stated unequivocally in 1972 that "total births will continue to increase over the next twenty years with a slower population growth rate."[2] The latest figures of the Bureau of the Census show that the number of births in 1970 was 3,739,000. By 1973, it had slumped to a bit over 3 million, where it has remained through 1977—despite the marked rise in the number of potentially fertile women within the population, and despite well-publicized increases in the sexual liberation of women. It can truthfully be said that never in the history of the world have so many done so much for so few!

This "birth dearth," as it has been labeled, combines with slackening investment and the widely promulgated vision of vanishing energy resources to produce an updated scenario of "secular stagnation." Secular stagnation was a theme that dominated the economic literature of the 1930s. According to the best estimates of such men as Alvin Hansen and Benjamin Higgins,[3] reduced population growth in the 1930s was reducing investment opportunities on the extensive margin and would likely discourage investment on the intensive margin. Hansen's original thesis was based on the perception that investment is required either to equip a growing labor force with new capital (the extensive margin) or to increase the capital–labor ratio for a given labor force (the intensive margin). Stated more formally, he took the identity, $K = L \times (K/L)$, where K is the capital stock and L is the labor force and differentiated the natural logarithms of both sides with respect to time to get

$$\frac{d \ln K}{dt} = \frac{d \ln L}{dt} + \frac{d \ln(K/L)}{dt}.$$

The term on the left side is approximately equal to the rate of growth of the capital stock over a given time period. If that time period is 1 year, the term is approximately equal to the ratio of net investment to capital

---

[1]Organization for Economic Cooperation and Development (1972, 1975, 1977).
[2]Morss and Reed (1972, p. 4).
[3]Hansen (1939) stated the thesis succinctly in 1939 and in expanded form with implications for government policy 2 years later (Hansen, 1941). Compare Keynes (1937), Myrdal (1940), Reddaway (1939), and Higgins (1944). The classic rebuttal of the thesis is Terborgh (1945).

stock. The first term on the right-hand side approximates the rate of growth of the labor force, and the second term approximates the rate of growth of the capital–labor ratio.

Hansen (1941, Chapter 1) attributed some 60% of American investment in the nineteenth century directly to the rate of growth of the labor force, the extensive margin for new investment, whereas only 40% came from the second term, or the intensive margin. If the barriers to immigration remained, the decline in the absolute number of births in the 1930s would eventually reduce the number of new laborers entering the labor force to the number leaving at retirement age. This eventually would eliminate what had been the greatest stimulus to investment in the nineteenth century. Only increased investment and other expenditures by the government or a dramatic reversal in population growth could stave off this decline of the West.

A number of factors account for the failure of Hansen's predictions to materialize before the 1970s. Perhaps the weakest link in Hansen's chain of reasoning was the link between declining births and declining entrants to the labor force. This can be broken in a number of ways. During the 1940s, there were:

1. An increased number of immigrants due to large numbers of Europeans qualifying for admission under the loopholes provided for refugees and spouses of American citizens
2. Increased participation rates in the labor force, especially for the female population

In the 1960s, the baby boom of the 1940s began to enter the labor force, and participation rates for younger women began to rise again. The vast military expenditures of World War II and the continued large scale of government expenditure after World War II for defense, education, highways, and medicine have also replaced private investment expenditures, not only as a source of autonomous expenditures for maintaining aggregate demand, but also as a locus of technological advance. In 1939, however, Hansen foresaw only the uncertain opportunities for raising the capital–labor ratio or replacing obsolete capital more rapidly. Now that the echo to the post–World War II baby boom is fading rapidly, defense budgets and overall government expenditures are being trimmed, the interstate highway system is largely completed, and the nation's petroleum reserves are being depleted, is it time for the realization of Hansen's stark vision of America's future?

The response of this chapter is no. Neither in the short run of the next 2 to 3 years nor in the long run of 20 to 30 years (when the age group 20–65 years old will have stabilized as a percentage of total population if fertility rates remain constant)[4] is it likely that the adverse effects of declining population growth upon investment demand will also lower the rate of growth of per capita income. Since investment demand is only important insofar as it helps maintain per capita income through full employment and continued technical progress, the theme of secular stagnation will not play well under these circumstances. Nevertheless, in the period between the short run and the long run—call it the trend transition (this will be defined more carefully)—some interesting possibilities arise that are quite different from past experience and that are potentially very disturbing. The most likely outcome for the 1980s will be an increase in the labor force from either (*a*) even higher participation rates for women than exist now, or (*b*) a relaxation of immigration restrictions, especially against Latin Americans. Neither of these is the Greek tragedy outlined by Hansen, but neither one is a lighthearted romance. Each will imply considerable change in the nature of the feedback from economic opportunities to fertility decisions in the native American households. In sum, a new era of economic–demographic interactions in American society is nearly upon us, and considerable research effort is required to anticipate the policy consequences that will emerge from it.

The argument of the chapter is developed by examining the theoretical relationships between investment demand and population growth, first in the short-run context of econometric models that attempt to forecast investment demand for the next 2 to 3 years, and then in the long-run context of mathematical growth models that compare different sustainable growth paths. The concept of trend transition is then developed and related to the large body of literature on the long-swing hypothesis. The question is explored as to whether past experiences of the American economy with trend transitions in population growth can inform us on the likely consequences of the current trend transition. The answer is no and yes: no, if the labor force is expanded primarily by increased participation rates of women; yes, if it is enlarged by immigrant workers. The final section of this chapter probes the likely characteristics of the new economic–demographic era if immigration restrictions are retained.

Population and Investment Demand in the Short Run

During the 1960s, a period when the growth of capital stock was accelerating as the baby boom of the 1940s entered the labor force and

[4]Coale (1970).

participation rates among women rose, a substantial literature on short-run investment demand arose. Two lines of development were pursued, one from the macroeconomic side, emphasizing the distributed lag accelerator model,[5] the other from the microeconomic side, emphasizing the neoclassical theory of the profit-maximizing firm.[6] The first posited that the desired level of capital stock was determined primarily by the expected levels of future output and was insensitive to interest rates or to the relative costs of capital and labor. The second argued that the desired level of capital stock for a firm was determined essentially by the relative prices of capital and output (and, by implication, the relative prices of labor).

The implications of the two approaches for the stagnation thesis varied as well: The accelerator models predicted that slowing population growth would reduce the rate of growth of capital stock unless offset by rising per capita income; the neoclassical models predicted that the outcome would hinge on the relative prices of labor, capital, and output, and that the effect of slowing population growth would reduce the relative price of capital, at least with respect to labor (provided savings rates did not decline). The relative price of capital to output would then depend on whether, on the average, capital goods industries were the more labor-intensive. The most sensible prediction would be a change in the composition of the economy's capital stock, the stock of machinery rising relative to the stock of nonresidential buildings, and both stocks rising relative to residential buildings. The outcome for total investment demand would be indeterminate without further information on relative prices.

Both classes of models gave good econometric results; as a result little remained but theoretical preferences to distinguish them, and the empirical models tested were each flawed in some theoretical respect. A way out of the impasse was discovered by Lucas (1967), who developed a general model capable of generating both the distributed lag accelerator and the neoclassical models as special cases. Empirical testing of the model has been conducted by Schramm (1970) and Nadiri and Rosen (1969, 1974). The model posits a production function for a firm with a number of inputs used in any time period, adjustment costs for each input that rise as the change in input increases, and a desire to maximize present value of the expected future stream of net profits. If the production function is $F(\mathbf{X}_t)$ in any time period t, the adjustment cost function is

---

[5]The major proponent of the distributed lag accelerator models has been Robert Eisner. Especially useful are Eisner (1960, 1964), Eisner and Nadiri (1968), and Eisner and Strotz (1968).

[6]The neoclassical model has been tested extensively by Jorgenson (1967, 1968, 1971).

$C(\Delta X_t)$, and net revenues equal $pF(X_t) - s'X_t - pC(\Delta X_t)$ where X, ΔX, and s are column vectors of all inputs, change in inputs, and their unit prices, and p is the price of the one good produced; then the present value, P, of the firm is given by the expression

$$P = \sum_{t=1}^{T} (1 + r)^{-t} \{pF(X_t) - s'X_t - pC(\Delta X_t)\}.$$

To maximize present value, the firm must set

$$\frac{\partial F(X_{i,t})}{\partial X_{i,t}} = \frac{s_i}{p} + (1 + r) \frac{\partial C(\Delta X_{i,t-1})}{\partial X_{i,t}} + \frac{\partial C(\Delta X_{i,t})}{\partial X_{i,t}}.$$

This expression simply means that to maximize profits over time, a firm must set the marginal product of each input equal to the marginal cost of each input *plus* the costs of adjusting the level of the input more or less rapidly. In the case of labor, adjustment costs include overtime payments to experienced workers and on-the-job expenses of training new labor, as well as the search costs for additional workers.

Solving these first-order conditions for the time path of each input can then be accomplished once functional forms for the production function and the adjustment cost function are specified. An input-adjustment equation system can then be derived that will take the following general form: $\Delta X = B(X^* - X)$, where B is a matrix of adjustment coefficients that depend upon the production function, the adjustment cost function, and the discount rate, and X^* is the desired value of X. The formulation combines elements of the distributed lag accelerator model (ΔK is a function of the difference between the desired and actual capital stock) and the neoclassical model (K^* depends on relative prices and the user cost of capital), with a full appreciation of the dependence of investment demand upon the demand for other inputs. The adjustment rate of capital stock depends then not only on the costs of enlarging capital stock but also on the costs of increasing all other inputs as well, including labor.

The results of Nadiri and Rosen (1974) indicate that, for U.S. manufacturing investment in the period 1947–1970, cross-adjustment or feedback effects between capital stock and one or more other inputs existed and were significant. In general, utilization rates of labor and capital responded most rapidly to changes in factor demand, usually overshooting their equilibrium values, then production employment, inventory, and nonproduction employment inputs responded in turn, until finally capital stock responded. Sales effects were found to be much larger than price effects, but the period of testing predated the price changes which occurred in the 1970s. Schramm (1970) also concluded that adjustment costs in changing the input of labor significantly affected the pace of U.S. manufacturing investment. His study covered the period 1949–1962.

No accurate predictions can be made at this time with the class of interrelated factor demand models just described, however. The primary reason is that they all postulate a stable mechanism of price expectations that is given exogenously for the rest of the analysis. The price experience of the mid-1970s has been so unstable that forecasts by these models of even short-run investment demand have been very erratic and less accurate than naive models of mechanical trend projections.[7] A secondary reason is that estimation of the parameter values has to date been hampered by problems of serial correlation in the observed variables. Recent developments in time series analysis, especially the Box–Jenkins techniques, permit a more sophisticated interplay of structural parameter estimates and stochastic disturbance terms. In particular, accurate estimation of lag response patterns for each of the interrelated input variables is greatly facilitated by the flexibility of ARIMA (autoregressive integrated moving average) models.[8]

The significance of the interrelated factor demand models for the secular stagnation thesis is striking. While denying the quantitative importance of the original path Hansen described from declining population growth to investment, they suggest an alternative causal route that ends up at the same result—slackening investment demand in response to slower population growth. If the reduced investment demand is not offset by appropriate policy measures, unemployment could rise. The likelihood of such a paradox arising (scarce labor supplies creating redundant labor supply) must be judged remote, but if it did occur, the rise in unemployment could cause a temporary reduction in per capita income. Again, however, the link between population growth and investment demand depends upon the effect of population growth upon labor force growth. Whereas eventually the birth dearth of the 1970s may reduce the growth of the labor force and reduce the pace of capital accumulation, an increased participation rate of women who normally would be having babies could actually accelerate the growth of the labor force and encourage an investment boom in the 1980s. These effects may

---

[7]Some doubts about the predictive accuracy of econometric models were already being expressed in the late 1960s. See, for example, Cooper and Jorgenson (1969) and Stekler (1968). By the end of the 1960s, all forecasting models were in complete disarray. See Liebling and Russel (1969).

[8]Zellner and Palme (1974).

or may not be reinforced by the influence of slowing population growth on the target levels of capital stock desired. This is a question more appropriately handled in the context of long-run growth models, however.

Population and Investment Demand in the Long Run

The effect of slower population growth upon the optimal level of capital stock and its rate of growth over time depends critically upon the type of growth model employed. Moreover, the relationship between growth of labor force and growth of capital stock is formulated differently depending on what question is asked. For example, the classical model of growth developed by David Ricardo was concerned more with the effects of rising costs of labor caused by continued population growth on an island with limited arable land. Would the rising real wage permit continued growth of the capital stock in the manufacturing sector? In long-run equilibrium, however, the real wage would be found at a level just high enough to "enable the labourers, one with another to subsist and to perpetuate their race, without either increase or diminution."[9] Varying the real wage then also varies the level of sustainable population—the numbers that can be supported by the amount of land under cultivation, the stock of capital in existence, and the rate of technological progress, both embodied and disembodied. A rising real wage would induce a rising population that could only be sustained if new land were brought into production, or if technological progress occurred. A decline in the rate of growth of population comparable to what we are experiencing today would be caused in turn by a failure of the real wage to rise at previous rates. The inference would be that rising real wages had limited the growth of profits and therefore the growth of capital stock embodying technological progress, eventually causing a reduction in the growth of real wages and then lower rates of population growth. The conclusion of the Ricardian analysis would be that declining population growth is accompanied by reduced investment demand relative to constant or rising population growth, but this is necessary to maintain the desired level of real wages in the long run when population growth must cease altogether.

In Harrod–Domar models, on the other hand, population growth

[9]David Ricardo, *The Principles of Political Economy and Taxation*, cited by Brems (1973, p. 12).

plays a more direct role in driving the growth of the economy. Lower population growth ultimately lowers the rate of growth of the labor force; this in turn lowers the feasible growth rate of output (assuming that the rate of technical progress is independent of the growth rate of the labor force or of the capital stock), which lowers the growth rate of the capital stock, and hence the level of investment. In a process of equilibration between feasible and sustainable growth rates, à la Hicks's (1950) trade-cycle model, lower population growth also lowers both autonomous investment and the accelerator component of investment. Autonomous investment determines the lower buffer level; the feasible growth rate determines the upper buffer; and the accelerator determines how rapidly output moves between the two buffers. When population growth declines, depressions in investment levels tend to last longer and go deeper, booms to be shorter in duration, and recovery growth rates to be lower. The level and long-run growth of per capita income is unaffected, but the periodic loss of employment opportunities becomes more severe. It is interesting to note that, if Harrod–Domar or Hicksian models permitted any feedback from economic conditions to population growth (they do not), the effect of lower population growth would be cumulative. Higher average unemployment rates would decrease the number of births further and possibly even increase the number of deaths.

In the neoclassical growth model, changes in the capital–labor ratio are permitted in response to changes in the relative prices of capital and labor. If the growth of population fell to zero and eventually the labor force stabilized,[10] the growth of output would be reduced by the labor elasticity of output times the previous growth rate of population. The growth of the capital stock would then be reduced to the rate of growth of technical progress divided by the labor elasticity of output. Investment demand would again be reduced, although the economy would still continue to grow, thanks to both the accumulation of capital (albeit at a slower rate) and the implementation of technical progress in the production processes. Interestingly, the real wage would be higher, although ultimately its growth rate would converge to the lower rate of growth of the capital stock.

If the possibility of unbalanced growth is permitted in the steady state (growth continues, but at a constant, and possibly different, rate for all parts of the economy), Brems (1973, Chapter 7) has found that a reduction in the proportionate rate of growth of the labor force reduces growth rates of output for each sector and, consequently, the rate of

---

[10]Brems (1973, pp. 67–68) analyzes this case explicitly.

growth of capital stock in each sector. Again, however, the real wage is raised, although its equilibrium growth rate is not. The full extent of the reduced growth of capital stock upon investment demand depends upon the relative rates of growth of each sector and their weights in investment demand.

To summarize, all four of the widely used growth models just analyzed predict that an economy already on a stationary growth path (unchanging growth rates in all economic variables) that experiences a slowdown in population growth also will eventually experience a slowdown in growth of capital stock and, hence, lower investment demand than would otherwise be the case. The result is generated in each case by deriving investment demand from the size of the capital stock required to maximize present net worth of the economy. In a closed economy at full employment, the effect of population growth is solely upon the amount of labor available to operate the capital stock in the production processes. Slower population growth reduces the growth of the labor force, and this makes it more profitable to slow down the rate of growth of capital stock. The lower rate of growth of capital stock, although implying reduced investment demand, does not necessarily mean lower per capita income, however. In the process of shifting from one steady-state growth path to another, the initiation of the shift from the side of population growth implies, in the last two models, a higher capital-labor ratio, which in turn is consistent with a higher level of per capita income. Capital stock can and should continue to grow at the previous high rate until the higher capital–labor ratio is reached. During this trend transition period, in other words, investment demand should continue unabated, helping generate a higher level of per capita income. When the new optimal capital–labor ratio is reached, the growth of capital stock will be reduced to match the lower growth rate of the labor force. Per capita income may continue to grow, but at a lower rate determined by the growth of technical progress.

Problems of the Trend Transition

The growth models all take as given a prior decline in the growth rate of the labor force. The new, lower growth rate is then assumed to remain constant and unresponsive to the changes in the economy that follow. No economist really believes this will be the case; the assumption is made merely to facilitate the analytical solution. If the growth rate of the labor force is influenced in turn by changes in the growth rate of other variables in the economy, the analytical solution is complicated by the existence of feedback from the economic variables to the demographic determinants of the growth of the labor force. The existence of feedback from the economic side to the demographic in these cases, however, implies a tendency to change the long-run equilibrium growth path of the economy. This can happen whether the feedback is positive or negative. Suppose that a speed-up in the growth of per capita income, albeit temporary in the context of these long-run growth models, induces higher fertility rates and lower death rates. Since the effect of these demographic changes would only appear in the labor force some 15–20 years later, when the new growth path would have been achieved, a series of trend alternations might be induced with a periodicity of roughly 15–30 years. Suppose, on the other hand, that the increase in the growth of per capita income is produced not by higher participation rates of men in the labor force or by nonfertile women, but instead by a larger proportion of fertile women joining the labor force. The acceleration in per capita income might then induce lower fertility rates.[11] This type of phenomenon would again generate problems during the trend transition, basically by prolonging the period of transition to the lower equilibrium rate of growth of capital stock.

The problem of economic-to-demographic feedback during the trend transition emerges, therefore, as the most interesting, whether we approach the question of the influence of slowing population growth upon investment demand from the short- or the long-run point of view. Fortunately, the past history of the U.S. economy is replete with similar episodes of declining population growth that can be examined to determine what the most likely outcomes will be. Unfortunately, it appears that the outcome of the current episode of declining population growth (as well as that of the 1930s) may not be predictable from earlier experiences.

Slower Population Growth and Investment Demand during Trend Transitions: The Long-Swing Hypothesis Revisited

Apparent trend transitions in the rate of American population growth have appeared repeatedly in American history. It is easy to overlook this fact, since previous trends have often been resumed, creating an even longer trend period for analysis. Obviously, we are living through such an apparent trend transition in the late-1970s as the fertility rates of American women fall to unprecedented levels. We cannot tell if higher

[11]The initial work on this topic is by Mincer (1963).

fertility levels will resume in the 1980s or if an entirely new demographic era will emerge. Both resumptions and terminations of demographic trends have, however, occurred in the American past and have been analyzed closely. A brief review of these analyses will suggest some of the pertinent issues that may need to be dealt with in our situation.

The resumption of previous trends in population increase occurred repeatedly during the nineteenth century. The most dramatic source of population increase came to be periodic waves of immigrants, chiefly from Europe, and Easterlin (1965) has shown that waves of immigrants also coincided with similar and reinforcing ripples of births in the native population. In later work, Easterlin (1968) argued that both the waves in immigration and the ripples in births were demographic responses to changed domestic economic conditions that increased the opportunities for employment. The demographic responses, in turn, created a demand for population-related investment, especially in residential construction, but also in commercial building and social infrastructure such as canals, railroads, highways, port facilities, central power plants, and the like. As well as further increasing employment opportunities, this population-sensitive investment made other forms of investment more attractive, especially in the manufacturing sector. The process was cumulative until the backlog of delayed household formation at home and of delayed migration from abroad had been worked through. Then rising labor costs eventually choked off further growth in investment demand, and the reduced growth of investment demand led rather quickly to a cumulative decline in employment opportunities. This caused a fresh backlog of deferred household formation and international migration to begin building up. The buildup continued in the nineteenth century until a fresh set of investment opportunities appeared sufficiently profitable to set off a new investment boom.

In my own work (Neal, 1974, 1976; Klotz and Neal, 1973), which has systematically applied spectral and cross-spectral analysis to Easterlin's version of the long-swing hypothesis, I have found it more useful to think of the long swing in economic–demographic interactions as initiated by the demographic upsurge rather than by an autonomous increase in investment demand. The reason is that long swings are clearly evident in most population variables subjected to spectral analysis, but not in most economic variables, including gross private domestic investment. If the long swings in population increase (and the constituent components of births, deaths, and net migration) drive the economic variables, the responses of the economic variables can take any of several forms. These can be classified broadly as price, quantity, and income response. Typically, a given economic time series represents only

Is Secular Stagnation Just around the Corner? Survey of Investment Demand 113

one of these possible response paths (e.g., per capita income). To varying degrees, the demographic impulse to the economic system as a whole will be partially absorbed along other response paths (size of labor force and level of money wages, for instance). Over a series of successive long swings it would be surprising, given these possibilities, if a pronounced, dominating, long swing appeared in every one of the economic variables, and not too surprising if the long-swing frequency failed to dominate the other frequencies in the power spectra of all the economic variables.[12]

In any event, if there is significant economic–demographic interaction occurring in the long-swing frequencies, cross-spectral analysis of two such related series should reveal significant peaks in the coherence statistics at the long-swing frequencies.[13] Performing such analysis on the relevant variables from the Easterlin model, Klotz and I (Klotz and Neal, 1973, p. 295) did find strong support for the existence of such a structural relationship in the United States over the period 1880–1965. All elements of the Easterlin model—GNP, labor force, marriages, gross capital formation, and residential construction—had strong coherence values at the long-swing frequencies.[14] Furthermore, the apparent direction of causation predicted by Easterlin was confirmed, except in the case of employment and household formation. There, the results seemed to indicate that fluctuations in household formation, with a periodicity of anywhere from 16 to 24 years, led rather than followed similar fluctuations in employment.

Applying these results directly to the situation of the 1970s suggests that the 1970s are a period of declining growth in marriages,[15] which has generated a longer-term slump in residential construction and other forms of population-sensitive investment (schools, hospitals, highways, and airports) which, with a lag, is responsible for the current sluggishness of business investment and the relatively slower rates of growth of GNP than in the 1960s. Sometime in the mid-1980s, however, household formation should pick up again, not only from the maturing of the babies born in the late 1950s but also from the growing backlog of potential, and as yet formally unmated, marriage partners. This, if the past

---

[12]The power spectra show how much of the total variance of a time series is attributable to each oscillation of various lengths.

[13]Coherence in cross-spectral analysis is equivalent to the coefficient of determination, or R^2, in regression analysis.

[14]Long swings are in the low-frequency range of the spectrum, where only a small part of the oscillation can be observed during one time unit.

[15]In the early 1970s marriage rates (per 1000 unmarried women 15 years and older) fell from 77.9 in 1972 to 72.0 in 1974; earlier they had risen from 71.2 in 1962 to 80.0 in 1969. See U.S. Bureau of the Census (1975a, 1976b).

model of economic–demographic interactions is still applicable, will stimulate increased residential construction as well as increased births and/or immigration (including illegal and, hence, uncounted immigrants). Another prosperous period in the American economy will be under way, analogous to the 1880s, the 1900s, the 1920s, the 1940s, and the 1960s.

Before any predictions, much less any policy conclusions, can be drawn from this scenario, however, we must explore the question of whether such economic–demographic interactions still occur in American society. Abramovitz, for example, has proclaimed the passing of the Kuznets cycle either with World War I or with the abandonment of the gold standard by the United States in 1933. Abramovitz (1968) has concluded, "the Kuznets cycle in America lived, it flourished, it had its day, but its day is past. . . . *Requiescat in pace*. Gone but not forgotten [p. 369]." To explore this question more closely, I have charted the course of the major economic and demographic variables that are supposed to have interacted in the Kuznets cycle.

Figure 5.1 shows the general pattern that can be found in these variables, taking as an example of the economic variables Gross Private Domestic Investment and, as an example of the demographic variables, marriages. They are plotted on a semilogarithmic scale for easier determination of the various trends and trend-breaks. A straight line on this figure indicates a constant growth rate equal to the slope of the line. For spectral analysis, it is necessary to remove time trends in order to approximate the characteristics of a stationary time series. Figures 5.2 and 5.3 show the results of doing this with one very robust technique—first-differencing the natural logarithms of the variables. This is equivalent to looking at the annual growth rates of the variables instead of at their levels. The trend line is plotted to indicate whether the growth rates have tended to rise or fall over time. Only in the case of two variables—employment and real wage—did a visible trend remain. In neither case was the trend significantly different from zero, although it may be worth noting that the trend was upward in real wages and downward in employment.

In Figure 5.1 trend-breaks can be discerned by a statistically significant change in the average slope of the graph. In particular, the influences of World War I, the Great Depression, and World War II show up in each series. Formal statistical tests for the existence of a significant trend-break at each of these possible points were positive in nearly every case.

It is this kind of trend-break most of us have in mind when we use the term. Modern time-series analysis suggests, however, a number of problems with this kind of calculation. In decreasing order of obviousness,

Is Secular Stagnation Just around the Corner? Survey of Investment Demand

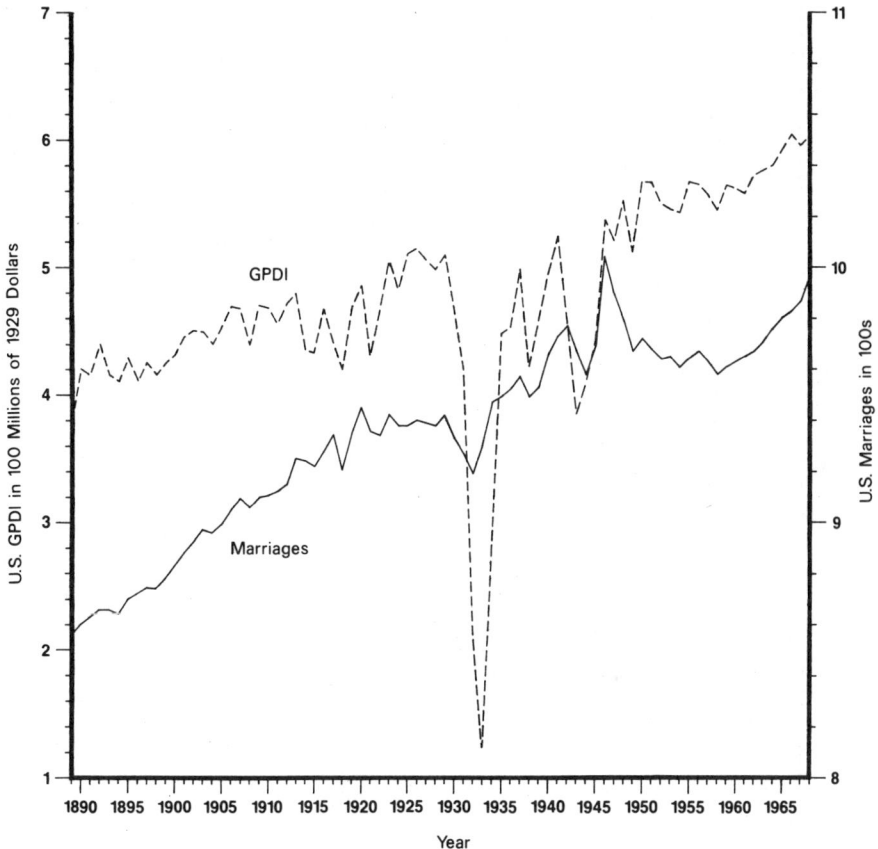

Figure 5.1. U.S. Gross Private Domestic Investment (GPDI) and marriages, 1889–1968. Ordinates are expressed in natural logarithms.

they are:

1. The time period for the trend calculation may be too short to give reliable results.
2. The most accurate trend calculation is likely to be a polynomial in time, giving increasingly large errors of prediction.
3. Any time trend will have serial correlation in the residuals, causing the calculated sample variance to understate the true variance.
4. The observed serial correlation may well be understated for the calculated regression if, as Klotz (1973) has argued, the underlying mechanism is an explosive first-order Markov process.

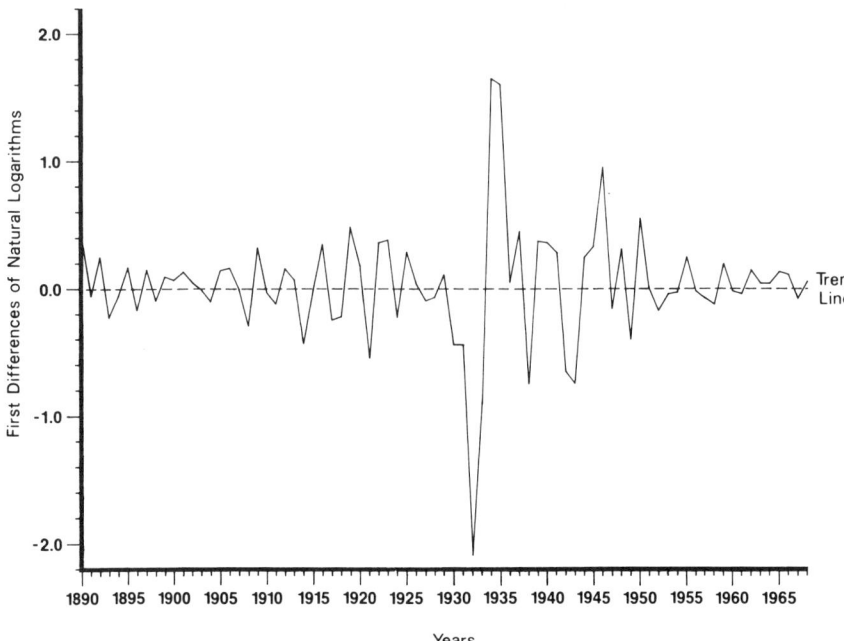

Figure 5.2. Annual growth rates in Gross Private Domestic Investment, 1890–1968.

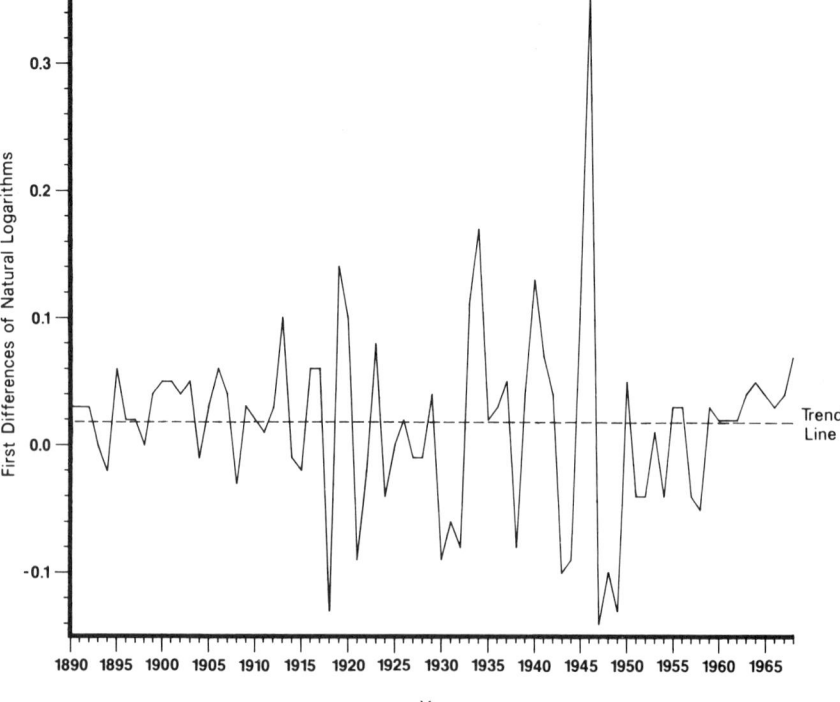

Figure 5.3. Annual growth rates in marriages, 1890–1968.

Table 5.1 shows the results of testing for a trend-break at the Great Depression in each of seven series when the first differences of the natural logarithms are calculated. The "z-tests" test for significant differences in the mean of the series as calculated for each subperiod (the mean equals the average annual growth rate), while the "F-tests" test for significant differences in the variance of the series between the two subperiods. Only in the case of the number of households was a trend-break detected for the mean of the series. For the variance of the series, the effects of the World Wars caused large disturbances, which explains why the F-tests rejected the hypothesis of equality of variance between the two subperiods for the real wage, the number of households, the number of marriages, and the level of investment demand. In sum, the removal of the trend in each series by simply taking first differences of natural logarithms effectively removes trend in the mean but not in the variance. The effects of nonstationarity in variance, however, have not in practice proven to be strong enough to affect the results of cross-spectral analysis.[16]

Even so, it is still possible that the nature of economic–demographic interactions has changed since the Great Depression. If so, this would produce changes in the low frequency coherence statistics among the variables of the Easterlin model. Table 5.2 displays these for two subperiods, 1890–1929 and 1930–1968. The Great Depression is chosen as a break point, since it conveniently gives an equal number of observations for each subperiod. Analysis of different break points with the longer time series available for Sweden and the United Kingdom, however, indicates that the Great Depression is the appropriate dividing point.

The following diagram summarizes the results of Table 5.2.

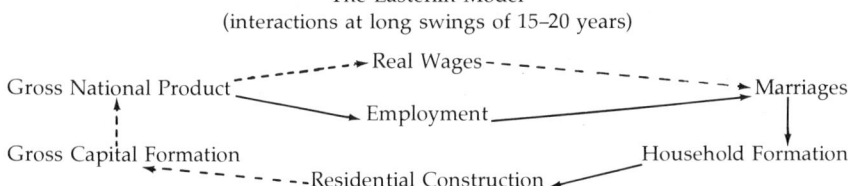

Dashed lines are used to connect variables whose coherence has changed appreciably since 1930; solid lines indicate no great change from before and after the depression. A number of striking changes has occurred. The coherence between GNP and the real wage index has been reduced, as has the coherence between GNP and total private

---

[16]See the results reported in Neal (1974).

TABLE 5.1.
Summary of U.S. Statistics: Testing Equality of Means and Variances: 1890–1929 and 1930–1968

Variable	z-statistic	Accept/reject equality of means	F-statistic	Accept/reject equality of variance
(1) Real wage	.7749	Accept	1.806	Reject at 5% Accept at 1%
(2) GNP	.2167	Accept	1.103	Accept
(3) Number of households	4.71	Reject	3.21	Reject
(4) Number of marriages	.4051	Accept	3.36	Reject
(5) Residential construction	.1892	Accept	1.29	Accept
(6) Gross private domestic investment	.02055	Accept	7.30	Reject
(7) Employment index	1.36	Accept	1.44	Accept

TABLE 5.2.
Low-Frequency Coherence Statistics between Economic and Demographic Variables 1890–1929, Compared with 1930–1968

	1890–1929	1930–1968		1890–1929	1930–1968
	GNP versus Real wage[a]			Real wage versus Marriages	
$\omega = 0$	.57	.49	$\omega = 0$	.75	.08
$= 1$	.68	.56	$= 1$	.74	.11
$= 2$	1.19	.74	$= 2$	1.12	.43
$= 3$	.79	.85	$= 3$	.74	.15
	GNP versus Employment			Employment versus Marriages	
$\omega = 0$	.88	.98	$\omega = 0$	.54	.54
$= 1$	.89	.96	$= 1$	.53	.62
$= 2$	.90	.93	$= 2$	1.00	1.09
$= 3$	.94	.89	$= 3$	.78	.68
	GNP versus Gross capital formation			Marriages versus Household formation	
$\omega = 0$	.48	.66	$\omega = 0$	.24	.37
$= 1$	.53	.55	$= 1$	.41	.49
$= 2$	.79	.45	$= 2$	.84	.65
$= 3$	.85	.46	$= 3$	.72	.57
	Gross capital formation versus Residential construction			Household formation versus Residential construction	
$\omega = 0$	.68	.87	$\omega = 0$	.64	.59
$= 1$	.60	.88	$= 1$	.83	.76
$= 2$	.42	.85	$= 2$	.98	.83
$= 3$	.43	.77	$= 3$	.67	.77

[a] ω indicates what fraction of the cycle has elapsed in 2 years. Since only 12 lags were used $\omega = 2$ means that $2/12$ of the cycle occurs every 2 years for an average length of 12 years. This is the closest one can come to centering on the long-swing frequency of 18 years when so few lags are used.

investment and between real wages and marriages. The link between residential construction and gross private domestic investment has been strengthened, however. Other major elements of the Easterlin process have retained much the same correlation at low frequencies both before and after the Great Depression. The results suggest overall that the specifically economic interactions have changed, but not the economic–demographic and especially the demographic interactions. The major exception is the breakup in the relationship between the real wage and marriages.

It must be remembered that all these results are for the low frequencies only. Other changes have occurred in all these relationships at the higher frequencies. These may portend future changes in the lower frequencies, or they may not. The relationship between household formation and marriages should be weakening, for example, as the headship rate in the population as a whole increases. A substantial reduction in the coherence between these two series was found, but only for the higher frequencies. Finally, it must be noted that the number of lags used (12) in calculating the coherence statistics of Table 5.2 are too few to permit isolation of the long-swing frequency either from the trend or from higher frequencies.

With all these qualifications as well as the initial welter of perplexing results, it is difficult to assess what new form of long swing economic-demographic interaction is emerging, if any. It is clear that, if an important and systematic interaction remains, it will be substantially different in form from the now classic Kuznets cycle of the nineteenth century. Immigration restrictions, if nothing else, prevent the kind of fluctuations in population increase that characterized the nineteenth century.

Emerging Characteristics of the New Economic-Demographic Era

Not enough time has elapsed in this new epoch to permit application of modern time-series analysis to determine the characteristics of the new form of recurring long swings or trend transitions. If a new form is emerging, however, which will tend to recur at long, irregular intervals, it is clear that its distinguishing feature, in contrast to previous Kuznets cycles, will be the relationship between GNP and births. Since the fertility rate of American women is currently undergoing a substantial reduction that will apparently become a permanent feature of American society, it is especially difficult to infer longer-run consequences from the patterns of the last decade. The only possibility for empirical induction is to assume that the relatively minor fluctuations that have occurred in the past 10 years in births are, in their rapid descent to new, lower levels, responses to economic conditions, and not merely reactions to cultural idiosyncrasies such as the "Pill scare" of 1968 and 1969 or the conjectured effects of marijuana consumption on male virility.

Figure 5.4 displays the post-World War II behavior of five variables whose interaction will determine many of the essential features of the next decade. They are the annual absolute changes in (a) real GNP (billions of 1958 dollars); (b) number of live births (inverted scale); (c) real stock of private nonresidential fixed capital (billions of 1958 dollars); (d) total civilian labor force, and (e) total female labor force. Changes in capital stock and labor force are closely correlated for the period as a whole, except for the mid-1960s, when the change in capital stock in-

Is Secular Stagnation Just around the Corner? Survey of Investment Demand 121

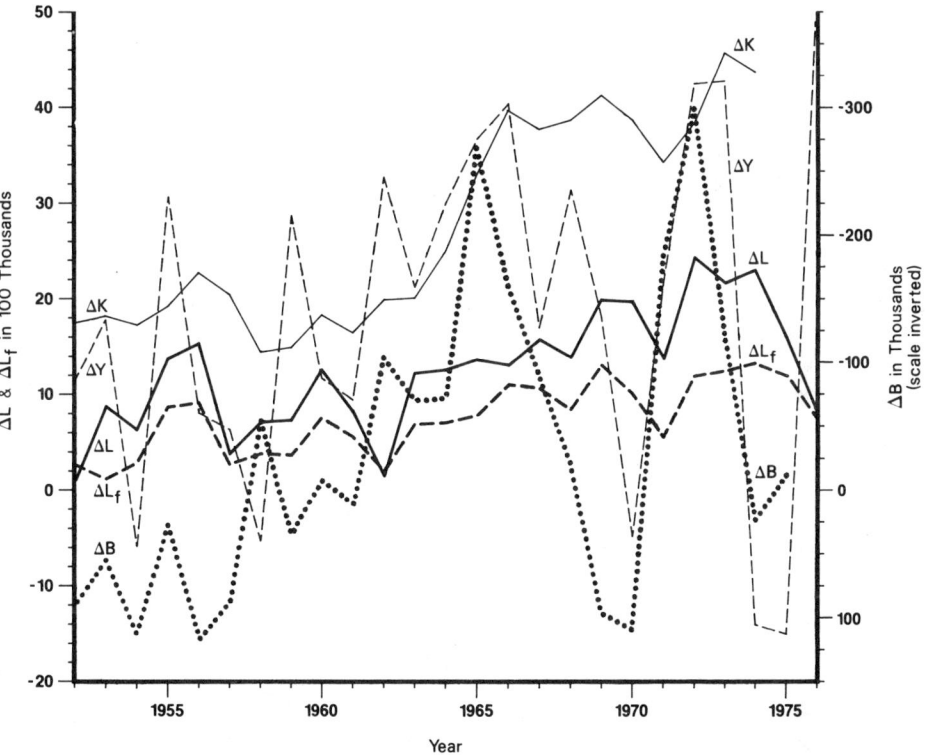

Figure 5.4. Annual changes in the level of real output (Y), births (B; inverted), capital stock (K), labor force (L), and female labor force (L_f), 1952–1976.

creased sharply to an average level double its previous average. Changes in both capital and labor are closely correlated with changes in the level of real output, but with a lag averaging 1 year. The changes in the total labor force correlate closely with changes in the female labor force. The latter, moreover, come increasingly to dominate the changes in the total labor force. The change in births, from the mid-1950s on, shows a close correlation with the change in real output, especially if it is plotted on an inverse scale. Apparently, American society has entered a period when an increase in the flow of real output is associated with a decrease in the flow of newborn babies, whereas a decrease in output means an increase in births. This type of inverse correlation is, as far as I know, unprecedented in American history.[17]

[17]Previous studies typically have found positive correlations with variable lags. See Easterlin (1968) and Silver (1965).

It is not immediately apparent why this inverse correlation has begun to show up. Until the behavioral determinants of this new pattern are understood, it will not be possible to say whether it will continue into the 1980s or whether the older positive correlation between births and output will be resumed. Some of the possible determinants that should be explored, however, are the rising labor force participation rates of women, especially women in the prime childbearing ages. From 1950 to 1975 there has been a clear upward trend in participation rates of women, whereas the birth rate has trended down. Fluctuations in the unemployment rate of women may have come to play an increasing role in determining the timing of planned births. The simple economic explanation of this inverse association between births and women's employment outside the home is that the opportunity cost of a new child is increased by the amount of the mother's earnings. If the mother is laid off, the opportunity cost drops sharply, and this increases the probability of a birth occurring during the next year. Testing for this possibility is complicated by the rapid change that has occurred in the relative importance of unemployment for women's decisions on childbearing. If it does play a significant role, it can only have begun to do so in the very recent past. There is also the problem that women's unemployment may be the result of childbearing, and not the cause.

Future Prospects

Much more work needs to be done on the precise form, strength, and implications of these relationships. If the economic–demographic interactions of the late 1960s and 1970s continue into the 1980s, they will alter dramatically the operation of our economic system. Let us assume that the combined demands of pollution abatement and the implementation of alternative energy sources induce a strong investment boom in the near future, which continues into the early 1980s. This will require a rapid increase in our labor force. This can only be met, in the absence of reduced immigration barriers, by an increased participation rate of women in the labor force, especially by women in the fertile age cohorts. Ample resources of potential labor supply do exist, however, in the large numbers of younger women currently not counted as part of the labor force. There is thus little reason why an investment boom in the immediate future should be choked off by the difficulties of staffing an enlarged capital stock.

The longer-run implications of this scenario are sobering, however. Such an increase in the female labor force will probably continue the downward trend of the birth rate. This will reduce the new entrants to the labor force in 20 years. Any future investment booms near the turn of the century will then tend to be choked off earlier by rising wage outlays caused by an inelastic labor supply. American savings at the end of the twentieth century, like those of the French at the end of the nineteenth century, will have to go abroad in search of new investment opportunities. Alternatively, immigration restrictions could be relaxed, permitting more foreign, unskilled laborers to enter the U.S. labor market. These laborers would be primarily Latin-American or Asian, however, and their entry in large numbers may create unacceptable or undesirable social stresses.

Objections to these scenarios can and undoubtedly will be raised. One possibility, developed at length by Terborgh (1945, Chapter 4) in the original riposte to Hansen's thesis of secular stagnation, is that savings of both households and firms will decrease pari passu with the decline in investment opportunities. In other words, a decline in investment expenditure is to a large extent offset by an increase in consumption expenditures. Empirical evidence on savings of households in advanced societies indicates that savings are not particularly responsive to numbers of children in the household, but are determined more by the level of per capita income and the degree of self-employment of households in nonincorporated business enterprises.[18] If these past relationships hold up in the future, household savings will tend to rise with the increase in household income generated by the increasing participation rate of women in the labor force. The reduction in number of children will have no effect (except as it may indirectly affect per capita income), and it is difficult to obtain any further reductions in the importance of such unincorporated enterprises as family farms and corner drugstores. The growing importance of the service sector, on the other hand, gives rise to opportunities for small family firms and for households with income from professional services of doctors, lawyers, educators, and

[18]Kelley (1972) reviewed both the theory and the empirical evidence for recent American experience. For supporting evidence from the late nineteenth century, see Neal and Uselding (1972). For a full discussion of the issue, see Simon (1977). Most models of consumption or saving behavior rely primarily upon per capita income. An important variant is the life-cycle model of Modigliani and Ando (1963) that permits the saving behavior of an individual to vary with age. The increasing weight of the older age groups in the American population suggests rising savings rates even without rising per capita income. An Organization for Economic Cooperation and Development (OECD) study (1972) showed the strong correlation in OECD countries between the rate of household sector saving and the proportion of unincorporated business enterprise in total output. See also Friedman and Kuznets (1945) and Friedman (1957).

government consultants. All these are increasingly uncertain sources of household income and should generate higher savings rates, regardless of reduced investment expenditures.

Savings of firms, assuming that operating expenses are met, are largely generated by the prospect of investment opportunities arising in the future, either from the need to replace existing capital or from the need to enlarge the capital stock used in producing for a larger market. The dominant American firms in the economy do not look merely to the American economy for their investment opportunities; Europe, Latin America, and, recently, the Middle East are scrutinized closely. So long as growing markets and/or elastic supplies of labor remain in those areas, American firms will find it profitable to continue saving from their internal revenues and to invest in new capital. The investment taking place, however, will be abroad and will promote continued rapid growth of those economies. The effect of this foreign investment on the American economy depends on the export markets it creates for American producers. Reduced growth of the economy will be avoided only if export demand increases sufficiently to offset the diversion of current saving abroad.

Another possibility for ameliorating the dampening effects of slowing population growth lies in the fact that its primary effect will be to reduce the demand for residential construction. Construction workers and materials will be released, therefore, to all forms of nonresidential investment. Insofar as nonresidential capital stock is more likely to embody technological advances, this kind of shift in the composition of gross private domestic investment may actually speed up the potential rate of growth of the economy. To date, however, this kind of tendency has failed to emerge clearly. One reason may be that average household size is declining so rapidly that the number of households, as Morrison's Chapter 9 of this volume shows, is growing more rapidly than total population. Another reason is that the growth of household income for all age groups and the growth of leisure time arising from earlier retirement in the older age groups have apparently increased the demand for secondary residences, especially in the form of mobile homes. Finally, inflation, combined with the progressive income tax schedule, has made home purchases increasingly attractive to affluent younger households seeking the tax advantages of mortgage interest payments and real estate taxes. Until these tendencies are played out, or reversed by appropriate policy actions, residential construction is likely to continue competing with other forms of investment for financing.

One final possibility that may alter the outcome of the current trend transition should also be mentioned. This arises from the increasing importance of investment in human capital relative to physical capital. Calculations by McMahon (1974) indicate that the rate of return on human capital has tended on average to remain higher than that on physical capital for most of the twentieth century. This helps explain the increasing diversion of the economy's resources from investment in physical capital to investment in human capital (i.e., the increase in expenditures on education, health, and welfare). These expenditures now equal those on physical capital, and insofar as technological progress may be embodied in the labor force rather than in the machines, they may be more important for maintaining or possibly increasing the rate of technical progress. This opens up an entirely new avenue of research into the effects of slowing population growth. It cannot be explored here, but it seems worth mentioning that McMahon's calculations also indicate that employment opportunities for younger workers are the chief determinants of fluctuations in the rate of return on investment in higher education. If an investment boom in the 1980s is prolonged by attracting college age men and women into the labor force and away from their studies, it may actually reduce the future rate of growth of technical progress.

All the possibilities examined above merit intensive research in the next few years. The economic–demographic experience in America during the remainder of the 1970s and through the 1980s will determine two things:

1. The nature of the long-run equilibrium on the new growth path the economy is approaching.
2. The nature of the new set of economic–demographic interactions that will characterize future trend transitions in the absence of changes in the immigration policy of the United States.

6

The Effects of Slowing Population Growth on Long-Run Economic Growth in the United States during the Next Half Century

RONALD G. RIDKER[1]

The interest in the economic consequences of a slowdown in population growth in the United States appears to stem from its possible policy implications: Is the slowdown something that should be encouraged or resisted; and how can its consequences best be accommodated? To discuss these consequences in a way that is relevant to help answer these questions, we cannot rely solely on theoretical or historical studies. Theory is useful to highlight the most important variables and relationships that must be studied and can sometimes indicate the most likely direction of changes. But in the present context, quantitative answers are needed not only because the policy implications will differ depending on the size and speed of the changes, but also because there are often too many offsetting forces at work to be able to say anything about their net effect without knowing the quantitative magnitudes of each. Historical studies might provide an indication of such magnitudes, but these policy questions pertain to the future, a future that will not replicate the

[1]The research for this chapter was supported by NIH Contract 1-HD-72813.

past if for no other reason than because of the population growth that has come before it. To be helpful, a study of the consequences of population growth must be quantitative and future-oriented; and, since population growth occurs quite slowly, it should have a fairly long time-horizon.

This chapter attempts to take these considerations to heart, at least in a limited way, by projecting the economic consequences of population growth in the United States during the next 50 years. Although this time horizon is too short to observe the full, ultimate consequences of a slowdown in population growth, anything longer would reduce our confidence in the results to a level too low to make the effort worthwhile. Our approach involves consideration of likely developments in each of the major factors that can influence the situation in order to determine which assumptions are most reasonable to include in the projection exercise. These assumptions are then incorporated into a model of the U.S. economy that is run with alternative population projections to determine what difference the latter make.

The model used for this purpose, RFF/SEAS (Resources for the Future/Strategic Environmental Assessment System), is actually a system of interlinked models, the core of which is the University of Maryland's dynamic input–output model of the U.S. economy (Almon et al., 1974). Other models, some developed in the original SEAS project sponsored by the Environmental Protection Agency and later modified by RFF, and others added by RFF (RFF/NIH Project Report, 1978), include components involving physical and monetary variables associated with energy, nonfuel minerals, transportation, and the environment (pollution, abatement costs, and environmental quality) at both the national and regional level. The system includes 185 sectors, all major fuels, some 20 nonfuel minerals, and 42 pollutants. All the coefficients in the model are subject to change over time, some on the basis of econometrically fitted equations with time trends or lagged variables, but most on the basis of exogenously specified changes in population and labor force characteristics, technology, tastes, and so on, determined on the basis of special studies.

Determinants of Economic Growth

Given the focus just described, we cannot concentrate solely on the effects of population, assuming other factors such as technology, tastes, institutions, availability of raw materials, and the like remain constant. This is clearly not the case over a 50-year period, and changes in such factors can strongly affect the nature and extent of the population impact. Moreover, such changes are unlikely to occur independently of each other. In what follows, we begin by discussing what we believe to be the principal determinants of economic growth and how they are likely to change over time under alternative assumptions about population growth. At the end, we return to discuss other determinants and interrelations among the variables as possible qualifications to the principal discussion.

Population and Labor Force

At the time the model on which this study is based was developed, four comparable population projection series were available from the U.S. Bureau of the Census (1972b).[2] Among these, Series D comes closest to reflecting a continuation of trends during the last 50 years. Between 1925 and 1975, the U.S. population increased by 68%, approximately 1% per year. According to Series D, which assumes an average of 2.5 births per woman, it will grow by 72% during the next 50 years, averaging 1.08% per year. To contrast this projection with one incorporating a slowdown in the rate of growth, there are two convenient alternatives: Series E (2.1 births per woman), in which population grows by 42% (.70% per year), and Series F (1.8 births per woman), in which it grows by 24% (.43% per year). Both are utilized in this chapter, Series F because it provides the largest contrast with Series D, and Series E because it comes closest to what we believe to be the most likely.[3]

Table 6.1 illustrates population size by principal age groups for these three projections. While the differences in projected sizes by the year 2025 are quite significant, especially in the younger age groups, the changes over time are fairly regular and slow. Three exceptions to this statement might be noted. The first pertains to the more or less rapid expansion of the retired population that is currently occurring. This is, of course, causing pension funding problems and changes in the composition of demand that we are not used to. But since the labor force during this 1972–1985 period is expanding at a greater rate, the aggregate eco-

[2] In October 1975 these series were replaced with three new ones (U.S. Bureau of the Census, 1975b) incorporating complete cohort fertility assumptions of 2.7, 2.1, and 1.7, and the same mortality and immigration assumptions. For our purposes, these new series are not sufficiently different from the old Series D, E, and F to warrant changing the model.

[3] "Most likely" is being used with respect to fertility rates. Net immigration rates (including illegal immigration) may be considerably higher, and mortality rates could be somewhat lower than those incorporated in any of these projections.

TABLE 6.1.
Population by Age Groupings and Median Age, Alternative Projections, 1972–2025[a]

	1972	D 1985	D 2000	D 2025	E 1985	E 2000	E 2025	F 1985	F 2000	F 2025
Population (millions)										
School age, 0-19	76.8	82.3	97.8	124.9	74.0	80.7	84.6	69.2	69.3	62.8
Working age, 20-64	111.0	135.7	159.3	194.5	135.7	154.8	171.1	135.7	152.6	154.0
(Young, 20-44)	(68.3)	(92.3)	(101.1)	(122.4)	(92.3)	(96.6)	(101.7)	(92.3)	(94.4)	(86.7)
(Old, 45-64)	(42.7)	(43.4)	(58.2)	(72.2)	(43.4)	(58.2)	(69.5)	(43.4)	(58.2)	(67.3)
Retired, 65+	20.9	25.9	28.8	48.1	25.9	28.8	48.1	25.9	28.8	48.1
Total	208.8	243.9	286.0	367.5	235.7	264.4	303.8	230.9	250.7	264.9
Median age	28.1	29.6	31.1	31.1	30.6	34.0	36.8	31.2	35.8	41.7
Percentage distribution										
School age, 0-19	36.8	33.7	34.2	34.0	31.4	30.5	27.8	30.0	27.6	23.7
Working age, 20-64	53.2	55.6	55.7	52.9	57.6	58.6	56.3	58.8	60.9	58.1
(Young, 20-44)	(32.7)	(37.9)	(35.4)	(33.3)	(39.2)	(36.5)	(33.5)	(40.0)	(37.6)	(32.7)
(Old, 45-64)	(20.4)	(17.8)	(20.4)	(19.6)	(18.4)	(22.0)	(22.8)	(18.8)	(23.2)	(25.4)
Retired, 65+	10.0	10.6	10.1	13.1	11.0	10.9	15.8	11.2	11.5	18.2
Total	100.0	100.0	100.0	100.0	100.0	100.0	100.0	100.0	100.0	100.0
Annual rate of change from previous year specified										
School age, 0-19		.5	1.2	1.0	-.3	.6	.2	-.8	.0	-.4
Working age, 20-64		1.6	1.1	.8	1.6	.9	.4	1.6	.8	.0
(Young, 20-44)		(2.3)	(.6)	(.8)	(2.3)	(.3)	(.2)	(2.3)	(.1)	(-.3)
(Old, 45-64)		(.1)	(2.0)	(.9)	(.1)	(1.9)	(.7)	(.1)	(2.0)	(.6)
Retired, 65+		1.7	.7	2.1	1.7	.7	2.1	1.7	.7	2.1
Total		1.2	1.1	1.0	.9	.8	.6	.8	.5	.2

[a]Population and median age, 1972–2000, from U.S. Bureau of the Census (1972b). Later years developed by the author.

nomic burden is somewhat mitigated. The second pertains to the effects of the postwar baby boom that raises and then lowers growth rates of different age groups as it moves through the economy. Up to 2010 or so, this effect is beneficial since it is the labor force ages that experience the most rapid increases. It is only thereafter that the retired age group begins expanding at a more rapid rate. While this could be disruptive, there are, as we shall see, ways to offset its aggregate economic effects and considerable time to plan to do so. The third possible exception arises from the absolute reductions that occur in the younger age groups in Series E and F. But the decline is temporary in Series E, and its rate is relatively small in both series.

Of more significance for the economy are changes in the labor force over time, changes that are influenced not only by the size of certain age groups but also by changes in participation rates for different ages and sexes. The figures on the labor force presented in Table 6.2 assume that average annual changes in labor force participation rates for men at different ages and for women of different ages with and without children under 5 continue in the future but at diminishing rates of change until they approximate zero in 2020.

The result, comparing 1972 with 2025, is a slower decline in the rate of growth of the labor force than of the population as a whole. In part, this result arises because of the movement of the cohorts associated with the post-World War II baby boom through the age groups, but it is also associated with the increase in the number of women in the labor force as fertility drops. The median age and the age distribution of the labor force also change, but not by very much or very fast, especially after 1985.

Labor Productivity

Labor productivity, by definition, equals hours worked per year times output per man-hour. The latter, in particular, is determined by a wide variety of factors: characteristics of the labor force such as its age, sex, and educational and occupational composition; the availability of other inputs into the production process (capital, raw materials, and land); and technology, that is, the recipe that explains how these inputs combine with labor to produce output. This section focuses on changes in hours worked per year and in the characteristics of the labor force, assuming for the moment that other factors progress more or less as they have in the past. These other factors are discussed in remaining sections, and additional adjustments in labor productivity are introduced where appropriate.

TABLE 6.2.
Labor Force and Dependency Ratios, Alternative Projections, 1972–2025[a]

	1972	D			E			F		
		1985	2000	2025	1985	2000	2025	1985	2000	2025
Labor Force (millions)	89.0	106.5	128.1	161.3	107.7	124.3	139.1	108.2	122.3	125.1
Percentage female	37.4	38.4	38.9	38.6	38.7	39.2	39.1	39.0	39.5	39.4
Percentage less than age 45	63.2[b]	67.8[c]	65.7	64.9[d]	68.0[c]	64.4	61.0[d]	68.2[c]	63.7	57.7[d]
Median age										
Males	35.6[e]		37.8	37.6		38.3	38.7		38.7	40.9
Females	35.8[e]		38.1	37.8		38.8	39.3		40.2	41.5
(Pop. − L.F.) ÷ L.F. (%)	135	129	123	128	119	113	118	113	105	112
Pop. (0–19) ÷ L.F. (%)	86	77	76	77	69	65	61	64	57	50
Pop. (65+) ÷ L.F. (%)	24	24	23	30	24	23	35	24	24	39

[a] Alterman (1976).
[b] For 1970.
[c] For 1980.
[d] For 2020.
[e] For 1975.

AVERAGE HOURS AND UNEMPLOYMENT

For most of the post-World War II period, average hours declined by about .5% per year in the farm sector and about .35% per year in the private nonfarm sector. Average hours in the public sector declined much more rapidly during the late 1950s and 1960s as a result of the increase in part-time employment of women and teenagers. But with the more complete absorption of women in the labor force and the decline in the proportion of teenagers in the population, this rate is likely to fall to that of the private nonfarm sector. With employment in the farm sector declining in importance, its weight in the average reduction in hours will decline. As a consequence, we have projected work hours to decline by .34% per year between 1975 and 1985, the same rate as that used by the Bureau of Labor Statistics for this time period, and by .3% thereafter. If taken in a shorter work week, this assumption means that work hours per week, which averaged about 38 in 1970, would decline to 33 in 2025; if there were no decline in hours per week, this would mean working 41 weeks per year instead of 48.

So far as unemployment is concerned, the principal factor to consider is a possible change in the ability of the government to maintain aggregate demand at the appropriate level, and this in turn depends, among other things, on the extent and speed of changes in aggregate demand and supply that would occur in the absence of government action. To what extent might demographic changes affect this situation?

If a decline in the birth rate were to occur rapidly, there could be an increase in the supply of labor (because of women entering the labor force) at the same time as there is a decrease in demand for labor (because of fewer children requiring goods and services) during a transition period lasting 20–25 years. But in the specific demographic circumstances of the United States, significant downward pressure on the labor market as a consequence of demographic changes appears unlikely. A crude index of this pressure is the percentage that the labor force is of the total population. In 1975, this index was 44; under the F population series, it would rise to 47 in 1985 and 49 in 2000 and then fall back to 47% in 2025. A more refined index that takes into account the possibility that the goods and services demanded by the elderly may be more labor-intensive than those demanded by the young would indicate even less downward pressure on the labor market and indeed might even indicate a slight upward pressure.[4] It is hard to argue that the government will find it difficult to offset such effects. For all runs of the model, therefore,

---

[4]See Chapter 4 of this volume by Wachter and Wachter for a more comprehensive and detailed discussion of related points.

we assume that the unemployment rate returns to 4-4.5% by 1980 and remains within that range thereafter.

MAN-HOUR PRODUCTIVITY AND LABOR FORCE CHARACTERISTICS

In essence, our procedure for estimating man-hour productivity is to project a trend rate of growth in productivity and then to modify this projection by, first, projected changes in the proportion of employment in the agricultural and government sectors, and second, projected changes in the age, sex, and educational characteristics of the labor force. In many studies (U.S. Bureau of Labor Statistics, 1974), the 1948–1968 period is used as a basis for establishing a basic, long-term trend. But the substantial shortfall that has occurred since 1968 has raised doubts about the continued appropriateness of this trend, doubts that have been reinforced by the increases in energy prices occurring since 1973. For present purposes, we assume that from 1968 onward the 1948–1968 trend has been shifted downward by .3% per year and that only half of the shortfall from this new trend is made up by 1980. Whereas in other work we have experimented with a somewhat higher rate of growth, this pattern appears more plausible at the present time.

The government sector, for which no productivity gain normally is assumed, is projected to grow less rapidly in the future because of the decline in employment in the education and military sectors. While this factor partially eliminates a drag on the rate of growth in productivity inherent in past trends, it is to some extent offset by declines in the positive contribution of the agricultural sector that has been present due to the elimination of marginal farmers. The net effect, reported in Alterman (1976), is small and can be ignored for present purposes since it is not affected by differences in population projections.

Of more relevance in this chapter is the effect of changes in the age, sex, and educational characteristics of the labor force. Our procedure here is to estimate how average wages would change if wages by age, sex, and educational subcategories were weighted together using future labor force numbers in each subcategory as new weights.[5] The result, for Series E, indicates that the trend rate of man-hour productivity should be adjusted upward by .14 percentage points during the 1980–1990 period and thereafter gradually decline to a downward adjustment of

[5]This procedure follows that of Denison (1974) and is spelled out in Alterman (1976). It assumes that wages are a good proxy for labor productivity and that the wage structure remains constant over time; both simplifications are necessitated by the fact that we do not have a detailed model of the operation of the labor market.

−.15 by 2020–2025. The upward revision occurs because the slight decline in the role of education is more than offset by a positive adjustment in the age and sex factors. The latter is due to a dampening in the rate of increase in labor force participation among women plus the relative increase in the proportion of young to old workers during this period. Beyond 1990, however, these factors become smaller and smaller, so that the continued decline in the role of education, relative to the base period, causes the net adjustment factor to turn negative.

The net effect of all these adjustments is a slowdown in the rate of growth of GNP per employee. In contrast to an annual rate of growth of 2.42% during the 1948–1968 period, it is projected to grow at 2.40% per year during the 1975–1980 period, 2.00% during the next 5-year period, 1.98% between 1985 and 2000, and 1.79% during the next 25 years.[6]

Technology

The previous section considered the choice of assumptions about labor productivity, implicitly assuming that appropriate technological changes would be forthcoming to justify the choice made. We must now consider whether that assumption is warranted, in particular whether changes in economies of scale or innovativeness associated with population changes are likely to be present. In addition, we must consider the possibility that changes in population could result in the substitution of one technological process for another in order to accommodate to the needs of different populations.

The problem, of course, is absence of information about what the future may have in store. Economies of scale clearly were present in the United States in the eighteenth and nineteenth centuries, a consequence of abundant open lands, untapped minerals and timber, and nondivisible investments in transport and communications that could be more effectively exploited with additional labor. But this easily tapped frontier has all but disappeared. Of more importance in the future will be the magnitude of effective demand which, in addition to sheer numbers, is influenced by income levels (internationally as well as domestically), the degree to which tastes are homogeneous, and the extent to which firms are able to take advantage of specialization through horizontal integration, vertical disintegration, and international trade. Thus, while it may

[6]Differences between the population series, especially between Series E and F, turn out to be small and partially offsetting. As a consequence, the same rates of growth in output per employee are assumed for the different series.

be appropriate to introduce some shift downward in the trend rate of growth in labor productivity as we have done in the previous section, there is little basis for assuming that the extent of this shift will be significantly affected by different assumptions about the rate of population growth within the range of rates we are investigating.

On the other hand, there is the possibility of growing diseconomies associated with the effects of congestion and crowding on relatively fixed resources, and it is somewhat more likely that such diseconomies will be affected by population growth rates within our range of rates. The two dimensions of such diseconomies we are able to take into account are discussed shortly, when considering the possible impacts of growing shortages of energy and of amounts of pollution that must be disposed of.

So far as inventiveness is concerned, we have a choice between demand- and supply-oriented theories, both suggesting that technological progress is positively related to population growth. Demand-based theories argue that increased population growth generates problems calling for solutions that in turn stimulate inventive activity at a faster rate than does a stationary population (Schmookler, 1966). Supply-oriented theories are either related to the law of large numbers—the larger the population, the larger the number of people with inventive and innovative skills (Kuznets, 1960)—or to the hypothesis that younger populations are more innovative (Sweezy and Owens, 1974).

Though there have been a few tests of these hypotheses and some of them find a positive correlation between inventiveness and population size or growth rate,[7] they are not very convincing. "Inventiveness" is not well defined and measured, and there are too many intervening variables that cannot be held constant. Such variables include the type of and quantity of education, the financial support provided to inventors and innovators, the possibilities of international division of labor in knowledge creation and its dissemination, and the way research is organized and integrated into the political and financial structure of a

---

[7]On the effects of population size and density, see Kelley (1972), who reviews the evidence and carries out several statistical tests of his own. Using patents per 1000 population as a proxy for inventiveness, some support can be found for the hypothesis within a limited range of population sizes and densities; but none of the tests is able to hold constant other potentially important variables. On the effects of age distribution, see Sweezy and Owens (1974), who show that, for population growth rates within the range zero to 1.5% per year, there is virtually no difference in the proportion of the population in the age group most likely to receive Nobel prizes. They also find no evidence for the 1959–1963 and 1963–1970 periods in Europe that the rate of growth of the labor force and in labor productivity are positively correlated.

society. Surely, all these factors are more important than population size, density, or growth at this stage in U.S. history. In addition, there is an optimistic bias built into these theories, especially on the demand side; population growth is assumed to throw up challenges that are not just met but "overresponded to" so that the per capita growth rate does more than hold its own. But it is just as possible that, beyond a certain point, population growth and density could lead to an overload of problems that the scientific community cannot keep up with. It seems safest to conclude that the rate of innovation is not likely to be affected by probable demographic changes during the next 50 years.

Finally, we come to specific technological changes, such as the introduction of the breeder reactor and new methods for constructing high-rise apartment buildings. Such changes must be introduced wherever they can be identified, because they can have dramatic effects on resource requirements and environmental pressures. But can such changes be related to different population growth rates? In principle, of course, they are likely to be related. The greater the population density, the more incentive there is to innovate in areas associated with high-rise buildings and mass transit; the older the population, the more incentive to improve medical technology associated with aging; the more the demands of a growing population press on limited resources, the more likely it is that efforts will be made to find substitutes in both production and consumption.

But we have no basis on which to estimate the quantitative nature of such relationships. The best we have been able to do is to develop one set of specific technological changes that are likely to occur during the next 50 years and to introduce them into all runs of the model, independent of changes in population growth rates. In general the changes introduced assume that technology progresses in evolutionary ways: Best practice slowly becomes average practice, processes and products now at the pilot or demonstration state become commercial and begin being used, and techniques still in the laboratory or experimental stage are brought on stream with appropriate time lags. Six main areas were emphasized: energy supply and conversion technologies, the substitution of concrete for lumber and steel in construction, increasing use of plastics and aluminum, improved efficiency of automobiles and the introduction of electric cars in significant numbers after 2000, process changes in primary metals production that improve efficiency and reduce residuals, and extensive development of communications and its partial substitution for some types of transportation. Judgments about development and diffusion rates were deliberately made conservative.

Thus, to the extent that population growth leads to problems, the severity of these problems is exaggerated because of this conservative bias.

Savings Rate

The savings rate is, of course, a critical variable in determining the amount of capital that labor has to work with and, hence, the rate of growth in output. If it is affected to any appreciable extent by changes in population growth rates, the economic consequences over a 50-year period could be quite significant.

So far as household savings are concerned, it is typically assumed that expenditures on children make it more difficult for parents to save. But in specific contexts this may not be the case. Children may be a substitute for other forms of consumption instead of for savings; they may contribute to family income or stimulate parents to work harder and longer (or in the case of the mother, less); and they may encourage the accumulation of certain forms of capital (e.g., education rather than other assets) and the amassing of estates. The issue cannot be settled without empirical evidence. But that evidence is sparce and ambiguous. Some studies indicate a negative relationship after controlling for income; others suggest that family savings rates increase with the first and second child and drop thereafter;[8] and one that focuses on the effects on family income finds no effect after controlling for the trade-off between work on the part of the wife and the husband (Simon, 1971).

But whatever the relationship, household savings represent a small, and probably diminishing, fraction of total savings in the U.S. economy. Over 80% of the private sector's new capital comes from sources internal to the investing sector, and this percentage has been rising over time. While these savings may be influenced by population growth because of the latter's effect on aggregate demand and profit rates, they also are influenced by monetary and fiscal policy. If the government acts to maintain full employment, it will more or less automatically compensate for any changes in aggregate demand and profit rates associated with changes in population growth rates.

These considerations lead us to conclude that we should not attempt to make the savings rate a direct function of changes in population growth rates over time and between runs. Instead, we have permitted savings to take on whatever value is necessary to satisfy the investment requirements found to exist. Of course, since investment requirements

---

[8]See Kelley (1972, 1976b) for an elaboration of these points and a review of the empirical studies.

vary with population, savings are indirectly related, but now on the requirements side rather than on the supply side of the equation.

The Resource Base: Energy and the Environment

If population were to increase with no change in other variables (especially technology, tastes, and per capita incomes), the price of both natural and environmental resources would eventually rise; poorer quality mines would have to be called into production, and there would be larger amounts of residuals requiring abatement. Such increased costs would then affect the rate and character of economic growth. This possibility, which can of course occur for other reasons as well, is close to the heart of many concerns about population growth and must therefore be taken into account in our model.

So far as natural resources are concerned, we started with special studies attempting to project global demands and supplies and, hence, prices for critical raw materials and sources of energy. These studies led to our focusing on energy, since new discoveries and technological changes appear to be adequate to maintain a rough balance between demands and supplies of nonfuel minerals without major price increases during the next 50 years. Energy prices, on the other hand, are expected to rise over time in response to a complicated set of pressures both internal and external to the United States. Though a number of different patterns of price changes and responses were experimented with, the one used in the runs presented here assumes that, after the dramatic increase in world oil prices in 1973 and 1974 and the expected subsequent increase in domestic prices to catch up to the world level (a transition that is not expected to be complete before 1980 or so), energy prices in real terms are assumed to remain more or less constant until forced up by the fact that world production of oil and natural gas can no longer keep up with the growth in demand, an event that does not occur in our runs until after 2000.

These price changes should have two major effects on the economy. First, they will lead to a decline in the amount of energy used per unit of output (more rapid than would otherwise have occurred), which, in the absence of offsetting changes, results in a decline in labor productivity. Second, they ought to induce changes in technology and a more rapid turnover of the capital stock, replacing more with less energy-using capital, in order to offset as much of this decline in productivity as possible. Although virtually nothing is known about the magnitude of such effects, we hesitate to leave them out altogether since their cumulative effect could be significant over a 50-year period. Accordingly, we have introduced three sets of assumptions to account for them. The first pertains to price elasticities of demand for energy for various sectors of the economy and various time periods;[9] together with the price changes and runs of the model indicating changes in the relative importance of different sectors, they determine the extent to which the trend decline in the aggregate Btu/GNP ratio is accelerated. The second assumes that, for each 1% decline in the Btu/GNP ratio over what it otherwise would have been had the pre-1973 trend continued, labor productivity will be .2% less than otherwise. And the third assumes that a doubling of energy prices will cut the expected life of existing durable equipment by approximately one-third in the industrial sector and one-quarter in the commercial sector.[10] The consequences for the economy for different assumptions about population growth are given in a later section.

So far as increased environmental pressures are concerned, these have been taken care of by special submodels that estimate the amounts of residuals generated, the amounts emitted under alternative abatement policies, the costs of such abatement policies, and the resulting concentration levels and damages in various regions. The abatement costs, most of which involve increased investments in abatement equipment, are fed into the core economic model so that their macroeconomic consequences can be assessed (RFF/NIH Project Report, 1978, Appendix 1). Although this procedure leaves out the economic consequences of the pollution damages and other possible environmental and ecological effects, it does capture the principal economic effects of the major pollutants being controlled by the Environmental Protection Agency.

Composition of Demand

The last major category of determinants we must discuss involves changes in the composition of expenditures by both private consumers and the government, many categories of which may be strongly influenced by changes in demographic assumptions. An older population requires fewer schools, more medical care, and, perhaps, a different kind of housing. Retired persons may prefer to live in different parts of

---

[9]For example, for manufacturing sectors the price elasticity of demand for energy is assumed to be .7 after 15 years. For the commercial sector it is .4 after 20 years.

[10]A more detailed discussion of the materials in this and the preceding paragraph, plus a presentation of the effects of other assumptions (for example, a continuously rising price of oil) can be found in Chapter 6 of the RFF/NIH Project Report (1978) and in Ridker *et al.* (1978).

the country and, once there, travel frequently. Expenditures on new social overhead capital—roads, water, sanitation works, and the like—will decline if population growth or migration slows. Larger households may experience economies of scale in the purchase, preparation, and storage of food as well as in their purchase of household capital assets. Smaller families may demand different kinds of housing and furnishings and may migrate more frequently. In addition, as incomes continue to increase, we must take account of possible saturation in the number of things possessed and shifts toward an emphasis on quality and services instead.

The core economic model contains equations that take some of these factors into account (Almon et al., 1974). However, the parameters of these equations were estimated on the basis of the 1961 Survey of Consumer Expenditures (which has now been superseded) plus time series data for the period 1947–1970. Emphasis was placed on equations that are sensitive to changes in per capita income and total population, with changes in age composition, size of household, and shifts in location playing little or no role; and no allowance was made for factors such as saturation that cannot be observed in the available data.

Although these shortcomings are in the process of being corrected, we have no choice in this chapter but to use this framework, supplemented as best we can by judgmental considerations. In the main, private expenditure patterns are assumed to change slowly over time in ways that would appear quite conservative and comfortable to the average person today. The housing mix is assumed to continue shifting toward medium- and high-density construction. The private automobile is assumed to remain the preferred mode of transportation for short- and medium-distance trips. But automobile purchases, as well as those of a number of other durables and semidurables, are assumed to be subject to saturation—saturation so far as the number of physical units purchased is concerned but not necessarily in terms of dollars spent on each unit, which sum can continue increasing to reflect change in quality. For example, auto ownership is expected to increase until it reaches one car per person of driving age, and expenditures per person are expected to increase almost three times between 1975 and 2025, roughly in line with the increase in disposable income per capita. While the proportion of total expenditures on such items falls, those on recreation, medical and other services, plus some newer commodities, absorb the slack.

Public expenditures are projected on an item-by-item basis. For current account categories, per capita expenditures (for education, per pupil expenditures, etc.) are assumed to be increasing functions of per capita income, using historical data as a guide. Capital account items are based on historical trends modified for different rates of growth in GNP or are specified exogenously.

Other Determinants

There are, of course, other important determinants of long-run economic growth. The amount of expenditure devoted to military and space exploration, the terms on which the United States can acquire resources and finished commodities from abroad, institutional changes, changes in tastes and life styles, and changes in the direction and rate of internal migration are all cases in point. For all such factors we have explicitly or implicitly made assumptions that will make the future fairly familiar to the individual of today. There are no institutional changes, no changes in tastes within specific income and age classes, no policy changes other than those already mentioned. Military expenditures are assumed to grow at an elasticity of .8 with respect to per capita GNP, the basic presumption being that, in the long run, a rich nation will treat defense much as the rich individual treats insurance, purchasing as much as he feels he can afford, but not quite in proportion to increases in income. Heavy investments to put the national highway system in place are assumed to be about completed, and so on. Although few of these factors are likely to change with changes in population, they may well affect the relationships between population changes and other variables. But for the purpose of this exercise, no changes in these assumptions were investigated; one set was chosen and kept constant across the three population series presented.[11]

Results

The results vary somewhat depending on the level of aggregation, both sectoral and regional, and on whether we are looking at physical or monetary flows. It is best, therefore, to present them item-by-item before attempting to draw broader generalizations about the overall impacts of a slowdown in population growth. In general, the discussion will start with a description of what happens over time using population Series E as a standard and then consider the impacts of shifting between series in the year 2025. While results for 1985 and 2000 are presented in some cases, the long-run impacts of population are difficult to judge

[11] The effect of varying a number of these assumptions will be reported on in the future.

from these earlier years because of transitory factors such as temporarily larger labor force in the slower growing population series, the 1973–1974 oil price changes, and legislated environmental standards scheduled for implementation in the next 5–10 years.

Macroeconomic Impacts

Table 6.3 provides an indication of how major macroeconomic variables and related indexes are likely to move over time. In contrast to a rate of growth of 4% for most of the 1950s and 1960s, GNP is likely to grow somewhat more slowly in the future, averaging 3.6% per year in the 1975–1985 period, 2.9% during the next 15 years, and 2.3% during the first quarter of the next century (assuming Series E population). This slowdown results from the combined impact of changes in the rate of growth of the population and the labor force, plus changes in labor productivity arising from shifts in the composition of the labor force and of output, and a number of transitional factors related to higher energy and environmental clean-up costs. During the 1975–1985 period the smaller population series leads to greater output because the labor force is expanded by women with fewer children; thereafter the smaller population leads to a smaller GNP, as one would expect. GNP per capita and consumption per capita grow continuously over time, fastest in the 1985–2000 period and slowest in the 2000–2025 period. As expected, they are larger the smaller is the population.

These results occur simply because the population size contracts more rapidly than does the labor force as one moves across projection series, from D to F, in a given year. In principle it could also occur if labor productivity were to increase as the population falls in size, which in turn could happen if the composition of the labor force improved or if the capital–labor ratio increased. But we have already observed (see Footnote 6) that differences in output per employee are too small to take into account across runs, and no adjustment for changes in the capital–labor ratio in a given year was made.[12] It is possible for this ratio to increase because of a decrease in the dependency ratio (see Table 6.2), which ought to give rise to more savings, lower interest rates, and higher investment levels. But such an effect may not occur because of changes in the composition of the dependent population (for example, if older dependents, whose numbers increase more rapidly, consume sufficiently greater amounts than do younger dependents). In fact, we find

---

[12]The minor differences in the ratio of GNP per laborer, less than 1% in 2025, is a result of the way the model is targeted, not of functional relationships built in the model.

TABLE 6.3.
GNP and Principal Components, Alternative Population Projections, 1975–2025

	1975	1985			2000			2025		
		D	E	F	D	E	F	D	E	F
GNP and Components (Bill. 71$)										
GNP	1,108	1,569	1,575	1,591	2,513	2,429	2,408	4,918	4,243	3,845
Private consumption	685	955	955	972	1,590	1,547	1,540	3,179	2,780	2,571
Private investment	167	285	286	289	399	380	388	804	665	612
Government	237	318	317	320	512	488	475	907	759	678
Exports	96	120	129	120	211	207	210	483	445	386
Imports	75	118	121	120	211	205	205	482	423	401
Inventory change	−3	9	9	9	13	11	11	27	18	10
Percentage of GNP										
Private consumption	61.8	60.9	60.6	61.1	63.3	63.7	64.0	64.6	65.5	66.9
Private investment	15.1	18.2	18.2	18.2	15.9	15.6	16.1	16.3	15.7	15.9
Government	21.4	20.3	20.1	20.1	20.4	20.1	19.7	18.4	17.9	17.6
Exports minus imports	1.9	.1	.5	—	—	.1	.2	—	.5	−.4
Inventory change	−.3	.6	.6	.6	.5	.5	.5	.5	.4	.3
Indexes										
GNP/Population (71$)	5,180	6,433	6,682	6,890	8,787	9,187	9,605	13,382	13,966	14,515
Consumption/Population (71$)	3,202	3,916	4,052	4,210	5,559	5,851	6,143	8,650	9,151	9,706
Capital–labor ratio (71$)	8,275	—	—	—	14,491	14,732	14,732	24,090	—	25,295

that the capital–labor ratio in 2025 is higher for Series F than for Series D, but by only 5%. The fact that we have ignored this influence on labor productivity is, therefore, of little consequence for our results.

Consumption as a percentage of GNP declines between 1975 and 1985 because of increased investment requirements for energy and environmental purposes, but rises fairly steadily thereafter. Although there is a tendency for this percentage to be larger the smaller is the population, the difference even in 2025 is quite small. Investment as a percentage of GNP is more volatile, as one would expect, and differences between runs are small and not systematic from period to period.

The relative importance of the government sector falls over time, having a slight tendency to be smaller the smaller the population is. Whereas the size of the government sector tends to grow with development in countries with lower per capita incomes (Kelley, 1976a), our result is in line with what some analysts believe is most likely in the postindustrial stages of economic growth (Heber, 1967; Williamson, 1961). But it should be noted that these expenditures are only on goods and services; transfer payments, which are likely to grow over time given social security and other commitments built into current legislation, are not included in the government sector.

Composition of Expenditures

EDUCATION AND HEALTH

Because of the shift in age composition from young to old, one might expect a comparable shift in expenditures away from education and toward health. But as disclosed by Table 6.4, which combines both public and private expenditures for these two items, educational expenditures more or less parallel the rise in GNP, whereas health expenditures grow somewhat more rapidly. In a given year a shift downward in the population growth rates does tend to decrease the percentage of GNP spent on education and increase the percentage spent on health, but this effect is relatively small.

These results are based on historic relationships between these expenditures on the one side and per capita income and population on the other. While the increase in per person health expenditures appears plausible given the shift in age composition, the increase in per pupil educational expenditures can be challenged on grounds that it is unlikely to continue increasing with income per capita for the next 50 years as it has during the last 20 or so. But there could well be an offsetting increase in the number of pupils as a consequence of expanding adult education programs, partly for retraining and partly as an adjunct of

TABLE 6.4.
Educational and Health Expenditures, Public Plus Private, Alternative Population Projections, 1975–2025

	1975	2000			2025		
		D	E	F	D	E	F
Education							
Per capita (71$)	367	736	743	754	1075	1040	1048
Per pupil (71$)[a]	1333	2873	3190	3514	4294	4914	5640
Percentage of GNP	7.1	8.4	8.1	7.8	8.0	7.4	7.2
Health							
Per capita (71$)	376	878	935	994	1406	1507	1618
Percentage of GNP	7.3	10.0	10.2	10.3	10.5	10.8	11.1

[a] Expenditures divided by population ages 5–19.

recreational and retirement activities. Thus, the net effect could be an expansion of total educational expenditures along the lines envisioned, even though it comes about in a somewhat different way.[13]

OTHER PRIVATE CONSUMPTION

Table 6.5 presents a detailed breakdown of private consumption expenditures (including the private components of medical and educational expenditures discussed previously). Since expenditures in all categories continue to increase over time, though some at substantially dampened rates, few businesses are likely to experience any absolute declines in their markets. This conclusion is reinforced by a more detailed look at prospects for individual industries (Howard and Lehmann, 1972; Jones, 1972).

The effects of population changes over time and across runs are summarized in Figure 6.1, which records the direction of change in the percentage of expenditures made on various categories. For example, these percentages decrease both over time and across runs when moving from higher to lower population projections for food and fuels, and they increase for medical services, recreation, education, and miscellaneous commodities and services. Expenditures on motor vehicles are left out because that percentage shows no significant change between 1975 and 2025 or across runs.

These results appear to be at variance with several studies that find

[13] See Appleman et al. (1972) for a more detailed discussion that reaches similar conclusions.

TABLE 6.5.
Composition of Consumption Expenditures, Alternative Population Projections, 1975–2025

	1975		2000						2025					
			D		E		F		D		E		F	
	Billions 71$	%	Billions 71$	%	Billions 71$	%	Billions 71$	%	Billions 71$	%	Billions 71$	%	Billions 71$	%
Food	71	10.5	119	7.5	112	7.3	108	7.1	224	7.1	188	6.8	167	6.6
Beverages and tobacco	21	3.1	29	1.8	28	1.8	29	1.9	45	1.4	40	1.5	39	1.5
Clothing and footwear	25	3.7	54	3.4	54	3.6	56	3.7	94	3.0	86	3.1	82	3.2
Gross rent and real estate	101	15.0	260	16.5	251	16.4	248	16.3	502	15.9	435	15.8	398	15.6
Fuel, power, and gasoline	34	5.1	55	3.5	51	3.3	49	3.2	78	2.5	64	2.3	56	2.2
Household operations, furniture, appliances, etc.	38	5.7	84	5.4	83	5.4	84	5.5	156	4.9	139	5.0	131	5.1
Medical care	50	7.4	152	9.7	147	9.6	147	9.6	320	10.2	281	10.2	261	10.2
Motor vehicles, parts, tires, repairs	42	6.2	91	5.8	89	5.8	88	5.8	202	6.4	176	6.4	162	6.3
Other transportation and communication	25	3.7	88	5.6	85	5.6	85	5.6	221	7.0	192	7.0	176	6.9
Recreation	21	3.1	48	3.1	48	3.1	48	3.1	100	3.2	89	3.2	85	3.3
Private schools	23	3.5	72	4.6	73	4.8	74	4.8	143	4.5	128	4.6	121	4.7
Other commodities	5	.7	14	.9	14	.9	15	1.0	26	.9	23	.9	23	.9
Other services	217	32.3	507	32.2	495	32.4	495	32.4	1040	33.0	916	33.2	851	33.4
Total private consumption	673	100.0	1573	100.0	1530	100.0	1526	100.0	3151	100.0	2757	100.0	2552	100.0

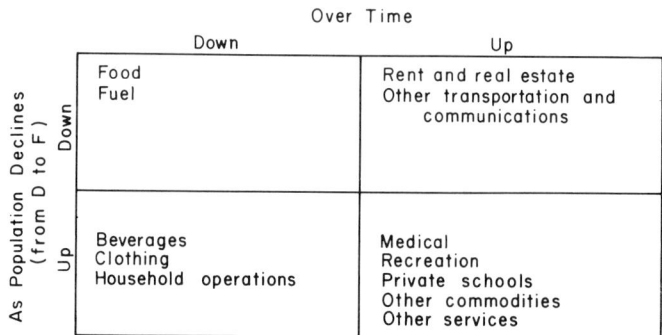

Figure 6.1. Changes as a percentage of total consumption.

little if any difference in consumption expenditures for most items under alternative assumptions about population growth rates.[14] Apparently, this result occurs because the demographic effects (e.g., changes in age structure) tend to offset the effects of changes in income per capita. The different results obtained here may be explained by the fact that we have not as yet taken such demographic effects into account in a systematic way.

Energy

Table 6.6 presents the results for the energy sector, results that are, it should be remembered, sensitive to assumptions about prices, policies, technology, response elasticities, and the level and composition of output, in addition to population. For example, the gross Btu/GNP ratio is projected to fall over time, depending on factors that are independent of population change.

Total energy consumption increases over time less rapidly than GNP and GNP per capita, but more rapidly so than does population. Nevertheless, it would be substantially smaller in 2025 if population were to grow less rapidly. If Series F population were to prevail instead of Series D, for example, consumption in that year would be 22% less compared to a population difference of 28%. Reliance on imports would be 26% less, and on nuclear power and coal 22 and 21% less, respectively.

[14]See especially Espenshade (1978), but also Eilenstine and Cunningham (1972), and Resek and Siegel (1974).

Differences with respect to other fuel forms are negligible because supply constraints dominate in determining their level of production.

But these reduced consumption levels would have little effect on energy prices, in particular on world petroleum prices. To have much effect, the cumulative savings must be a substantial portion of world consumption over a series of years. But world consumption is growing faster than that of the United States. Even if cumulated from 1975 to 2025, the savings that would occur if the U.S. population were to follow Series F rather than Series D would represent less than a year's world consumption in 2025.

TABLE 6.6.
Energy Production and Use, Alternative Population Projections, 1975–2025

	1975 Bureau of Mines	1975[a] E	2000 D	2000 E	2000 F	2025 D	2025 E	2025 F
Btu/GNP ratio–gross (1000 Btu)		54.2	47.3	47.0	46.7	40.0	40.4	40.0
Production–gross (10^{15} Btu)								
Coal–direct	15.4	15.5	24.6	23.7	23.1	41.5	37.6	33.0
Coal–liquified	—	—	—	—	—	9.7	8.4	7.6
Coal–gasified	—	—	—	—	—	.6	.5	.5
Petroleum	17.7	20.2	11.2	11.2	11.2	6.1	6.1	6.1
Natural gas	19.6	21.4	12.0	12.0	12.0	5.6	5.6	5.6
Shale oil	—	—	—	—	—	11.0	9.5	8.6
Hydro	3.2	2.9	3.2	3.2	3.2	3.3	3.3	3.3
Geothermal	—	—	1.1	1.1	1.1	2.9	2.9	2.9
Solar (space conditioning)	—	—	1.1	1.1	1.1	6.4	6.4	6.4
Nuclear power	1.8	2.2	23.8	22.7	22.3	47.3	40.9	36.6
Total–gross	57.7	62.2	77.0	74.9	74.0	134.4	121.1	110.4
Imports	13.9	15.3	45.6	43.1	42.3	72.3	61.4	53.4
Exports	2.3	2.5	3.7	3.7	3.7	11.2	11.1	10.9
Total use–gross[b,c]	70.6	74.9	118.9	114.2	112.5	195.5	171.4	152.9
Total use–net	56.9	60.1	88.3	85.3	83.9	145.5	128.4	114.2
Electricity–gross[b]	20.2	20.8	45.8	43.6	42.9	74.9	64.8	57.9
Electricity–net	6.6	6.0	15.2	14.6	14.2	28.1	24.6	21.8

[a]Since the model starts operating in 1971, the 1975 figures may deviate somewhat from the actual. Bureau of Mines estimates for 1975 are therefore provided.

[b]The difference between gross and net energy use is conversion and distribution losses.

[c]Discrepancies between total use (gross) and gross production plus imports minus exports result from miscellaneous and unallocated categories in 1975 Bureau of Mines data and rounding in projected data.

Environment

Table 6.7 presents the results for a number of variables pertaining to the environment for a specified control strategy that assumes a modest degree of slippage in enforcement of environmental standards (Ridker and Watson, 1978). Given this policy, emissions of many major air and water pollutants will be reduced significantly over time, and the effect of population growth is thereby dampened. Differences due to alternative population assumptions in a given year become sizable in percentage terms by 2025, but only because the base by that time is so low. For items less subject to control, where emissions are likely to increase over time, the effect of population can be seen more clearly. If the population were 28% less in 2025 (Series F instead of D), emissions of dissolved solids would be 25% less, thermal loadings 16% less, agricultural runoff 17-24% less depending on the item, radionuclide emissions 23% less, and spent nuclear fuel (that must be permanently and securely stored if not recycled) 15% less.

Of more economic importance are the figures for costs of control and damages (Ridker and Watson, 1978). As can be seen, the sum of these items—the total social costs of pollution to the extent we have been able to capture them—increases over time at rates approximately the same as for total energy consumption, with damage costs being held more or less constant by use of increasingly expensive control measures. Had a stricter environmental policy been assumed, total costs would have risen less rapidly, damage costs declining more than control costs increase. These total costs, and in particular the damage costs, appear to be highly sensitive to changes in population assumptions: Compared to a 28% fall in population size between Series D and F in 2025, total costs fall 29%, and damages fall 42%. This high degree of sensitivity results from the fact that damages are a function not only of emissions, which in turn are influenced by population and economic growth, but also of the number of people around to experience them, that is, per capita damages as well as total damages are a function of population growth. In contrast, control costs vary only with respect to emissions and hence are not as sensitive to population changes.

But this way of stating the results exaggerates the value of shifting between the population series. Control and land reclamation costs have already been factored into GNP; since they are always a small fraction of GNP, rising from .8% in 1975 to between 1.62% (Series D) and 1.65% (Series F) in 2025, their effect on long-run growth is not very significant. Similarly, damage costs, which have more effect on the satisfaction derived by consumers than on the ability to produce, are a small—and

TABLE 6.7.
Environmental Indexes,[a] Alternative Population Projections, 1975–2025

	1975	2000			2025		
		D	E	F	D	E	F
Air pollution emissions (10^6 tons)							
Particulates	24.3	3.1	2.9	2.9	2.4	2.1	1.8
SO_x	37.5	31.0	27.9	29.3	24.4	19.8	18.6
NO_x	18.5	15.6	14.2	14.7	18.8	16.0	14.3
HC	20.8	7.1	6.9	6.9	6.9	6.3	5.5
CO	87.6	16.4	16.1	15.9	19.0	17.6	15.3
Water pollution emissions (10^6 tons)							
BOD	4.0	2.3	2.2	2.1	1.3	1.1	1.0
COD	3.9	3.0	2.9	2.9	2.9	2.4	2.2
Suspended solids	11.2	2.8	2.7	2.6	1.2	1.0	1.0
Dissolved solids	22.2	23.6	21.6	21.6	34.7	29.4	26.1
Thermal (10^{15} Btu)	6.0	4.8	4.2	4.4	5.6	5.2	4.7

TABLE 6.7. (Continued)

	1975	2000 D	2000 E	2000 F	2025 D	2025 E	2025 F
Agricultural runoff							
Sediment (10⁶ tons)	41.9	58.9	56.1	54.9	88.5	76.3	68.0
Pesticides (10³ tons)	.2	.4	.4	.4	.6	.6	.5
Fertilizers (10³ tons)	4.5	10.9	10.3	10.0	16.6	14.2	12.6
Land disturbance[b] (10³ acres)	1209	1881	1872	1857	2395	2268	2113
Nuclear							
Radionuclide emissions (10⁶ curies)	3.4	40.9	39.0	38.3	91.8	79.4	71.1
Spent fuel, cumulative[c] (10³ tons)	1.1	183.6	175.7	172.8	731.0	669.1	624.1
Cost of controls and damages (Billions 71$)							
Pollution control	9.20	39.50	38.10	37.80	79.50	68.20	63.60
Land reclamation	.15	.17	.16	.16	.28	.25	.22
Damages	47.70	50.70	47.90	47.30	59.70	44.60	34.70
Total	57.05	90.37	86.16	85.26	139.48	113.05	98.52

[a]Assumes some slippage in the enforcement of legislated environmental regulations plus some upgrading of standards after 2000.
[b]Land used for mining purposes.
[c]Cumulative from 1975. Assumes that light-metal-fast-breeder reactors and fusion reactors generate the same amount of waste as light-water reactors.

falling—fraction of consumption, falling from 6.9% in 1975 to between 1.9% (Series D) and 1.3% (Series F) in 2025.

Other Consequences: Regional Impacts

There are, of course, other consequences of the changes in population growth rates that could affect long-run economic growth. One pertains to regional consequences that could be dramatic for specific regions losing or gaining population or where more or less coal and other minerals will have to be mined. It would take us too far afield to discuss these impacts quantitatively, but it should be kept in mind that resistance to local developments can affect national economic growth. The smaller the population, the fewer the number of sites that must be found for power plants and mines, and the less likely that economic growth will be held up by local resistance.

The quantitative importance of this point depends on the adaptability of the American economy, which may also be affected by population change. If capital and labor are willing to move to new sectors and regions, and if consumers are willing to change expenditure patterns and living styles as easily as they have in the past, the impact on national growth rates will not be great. But an older population may be less flexible in these respects. Some aspects of this inflexibility can be offset by policy changes, for example, retraining and resettlement programs.[15] Moreover, the older the population, the slower is its rate of growth, the less the local pressures will be, and the more time there will be to resolve such problems. Although it is quite possible that local resistance to growth will at times affect national economic growth, these considerations lead us to believe that differences in population growth rates within the range specified, as opposed to other factors affecting this situation, will not be very significant.

Conclusions and Qualifications

Of the various indexes of economic growth we have presented, the most important from a welfare perspective is consumption per capita, or consumption per capita corrected for pollution damages. If population growth continues at about the same rate it has grown during the last 50 years (Series D), per capita consumption will grow by about 2.0% per

---

[15]However, European experiments with resettlement apparently have achieved mixed results. See Sundquist (1975).

year, the same rate it grew between 1952 and 1975 (slower than the 2.4% experienced since 1960, but, because of World War II, faster than since 1929). If population growth slows to that represented by Series F, consumption per capita will grow by 2.2% per year on the average, by 2025 becoming 12% greater than in Series D (13% greater if corrected for pollution damages). These are hardly very dramatic results, surely not a basis for preferring one over the other population growth rate when noneconomic considerations are added. Unless the average consumer were suddenly transported from one scenario to the other in the terminal year, the individual is unlikely to notice the difference.

As we disaggregate, looking at certain sectors or regions of the country and at specific resources such as coal and specific pollutants such as hydrocarbons, the impact of a change in population growth is frequently greater. But the more disaggregated we become, the less important the variable is to national economic growth, the principal concern of this chapter.

One explanation for this small difference is that we have not projected far enough into the future. Had our time horizon been 75 or 100 years, the economic differences between Series D and F might be driven home with considerably more force. But resource and environmental constraints are not sufficiently binding in 2025 to make a significant difference. An alternative way of making the same point is to emphasize the narrowness of the range of population projections. Had we compared a continuation of past trends with no growth in the population during the next 50 years, the impact would have been more dramatic; for example, there would have been a much clearer and more significant impact on world oil prices.

But the acceptance of these explanations is unlikely to lead us to change the policy implications of our findings. It is practically impossible to project 50 years into the future with any modicum of confidence; to push the analysis further when we have no conception of what might happen to technology and tastes, not to mention population growth itself, would be meaningless. And within the next half century, it does not appear likely that population growth rates will in fact fall outside the relatively narrow range specified.

There remains a real possibility that our methodology and assumptions have led us to understate the difference that population growth might make. The difference would have been greater: if there were a constraint on the aggregate savings rate or if this rate varied inversely with population size; if the date at which world production of petroleum, or other fuels or minerals, can no longer keep up with demand without an increase in relative prices occurs earlier than we have assumed; if investment requirements necessary to develop new sources of energy and to introduce energy-saving forms of capital prove to be greater than assumed; if changes in the composition of demand are greater and have adverse effects on labor productivity; if environmental and ecological problems, some of which have not been included in our analysis, prove to be more intractable; if difficulties in siting mines and power plants are more closely linked to differences in population growth rates than assumed; or if more rapid population growth leads to a general overload of problems requiring solution.

But there could be important biases on the other side of the coin as well. Differences in consumption per capita would be less: if hours of work varied inversely with income per capita; if it is true that demographic effects not captured in our consumption functions offset the income effects, as the authors cited in Footnote 14 have found; if unemployment increased with an increase in the percentage of population in the labor force;[16] if there were more economies of scale to exploit; or if the rate of innovation increased with the rate of population growth. Population growth might slow down as income per capita rises, in which case failure to take this into account leads to an overstatement of differences. And it should not be difficult for the government to anticipate and appropriately plan for at least the more obvious demographic changes in the offing, for example, the relatively rapid rate of growth in the retired population after 2010 or so, and the small but absolute decline in younger age groups in Series E and F during certain periods.

There is no way to determine how these offsetting possibilities might balance out. Thus, we must conclude that, although there are great uncertainties that make it difficult to hold this view very strongly, our best guess is that the kind of slowdown in population growth that the United States is likely to experience during the next 50 years is unlikely to have a significant effect on this country's long-term economic growth. The more adequate the planning is to accommodate this slowdown, the more confidence we can have in this conclusion.

---

[16]Unemployment would then be greater, and that would make output and consumption per capita less under Series F than Series D assumptions.

7

Social Security and Aging Populations

ALFRED M. PITTS[1]

The debate over the need for fundamental reform in the social security system represents a decided break with the history of broad support that the program has received since 1935. With one notable exception,[2] past criticism of the system concerned itself primarily with the adequacy of social security benefits and with the equity of specific provisions of the Social Security Act. These early controversies were aimed largely at fine tuning the existing system. In contrast, today's debate questions its basic principles. The relationship between the benefits and contributions, the retirement test, and pay-as-you-go financing are major topics that dominate current discussions. None of these fundamental elements of the social security system has ever been challenged as widely as it is presently.

Among economists, heightened interest in social security derives in part from theoretical insights into its effects upon personal savings, which suggest that pay-as-you-go financing may have an adverse effect upon economic growth (Feldstein, 1974, 1976). In addition, increased

---

[1]The research for this chapter was partly supported by Administration on Aging Grant 90-A-1029/01. The chapter was written prior to 1977 Congressional revisions of the Social Security Act which, besides increasing the payroll tax, loosened the OASDI earnings test and decoupled the benefit formula.

[2]The exception is the public debate over the issue of full-reserve versus pay-as-you-go financing, which occurred in the late 1940s and early 1950s.

government reliance upon means-tested income maintenance programs to combat poverty among the aged raises serious questions about the proper role of social security in offsetting reductions in personal income due to retirement.

A more pressing stimulus for a major reevaluation of the social security system at the present time, however, can be found in the system's financial situation. For the first time in its history, the Old-Age, Survivors, and Disability Insurance (OASDI) faces an immediate prospect of large and growing annual deficits. While it is true that the system cannot go "bankrupt" in the usual sense of that term, its projected fiscal imbalance could imply a need for painful increases in the payroll tax, major commitments of general revenue funds, an intensification of various inequities in the system, or a reduction in real benefits.

Of the various factors that underlie OASDI's plight, this chapter concerns itself with the one presently regarded as most responsible for the program's long-term outlook: the slowing of U.S. population growth.

In the first part of this chapter, we assess the relative significance of demographic change as a factor in the prospective evolution of social security benefit costs. Following a brief review of salient OASDI objectives and characteristics, we trace out the manner in which the burden of retirement benefits can be expected to respond to the likely future aging of the U.S. population. Our exegesis will draw upon published OASDI cost forecasts, first, in order to develop base-line comparisons of the relative contributions of various cost determinants and, second, in order to assure that our speculation as to the likely future impact of demographic change reflects the particular institutional characteristics of the OASDI program. Our conclusion is that, given the existing formula for awarding and financing social security benefits, changes in the evolution of U.S. population growth that have already occurred have probably rendered inevitable a sharp rise in the per capita burden of OASDI, beginning roughly in the year 2005.

The second part of this chapter examines the impact of an aging population on social security costs from a less institutionally focused perspective. A principal finding that currently characterizes much economic thought regarding the functioning of social security is that the impact of benefit costs is mediated by the manner in which retirement benefits are financed. The dominant paradigm for examining the "burden" of social security is presently one that reduces the issue to a question of intergenerational equity. After briefly sketching the theoretical underpinnings of the intergenerational transfer model, we summarize its implications for an era in which population growth is likely to diminish.

In the closing two sections of our discussion we suggest that the distinctions that economists have made among alternative strategies for financing social security costs are perhaps overdrawn and reflect a confusion between the means and ends of social security. We conclude that, if all of the objectives of social security are taken into account properly, the rising per capita burden of OASDI costs, which is the likely consequence of population aging, is not necessarily vitiated by a movement away from pay-as-you-go.

Slowing Population Growth and the Social Security System

Social Security Today

The magnitude of social security's role in today's economy cannot be denied, regardless of how one views the system. Coverage now extends to over 90% of the working population and a roughly equal proportion of the nation's total civilian payroll. In 1975, payroll taxes for OASDI and Medicare equaled nearly 81% of the federal government's personal income tax receipts, roughly equaled total personal savings, and were almost triple the contributions to private pension funds. Annual benefits paid currently exceed $80 billion, and the present value of future obligations under social security has been variously estimated at between $2.5 and $4 trillion. In fiscal 1974, OASDI outlays comprised 42% of the total federal public welfare budget (U.S. Congress, Joint Economic Committee, 1974).

The effect of social security upon the economic welfare of the aged is equivalently significant. The proportion of preretirement earnings replaced by social security benefits among single, elderly males retiring in 1972 was 45%; for the newly retired male, age 65, with a dependent spouse also age 65, the replacement ratio was 68% (1975 Advisory Council). Compared with other income sources, 30% of the incomes received by aged couples in 1967 consisted of social security benefits, 40% for nonmarried beneficiaries. Without social security, only one-fifth of all beneficiary couples would have had enough income to afford the Bureau of Labor Statistics' "moderate" budget or better, a proportion that drops to 10% among nonmarried beneficiaries (Bixby, 1970). Evidence of poverty among the aged (Thompson, 1973) suggests that social security's role in preventing poverty has not diminished. Of course, in the absence of a social security system, it is likely that individual saving patterns over a working lifetime would be altered in order to provide some source of postretirement income.

Direct federal contributions to old-age security are spread among four principal cash benefit programs: OASDI, government pension plans, Medicare, and direct assistance grants (chiefly, the Supplemental Security Income program). Fiscal 1974 disbursements under each of these programs are itemized in Table 7.1. A fifth component of this system is ERISA, the Employee Retirement Income Security Act of 1974. Taken together, these programs serve three primary old-age security objectives:

1. To guarantee a basic, minimum level of income to retired or disabled workers and their dependents
2. To offset partially the loss of earnings experienced upon retirement or disability
3. To supplement retirement benefits received from private pension funds and other retirement savings, both directly via cash benefits, and indirectly by enforcing minimum vesting, portability, and

TABLE 7.1.
Federal Outlays for Selected Old-Age Assistance Programs, Fiscal 1974[a]

Program	Disbursements[b] ($ millions)	Percentage of total
Total, all programs	83,845	100.0
Social security (OASDI)		
Old-age insurance	34,540	41.2
Survivors insurance	12,863	15.3
Disability insurance	6,104	7.3
Other benefits[c]	1,281	1.5
Other federal pension programs		
Veterans pensions[d]	2,652	3.2
Federal retirement	4,953	5.9
Military retirement	5,106	6.1
Railroad retirement	2,534	3.0
Medicare	11,410	13.6
Direct assistance grants		
Supplemental security income[e]	1,850	2.2
Other old-age assistance grants	552	.7

[a] Joint Economic Committee (1974).
[b] Includes outlay for administrative costs.
[c] Includes special age 72 benefits and cash benefits to permanently disabled coal miners.
[d] Includes survivors benefits of $1.17 billion.
[e] First year of operation.

funding standards for private pension plans and granting preferred tax treatment for private retirement savings

Salient Features of OASDI

The federal old-age assistance programs just discussed share an overlapping mix of the three general social welfare objectives. Moreover, OASDI performs a variety of income assistance functions that extend beyond the replacement of preretirement earnings. Since we shall be using OASDI as an analog for a specific class of income assistance programs, it might be useful to summarize those provisions that distinguish it from other old-age security programs. The provisions include:

1. The provision of retirement annuities to the aged and their dependents. Receipt of benefits under OASDI is, for the most part, conditioned upon substantial withdrawal from the labor force after age 62. Benefits are reduced for aged persons older than 62 who continue to receive wage income; such workers can, however, elect to defer receipt of any benefits, thereby increasing the amount of their benefits when they do retire. The retirement test distinguishes OASDI from SSI, which is means-tested (and thus provides benefits to the aged, working poor), and from most other retirement pension schemes under which individuals can collect benefits based upon past service for a former employer while still earning wages from another employer.

2. Benefits based upon past earnings. Recipients generally are required to have been engaged in covered employment for a minimum length of time,[3] and benefit levels are scaled against average monthly wages earned in past, covered employment. Unlike SSI, OASDI benefits are awarded primarily to only those retirees who have had a lengthy history of labor force participation. Unlike most other pensions plans, the level of OASDI benefits depends upon one's past earnings history, rather than upon past contributions.

3. A progressive benefit structure financed by a fixed payroll tax. OASDI is intended to supplement, rather than replace, personal retirement savings. Wages are covered only up to a certain maximum, beyond which OASDI coverage would "interfere with the private savings element [1975 Advisory Council, p. 62]." At the bottom of the income scale, a minimum benefit is awarded to otherwise eligible beneficiaries whose entitled benefit does not exceed the minimum; the objective here is to extend retirement coverage to those among the working poor whose

---

[3]Eligibility for dependent and survivors benefits is mainly conditioned upon the employment history of the supporting wage earner.

preretirement incomes were too low to have furnished an adequate margin for personal savings during their working years. In addition, the payroll tax is invariant with the covered wage level.

4. Universal, compulsory coverage. Very few sectors of employment are still exempt from coverage under OASDI. Compulsory contributions are required both from high-income workers in covered employment, who have substantial retirement savings, and from covered low-income workers, who are not entitled to opt out from OASDI coverage in favor of direct public assistance grants in their old age.

5. Pay-as-you-go financing. OASDI's current beneficiaries are paid from the contributions of current workers. The OASDI trust funds serve only to smooth out short-term financing shortfalls and surpluses, and are not to be properly regarded as generating interest income with which to finance benefits on an actuarial basis.

Taken together, these provisions define the general institutional model implicit in our illustrative use of the OASDI program in the pages that follow. Summarizing its salient elements, then: The system provides benefits to former workers (and to the dependents of former workers), whose monetized contribution to total national output has largely ceased and whose contribution to the economy prior to retirement was, in some sense, "substantial." For these retirees, benefits are viewed as a guaranteed supplement to income from realized private retirement savings, with the proportion of preretirement income replaced by benefits being inversely related to the individual retiree's preretirement, lifetime "savings margin." Furthermore, the consumption of income-inelastic components of the retiree's budget, which are subject to price-level changes frequently exceeding the general rate of inflation, is subsidized by programs other than OASDI (Medicare, the food stamps program, etc.).

Current benefits paid to current beneficiaries are financed through a fixed proportional, earmarked tax on the earnings of current workers. The earnings of all workers, up to a certain maximum amount, are subject to the tax. The tax payments of employees are matched by a payroll tax on employers, with the combined tax rate set at a level such that total tax receipts equal total benefits paid (plus OASDI's administrative costs) on a current basis, with benefits indexed to the general price level.

Dimensions of the Social Security "Crisis"

To a certain extent, the prospects of substantial short- and long-term social security deficits caught both the public and social security planners by surprise. In 1971, the Quadrennial Advisory Council of Social Security came to its usual sanguine conclusion regarding OASDI, that "adequate provision has been made in the law to meet all the costs of the cash benefits program both in the short run and over the long range future; the cash benefits program is actuarially sound [1971 Advisory Council, p. xiv]." As late as the end of fiscal 1973, the OASDI Board of Trustees concurred with this view (1973 *Annual Report,* pp. 31–32).

Not much later, however, the 1975 Advisory Council's assessment was more guarded: "The (OASDI) cash benefits program needs a comparatively small amount of additional financing immediately in order to maintain the trust fund levels. Beginning about 30 years from now, in 2005, the program faces serious deficits. . . . [A projected long-term] deficit of 2.98 percent presents a serious problem to the system [1975 Advisory Council, pp. xvii, 99, and 112]." The Council advised that unless corrective measures were taken the OASDI trust funds would be exhausted by 1985, and by 2045 benefit payments would annually exceed contributions by 34.5%. The 1976 OASDI cost projections are even more pessimistic, indicating trust fund exhaustion possibly as early as 1981, with benefits exceeding contributions by 134% in 2050 (Board of Trustees, 1976, pp. 24 and 48).

The sudden change in OASDI's fiscal prospects coincided with major changes in the Board of Trustees' long-term outlook on the economic and demographic future confronting the system. As indicated in Table 7.2, the 1976 trustees report foresaw much lower future fertility levels, higher rates of inflation, and slower growth in real wages over the long run, than were envisioned in 1973. In the near term, unexpectedly high levels of inflation and unemployment are having the joint effect of raising total benefit costs while reducing payroll tax collections below anticipated levels, thereby rapidly depleting the trust fund. Finally, the cost impact of all of these adverse factors is being exacerbated by a 1972 change in the OASDI benefit formula that inadvertently overcompensates beneficiaries for real income losses due to inflation.

In order to isolate the net effect of slowing population growth from that induced by changes in other OASDI cost parameters, it would be useful, first, to review the manner in which benefit levels are determined under the system.

The Benefit Formula

Retirement benefits under OASDI are awarded in proportion to a beneficiary's Average Monthly Wage (AMW). The proportions are formulated as marginal replacement ratios; these are set by law as a margi-

TABLE 7.2.
Long-Run OASDI Current Cost Projections, 1975–2050 (Present Overindexed System)[a]

		OASDI costs[b] as percentage of taxable payroll			
Calendar year	Combined tax rate under current law	1973 trustees report[c]	1974 trustees report	1975 trustees report	1976 trustees report
1973–1976[d]	9.9	9.7	10.7	10.9	10.7
1985	9.9	9.4	10.4	10.9	11.2
1995	9.9	8.9	11.3	11.6	12.9
2005	9.9	8.4	11.7	12.8	14.3
2015	11.9	9.1	14.1	16.1	18.4
2025	11.9	10.0	17.0	20.5	24.1
2035	11.9	9.7	17.7	22.2	27.0
2045	11.9	9.6	17.9	22.1	27.9
Average deficit[e]		—	3.0	5.3	8.0
Central assumptions:[f]					
TFR		2.60	2.10	2.10	1.90
CPI		2.75	3.00	4.00	4.00
Real wages		2.25	2.00	2.00	1.75

[a] Board of Trustees of the Federal Old-Age and Survivors Insurance and Disability Insurance Trust Funds (1973, pp. 35–43; 1974, pp. 69–89; 1975, pp. 34–56; 1976, pp. 61–75).
[b] Includes administrative costs.
[c] Cost projections include a ⅜% "contingency margin" added to projected costs annually between 1973 and 2010.
[d] Year of report.
[e] Average amount of additional tax (as a percentage of taxable payroll required to cover all costs projected for the next 75 years).
[f] TFR—ultimate total fertility rate; CPI—average annual rate of increase in the Consumer Price Index (in percentage); Real wages—average annual rate of increase in real wages (in percentage).

nally decreasing function of the AMW. "Average Monthly Wage" refers to an individual's average monthly lifetime, nominal earnings in covered employment. It is possible for a beneficiary to increase his or her AMW, and therefore his or her benefits, by continuing to work after first drawing benefits, but very few beneficiaries choose to do so.[4] Thus the AMW's of most beneficiaries are virtually fixed upon first drawing OASDI and tend to remain constant during each recipient's postretirement years.

Although individual AMW's are virtually fixed upon retirement, secu-

[4] In 1973, only 6.4% of all old-age beneficiaries reported earnings in excess of the $2400 exempt amount that year (Greenough and King, 1976, p. 83); those who had exempt earnings only are not likely to have substantially increased their AMW's.

lar increases in workers' earnings imply that newly entitled beneficiary cohorts will have successively higher AMW's. This would suggest that the average replacement ratio for the system as a whole should have declined over time, given the progressivity of the benefit schedule. However, the benefit schedule has been adjusted periodically so as to maintain the real average replacement ratio at a roughly constant level (Greenough and King, 1976, p. 83; Henle, 1972). As a consequence, average real benefits for the system as a whole historically have risen while the real benefit awarded each beneficiary has been approximately maintained at a constant level during each person's retirement years.

To the extent that these patterns in the historical evolution of benefit levels reflect the intent of the system, it can be seen that the OASDI benefit formula simultaneously serves three basic standards of generational equity and welfare:

1. Intercohort[5] constancy in the proportion of real preretirement earnings replaced by OASDI retirement benefits
2. Intracohort progressivity in replacement ratios, with regard to earnings before retirement
3. Intracohort constancy in real benefits received per recipient during the remainder of each beneficiary's lifetime

Prior to 1972, when secular trends in prices and wages led to unacceptable departures from these principles, Congressional revisions of the benefit formula effectively restored these relationships between replacement ratios and real OASDI benefits per recipient. The 1972 amendments to the Social Security Act sought to eliminate the need for legislative intervention by indexing the benefit schedule to the Consumer Price Index (CPI). However, the exact formula that was adopted had the unintended[6] effect of triggering a likely rise in future real earnings replacement ratios in a manner inconsistent with the preceding standards of generational equity.

[5] A "cohort" refers here to all beneficiaries who elect to begin drawing OASDI retirement benefits in a given year. To a certain extent, each cohort can be distinguished from other cohorts by the average age of its members; a high proportion of workers who reach the minimum eligibility age (now 62 years) choose to begin drawing benefits immediately upon reaching that age, or shortly thereafter (Lauriat and Rabin, 1970).

[6] No observer of whom this author is aware has seriously advocated the retention of the "overindexed" benefit formula, and those who have advanced proposals for "decoupling" the system almost unanimously have suggested alternative formulas that are consistent with the preceding three criteria of generational equity (see, for example, 1975 Advisory Council on Social Security, pp. 14-20 and pp. 47-53; OASDI Board of Trustees, 1976, pp. 44-47; Feldstein, 1975, pp. 78-79; Munnell, 1976, pp. 8-11; Greenough and King, 1976, pp. 100-103).

The interactions among price levels, wages, population growth, and replacement ratios under the current benefit formula need not be examined in detail here.[7] In brief, the present benefit formula indexes the marginal replacement ratios of the benefit schedule to the total percentage change in the CPI since 1975. As a result, the real benefits received by today's existing beneficiary cohorts will be maintained at a roughly constant level for the remainder of their lifetimes. However, the CPI-adjusted replacement ratios are then applied to average nominal earnings, and the AMW's of future beneficiary cohorts will embody cost-of-living increases in workers' earnings awarded after 1975, when the current formula went into effect. As a consequence, the benefit levels of future cohorts are doubly compensated for inflation: once, on the replacement ratio side of the benefit equation, and then again on the AMW side. The net effect of this "overindexing" is to set off an intergenerational rise in future replacement ratios, given future increases in nominal wages.[8] Because replacement ratios under the new system are thus a function of price changes, they are said to be "coupled" to the CPI.

The "coupling" issue is of interest here for several reasons. First, the manner in which benefits are indexed to prices affects the manner in which demographic change alters OASDI costs. Second, the coupled benefit formula went into effect only recently, having been legislated in 1972 and implemented in 1975; thus, current projections of OASDI costs (such as those in Table 7.2) reflect a variety of purely transitory influences that are peculiar to a social security system with a newly overindexed benefit formula. Finally, it is quite likely that the OASDI benefit formula will be decoupled in the near future.

Slowing Population Growth and OASDI Costs: Long-Term Effects

As a proportion of total covered payroll, current OASDI retirement costs can be denoted by C in the expression:

$$C = \frac{B \cdot \bar{r} \cdot \overline{W}_b}{L \cdot W_L}, \qquad (1)$$

where B is equal to the number of beneficiaries, $\bar{r}$ is equal to the proportion of average lifetime earnings replaced by OASDI, $\overline{W}_b$ is equal to the

---

[7]For a more detailed discussion of "overindexing," see Thompson, 1974, 1975.
[8]Benefits are not reduced if the CPI falls, however.

average nominal covered wage received during the lifetimes of current beneficiaries, L is the size of the work force, and W_L is the average covered nominal wage received by the current work force. Under pay-as-you-go, the payroll tax for OASDI is set so as to assure that, over the long run, total payroll tax receipts are equal to total benefit costs (including administrative costs). Thus, C is equal to the current payroll tax rate and is therefore a measure of the per worker cost of current benefits to the wage earners whose taxes finance it.

It can be shown that the principal long-term effect of a permanent decline in the rate of population growth is an increase in the relative proportions of older individuals in the affected population. The most direct consequence of this relative aging effect for OASDI costs flows from the resultant increase in the old-age dependency ratio (that is, the ratio of B to L, or its proxy, the ratio of persons 65 and over to those aged 20–64). As Eq. (1) implies, per worker social security costs will increase in proportion with the rise of the Old Age Dependency Ratio (OADR).

In addition to altering the ratio of beneficiaries to contributors, a slowdown in population growth will also shift the relative age distribution within the beneficiary population itself, giving added weight to beneficiaries in older retirement cohorts. If one assumes an economy that has been experiencing a continuous rise in average nominal wages, an aging of the beneficiary population will therefore somewhat offset the rise in per worker benefit costs associated with the increase in the OADR because older retirement cohorts will have successively lower AMWs. In general, however, this offset to per worker OASDI costs will be swamped by the OADR effect.

The principal distinction between a "decoupled" and "coupled" benefit formula has to do with the constancy of $\bar{r}$, the average proportion of lifetime earnings replaced by OASDI. Using a decoupled formula, [9] $\bar{r}$ remains constant, both intergenerationally and over time. Since all retirement cohorts will forever be facing the same replacement ratios, the average replacement ratio for the entire beneficiary population remains fixed, even if its age structure changes.

Under social security's coupled formula, however, the replacement ratio is tied to the aggregate price level. Given the most likely future trends in prices and wages, the replacement ratios for each future re-

---

[9] It is possible to suggest any number of procedures for decoupling the benefit formula. The "decoupled formula" assumed in this chapter is the one used in the 1976 *Annual Report* of the OASDI Board of Trustees (p. 53) which, in effect, employs a fixed schedule of marginal replacement ratios indexed to the total relative change in the CPI since the year in which each individual first drew benefits, rather than to the CPI in 1975 as was formerly the case.

tirement cohort will successively rise. This long-term rise in $\bar{r}$ for the beneficiary population as a whole, independently induced by inflation, could be offset somewhat by slowing population growth, since it would increase the relative number of older beneficiaries who have generally lower replacement rates.

Thus, two of the likely long-term effects of slowing population growth would have the same relative effect on OASDI per worker costs, regardless of whether the benefit formula is "coupled." First, costs will rise in proportion to the implicit increase in the old-age dependency ratio. Second, the rise in costs will be somewhat offset by a decline in the average AMW for the beneficiary population as a whole. In addition, with a coupled benefit formula, slowing population growth further offsets the rise in per worker OASDI costs attributable to higher dependency ratios by reducing the rate of increase in average replacement ratios.

Short-Term Influences on OASDI Costs

All of the OASDI cost projections in Table 7.2 display a similar pattern of increases in future per worker social security costs. The projected increases occur in three distinct phases, each approximately 25 years in length. For the remainder of this century, per worker costs increase quite slowly, necessitating in all cases less than a two percentage point total increase in the combined payroll tax. The rise in costs rapidly accelerates in the period 2000–2025, averaging roughly 1.3–2.0% per annum. After 2025, the rate of increase slackens; indeed, the 1973 and 1975 projections show a slight net decline in per worker costs after 2035. Fluctuations in the rate of growth of per worker costs after 2050 (not shown) occur within a fairly narrow band; given the coupled benefit formula implicit in all four projections, the rate of growth in per worker costs ultimately converges on the rate of growth of the average replacement ratio.

This pattern of change in per worker OASDI costs is coincident with expected future patterns of change in both the old-age dependency ratio and the average earnings replacement ratio. Fluctuations in the old-age dependency ratio largely reflect past changes in the level of fertility. Future changes in the replacement ratio derive from the coupling of the benefit formula to the CPI.

Historical data for the United States reveal a continuous secular decline in fertility since at least 1800 (Coale and Zelnick, 1963). The only exception of any importance is the short-term postwar upsurge, which peaked in 1959 at a total fertility rate (TFR) of 3.8. Since then, the United

States has been experiencing its most rapid decline in fertility, with the 1977 total fertility rate somewhat below replacement.

Consequently, projections of the U.S. old-age dependency ratio will reflect shifts in the relative balance of four distinct birth cohorts:

1. The pre-World War I cohort, which comprises today's OASDI beneficiaries; the growth rate of this group reflects the modest decline in fertility that took place roughly between 1890 and 1920, when the TFR fell from about 3.8 to 3.3
2. The "depression cohort," born between 1920 and 1940, when the decline accelerated
3. The "baby boom cohort," born between 1940 and 1960
4. The "birth dearth cohort," born after 1960

The cost projections presented in Table 7.2 for the most part assume that the decline in the total fertility rate will bottom out at about 1.75 in the late 1970s and rise to various postulated levels between 1990 and 2000, after which it will remain constant. Table 7.3 presents the projected old-age dependency ratios that underlie the future OASDI cost estimates in Table 7.2.

During the first 25 years of the projections, the OADR remains relatively stable, regardless of any assumed changes in the total fertility rate. A slight rise in the growth rate of the working population occurs as the successively larger birth cohorts of the baby boom reach age 20. The last of the baby boom birth cohorts will enter the labor force during 1980–1985; afterward, the growth rate of the population aged 20–64 will begin to slow as the relatively smaller birth dearth cohorts reach working age. Simultaneously, the growth rate of the beneficiary population continually drops as the successively smaller pre-World War I cohorts enter their retirement years. Thus, the overall pattern is one of relative stability in the old-age dependency ratio between the years 1975 and 2000, with the OADR falling slightly until 1980–1985 and then rising gently between 1985 and 2000–2005. This first phase will end with a fairly sharp, short-lived drop in the OADR as the depression cohort reaches retirement.

The second phase in the future evolution of the old-age dependency ratio, between 2000 and 2025, will be a period of explosive growth. Successively larger baby boom cohorts will begin to reach retirement in 2005, which almost immediately triggers a rapid rise in the rate of growth of the aged population. This coincides with an accelerating reduction in the rate of growth of the working population as the birth dearth cohorts come to comprise a progressively larger proportion of the working age population; indeed, the population aged 20–64 begins to

TABLE 7.3.
Projections of the Old-Age Dependency Ratio under Various Fertility Assumptions

	Population aged 65 and over as a percentage of population aged 20-64			
Calendar year	1973 trustees report	1974 trustees report	1975 trustees report	1976 trustees report
1975[a,b]	19.9	19.1	19.1	19.1
1985	18.7	19.2	18.9	19.0
1995	19.0	20.2	19.7	19.8
2005	16.2	18.9	18.8	18.9
2015	17.3	21.7	21.9	22.3
2025	21.8	27.7	28.7	29.8
2035	22.4	29.3	31.2	33.3
2045	22.4	27.7	28.6	31.8
Assumed ultimate total fertility rate	2.6	2.1[c]	2.1[d]	1.9[d]
Total percentage change in OADR[e]				
1975–2000	−7.3	2.6	1.0	1.0
2000–2025	29.0	41.3	49.5	54.4
2025–2050	4.6	2.2	−1.0	7.0
Total percentage change in OASDI costs[f]				
1975[g]–2000	−12.4	5.7	10.0	25.3
2000–2025	18.0	50.0	70.4	79.6
2025–2050	−4.3	5.5	9.7	18.7

[a] See Table 7.2.
[b] Observed.
[c] Assumes that the decline in TFR bottoms out in 1975 at 1.9 births per woman.
[d] Assumes that the decline in TFR bottoms out in 1980 at 1.75 births per woman.
[e] Old-age dependency ratio.
[f] OASDI benefit and administrative costs as a percentage of taxable payroll under the overindexed system; see Table 7.2.
[g] Year of report.

decline in absolute numbers after 2015. The upshot is a very rapid rise in the OADR between 2005 and 2025.

The final phase of the OADR adjustment to the post-1960 slowing of U.S. population growth occurs after 2025. The period 2025–2030 finds the last of the baby boom cohorts having reached retirement age. With the successively smaller birth dearth cohorts reaching old age afterward, the decline in the working-age population, already underway, is matched by a slowing rate of growth for the older population. After 2035, the rising number of aged deaths generated as the baby boom cohorts begin to reach extreme old age is no longer fully offset by birth dearth increments to the elderly population, and the rate of decline in the aged population comes to exceed that of the working population. As a result the OADR begins to fall, but at a steadily decreasing rate (after 2050), as the baby boom cohort dies off.

The preceding fluctuations in the rate of change reflect the transition to a theoretical stationary–stable population. With the fixity of vital rates after the year 2000 that is assumed in all of these projections, the old-age dependency ratio ultimately will attain a fixed level. How rapidly this stable level is reached depends upon the degree of discrepancy between the relative age distribution at the time when the fertility decline began and the ultimate, stable age distribution, or, alternatively, upon the magnitude and rapidity of the fertility decline.[10] Under the conditions just described, virtual stability in the U.S. population OADR will be attained roughly 80–100 years from now.

Given the relatively high sensitivity of the age distribution to fertility change and this country's history of quickly reversible fertility trends, any projection of the long-term OADR that will result from the slowing of U.S. population growth should be greeted with some skepticism. The near-term (to 2000) prospects for the old-age dependency ratio, however, are more certain.

First, the old-age dependency ratio over the next 25 years will not be affected by any deviations from recent fertility levels, no matter how sudden or sharp such future changes in fertility might be. Ceteris paribus, per worker OASDI costs will remain relatively stable for the remainder of this century. This is true simply because the earliest date at which a change in the number of births can affect the OADR is when those births attain working age.

Secondly, the impact on OASDI costs between 2000 and 2025 will be modulated by the fertility decline that already has occurred since 1960. Future birth cohorts will have to replace the future work force substantially before they can have much of an effect on the old-age dependency ratio.

Finally, a sharp fluctuation in the OADR between 2005 and 2035 is already unavoidable because of the quick succession of baby boom and birth dearth cohorts already born. This implies a sharp fluctuation over a very short time in the future growth rate of the aged population, given that more than 70% of all U.S. mortality is concentrated in the relatively few years of life remaining after age 65. Any imminent, sharp increase in fertility can partially attenuate the resultant destabilization of the OADR

---

[10]For a detailed discussion of these propositions, see Keyfitz (1971).

by enhancing the growth rate of the work force between 2005 and 2035, but it runs the risk of generating a second transitory destabilization of the dependency ratio at a later date unless the rise in fertility is a sustained one. At the very least, then, an anticipatory adjustment of OASDI trust fund levels seems unavoidable in the early part of the next century.

Another short-term influence on OASDI costs has to do with the recency of the 1972 coupling of earnings replacement ratios to changes in aggregate prices and wages. All of the cost projections in Table 7.2 assume the coupled benefit formula and a fixed, positive rate of growth in prices and wages after 1980. As a result, the replacement ratios for new beneficiary cohorts should rise steadily. Given the wage–price combination assumed in the 1976 projection, for example, the replacement ratio for a newly retired, single male aged 65 with the median AMW will rise from 42% in 1975 to 69% in 2050 (OASDI Board of Trustees, 1976, p. 47).

Over the long run, the rate of growth in the average replacement ratio would come to equal an eventually constant rate of growth in the replacement ratios for successive beneficiary cohorts. Over the short run, however, the rise in the average replacement ratio for the entire beneficiary population will deviate from this long-term rate for two reasons. First, earlier beneficiary cohorts will experience a slower increase in their replacement ratios than later ones because a smaller proportion of their AMWs will reflect cost-of-living increases awarded since 1975. Second, the rate of growth of the mean replacement ratio for the entire beneficiary population will fluctuate with the rate of population growth as it affects the balance of future retirees, with their high replacement ratios, to earlier beneficiary cohorts.

The net result of these two factors over the course of the projections examined in this chapter is that, although the mean replacement ratio for the entire beneficiary population grows in absolute magnitude, the rate of that growth is moderated by the growth rate of the population. Given the wage–price assumptions used in the 1974–1976 trustees projections, it adds relatively more to costs when the growth rate of the beneficiary population is relatively high. As the age structure of the population approaches stability, this second-order effect vanishes.

Table 7.4 compares OASDI cost projections for the present overindexed system with those that could be expected were the benefit formula decoupled. In effect, the cost figures show what the combined payroll tax would have to be, starting in 1975, in order to balance total costs against total contributions over the period indicated. As expected, coupling has

TABLE 7.4.
Long-Run OASDI Cost Estimates under Various Fertility Assumptions Using Overindexed System and "Decoupled" System[a,b]

System and period	Average OASDI costs as a percentage of covered wages, assuming ultimate total fertility rate of:			
	1.7	1.9	2.1	2.3
Present system				
1975–2000	11.8	11.8	11.8	11.8
1975–2025	15.1	14.9	14.7	14.6
1975–2050	19.8	18.9	18.2	17.5
Decoupled system				
1975–2000	11.6	11.6	11.6	11.6
1975–2025	13.4	13.2	13.1	13.0
1975–2050	15.9	15.3	14.7	14.2

[a] Board of Trustees of the Federal Old-Age and Survivors Insurance and Disability Insurance Trust Funds (1976, p. 71).

[b] Cost estimates include administrative costs, and they are arithmetic averages of the annual costs projected for the periods specified. The projections assume average annual increases in the CPI and in real wages of 4% and 1.75%, respectively.

very little effect on average OASDI per worker costs in the near future. After that, however, there occurs a rapid rise under both formulas, requiring a relatively greater tax increase to support the present coupled system. After 2050, the required payroll tax for the overindexed system would continue to rise after the population stabilizes; further tax increases would not be required to support a decoupled formula.

Relative Effects of Changes in Various OASDI Cost Parameters

It is possible that the projected trends in OASDI costs might be deflected by future deviations from the assumed levels of future fertility, wages, and prices upon which the projections are based. Furthermore, the 1973–1976 Board of Trustees projections embody assumptions regarding the future paths of a variety of heretofore unmentioned codeterminants of OASDI costs. Changes in any of these might also offset or exacerbate the likely future rise in per worker social security costs. In addition, we have thus far regarded a slowing of population growth as being synonymous with a sustained decline in future fertility levels; however, such an event might also be accompanied by changes in mortality or migration levels. All of these possibilities raise questions as to the comparative influences of changes in each of the basic determinants of OASDI costs.

Table 7.5 presents some results of a series of social security cost projections in which an attempt was made to compare the relative impact of independent changes in each of four OASDI determinants. Since it is likely that the present overindexed benefit formula will be abandoned in the near future, the projections presented here assume a decoupled benefit formula. They embody a "sensitivity analysis" approach to the assessment of relative cost impact. In brief, this procedure begins with a cost projection based upon a set of "central" assumed levels[11] for each of the cost-determining variables in the social security cost-forecasting model. Alternative projections are then prepared by changing the assumed value of each independent variable while holding all remaining variables constant at their central levels. Maximum and minimum values that the independent variables are allowed to assume define a "reasonable" range of long-term average values that a given variable might be expected to take on over the next 75 years.

The "mean elasticity" (ME) figures in the table represent the average percentage change in annual OASDI per worker costs corresponding to a 1% change in the value of the independent variable between the lowest and highest levels shown for each cost variable in Table 7.5. Interpreting the mean elasticity shown in the lower left-hand corner of the table, for example, an annual rate of increase in the CPI of 4.8% (i.e., a 140% increase over 2.0%) will be associated with an approximate decrease of 2.52% (140 × −.018) in average annual per worker OASDI costs between 1975 and 2000 (i.e., from 11.8 to 11.5% of taxable payroll), if all other cost determinants remain at their "central" levels during the period.

WAGES AND PRICES

Table 7.5 suggests that, in a decoupled system with intergenerationally constant real earnings replacement ratios, changes in prices and real wages would have relatively little impact on the per worker burden of social security. This is a basic characteristic of the decoupled benefit

[11]The central level assumed for each independent variable shown in Table 7.5 is the second one in the range of values listed there.

TABLE 7.5.
Sensitivity of OASDI Cost Projections to Changes in Selected Assumptions ("Decoupled System")[a]

Assumption	Average annual OASDI costs as a percentage of taxable payroll during:		
	1975–2000	1975–2025	1975–2050
Total fertility rate			
1.7	11.6	13.4	15.9
1.9	11.6	13.2	15.3
2.1	11.6	13.1	14.7
Mean elasticity	.007	−.095	−.323
Improvements in mortality rates			
No improvement	11.5	12.9	14.6
15% reduction	11.6	13.2	15.3
30% reduction	11.7	13.6	15.9
Mean elasticity	.058	.168	.316
Average annual growth in real wages			
1.00%	12.1	14.0	16.2
1.75%	11.6	13.2	15.3
2.50%	11.1	12.6	14.4
Mean elasticity	−.052	−.066	−.072
Average annual increase in CPI			
2%	11.8	13.6	15.7
4%	11.6	13.2	15.3
6%	11.4	13.0	14.9
Mean elasticity	−.018	−.022	−.024

[a] Board of Trustees of the Federal Old-Age and Survivors Insurance and Disability Insurance Trust Funds (1976, pp. 70–73).

formula: Changes in prices or real wages ultimately have no effect at all on the real per worker cost of OASDI.

The projections in Table 7.5, however, show the OASDI per worker burden changing slightly and inversely with changes in both prices and real wages. The explanation for these effects is to be found in two sources of "friction." First, changes in real wages will have a more immediate effect on the current average wage of workers than they will upon the average monthly wages of beneficiaries. Second, it is assumed that the current nominal wage will respond to changes in price levels more quickly than will the benefit schedule. These lags lead to a slight, transitory differential between the rates of growth of total benefits and total covered payroll (OASDI Board of Trustees, 1976, p. 72).

MORTALITY

The rate of mortality improvement shown in Table 7.5 refers to the relative difference between the age-adjusted crude death rate projected for 2050 and that observed in 1973. Mortality is projected to improve relatively more at the very young ages and at the over-65 ages than at the inbetween ages, and it is assumed that the rates change gradually between 1975 and 2000, with no changes occurring after the year 2000.

To the extent that a comparison between a "total mortality rate" (i.e., the age-adjusted crude death rate) and the total fertility rate is indicative, it is interesting to note that reductions in mortality would have a more immediate and proportionally equal or greater impact on OASDI costs than would roughly equivalent changes in total fertility. This is, of course, because future reductions in U.S. mortality must come primarily in the older age categories, as is assumed in these projections. Thus, any reductions are likely to increase the rate of growth of the aged population while leaving that of the working-age population relatively unchanged. The result is an immediate rise in the old-age dependency ratio.

Changes in fertility levels have a pervasive, although delayed, influence on age composition because they alter the rate of population flow into the bottom end—and therefore all subsequent parts—of the age distribution. In comparison, the impact of changes in mortality now tends to be relatively more selective, although more immediate; mortality fluctuations in developed societies tend to affect only the rate of cohort flow past the points in the age distribution at which such changes occur, because there is relatively little scope for mortality change during or before the childbearing ages.

IMMIGRATION

Relative to the effects of fertility and mortality change on age structure, the effects of a change in the level of migration are attenuated by two factors. First, to the extent that immigrant cohorts and their survivors come to assume the fertility and mortality behavior of the resident population, the size and age distribution of any one migration cohort will have little lasting influence on the long-term evolution of the resident population's age structure. Second, the effect on age composition of changes in the level of migration is further mediated, both in the short run and in the long run, by the degree of discrepancy between the relative age structure of the immigrants and that of the resident population. Where there is coincidence between their relative age structures, for example, immigration would alter equally the growth rates of all age cohorts in the resident population; the relative age composition of the latter therefore would not be altered, regardless of the level of migration.[12]

The level of annual legal immigration to the United States has been fairly stable and constant in total numbers over the past decade and a half, although a slight downward trend appears to be taking shape (Immigration and Naturalization Service, 1975). Consistent with recent experience, the current OASDI cost projections assume a fixed net influx of 400,000 immigrants per year from now to 2050.[13] The age composition of each immigrant cohort also is assumed to be fixed and considerably younger than that of either the current or any presently projected U.S. resident population. The age distribution of each new immigrant cohort is assumed to be unimodal, peaking at age 27 for males and age 23 for females. Thus, the old-age dependency ratio among new immigrants is assumed to be 3.8 per hundred persons aged 20-64, in contrast to the 19.1 estimated for the U.S. resident population in 1975 (Bayo and McKay, 1974; OASDI Board of Trustees, 1976).

Under such conditions, immigration should serve as a slight brake on any likely future rise in real per worker OASDI costs. Furthermore, for any given level of annual total immigration, the restraining influence of immigration should increase relatively as the discrepancy between the relatively younger age distribution of new immigrant cohorts and that of the aging resident population widens. The overall effect of immigration should be dampened in the long run, however, by the progressive integration of each new immigrant cohort and its offspring into the vital rates schedule and age structure of the resident population.

Empirical estimates of the OASDI per worker cost elasticity of immigration are consistent with these expectations. Based upon the central assumptions that were used in the 1975 trustees projections, a 1% increase in total immigration was found to be associated with $-.012\%$, $-.024\%$, and $-.029\%$ changes in average OASDI costs as a percentage of taxable payroll for the periods 1975-2000, 1975-2025, and 1975-2050, respectively (OASDI Board of Trustees, 1975).[14]

---

[12]For a more detailed discussion of the comparative dynamics of changes in mortality, fertility, and migration, see Keyfitz (1965, 1968), Rogers (1973), and Spengler (1963).

[13]Virtually all standard government projections of the U.S. population assume away any emigration or illegal immigration.

[14]The range assumed for annual total immigration was 300,000-500,000. ME estimates for immigration that are compatible with the central assumptions used in the 1976 sensitivity tests were not obtainable. It should be noted, however, that the ME's for fertility and mortality obtained in the 1975 tests were comparable in magnitude and trend to the 1976 values reported in Table 7.5.

FEMALE LABOR FORCE PARTICIPATION

Concomitant with the secular decline in U.S. fertility, there has occurred a fairly steady long-term rise in female labor force participation (Bureau of Economic Analysis, 1973; Bureau of Labor Statistics, 1975). All of the OASDI projections examined so far assume that this trend will continue; the 1976 trustees projections foresee a total increase of 22% between 1975 and 2050, at which time the female rate will be 73% of that of males, in contrast to the present 60% (OASDI Board of Trustees, 1976).

In the short run, an increase in female labor force participation should somewhat ease the burden of projected OASDI per worker costs by virtue of its immediate expansionary effect on the system's payroll tax base. Its long-term effect is less certain, however, if one assumes that most of the increase in labor force participation will occur among married women.

Very few of these new female entrants into the labor force are likely to represent net additions to the future beneficiary population. Even if they had never worked, almost all married elderly women would still qualify for their own benefits as wives of OASDI-eligible male retirees. Approximately 92% of all persons currently reaching age 65 are eligible for either primary or secondary OASDI benefits (1975 Advisory Council). The residual 8% consists mainly of workers in employment areas not covered by social security. Consequently, there is little scope for increases in female labor force participation to increase the overall size of the benefit population.

Virtually the only effect that increased female labor force participation could have on total benefit costs would be to increase the proportion of elderly wives who qualify for primary, retired worker benefits as opposed to secondary-spouse or secondary-widow benefits. Even here, the effect would likely be small, for two reasons.

First, a relatively large proportion of retiring women already qualify for primary benefits based on their past earnings records. By 1970, 68% of all women aged 40-49 already had enough quarters of covered employment to qualify them for retirement benefits at age 65 (Reno, 1973). Even with no further increase in participation rates, 75-80% of the present female labor force would meet minimum eligibility requirements by the time they retire. The 22% rise in female labor force participation assumed in the latest projections would at most increase ultimate eligibility to 85% (OASDI Board of Trustees, 1975, 1976).

More importantly, however, any increase in eligibility levels will have little effect upon OASDI costs unless it also is accompanied by a closing of the differential between the average lifetime earnings of husbands and wives. Accordingly, the effect of increased female labor force participation rates on total payroll tax receipts is also dependent on discrepancies between the size and age distributions of the male and female working-age populations and sex differentials in average wages and unemployment rates.

The elderly wife of a retired OASDI-eligible worker is entitled to a secondary benefit equal to 50% of her husband's benefit, 100% if she is widowed. Alternately, she may elect to receive a primary benefit based on her own earnings record if it exceeds the secondary benefit for which she is eligible and which is based upon her husband's earning record. The average benefit received by elderly beneficiaries in 1975 was $2209, $1234, and $2368 for the primary, secondary-spouse, and secondary-widow categories, respectively[15] (OASDI Board of Trustees, 1976). A very rough indication of the influence of female labor force participation rates and husband–wife differences in earned incomes and employment upon OASDI costs might be obtained as follows.

Assume that in 1975 all recipients of secondary benefits received instead a primary benefit equal to what they would have received had they experienced the same wage and employment histories as their spouses. About the only effect that this would have had upon 1975 benefit costs would have been to double the mean secondary-spouse benefit to $2468. Since these account for 12.4% of elderly beneficiaries, total benefit costs for fiscal 1975 would have been increased by 6.2%.

Similarly, had females experienced the same median earnings and unemployment rates as males experienced in 1975, a 22% increase in female labor force participation would have increased the total OASDI payroll tax yield by approximately 31.0%.[16] With no closing of the gap between male and female earnings and unemployment, a 22% change in female labor force participation would have yielded only a 5.7% increase in payroll tax collections. With no change in female labor supply but with a closing of the earnings–employment gap, the increase in 1975 tax collections might have been 20.7%.

Implicit in the preceding are decreases in the 1975 per worker cost of

---

[15]The secondary-benefit categories include benefits received by dependent husbands and widowers. The primary-benefit category here includes special benefits paid to noninsured persons aged 72 and over.

[16]The estimated U.S. male population aged 20–64 in 1975 was 57.0 million, that of females 59.5 million. Observed labor force participation rates for males and females of those ages were 89.1 and 53.8%, respectively; unemployment rates at those ages, 5.8 and 8.1%. Finally, the median earnings of full-time female workers in 1973 were 57% those of full-time working males (1975 Advisory Council, p. 74).

OASDI ranging from 5.4% (with a 22% increase in the female labor supply, no equalization of unemployment rates and wages, and no changes in beneficiary status) to 11.2% (with female wages and unemployment rates equal to those of males, all spouses drawing primary benefits, and no changes in labor supply) to 19.2% (with wage–employment equalization, all retirees receiving primary benefits, and a 22% increase in the female labor supply).

THE RETIREMENT AGE

Changes in the retirement age might be expected to have a particularly powerful effect on the per worker burden of social security costs because they can cause the size of the contributory and beneficiary populations to vary in opposite directions. Clark (1976a), using a stationary-state projection of the U.S. population, demonstrates that a drop in the retirement age from 65 to 60 years could, ceteris paribus, force a 48% long-term marginal increase in the payroll tax; such a reduction in the retirement age would bring about a 34% ultimate increase in the population of old-age beneficiaries and a 10% decrease in the working-age population. Similar speculative findings have also been reported by Rejda and Shepler (1973), among others.

There have been a number of proposals to increase the minimum eligibility age for OASDI retirement benefits. The 1975 Advisory Council on Social Security, for example, suggested that the payroll tax required to accomodate the likely future rise in benefit costs might be reduced by as much as 1.5 percentage points were the minimum age increased to 68 years. Munnell (1976, p. 16) reasons that "extending the retirement age would simultaneously ease the burden on future taxpayers and bolster the economic welfare of the elderly" if it were accompanied by the elimination of a variety of provisions that discourage labor force participation among the elderly.

Absent from most recent discussions of the retirement age issue seems to be any serious consideration of aggregate demand constraints on old-age employment. Altering the social security system so as to encourage later retirement can benefit the elderly population only to the extent that sufficient job opportunities would be available to the older worker. In contrast to Munnell's assertion (1976, p. 16) that an increase in the retirement age would improve the economic lot of the aged by "shortening the period over which they suffer reduced retirement income," Kreps et al. (1962, pp. 52 and 54), writing at a time when serious attention was given to encouraging early retirement, remind us that

More fundamentally, however, a gain in national product attributable to increased labor-force participation of older persons can occur only when these persons are a *net addition* to the [employed] work force.... In the growing residue of unemployment left by the recession of 1957–58 and 1960–61, the older worker has been particularly prominent.... [A slackening of labor demand] raises the question of adequate job opportunities for all workers; but the question is of particular significance to the older, and apparently somewhat more marginal, worker.

It can, of course, be argued that slowing population growth would ultimately shrink the pool of available manpower even with increased female labor force participation. In addition, the direct effect of slowing population growth on aggregate demand is presently an unsettled issue among economists. At the very least, however, calls for a raising of the OASDI eligibility age in the near future need to be balanced against existing evidence that a substantial proportion of those who elect to receive benefits at today's minimum age consists of workers who have been experiencing lengthy periods of unemployment and ill health immediately prior to claim. Data from the Survey of Newly Entitled Beneficiaries, for example, suggest that in 1968 about 20% of the males who first claimed reduced benefits at age 62 had not worked for at least 12 months prior to claim (McKinley and Frase, 1970): "It's almost as if they were in a queue waiting for the minimum age... to arrive [pp. 9–10]."

Furthermore, the disincentive effect of the earnings test is somewhat offset by the fact that it has little impact upon elderly workers who defer first claims; it affects only those retirees who are actually receiving OASDI benefit payments. Note that aged workers in stable full-time employment—that is, those most likely to have earnings that exceed the exempt amount and who would, therefore, be most discouraged by the earnings test—are also the ones most likely to defer first claim.

We conclude that findings as to the benefits of later retirement should be discounted against the likely employment prospects of the elderly worker. While a later retirement age would almost certainly reduce the future growth of OASDI benefit costs, it is not at all certain that it would expand the system's tax base to the extent postulated in much of the existing literature. Moreover, should aggregate demand be insufficient to engage fully an expanded old-age work force, an increase in the minimum OASDI eligibility age might simply shift the burden of old-age assistance costs from social security to other public welfare programs, without reducing its overall size.

Some General Observations

Before concluding this exegetical treatment of demographic influences on social security, several cautionary remarks are in order.

First, our conclusions regarding the inevitability of a future rise in the old-age dependency burden are highly conditional on the narrow range of fertility prospects that we have been considering. The same holds true for the relative sensitivity of OASDI costs to various types of sociodemographic and economic change. As Spengler (1963) quite clearly illustrates, it is only when fertility rates reach near-replacement levels that demographic factors other than fertility can have much of an impact on age structure. Low levels such as those assumed in much of the preceding discussion are historically atypical; even today, they could be regarded as exceptional (Wachter, 1975). Were the trend in U.S. fertility rates to reverse itself, with fertility rates ultimately reaching, for example, the levels that were attained in the late 1950s, any pessimism regarding the long-term future of social security costs might be unwarranted.

Second, this discussion of OASDI has largely ignored the disability and child-related benefit components of social security costs. In 1974, both consumed sizable portions of the total OASDI budget—11.2 and 11.4%, respectively (OASDI Board of Trustees, 1976). Both are expected to consume much smaller shares by 2050 if fertility remains low. Nevertheless, the existence of these benefits should be taken into account in more detailed assessments of demographic influences on OASDI, since they can confound some of the effects just noted. As an example, increased fertility, while reducing the ultimate balance of old-age beneficiaries to working-age contributors, could also increase the average number of secondary, child-related benefit claims generated by each worker's retirement or death.

Finally, there are the limitations of the OASDI forecasting model itself, not the least of which is its partial equilibrium focus. All of the cost determinants examined here are treated by the model as being exogenous to the social security system and as arising independently of each other. The possibility that an aging of the population might, for example, affect labor productivity and therefore the rate of growth in real wages is not considered. In its defense, it might be noted that much of the economic analysis of social security problems has suffered from this lack of scope, at least until recently.

More importantly, the model embodies a very specific set of institutional arrangements for financing and awarding social security benefits. The published projections therefore should be interpreted as reflecting a highly particularized set of responses to slowing population growth. They show what the consequences of population growth might be, given the existing pay-as-you-go system in the United States.

Pay-as-you-go is only one of a number of alternative strategies for financing social security costs. Since many of the other approaches respond differently to demographic change, they warrant some discussion here.

Slowing Population Growth and Pay-As-You-Go

It is not possible to describe in detail here all of the alternative financing arrangements that appear in the literature. Fortunately, they can largely be characterized as variants of three basic approaches: reserve (or "actuarial") funding, pay-as-you-go, and general revenue financing.

Keyfitz (1976, p. 1) has neatly summarized the basic principles of full-reserve funding:

> In pension funding with actuarial reserves..., each person's discounted prospective contributions are set equal to his discounted benefits less office loading, so that each person pays for himself. The sense in which any one individual pays for himself is not that his deductions are equal to his benefits, but rather that prospective values are equal, and for large bodies of policy-holders this is what counts. [For then each] cohort of people of a given age will come close to balancing [its own] deductions and benefits [over the entire course of its lifetime. Other cohorts can] be much larger or smaller without this making any difference [in the resources available to finance benefits for any other cohort].... As long as the insurer holds the calculated reserves and remains solvent, no problem of equity among cohorts or among generations can possibly arise.

> Each cohort gains from the fact that the insurer puts the reserve out at interest, and the interest is for most ages of much more consequence than the gain through some members of the cohort dying before they can collect. The community benefits by having the funds for long-term investment.

Each individual's reserve account is built up prior to retirement and drawn down only after retirement. The rate of return to each person's savings is equal to that earned by all other plan participants.

Under pay-as-you-go, no long-term investment reserve is ever created. All contributions to the plan are immediately paid out to meet the claims of current beneficiaries. If cost imbalances occur, the plan manager adjusts either, or both, the contribution rate or the benefit rate to bring total contributions back into line with total benefits on a current basis. Thus, under pay-as-you-go a plan's reserve balance will always equal zero, whereas under full-reserve funding the balance remains positive until the last beneficiary dies.

General revenue financing differs from pay-as-you-go only insofar as the incidence of the "contribution" is shifted. Under pay-as-you-go, the contributory tax is levied only upon those persons who will ultimately become the plan's beneficiaries. Under general revenue financing, the claims of current beneficiaries are met via a tax on the community at large.

The Social Insurance Paradox

The attractiveness of pay-as-you-go as a strategy for financing social security benefits arises from what has come to be known as the "social insurance paradox."

Assume that, under conditions of constant population growth, all individuals are contributing to a full-reserve funded pension plan. It can be shown that the reserve fund of a mature system would then be increasing at a rate equal to that of the population. At all times, therefore, current contributions to the plan would exceed current benefits, if the rate of population growth is positive. Premiums therefore could be reduced below the level required to equalize the present values of contributions and benefits at the prevailing interest rate, with plan receipts still continuing to exceed benefits paid. Everyone would then be receiving a larger pension than he had paid for. Premiums, in fact, could be reduced until the level was reached at which no further growth in reserves occurs. Thus the paradox noted by Aaron (1966, p. 372):

> For the nation as a whole, the present expected value of the sum of real net lifetime receipts is greater when reserves are not accumulated than when they are, although the national income at each point in time is unaffected.

Note that the advantage that the intergenerational transfer paradigm confers on pay-as-you-go vis-à-vis actuarial funding is a doubly qualified one. First, the relative merit of pay-as-you-go is partly conditional on the rate of population growth. If the rate of population growth declines, the real rate of return ultimately received by contributors will fall below that received by the current cohort of retired workers, at which point considerations of interpersonal equity arise. Second, the optimality conditions are premised on the absence of a store of value. If the income transfers are permitted to substitute for real savings, they could reduce the accumulation of productive capital, and thus reduce the rate of growth in real income. The possibility of such an offset to social welfare is explicitly not permitted in Samuelson's (1958) model of interest rate determination in a pure consumer loan economy.

Slowing Population Growth and Intergenerational Transfers

A number of studies have attempted to assess the impact of slowing population growth on the intergenerational transfers that are possible under pay-as-you-go. A study by Rejda and Shepler (1973) illustrates the approach that is generally taken in the current literature.

The questions they ask are relatively straightforward. How large an average increase in real per capita income would be required between 1970 and 2050 to support a ZPG-level aged population with no increase in the real burden of the transfer on active workers?

Rejda and Shepler take as their benefit equation the following expression:

$$B(t) = \frac{P(t) \cdot r(t) \cdot (1-c)}{R(t)}, \qquad (2)$$

where t is a given calendar year and

$B(t)$ = Real per capita OASDI benefits for the aged
$P(t)$ = Real per capita personal income
$r(t)$ = Percentage of $P(t)$ spent on OASDI
c = Administrative costs of OASDI as a percentage of $B(t)$, assumed to be constant
$R(t)$ = Old-age dependency ratio.

If the real burden on active workers is to be left unchanged, $B(t)$ and $r(t)$ must remain constant, which will be true only if the rate of increase in real per capita income is equal to the rate of increase in the dependency ratio. Assuming an age at entry into the labor force of 20 years and a retirement age of 65 years, the stable old-age dependency ratio projected under the 1975 Advisory Council's ZPG assumptions[17] will be .283, as opposed to .182 in 1970. Thus, no long-term intergenerational transfer of real per capita income need occur if the annual rate of growth in real per capita income averages approximately .6% during the period 1970–2050.

However, as noted earlier, real benefits have increased over time; between 1950 and 1972, they grew at an annual rate of 3.52% (Turchi, 1975). Thus, real per capita income would have to increase at a rate of 4.12% annually to prevent an increase in the real burden of OASDI costs. In contrast, the annual rate of growth in real per capita income (1958 dollars) averaged only 2.05% between 1950 and 1970 (Bureau of Economic Analysis, 1973).

Hogan (1974, 1976) points out that the rise in the old-age dependency ratio should be accompanied by a reduction in the proportion of young people. As a result, it should be possible to reduce government expenditures on youth-related programs. He estimates that, based on 1972

---

[17]Rejda and Shepler's results have been revised here to reflect more recent data.

spending levels, such reductions could more than offset the increase in old-age assistance costs while leaving per child expenditures unchanged. Work by Michael (1973), Kelley (1976) and others, however, suggests that, to the extent that a large portion of youth-related expenditures consists of expenditures on human capital, government may elect to deepen its investment in children rather than reduce its per capita child costs, particularly if the returns to such investment are subject to economies of scale.

Clark (1976b) and Turchi (1975) both raise a more fundamental issue. If the rate of increase in average real benefits remains at or above the increase in average real wages, then the real burden of OASDI payments must necessarily grow as the old-age dependency ratio increases. Since the maintenance of fixed replacement ratios implies that average real benefits and wages will both grow at the same rate in the long run, slowing population growth would make increasing pressure on real per capita incomes practically unavoidable.

Social Security and Personal Saving

Using the consumer-loan–tax-transfer model of social security, it can thus be shown that slowing population growth undermines the insurance paradox as a rationale for pay-as-you-go. By forcing today's workers ultimately to accept an implicity lower rate of return on their contributions than that received by the beneficiaries who were supported by their taxes, slowing population growth could lead to an increasingly inequitable redistribution of income away from the young.

Because pay-as-you-go involves an income transfer from net savers to net dissavers, social security should depress aggregate saving, assuming no change in the average propensities of workers and the aged to consume. One would expect this dampening effect to increase as a result of an aging of the population. In addition, however, there is the question of whether the existence of social security alters the marginal propensities of the working population to save.

Pechman *et al.* (1967) note that old-age security is only one of several motives for personal saving. They speculate that, with one of life's hazards covered, people may choose to increase their savings to meet other saving goals. Studies by Cagan (1965) and Katona (1965) using cross-sectional consumer data suggest that pension plans might stimulate voluntary saving. In addition, Munnell (1974b) notes that if one adds total social security contributions to U.S. time series data on personal savings, one finds that the ratio of savings to disposable income has risen over time.

The contrasting position given by Friedman (1957) is that "the availability of assistance from the State would clearly tend to reduce the need for private reserves and so to reduce planned saving [p. 123]." Empirical support comes from cross-national evidence (Aaron, 1967) and U.S. time series data (Feldstein, 1974, 1976; Munnell, 1974a,b). Feldstein and Munnell adopt the approach of extending the Ando–Modigliani life cycle consumption model to the consideration of future social security benefits as perceived wealth, with the retirement age a function of retirement savings. They reach three main conclusions. First, enforced saving should encourage earlier retirement, thus encouraging higher total savings. Second, the availability of social security "savings" should reduce the need for savings in other forms. Third, because pay-as-you-go transfers social security savings immediately to the system's beneficiaries, no real capital accumulation occurs. Munnell finds that the earlier retirement effect of social security has largely offset the savings substitution effect; Feldstein disagrees to some extent, but both agree that there is strong evidence to support the finding that pay-as-you-go depresses real capital accumulation.

The latter, enforced savings view of pay-as-you-go leads to a finding (Feldstein, 1976) that it reduces social welfare by substituting "an asset with a very low implicit rate of return for real capital accumulation with a much higher social rate of return [p. 85]." Slowing population growth would only exacerbate this effect.

Alternative Financing Approaches

It seems evident, then, that slowing population growth could exert heavy pressure against the real income of the young, both by increasing the relative size of the tax transfer that pay-as-you-go entails and by reducing the rate of capital accumulation. Would alternative financing strategies fare any better?

General Revenue and Full-Reserve Funding Alternatives

Rejda (1970), Cohen and Friedman (1972), and Rejda and Shepler (1973) argue that the United States' existing social security system would be improved if benefits were financed out of general revenues. Obviously, general revenue financing would only make explicit the intergenerational transfer that now occurs under pay-as-you-go, and, to the extent that the replacement ratio remains unaltered, would not reduce the magnitude of the transfer induced by slowing population growth.

Instead, proponents of the general revenue financing strategy argue that a regressive payroll tax is an inefficient way to negotiate an income transfer. The countervailing argument is that the benefit schedule's progressivity offsets the regressivity of the payroll tax, that general revenue financing would not affect social security's adverse influence on personal savings and capital accumulation, and that social security's objectives extend beyond that of guaranteeing a minimum income to the elderly.

Buchanan (1968), Browning (1973), Campbell (1969), and Feldstein (1975) all advocate actuarial funding as an improvement upon pay-as-you-go. Feldstein argues for reserve funding as a manner in which to negate the savings loss resulting from pay-as-you-go. Buchanan, Browning, and Campbell call for bonding schemes in which each contributor would receive a bond yielding either the prevailing long-term interest rate or a rate of return equal to the rate of growth of the economy. Campbell, in particular, sees this approach as a way to equalize the implicit rates of return earned by successive cohorts; thus, the bonding approach also has the merit of improved equity.

However, at least three considerations vitiate the advantages of and distinctions among pay-as-you-go, actuarial funding, and general revenue financing.

The Blanketing-In Problem

First, there is the "blanketing-in" problem—the awarding of benefits to individuals whose past contributions are insufficient to finance the benefits that they can expect to receive (Wilson, 1973).

In the private sector, these underfinanced benefits arise from the practice of awarding "past service credits" to employees who are present when a pension plan is first implemented, rather than basing the size of their pensions strictly on the amounts that they contribute subsequent to the plan's implementation. In effect, each employee present at the beginning receives a fictitious fund endowment equal to the amount that the person would have accumulated had the plan been in effect when the worker was first employed. Benefits based upon past service credits must eventually be financed by borrowing, by reducing the implicit rate of return received by current contributors, or—if a plan is directly managed by the employer—out of current profits.

Similarly, those who were in the work force in 1937, when social security was first implemented, eventually received benefits as though they had been contributing to social security throughout their working lives. Furthermore, expansion of social security coverage and benefit increases since 1937 have generated additional underfinanced benefit claims. A strong case can be made that, although the system originally was conceived as a reserve funded system, OASDI gradually drifted into pay-as-you-go as the trust fund was drawn down to cover these underfinanced benefits.

Blanketing-in thus blurs the distinction between pay-as-you-go social insurance and private, reserve-funded pension plans. To the extent that universality of coverage and fixed replacement ratios are considered as indispensable elements of social security, the distinctions between pay-as-you-go and actuarial funding become a matter of the degree, rather than of the mere existence, of underfinancing. In the private sector it can be quite high ("Pension Reform—A 'Boon' that's Backfiring for Many," 1975; "When Pension Liabilities Dampen Profits," 1975).

In terms of its impact on social equity, blanketing-in must ultimately force a future generation to accept a lower implicit rate of return on their "contributions" to social security, be these in the form of general taxes, social security payroll taxes, or contributions to a reserve-funded pension system. How the income transfers to blanketed-in beneficiaries are financed simply reflects the incidence and timing of the reduction. Funded from general revenues, blanketed-in benefits must be covered either by higher general taxes or by deficit financing. General tax funding causes the current generation to bear the lower rate of return implicit in the combination of higher taxes with no change in the ultimate benefits it will receive. Deficit financing shifts the burden to later generations of workers; in this case, the intergenerational incidence of the reduction in the implicit rate of return will be determined by the rate of debt retirement and the financing and magnitude of interest payments on the debt (Bowen *et al.*, 1960; Browning, 1973). The deficit finance model also applies if underfinanced benefits are paid from accumulated reserves in the case of actuarial funding.

Social Security Financing and Aggregate Savings

The literature on the comparative macroeconomic merits of the three approaches is somewhat ambiguous in its findings. Clearly, the only major difference between general revenue financing and pay-as-you-go is in the incidence of the tax used to finance retirement benefits. Since advocates of the former approach would have the incidence of the tax shifted from the low- and middle-income workers who now bear the greater burden of the tax to those with higher incomes, general revenue funding should reduce the level of saving, ceteris paribus (assuming that marginal, as well as average, propensities to consume decline with income). How a move toward full-reserve funding would affect savings in the event of slowing population growth is an issue implicitly raised in the literature dealing with the effects of private pension funds on the macroeconomy. And, again, the implications are not clear. As Blackburn (1967) and Turchi (1975) both suggest, an attempt to resolve this issue inevitably draws one into a reconsideration of the stagnationist controversies of the 1930s. Following Turchi's lead, then, "without a holistic approach to the impact of demographic change on the economy it may be impossible to make a meaningful assessment of future prospects [p. 85]" regarding the relative macroeconomic merits of the three financing proposals.

The Case for Reform and the Objectives of Social Security

> On the afternoon of January 16, after the President had already notified Congress that on the following day he would present a special message on economic security, he sent for Miss Perkins. He said there must be some mistake in a table which appeared in the report since he had not understood that a large deficit to be met out of general revenues would develop in the old age insurance system beginning in 1965... When informed that the table was correct, ... [the President] directed that the committee proceed to develop, as soon as possible, a completely self-sustaining old age insurance system
>
> [Altmeyer, 1966, p. 29].

> [President Roosevelt acknowledged the regressive nature of the payroll taxes. However:] "We put the payroll contributions there," he said, "so as to give the contributors a legal, moral, and political right to collect their pensions and unemployment benefits. With those taxes in there, no damn politician can ever scrap my Social Security system
>
> [Leuchtenburg, 1963, p. 133].

We thus conclude this brief review of the financing issue on a pessimistic note. It appears that slowing population growth will set in motion an increasingly one-sided intergenerational income transfer that ultimately cannot be avoided, regardless of how benefits are financed. Although financing arrangements can be manipulated to alter the timing and incidence of adverse effects, ultimately policymakers will be confronted by a choice between a rising tax burden and reductions in benefit levels. By undermining the social security paradox, an aging population forecloses pay-as-you-go as a Pareto-optimal solution to this dilemma, yet alternative financing arrangements will fare no better. The case for reform will depend upon other criteria.

The economics literature on social security is almost uniformly critical of the system. It generally presents the picture of a major social institution that is inefficient in the pursuit of its own stated objectives, inequitable in its redistribution of social product, and potentially malignant in its impact upon economic growth. The existence of many of social security's reported ills is beyond dispute, yet evidence of inefficiency and inequity alone is insufficient to establish the need for reform unless it properly accounts for all of the system's objectives. Otherwise, critical findings only document the existence of policy trade-offs; they cannot be accepted as evidence of policy failure. In this regard, much of the literature on social security is far from satisfying in that analysts frequently stress only selected OASDI objectives, while ignoring others.

OASDI is an integrated approach toward servicing at least three potentially conflicting social needs:

1. Income adequacy—the maintenance of adequate levels of retirement incomes
2. Enforced saving—the need for compelling workers to make satisfactory provision for their retirement
3. Income assurance—the need to shield workers from the potentially adverse effects of economic uncertainty on their retirement decisions

All too frequently, specific proposals that aim at the attainment of greater equity or efficiency in meeting one of these objectives would undermine the ability of the system to serve its other goals.

Some Current Dilemmas

Proponents of general revenue financing, for example, while often showing how the system could be improved in its pursuit of income adequacy, typically ignore social security's enforced savings motive. The need for compulsory saving is based upon the proposition that individuals might choose to reduce their level of saving or retire earlier if benefits were not tied to contributions, thus unfairly increasing the tax burden on the less profligate. If this result is to be avoided, contributors must be required to perceive that at least a portion of their taxes constitutes a contribution toward their own retirement saving. Although a straight transfer tied to a negative income tax, as proposed by Friedman, Rejda, and others, might alleviate the perceived inefficiency of financing a progressive system of benefits with a regressive tax, it would probably also undermine the existing linkage between benefits and contributions. Moreover, if the tax explicitly contains a saving component, it is not clear that the "regressivity" of the tax retains its usual conceptual meaning; since contributors to the system are receiving a specific guarantee of future consumption in exchange for their taxes, it makes little more analytical sense to speak of the "regressivity" of the payroll tax than it does to refer to the "regressivity" of milk prices.

If the tax transfer model of social security fails to account for the need for enforced savings, exponents of the enforced savings–reserve funding approach typically downplay the income adequacy and income assurance objectives. We have seen that a fully funded system becomes analytically indistinct from pay-as-you-go if one permits the creation of underfinanced benefit obligations. Yet underfinancing can arise from at least two sources that are not routinely considered in the existing economics literature.

Blanketing-in reflects a social decision that benefits provided to those retirees who have not contributed to social security throughout their working years should meet the same standard of income adequacy as do benefits accorded to continuously covered workers. Unless blanketed-in workers (including those who were already retired when the system was first implemented) are forced to finance their own benefits, there will necessarily occur an unequal intergenerational transfer of income, accompanied by interpersonal variations in the implicit rate of return to contributions. Once it has been decided that such benefits will be financed by an intergenerational consumer loan rather than out of the blanketed-in beneficiaries' own pockets, all that remains to be determined is when that "loan" will be retired by a reduction in some future generation's lifetime income and whether the incidence of the "loan redemption" will fall on current consumption or current saving when it occurs.

Of course, blanketing-in need have only a passing effect on rates of return, the level of consumption, or the rate of capital accumulation. By initially setting the payroll tax rate to exceed the "actuarial" tax rate, it is possible eventually to eliminate this source of underfinancing once and for all. In fact, this seems to have been what was intended when the Social Security Act was first passed (Altmeyer, 1966). The system is then freed to realize all of the benefits that have been claimed for full-reserve funding—but only in the absence of economic uncertainty.

An Alternative Model

It is paradoxical that although social security was initially promoted as a social insurance program, the income assurance functions of the system receive short shrift in present-day commentary on OASDI. Indeed, today's orthodoxy seems to demand that almost every article on social security, if it does not open on a note of crisis, at least begin with a dismissal of the "insurance myth." Clearly, social security does not *function* as do insurance firms in the private sector. It is not as clear, however, that the system fails to serve important insurance *objectives*.

In order to understand OASDI's income assurance role, it is necessary to distinguish between insurable risks and genuine economic uncertainty. Insurable risk refers to those contingencies of which the aggregate volume of individually random events is known with reasonable certainty. Without fully reiterating the economic case for insurance, suffice it to say that the pay-as-you-go system of social security suboptimally serves standards of insurance equity that would be better served by a fully funded system. Consequently, the need to cover such risks cannot be cited as a rationale for the existing system.

Economic uncertainty, on the other hand, refers to those contingencies that are not genuinely random, or the aggregate volume of which is unknown. Many of these latter contingencies (e.g., lifetime unemployment patterns, age–income profiles, future prices) must be anticipated with some certainty and precision if the individual is to make adequate provision for retirement; "bad guesses," the costs of obtaining good prior information, and other prediction problems pose an ever-present threat to the efficiency of retirement saving, even if savers are not profligate or shortsighted. It is *these* "risks" that are cited as indicating a need for social insurance, and not the narrower class of insurable contingencies to which orthodox dismissals of the insurance analogy refer.

Private insurers will be quite averse to bearing these "risks," since there is no guarantee that their potential liabilities can be recovered out of the resources of the insured before the "risk pool" dies out. Government is, within limits, in a better position to cover such unplanned contingencies because it can spread the potential costs of such risks over the lifetime of an entire society. Although the eventual losses that might accrue to uncertainty cannot easily be anticipated, there is one direct measure of such costs—the extent to which retirement incomes fall short of some socially agreed upon level of adequacy. These and other considerations suggest a view of social insurance in which government, acting as an "insurer of last resort," retrospectively compensates retirement savers for unplanned savings losses arising from the presence of economic uncertainty. Thus, we are left with two alternative models of social insurance that permit somewhat different interpretations of social security's problems.

The orthodox model—Samuelson's (1958) Hobbes–Rousseau social contract—envisions the system as an attempt to compel an income transfer from the currently young to the currently old. The equity of the transfer depends upon whether society can continue to pay each currently young worker a stipend that, over the course of the person's retirement years, is greater than or equal to the opportunity cost of all income transferred during the working years. Since slowing population growth ends all possibility of equity in these terms,[18] continuation of pay-as-you-go cannot be justified. In effect, the justification for the system rests upon a "demographic wager" on the social insurance paradox, perhaps reinforced by an ethical consensus that the young *should* support the elderly. Reserve funding, on the other hand, represents a more risk-averse policy under which each person saves only for his own retirement; no possibility of an inequitable transfer can arise, but society gives up the opportunity of benefiting from the paradox.

Our alternative model of the system differs from this "orthodox" approach in at least four ways.

First, the nature and justification of the intergenerational transfer are more specific. Instead of representing a prospective wager on the social insurance paradox, the income transfers retrospectively compensate yesterday's savers for any net adverse uncertainty effects on the efficiency of their prior retirement savings decisions.

Second, the "insurer of last resort" model requires no specific concern with insurance equity. Today's savers derive current utility from the knowledge that their savings are guaranteed to net them an adequate retirement income. Since individuals are differentially subject to uncertain contingencies, the guarantee necessarily implies interpersonal variations in the rate of return to social security contributions.

Third, the degree of funding simply reflects past decisions as to whether the transfers required to redeem the guarantee were to be negotiated as offsets to current saving or as offsets to current consumption. In this view, the choice between a funded system and pay-as-you-go is not an either–or decision to be resolved on the basis of equity considerations. Rather, the "fundedness" of the system is determined passively on the basis of purely situational criteria, insofar as the inci-

---

[18]The indexing of benefits rules out any possibility that inequity can be overcome via economic growth.

dence of social security transfers on current savings or current consumption is made consistent with the prevailing needs of fiscal, monetary, and manpower policy in general.

Finally, one should not forget that the social security system was established toward the end of a depression that wiped out the savings of millions of workers. These workers are only now passing out of the system. It may very well be that today's pay-as-you-go system reflects the historical fact that the United States elected for the most part to reimburse the workers of the depression for their savings losses between 1929 and 1937 and before out of aggregate savings generated between 1937 and 1977.[19] If this was the case, then our model suggests that advocates of full-reserve funding who point to the consequences of pay-as-you-go for capital formation as signaling the need for reform, must, in effect, be asserting one or more of the following:

1. Past transfers to cover blanketed-in benefits should have been financed out of current consumption between 1937 and 1977.
2. Past benefit levels have been "too lavish" in some sense.
3. Today's situational conditions call for greater capital formation (thus we should reduce our own consumption to cover social security transfers).
4. For ethical reasons, we should no longer reduce the incomes of future generations by reducing today's savings to cover social security transfer.

These are different propositions, from a policy standpoint, than those that assert that the investment dampening effect of pay-as-you-go, or its intrinsic inequity in an era of slowing population growth, or its bias toward unwarranted benefit increases alone constitute a priori grounds for abandoning the system.

Conclusion

Our alternative model, we would argue, provides a more holistic framework for analysis than do more orthodox treatments of social security issues. By making the objectives of the system more explicit, the

---

[19]The case for this hypothesis is strengthened when one considers that social security was originally fully funded. Indeed, the payroll tax was originally set at levels above the actuarial tax rate. If F.D.R. had had his way, all blanketed-in benefits would eventually have been covered out of a levy on the preretirement consumption of those who were in the labor force between 1937 and 1985. This policy was effectively vetoed by Congress, which failed to authorize payroll tax hikes scheduled for the mid-1940s to the early 1950s (Altmeyer, 1966).

trade-offs of social insurance policy become more apparent. By viewing the "reserve fund" as merely a benchmark reflecting past decisions on the allocation of past resources between saving and consumption, it evades the underfinancing dilemmas encountered by the standard approach even as it admits the need for enforced savings.

It does not, however, change our basic conclusion that slowing population growth will make it more difficult to pursue retirement-related income maintenance policies. Nor does it preclude increasing intergenerational inequity, in the sense that the implicit rate of return, as formalized in the literature, will differ among individuals. We would, however, suggest that the orthodox conception of insurance inequity is irrelevant to the objectives of social insurance. It is difficult to see how a policy that jointly strives for income adequacy and income assurance could avoid unequal intergenerational transfers if "equity" retains its orthodox, insurance equity meaning. Yet both objectives are integral to the system. Therefore, we propose to accept the unequalness of intergenerational transfers as given and then erect a framework for evaluating the system based upon criteria that, it is hoped, are more useful from a policy standpoint.

Besides establishing that intergenerational income exchanges will become more unequal when a population ages, the analytical approaches taken in the existing social insurance literature may have little else to offer in the way of creative insights into the effects of demographic change on social security. As things now stand, one is left with the dilemma of choosing between equity and efficiency on the basis of criteria that are left unclear in existing analyses. It appears that concern for a large number of very limited issues—intergenerational equity, short-term efficiency, voting bias, etc.—has obscured the need to deal with the fundamental problem that social insurance attempts to address: that of assuring adequate retirement incomes in a humane, uncertain world. Particularly in this area of social policy, prescriptions that are based upon partial equilibrium solutions to small problems and that ignore basic objectives run a clear risk of long-term disaster. We need to do much better.

8

The Impact of Demographic Change on the Distribution of Earned Income and the AFDC Program: 1975-1985

RICHARD F. WERTHEIMER II and SHEILA R. ZEDLEWSKI

Introduction

The major purpose of this chapter is to forecast the future cost and caseload of the Aid to Families with Dependent Children (AFDC) program through the year 1985.[1] Nine alternative forecasts have been made—each conditional upon a unique combination of demographic and economic assumptions. The major findings of the research include the following:

[1] An expanded version of this chapter is available as an Urban Institute Paper on Income Security, 985-1 (December 1976), from The Urban Institute, 2100 M Street NW, Washington, D.C. 20037. The research reported herein was performed pursuant to a grant from the Department of Health, Education, and Welfare, Washington, D.C. The opinions and conclusions expressed herein are solely those of the authors and should not be construed as representing the opinions or policy of any agency of the United States Government. The interpretations and conclusions are those of the authors and should not be attributed to the Urban Institute, its trustees, or to any other organizations that support its research.

1. The growth in the AFDC caseload will be affected greatly by the birth rate, the marriage rate, and the divorce rate prevailing during the next 10 years.
2. If society moves toward greater family stability and AFDC benefits are increased only at the same rate as the cost of living, the AFDC caseload may not increase at all.
3. If society moves toward less family stability, the AFDC caseload may grow by more than 50% even if AFDC benefits increase only at the same rate as the cost of living.
4. The number of families headed by women is likely to grow under a wide range of demographic assumptions. Under most assumptions, by 1985 female-headed families will constitute a larger share of American families than they do today.
5. The number of families with low incomes is highly sensitive to the divorce rate. If high divorce rates prevail over the 1976–1985 decade, there will be 2.5 million more families with low incomes (under $4000 in 1958 dollars) in 1985 than if low divorce rates prevail over this decade.

The Urban Institute Dynamic Simulation of Income Model (DYNASIM) has been the major analytical tool for this set of forecasts. DYNASIM is a flexible vehicle for incorporating the major demographic and economic trends taking place at present and forecasting their implications for a representative sample of the U.S. population. Each element of DYNASIM is based upon how members of the U.S. population have been observed to behave. Censuses, current population surveys, and panel studies all have been used to derive the behavioral relationships that are joined together in DYNASIM.

The second section of this chapter describes some of the critical features of DYNASIM that impact on this set of simulations. The third section gives many of the specific assumptions of the nine simulations performed. The final section presents the detailed findings.

Critical Features of DYNASIM

In this section, we describe those features of DYNASIM that are critical to an understanding of the simulation experiments that were undertaken.[2] We shall discuss in turn the demographic operating characteris-

---

[2] A complete description of DYNASIM is given in Orcutt et al. (1976).

tics, the dynamics of family structure, and the government-transfers operating characteristics.

Demographic Operating Characteristics

BIRTH

Each simulation year, DYNASIM calculates a probability of giving birth for each female aged 14-49. First, it is determined whether a woman desires another child. Unmarried women are all assumed not to want a child. The probability that a married woman desires another child depends upon her current number of children. A random draw determines if she desires another child. If she does, her probability of giving birth depends upon her age. For women who do not desire a child, the probability of giving birth is reduced to account for reduced sexual activity and contraception. The reduction factor is a function of race and education in order to account for differences in contraceptive efficiency. Finally, the probability for all women can be raised proportionately by multiplicative parameters that can be used to "align" the total number of births to any predetermined total while leaving unchanged the distribution of births among various groups of women. A random draw determines if a birth takes place.

MARRIAGE

The probability of a person's getting married for the first time is a function of the person's age, race, sex, year of birth, the current simulation year, and the person's education, hours worked, wage rate, and transfer income. Persons who have been previously married have a calculated probability of remarriage based upon their age, sex, the current simulation year, current marital status (i.e., widowed or divorced), and the year of their most recent change in marital status. A random draw determines whether the person enters the marriage union process. Persons who have been selected for marriage are matched in the marriage union module. An algorithm matches men to women on the basis of their race, age, education, and region of residence.

DIVORCE

The probability of divorce is a function of the duration of the marriage, the year of the marriage, the current simulation year, the man's race, age, disability status, and unemployment status, the wife's earnings, and the family's region and the size of the city they live in. A random draw determines whether the couple is divorced.

The Dynamics of Family Structure

The simulation of demographic events outlined in the preceding paragraphs has important consequences for the grouping of persons into families. In DYNASIM persons are grouped into *nuclear* families. Nuclear families are either single individuals or married couples and their children. Whenever a simulated event occurs that would cause a nuclear family to grow into an extended family (such as the birth to a daughter of an illegitimate child), the extended family is immediately divided into its nuclear components. This difference in definition of family has important consequences for the *number* of families. A DYNASIM population will have more families in it than a Census population. However, in most applications of DYNASIM, the *number* of families is not as important as the *differences* in the number of families between one experiment and another. In general, we can expect that differences in divorce rates or marriage rates in DYNASIM will generate differences in the number of nuclear families that will be roughly equivalent to the differences in the number of families using the Census definition.[3]

CONSEQUENCE OF BIRTH

If a child is simulated to be born to a single woman living by herself, the child becomes a new member of what has become a two-person family. This is one way in which the number of female-headed families grows. If a child is born to a single woman living with her parents, she and the baby become a new two-person family—also a female-headed family. Because of this dynamic restructuring, the growth of female-headed families is linked to the birth rate. While a high birth rate does not increase the *ratio* of illegitimate to legitimate births, it does increase the number of illegitimate births and consequently the number of female-headed families.

---

[3]DYNASIM works on a nuclear-family basis because the dynamics of the restructuring of extended families are difficult to simulate. For example, aging persons would have to be matched selectively with families to simulate elderly parents moving back with their children. A similar process would have to be followed for adults moving in with siblings. Conversely, a wide variety of family "exits" also would have to be simulated. Simulating these changes is technically feasible but was felt to have a low payoff relative to its cost—particularly considering the fact that the Census definitions of family also do not capture extended families accurately.

CONSEQUENCES OF MARRIAGE

High marriage rates hold down the rate of formation of female-headed families since, the higher the proportion of women who are married, the smaller the proportion of illegitimate births. Conversely, high marriage rates increase the rate of elimination of female-headed families, since the heads of these families will be more likely to get married.

CONSEQUENCES OF DIVORCE

In the event of a simulated divorce, the husband becomes a single individual making up his own nuclear family, whereas the wife and the children (if any) become a female-headed family. One family has become two. Thus, divorce is an important factor in the growth of the total number of families as well as of the number of female-headed families. However, over time, one or both of the divorced spouses may remarry. Thus, there is a natural dampening effect upon the growth of female-headed families.

Government Transfers Operating Characteristics

The programs included in the transfers operating characteristics are: social security (SSA), pensions, supplemental security income (SSI), unemployment compensation, aid to families with dependent children (AFDC), and food stamps. The unemployment compensation, AFDC, and food stamps programs are assumed to be affected by changes in births, marriages, and divorces.[4] First of all, the caseload of the unemployment insurance program will increase or decrease depending on the extent of labor-force participation of females.[5] Because the unemployment rate is exogenous to the model, the number of persons experiencing unemployment is proportional to the size of the labor force. Thus, if more females are heads of families in one simulation than in another, they will tend to work more and to experience unemployment. If they are simulated to be covered under the unemployment insurance system, they may receive this transfer payment.

[4]The first three transfer programs mentioned—SSA, pensions, and SSI—have as their primary recipient group the aged. Changes in births, marriages, and divorces have little effect on their costs or caseloads in the 1975-1985 time frame of the simulation experiments because these demographic events are most likely to take place in a relatively young age group.

[5]Each person's wage rate, labor force participation, and unemployment status are computed in a labor market model, and these in turn determine the distribution of earnings among persons and families.

The AFDC transfer program is very sensitive to changes in fertility, divorce, or marriage rates. These rates determine the number of female-headed families in the population, and it is this group that the AFDC program was designed to serve. To be eligible for benefits under this program, dependent children must reside in the family, and the family's economic resources—earnings (less work expenses), asset income, and other transfer payments—must fall below the "standard of need" established in their state. Benefits are assigned to the family on the basis of this standard.

The number of families participating in the food stamp program is also sensitive to changes in the demographic sector of the model. This occurs primarily because families who receive AFDC transfer payments are automatically eligible to purchase food stamps.

Key Assumptions and Mechanics of the Simulations

Any forecast of the future is a product of the assumptions that the forecaster has made. When using DYNASIM to predict the future, the forecaster is for the most part assuming that the behavioral relationships embedded in the operating characteristics of the model remain unchanged over time. However, certain key assumptions are directly under the control of the forecaster. What these key assumptions are and how they are incorporated into the simulation process is the subject of this section.

Alignment: 1970–1974

There is no guarantee that when DYNASIM is run over an historic period that it will produce aggregate statistics that agree with aggregate statistics drawn from the Current Population Survey (CPS) or other sources of aggregate data. Inconsistencies can arise for a variety of reasons. They include:

1. Differences in the concept being measured
2. Errors in the initial DYNASIM survey population
3. Errors in the statistics to which DYNASIM is being compared
4. Errors in the DYNASIM operating characteristics

The first type of inconsistency can be dealt with by adjusting the historical statistics to make them consistent conceptually with the statistics produced by DYNASIM, or vice versa.[6] We have chosen to deal with the latter three sources of inconsistency through a process called "alignment." If the aggregate statistic is the total number of events (such as births or marriages) that have occurred during the year, we can align the expected number of events produced by DYNASIM to the historical number of events by raising or lowering the probability of the events occurring by the percentage discrepancy between the unaligned DYNASIM total expected events and the historical number of events. For example, if the total number of births produced by DYNASIM in 1973 were 10% below the actual number of births in that year, we could raise the probability of giving birth by 10% for all women of childbearing age. In this way the relative distribution of probabilities remains unchanged.

In this fashion we have aligned many important outputs of DYNASIM over the period 1970–1974. They include births, marriages, divorces, deaths, labor-force participation, wage rates, unemployment, and the caseloads of several government transfer programs.[7]

Base Run: 1975–1985

In addition to being a calibration device for the period 1970–1974, the alignment process provides guidance for adjusting the model's parameters for simulations into the future. For example, if DYNASIM's predictions for a particular national aggregate are consistently 10% too low, it is a reasonable supposition that they will continue to be 10% too low in the future. Similarly, if there is a trend in the adjustment factor needed to align DYNASIM, it is a reasonable guess that the trend will persist for at least sometime into the future. This subsection draws upon the alignment process as well as other insights to present the assumptions made in constructing the base run of the model from 1975 to 1985.

DEMOGRAPHIC ASSUMPTIONS

The demographic assumptions can best be summarized by examining the number of key demographic events predicted by DYNASIM over the

---

[6]For example, the standard labor force statistic for a particular year is the number of persons in the labor force during the survey week of each month averaged across the 12 months of the year. This can be adjusted to the DYNASIM concept of labor force—the number of persons participating in the labor force at some time during the year.

[7]In the case of government transfer programs, the DYNASIM-produced caseload can be aligned to the administrative statistics by adjusting the rate of participation in the program. Comparisons of aligned DYNASIM statistics and historical statistics for 1970–1974 are shown in the longer version of this chapter (see Footnote 1).

period 1975–1985. These are shown in Table 8.1. The probabilities of birth were adjusted to align the predicted number of births to the Series II projections of the U.S. Bureau of the Census (1975b). These projections assume a completed fertility rate of 2.1 children per woman for each cohort of women. The adjustments made to align the total number of deaths over the first 5 years of the 1970s were small. Since we are confident that the probability of mortality produced by DYNASIM is accurate, we concluded that the discrepancy between the predicted number of deaths and the actual number of deaths was due to idiosyncrasies of the sample. Thus, we allowed the annual percentage adjustments in death probabilities to decline linearly from their 1974 values to zero by 1985.

Marriage and divorce rates have been exhibiting strong trends in opposite directions over recent years. The probability of marriage has been falling, and the probability of divorce has been rising.[8] DYNASIM, for the most part, does not pick up these trends. Therefore, over the early 1970s, there was a need to adjust the probability of marriage downward year by year and to adjust the probability of divorce upward in order to align DYNASIM predictions to aggregate statistics. Rather than assuming that these trends would persist at the same rate through 1985, we dampened the trend in the adjustment factors down to zero in the first few years of simulation and projected no trend during the last 8 years, 1977–1985. Table 8.1 shows that the number of marriages rises year by year in the base run (unlike the period 1970–1974, when the number was relatively constant). The number of divorces stays relatively constant until the 1980s, when it begins to rise, reflecting the larger number of marriages at risk.

LABOR ASSUMPTIONS

The labor assumptions were derived mainly from forecasts of The Urban Institute's Group Transition Model.[9] The model provides monthly estimates of the employment, unemployment, and nonparticipation levels of 16 age–race–sex groups from behavioral relationships that predict monthly transition rates between the three labor force categories. Each transition rate is a function of aggregate job opportunities, trends, and seasonal factors. This model's forecasts were used instead of DYNASIM's own forecasts in order to pick up the different cyclical fluctuations in vulnerability to unemployment experienced by

[8]See U.S. Bureau of the Census (1974, pp. 1–5).
[9]See Smith (1974).

TABLE 8.1.
Births, Deaths, Marriages, and Divorces in the Base Run,
1975–1985 (numbers in 1000s)

Year	Births	Deaths	Marriages	Divorces
1975	3200	1940	2130	1290
1976	3400	1970	2120	1340
1977	3570	2030	2200	1330
1978	3720	2080	2290	1320
1979	3860	2120	2370	1320
1980	3980	2130	2420	1330
1981	4060	2180	2510	1310
1982	4100	2230	2550	1340
1983	4140	2270	2590	1360
1984	4200	2340	2580	1390
1985	4170	2390	2500	1420

the four major race–sex groups. The underlying assumption on unemployment was that the rate would gradually drop to 5% by 1980.[10]

Only modest adjustments were necessary during the 1970–1973 period to align DYNASIM's prediction of average earnings by race and sex to historical statistics. We have used the 1973 percentage adjustment for all years afterward. This means we have assumed that sex and race differentials (holding age, education, location, marital status, and the like constant) would remain unchanged through 1985.

TRANSFER ASSUMPTIONS

The categorical rules defining the various transfer programs (i.e., eligibility requirements other than monetary ones) were assumed to remain as specified in 1974 for the future period 1975–1985. The projections of income eligibility standards and benefit amounts vary depending on the particular transfer program. By law, the monetary parameters of the social security program and the supplemental security program are indexed to the Consumer Price Index (CPI) starting in 1975. The inflation rate is projected to fall from 8% in 1975 to about 4% in 1978 and then to remain there for the remainder of the period.[11]

The monetary parameters of the other transfer programs simulated

[10]This was the Administration assumption as of May, 1975. See U.S. Office of Management and Budget (1975).

[11]This was the assumption issued by the Office of Management and Budget (1975) in May, 1975.

are subject to annual administrative policy decisions of the federal government and the individual states. Some modest growth in the program parameters was assumed. The parameters of the unemployment compensation program were projected to have a modest and gradual increase of 15% over the 11-year simulation period. The dollar value of pension payments was assumed to keep pace with the CPI, reflecting the general trend in this diverse group of transfer payments. For the base run and the eight demographic experiments, the monetary parameters of the AFDC program were increased by the CPI in each year. Although an indexing scheme is not in effect for this program, it was felt that this type of increase would most likely parallel the future progress of the program.

Participation trends for the various transfer programs in the period 1970-1974 were used to project program participation for future years. For three of the programs—SSA, AFDC, and pensions—the participation rate necessary to match the historical caseload in 1974 was 1.0. This rate was assumed constant through 1985. For the remaining three programs—SSI, unemployment compensation, and food stamps—the participation trend over the period 1970-1974 was projected to continue and then level off in the 1980s.

Specification of the Nine Experiments

The base run can be thought of as a "middle-of-the-road" set of assumptions representing a best guess of the correct parameter values. However, the volatility of fertility rates, marriage rates, and divorce rates means that the point estimates made in the base run have a wide margin of error and should not be considered an unconditional forecast.

To estimate the sensitivity of the AFDC cost and caseload to alternative assumptions about the rates of fertility, marriage, and divorce, six additional experimental simulations were performed. For each of the three factors under consideration, we have selected a high, medium, and low rate. In the case of fertility we have chosen the Census Series I projection of births as our high rate, the Series II projection as our medium rate, and the Series III projection as our low rate. The Series I projection assumes a completed fertility rate of 2.7 children per woman, while the Series III projection assumes a 1.7 completed fertility rate. In the case of marriage and divorce, the high rate was set at 30% above the base run rate for each year, and the low rate was set 30% below the base run rate. This was done by raising or lowering each individual predicted marriage or divorce probability by 30% for each year of the simulation.

These alternative assumptions generated alternative levels of births, marriages, and divorces in different simulations.

In order to be able to calculate a rough elasticity of AFDC cost and caseload with respect to each of the three factors, six of the experiments use the middle rate assumption for two of the three factors and either the high or low rate for the third. This yields three points to calculate the elasticity of the AFDC caseload with respect to, say, the fertility rate— the calculation being performed with marriage and divorce rates held at their middle level.

Two additional simulations were designed to represent low family stability (high fertility rate, low marriage rate, and high divorce rate) and high family stability (low fertility rate, high marriage rate, and low divorce rate). The experimental design is summarized in Table 8.2.

Simulation Procedure

Each of the nine simulations took place over the same 11-year period (1975–1985), using the same initial population (the 1970 Census 1–10,000 sample aged through 1974). To the extent possible, the Monte Carlo variance from one run to another was eliminated by using the same stream of random numbers for each person for each drawing.[12]

Surveys of the simulated population were taken in 1974, 1980, and 1985. This permits calculation of detailed distributions for these 3 years only. In addition, a limited amount of time series information was generated annually. This includes the caseload and cost of the AFDC program, as well as the information normally used for alignment purposes.

Results

The different sets of demographic assumptions in the nine simulations lead to dramatically different groupings of persons among families. The differences in family structure, in turn, are responsible for substantial differences in the cost and caseload of AFDC, the distribution of income, and the supply of family labor.

Since changes in family structure are largely responsible for the remaining changes, they will be discussed first. Second, changes in the distribution of income will be analyzed with particular attention to the adequacy of family income. Finally, we shall explore the sensitivity of AFDC to the alternative assumptions.

[12]See Orcutt et al. (1976, Chapter 1) for an explanation of how this is done.

TABLE 8.2.
Specification of the Base Run and the Eight Experiments

Experiment number	Fertility rate	Marriage rate	Divorce rate
Base run	M[a]	M	M
1 (low stability)	H	L	H
2 (high stability)	L	H	L
3	M	M	H
4	M	M	L
5	M	H	M
6	M	L	M
7	H	M	M
8	L	M	M

[a]The letters M, H, and L stand for the medium, high, and low variants, respectively, of the fertility, marriage, and divorce rates.

Changes in Family Structure

FAMILY SIZE

One of the most striking differences that the alternative fertility, marriage, and divorce rate assumptions make is in the 11-year change in the number of families, persons, and average family size. Table 8.3 shows the percentage change in each of these three measures. In all nine simulations the percentage increase in the number of families is greater than the percentage increase in the number of persons. Consequently, family size falls in all nine cases. This universal tendency for family size to fall is probably caused by the increasing share of the elderly in the U.S. population, combined with relatively low birth rates. Relatively high divorce rates and relatively low marriage rates (compared with the 1950s and 1960s) also are playing a role in reducing family size.

That birth rates, marriage rates, and divorce rates are an important factor can be seen by comparing the high and low experiments for each of these three factors. The decline in family size is nearly twice as large in the low birth rate simulation as in the high birth rate simulation. The decline is more than twice as large in the high divorce rate experiment than in the low divorce rate experiment. The difference is smaller but still in the expected direction in the high and low marriage rate experiments.

This finding, that the number of families will grow more rapidly than the population, can have important economic implications. One of the

TABLE 8.3.
Percentage Change in the Number of Families, Number of Persons, and Average Family Size, 1974-1985

		Simulation experiment							
	Base run	High birth rate	Low birth rate	High divorce rate	Low divorce rate	High marriage rate	Low marriage rate	Low family stability	High family stability
Percentage change in number of families	20.5	20.9	20.0	22.9	17.8	20.5	20.0	23.6	17.6
Percentage change in number of persons	11.0	14.4	8.0	10.2	11.9	13.1	8.9	11.0	10.5
Percentage change in average family size	−7.9	−5.4	−10.0	−10.3	−5.0	−6.1	−9.3	−10.2	−6.0

most important is that growth in real *per capita* national income will not get translated into equivalent increases in average *family* income. For example, in the base run, real per capita national income grew by 28% over the 11-year simulation, whereas real family income grew by only 18%.

FEMALE-HEADED FAMILIES

Not only does the number of families grow more rapidly than the population, but the number of families headed by females grows more rapidly than the total number of families in all but one of the simulations.[13] In the base run, female-headed families grew from roughly 7% to about 9% of all families over the 11-year period. This amounted to more than a 50% increase in the number of families headed by women. Even in the high stability experiment, where the fraction of families headed by women remained constant, the number of female-headed families grew by 12% over the 11-year period simulated.

The high and low fertility simulations showed noticeable but not large differences in the fraction of families headed by women. High fertility rates stimulate the growth of female-headed families because, in DYNASIM, an illegitimate birth triggers the formation of a new family if the mother was living with her parents. This result may be somewhat overstated, because in practice some new mothers of illegitimate babies elect to continue living with their parents—at least temporarily.

The alternative marriage rate simulations had a somewhat larger effect. By 1985, 10% of all families were headed by females in the low marriage rate experiment, compared with 9% in the base run and 8% in the high marriage rate experiment. Higher marriage rates retard the growth of female-headed families both because they reduce the number of illegitimate births (since young women get married earlier) and because they increase the probability of remarriage for divorced and widowed women.

The alternative divorce rate simulations had a slightly larger effect than the alternative marriage rate simulations. In particular, the low divorce rate experiment raised the fraction of female-headed families less than the high marriage rate experiments. This asymmetry probably results from the fact that lower divorce rates are directly affecting mostly families with children, whereas higher marriage rates are to a large extent affecting single women, most of whom do not have children. In other words, divorce automatically creates a female-headed family

---

[13]The exception is the high family stability experiment where the growth rates are about the same.

whenever the family has children present. A marriage directly eliminates a female-headed family only if the woman already has children. It also may prevent formation of a female-headed family by preventing an illegitimate first child.

As expected, the high and low family stability experiments had the largest effects upon formation and retention of female-headed families. In the low stability experiment nearly 12% of all families were female-headed by 1985. On the other hand, in the high stability experiment the fraction of families headed by females actually declined to slightly under 6% by 1985.

In summary, the formation of female-headed families was highly sensitive to the alternative demographic assumptions. As we shall see, this has important implications for the distribution of income among families and for the cost and caseload of the AFDC program.

MARITAL STATUS

The alternative demographic assumptions have important direct impacts upon the distribution of the population by marital status. Table 8.4 shows the distribution of persons in 1985 among three marital status categories in the high and low family stability simulations. The relatively high marriage and low divorce probabilities in the high stability experiment resulted in a far higher number of married persons and a far lower number of single and divorced persons than the low stability experiment. This is particularly true in the 18–54 age groups, where changes in marital status are most likely. One of the most striking statistics is the number of single persons in the 25–34 age category. The alternative

TABLE 8.4.
Persons by Age and Marital Status in 1985 in the High and Low Stability Simulations (numbers in 1000s)

Marital status and simulation type		Age					
		Less than 18	18–24	25–34	35–54	55–64	65 and over
Married	Low	222	7,188	19,001	31,834	13,996	14,692
	High	465	11,746	29,448	39,776	15,462	15,949
Divorced	Low	0	802	8,143	15,484	4,256	2,800
	High	0	729	4,552	8,407	2,808	2,240
Single	Low	14,386	19,032	12,992	4,119	1,436	1,796
	High	14,142	14,492	6,127	3,442	1,436	1,774

marriage rate assumptions led to twice as many single persons in the low stability simulation as in the high stability simulation. There are also nearly twice as many divorced persons in the low stability simulation and, consequently, over 10 million fewer married persons.

Changes in the Distribution of Income

It is becoming increasingly well documented that marital status changes and decisions to have children can have profound impacts on an individual's economic well-being.[14] In general, marriage or remarriage has a beneficial effect on economic status and divorce has a serious negative effect. This occurs primarily because a married couple has the opportunity to pool all of its economic resources, including labor supply, earnings, and other assets. In contrast, a single-person family can rely on only one person's resources for support. The decision to have children, of course, has a heavy impact on per capita family income. It also may be the determinant as to whether one devotes time to childbearing or to labor force activities.

These types of demographic changes usually affect women more than men, because a female's earning capacity is typically lower than a man's, and she is generally the primary custodian of any dependent children. Duncan and Morgan (1975, p. 5) have shown that the threat of poverty was four times greater for women who were divorced or widowed and did not remarry than it was for women who either remarried or remained married during the 7 years of the survey.

The results of the simulations are useful in outlining the magnitude of these effects for the forecast period 1975–1985. The data shown here are for 1985, thus highlighting the cumulative effects of different rates of birth or marital status changes during the period. The changes in the distribution of income of all families in the population which occurred in the eight simulations is shown in Table 8.5. One can see the number of families falling into each income interval, where income includes the earnings, transfers, and asset income of all members of the family. The table shows the high and low rate results for each demographic factor, along with the high and low family stability simulations. The simulation that produces greater family stability is shown on the left and compared against its companion simulation on the right in which there is greater family instability, and the last column shows the percentage difference between the two. The birth rate experiments do not produce changes in

[14]Duncan and Morgan (1975).

TABLE 8.5.
The Effect of Demographic Change on the Distribution of Total Family Income in 1985

Income[a]	Low	High	Percentage change
Birth experiments			
0–4000	28,074[b]	27,978	−0.3
4001–8000	20,375	20,638	+1.3
8001–12000	15,621	15,601	−0.1
12001–16000	11,332	11,533	+1.8
>16000	23,976	24,230	+2.3
Total	99,478	101,076	+1.6
Marriage experiments			
0–4000	28,264	27,832	+1.6
4001–8000	21,071	20,173	+4.5
8001–12000	14,956	15,927	−6.1
12001–16000	11,269	12,041	−6.4
>16000	23,870	23,754	+0.5
Total	99,430	99,727	−0.3
Divorce experiments			
0–4000	26,648	29,088	+9.2
4001–8000	19,761	21,673	+9.7
8001–12000	15,431	15,980	+3.6
12001–16000	11,459	11,702	+2.1
>16000	24,218	23,311	−3.7
Total	97,519	101,754	+4.3
Family stability experiments			
0–4000	30,016	26,247	+14.4
4001–8000	21,800	19,678	+10.8
8001–12000	15,483	15,600	−0.8
12001–16000	11,385	11,713	−2.8
>16000	23,479	24,145	−2.8
Total	102,166	97,382	+4.9

[a] In 1958 dollars.
[b] In thousands of families.

family stability per se, except in the sense that more families exist in the simulation with the higher birth rate because of illegitimacy.

With the exception of the birth rate experiments, family instability leads to an increase in the number of families falling into the lower end of the income distribution. In addition, there is a slight tendency toward a decrease in the number of families falling into the highest end of the distribution, particularly those with an income greater than $20,000. In the low marriage rate experiment, 1.3 million more families fall into income brackets below $8000 than in the high marriage rate experiment, despite the fact that the total number of families in the population is less by a small percentage.

The divorce rate experiments show an even greater change in the distribution of income. In the high divorce rate case there are 4.3% more families, representing an increase of 4.2 million families. Despite this increase, the number of families with incomes in excess of $16,000 is less by nearly 1 million. However, the number of families falling into the lowest two income intervals is up by 4.4 million, slightly over 9%. A comparison of the high and low family stability experiments shows similar but even more striking results, because both the marriage and the divorce instability effects are combined. In fact, in the low stability simulation, the number of families who are poor or near poor (incomes of $4000 or below) has increased by 3.77 million. Inconclusive changes in the distribution of income occurred in the birth rate experiments, because the effects on family stability are small, as mentioned earlier.

In sum, the results of these simulations show that the degree of family stability has a strong influence on the economic status of families. Higher rates of instability mean downward shifts in the distribution of income, creating more low-income families and fewer high-income families.

An analysis of income distribution by family type reveals that female-headed families with children are expected to fare worst of all. By 1985 over half of these families are projected to have incomes of $4000 or less (measured in 1958 dollars), and their mean income of approximately $6000 is less than half that of husband–wife families. Moreover, the low family stability simulation implies 83% more female-headed families with children by 1985 than does the high stability simulation. Nearly half of this increase falls in the $4000 and below income category. Although the low stability simulation suggests a slight improvement in the income position of female-headed families with children over the high stability case—this occurs primarily because in the DYNASIM model women who are economically independent tend to get divorced more frequently than those who are not—it still projects that 51% of these families will be poor or near poor by 1985.

Aid to Families with Dependent Children

BASE RUN PROJECTION

DYNASIM's projection of the AFDC caseload is affected by all sectors of the model. It embodies the complex set of assumptions relating to the demography of the population, the labor force sector projections, and macroeconomic factors. Of course, the assumptions of the AFDC model itself are important. Essentially, the base run simulation incorporated conservative assumptions—the rates of birth, marriage, and divorce were assumed to remain constant after 1977, female labor force participation was expected to grow, and unemployment and inflation were predicted to dampen to rates of 5 and 4%, respectively, from relatively high 1974 levels. The economic parameters of the AFDC model were projected to grow at the rate of inflation.

Column three of Table 8.6 shows the caseload growth of the AFDC program from 1975 to 1985 under these assumptions. In the first 5 years of the simulation, the AFDC caseload exhibits no clear growth trend. This reflects the trends exhibited in marriages, divorces, and births during this period. Marriages show a continuous but slow rise, while divorces remain constant over the latter half of the 1970s. Both of these trends have a dampening effect on the AFDC caseload because the rate at which female-headed families are formed is slowed. Births show a slow but steady rise during the same period. This tends to increase the AFDC caseload because marriages at risk for divorce are more likely to have children, and female-headed families are formed via illegitimate births. Thus, these demographic trends somewhat offset each other.

Beginning in 1980, however, the AFDC caseload shows a positive growth trend, increasing by approximately 15% by 1985. This growth reflects the increasing trend in the number of divorces that take place in this period. Because marriages have been increasing over the entire 11-year period, more divorces begin to occur simply because there are

TABLE 8.6.
AFDC Program Projections: Base Run Assumptions

Year	Caseload (1000s of families)	Average payment (1958 dollars)	Caseload growth (1974 = 100)
1975	3371	1480	103.7
1976	3336	1505	102.6
1977	3227	1453	99.3
1978	3505	1390	107.8
1979	3323	1427	102.2
1980	3454	1412	106.3
1981	3555	1420	109.4
1982	3593	1415	110.6
1983	3830	1455	117.8
1984	3837	1495	118.1
1985	3727	1470	114.7

more married couples in the population at risk for divorce. The AFDC caseload growth also is increased by a continuation of the steady increase in births mentioned earlier.

Columns one and two of Table 8.6 show the absolute AFDC caseload measured in number of families and the average AFDC payment, respectively. It should be noted that DYNASIM slightly underestimates the AFDC caseload for the historical period. For example, in 1974 the caseload was about 2% below the actual reported one, although a 100% participation rate was used. The reason for the underestimation is that DYNASIM is an annual model and cannot capture part-year participants. It is expected that the size of this bias should remain constant over the 1975-1985 forecast period. The average AFDC payment projection, shown in 1958 dollars, remains relatively constant. This reflects the fact that benefit formulas were projected to keep pace with inflation. In addition, it shows that there is no trend toward an increasing or decreasing size of a typical AFDC family during this period.

EFFECT OF THE DEMOGRAPHIC EXPERIMENTS

The AFDC transfer program is sensitive to changes in the demography. Any demographic event that leads to the formation of a female-headed family with dependent children also leads to a family at risk for AFDC. A birth to a single woman always creates a female-headed family. A birth to a married woman may contribute indirectly to an increase in this type of family, because of the possibility of a subsequent marriage dissolution. The marriage rate also affects the rate at which AFDC families are formed. Low marriage rates decrease the rate at which the current stock of female-headed families is dissipated via remarriage and increase the number of single women at risk for illegitimate births. These effects in turn can increase the AFDC caseload or at least prevent some families from moving off the rolls. On the other hand, low marriage rates mean that fewer children are born and, in the longer run, that fewer divorces can occur. These effects decrease the number of female-headed families in the population. Thus, low marriage rates have opposing effects on the AFDC caseload, but we expect the first effect discussed to be the stronger of the two. High marriage rates work in the opposite direction. The rate at which divorces occur in the population has the clearest, most direct effect on the AFDC caseload. When a divorce occurs and children are present, the female-headed split-off family is at risk for AFDC.

Table 8.7 shows the percentage change from the base run in the AFDC caseload in the eight demographic experiments for each simulation year. Columns one and two show the percentage change in the caseload

TABLE 8.7.
Percentage Change in AFDC Caseload from the Base Run

Year	Simulation experiment					
	Low births	High births	Low marriages	High marriages	Low divorces	High divorces
1975	−.9	.9	1.5	−2.1	−3.4	4.0
1976	−1.3	2.2	5.0	−3.1	−4.0	7.2
1977	−1.6	3.9	7.4	−.6	−4.5	9.7
1978	−3.9	5.0	3.9	−5.1	−4.8	7.4
1979	−3.5	6.6	4.7	−6.9	−8.2	11.0
1980	−5.2	4.3	8.5	−4.5	−8.2	9.4
1981	−6.5	6.2	8.3	−7.1	−10.0	11.2
1982	−9.7	9.0	9.1	−5.0	−12.3	10.2
1983	−7.9	9.9	8.3	−8.8	−13.4	6.1
1984	−9.3	8.8	6.1	−7.7	−13.5	8.3
1985	−6.2	11.1	11.1	−3.4	−8.5	12.2
Average percentage change	−5.1	6.2	6.7	−4.9	−8.3	8.8
Average caseload change (in 1000s)	−184.09	222.36	238.73	−177.45	−296.45	309.73

under the low birth assumption (a completed fertility rate of 1.7 children per woman) and the high birth assumption (a completed fertility rate of 2.7 children per woman). Columns three and four show the percentage change in the caseload under a low marriage rate (30% below the base run) and a high marriage rate (30% above the base run). Similarly, columns five and six show the percentage change in the caseload under a low divorce rate assumption (30% below the base run) and a high rate assumption (30% above the base run).

One can observe a substantial change in the caseload under each of these assumptions as compared to the base run caseload. On the average, over the 11-year period, the low birth assumption decreased the caseload by 5% in each year, whereas the high birth assumption increased the caseload by about 6%. The average percentage change in the AFDC caseload in the marriage experiments was about the same as that in the birth experiments. As expected, changes in the divorce rate show the greatest effect on the AFDC caseload. In the low divorce experiment, the annual caseload decreased by 8.3% on the average. This change represents a decrease in the caseload of about 300,000 families per year. A similar effect, but in the opposite direction, is shown for the high divorce experiment.

There is an apparent acceleration in the change in the AFDC caseload over the 11-year period, particularly in the marriage and divorce experiments. For example, under the low marriage assumption the AFDC caseload change moved from 1.5% in 1975 to 11.1% in 1985. This effect is caused by the fact that, ceteris paribus, a family tends to stay on the welfare rolls from one year to the next. Thus, if the number of families receiving AFDC is increased in one year, some of these families will also receive AFDC in subsequent years. A decrease in the caseload also tends to show a cumulative effect because of a dampening of this growth trend.

Table 8.8 shows the elasticity of the AFDC caseload with respect to each of the demographic changes. These elasticities were computed as the percentage change in the number of families receiving AFDC divided by the percentage change in the particular demographic event. This table shows a more equal effect of births, marriages, and divorces on the AFDC caseload than does Table 8.7.

The data disclose that the average elasticity of the AFDC caseload with

TABLE 8.8.
AFDC Caseload Elasticities[a]

	Simulation experiment					
Year	High births	Low births	High marriages	Low marriages	High divorces	Low divorces
1975	.046	.080	−.070	−.056	.132	.113
1976	.122	.082	−.124	−.184	.254	.137
1977	.217	.096	−.027	−.287	.362	.160
1978	.318	.250	−.264	−.158	.287	.174
1979	.429	.198	−.383	−.200	.440	.307
1980	.279	.371	−.265	−.390	.376	.323
1981	.371	.451	−.452	−.382	.459	.394
1982	.479	.678	−.345	−.438	.434	.492
1983	.384	.594	−.611	−.405	.257	.549
1984	.442	.554	−.490	−.313	.409	.536
1985	.529	.425	−.227	−.569	.595	.339
Average (1975–1985)	.329	.344	−.296	−.311	.364	.320

[a]The calculation of elasticities for each demographic variable—births, marriages, or divorces—holds the other two variables at their middle levels.

respect to each of the demographic factors is around .3. That is, for each 10% change in births, marriages, or divorces, the number of families receiving AFDC changes by approximately 3% in the appropriate direction.

EXTREME FAMILY STABILITY EXPERIMENTS

The AFDC caseload was also studied in the high family stability and the low family stability simulations. Since these experiments compound the effects displayed in Table 8.7, they lead to the most dramatic changes in the AFDC caseload, as shown in Table 8.9. By 1985, the AFDC caseload is 23% or 865,000 families lower under high family stability assumptions than in the base run. On the other hand, the AFDC caseload is 1.26 million families, or 34% higher by 1985 under the low family stability assumptions than in the base run.

The tendency for the AFDC caseload to grow in the low stability case is somewhat larger than the tendency for it to decrease under high stability. Three factors that are supported by recent data and built into DYNASIM contribute to this tendency. First, the receipt of welfare decreases a woman's first marriage probability. Therefore, a female with an illegitimate child who receives AFDC is less likely to marry than one who does not receive AFDC. Second, the receipt of transfer payments in one year has a depressing effect on the labor-force participation probability in the next year, making it less likely that a family will attain self-support. Third, the AFDC program itself makes it more difficult to get on the rolls than to stay on. In order to receive AFDC initially a family must pass the full standard test that counts all of the head's earnings in the needs test. However, once a payment is received, the first $360 and ⅓ of the remainder of the head's earnings are excluded from the qualifying test. Thus, the family's earnings may increase substantially before they exceed the maximum allowable amount.

Table 8.9 also shows the percentage difference in the AFDC caseload between the low stability and the high stability experiments. We see a 74% increase in the caseload in 1985 in the low family stability conditions over the high family stability conditions. Figure 8.1 plots the actual AFDC caseloads for the high stability, base, and low stability simulations from 1974 through 1985. The high stability simulation shows a declining trend in the AFDC caseload to a level of about 2.9 million families in 1985. This is significantly below even the actual caseload of about 3.3 million families in 1974. The low family stability simulation shows an increasing trend in the AFDC caseload for the entire period. By 1985, about 5 million families are projected as receiving AFDC as compared to 3.7 million in the base run.

SOME REGRESSION RESULTS

An additional way to summarize the effect of births, marriages, and divorces on the AFDC caseload is to examine their significance via regression analysis. Such analysis is, of course, *descriptive* of the DYNASIM predictions rather than being a *predictive* model itself. Since DYNASIM forecasts are used for both the explanatory and dependent variables, and since the great majority of human behavior was "held constant" in the various experimental runs, a regression of this sort is only possible once the DYNASIM forecasts have already been made. Thus, it should be considered a form of a shorthand for the relationship in DYNASIM between the AFDC caseload and the factors which were allowed to vary.

Four time series—the total number of AFDC families, births, marriages, and divorces—for the period 1975–1985 from each of the nine simulations were pooled to form a data base of 99 observations. The following simple model was estimated:

$$Y_t = B_0 + B_1 Y_{t-1} + B_2 X_{1t} + B_3 X_{2t} + B_4 X_{3t} + U_t$$

where Y_t equals the AFDC caseload in period t, X_{1t} through X_{3t} equal the level of births, marriages, and divorces, respectively, in period t, and U_t

TABLE 8.9.
Impact of High and Low Family Stability on the AFDC Caseload

Year	Change from base run to high stability		Change from base run to low stability		Change from high stability to low stability	
	Number of families (1000s)	Percentage	Number of families (1000s)	Percentage	Number of families (1000s)	Percentage
1975	−217	−6.4	218	6.5	435	13.8
1976	−353	−10.6	468	14.0	821	27.5
1977	−395	−12.2	583	18.1	978	34.5
1978	−605	−17.3	604	17.2	1209	41.7
1979	−648	−19.5	721	21.7	1369	51.2
1980	−670	−19.4	806	23.3	1476	53.0
1981	−807	−22.7	954	26.8	1761	64.1
1982	−914	−25.4	1050	29.2	1964	73.3
1983	−1020	−26.6	842	22.0	1862	66.3
1984	−970	−25.3	1086	28.3	2056	71.7
1985	−865	−23.2	1257	33.7	2122	74.1
Average (1975–1985)	−678.5	−19.0	780.8	21.9	1459.4	51.9

The Distribution of Earned Income and the AFDC Program: 1975–1985　　221

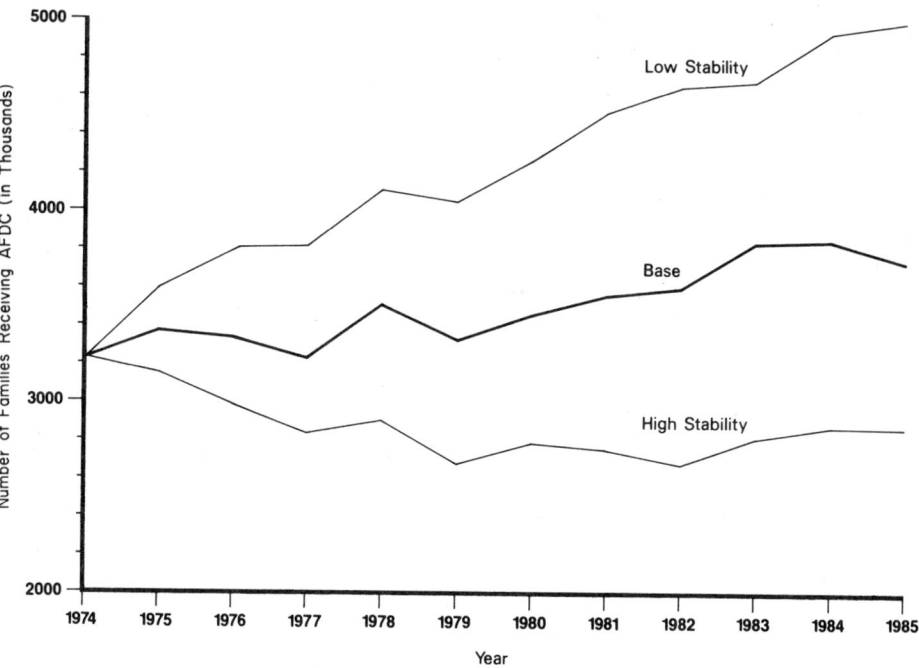

Figure 8.1. The number of families receiving AFDC in three simulations (1974–1985).

is a random error term. This model states that, given these aggregate data, a significant factor in predicting the AFDC caseload in year t is the caseload in year $t-1$. This reflects the fact that, as discussed earlier, there exists substantial inertia in the welfare rolls. Generally, a family moves off the rolls in one of three ways.[15] First, the children in the family may reach the age at which the family no longer qualifies for AFDC. Second, the head of the family may reach a level of earnings that disqualifies the family. Third, the head of the family may remarry. The first phenomenon is a slow and ongoing one, but in any one year affects only a small percentage of the AFDC families. The likelihood that the second phenomenon will occur in any one year is also low, as discussed previously. The third phenomenon, remarriage, is the most likely of the three to occur and is measured by the marriage variable in the equation.

The three demographic variables are expected to have fairly immediate effects on the caseload. Some proportion of the marriages will result in the removal of AFDC families from the program, and some

[15]This discussion ignores the fact that some AFDC families qualify because of the father's unemployment or disability.

TABLE 8.10.
AFDC Caseload Regression

Explanatory variable	Regression coefficient[a]	t-statistic	$\bar{R}^2$	Standard error
$AFDC_{t-1}$	.9432	27.126	.93	130.0
Births	.0903	2.611		
Marriages	−.1570	3.211		
Divorces	.2003	2.378		

[a] All coefficients significant at the .01 level.

proportion of the divorces will result in an increase in the number of AFDC families. This is because these events precede the determination of eligibility for AFDC in the simulation. Similarly, some proportion of the births will be illegitimate and result in an increase in the number of families that receive AFDC in the same simulation year. Additionally, since the birth module precedes the divorce module, an immediate effect may be seen in the increase of the number of families with children at risk for divorce.

The regression equation results are shown in Table 8.10. All three demographic factors have significant (at the .01 level) effects on the AFDC caseload. In addition, the coefficients are in the expected direction. Marriages tend to reduce the caseload, whereas births and divorces tend to raise it. Ninety-three percent of the variation in the AFDC caseload was explained by the equation, but the lagged AFDC caseload variable explained the largest share of this.[16]

In summary, this section uses three measures—simple percentage changes, elasticities, and regression analysis—to show the sensitivity of the AFDC caseload to changes in birth rates, marriage rates, and divorce

---

[16] Since this regression equation incorporates a lagged dependent variable, the coefficients are biased in small samples but asymptotically consistent. That is, as the sample size approaches infinity, the bias disappears. The degree of autocorrelation in the error terms was estimated to see if correction procedures were needed. The first-order autocorrelation coefficient (γ) was computed by averaging over the nine experiments as follows:

$$\gamma = \frac{n}{n-1} \frac{\sum_{k=1}^{K} \sum_{t=2}^{n} U_{kt} U_{kt-1}}{\sum_{k=1}^{K} \sum_{t=1}^{n} U_{kt}^2}$$

The value of γ, .36, was evaluated as being small enough to rule out any correction procedures. This formula follows Johnston (1972, pp. 304–310).

rates. All three measures show that the caseload is highly sensitive to these factors, because together they are the primary determinants of the rate of formation or dissolution of female-headed families with dependent children, the group that is the primary recipient of AFDC transfer payments.

9

Emerging Public Concerns over U.S. Population Movements in an Era of Slowing Growth

PETER A. MORRISON[1]

Introduction

It is time to honor a prophet in his own country: Dr. John S. Billings. In an article entitled "The Diminished Birth-Rate in the United States" he called attention to "the deliberate and voluntary avoidance or prevention of childbearing on the part of a steadily increasing number of married people, who not only prefer to have few children, but who know how to obtain their wish." He ventured the following interpretation of this trend:

> Young women are gradually being imbued with the idea that marriage and motherhood are not to be their chief objects in life, or the sole methods of obtaining subsistence; ... that housekeeping is a sort of domestic slavery, and that it is best to remain unmarried until someone offers who has the means to gratify their educated tastes. ... If this view of the case is correct, the birth-rate will not only continue low in the United States compared with former years, but it will probably become lower.

[1]This chapter draws on research supported by a grant from the Economic Development Administration, U.S. Department of Commerce. Views expressed here are the author's own and are not necessarily shared by Rand or its research sponsors.

225

Dr. Billings, a physician who also served as chief librarian of the New York Public Library, set forth these views in the June 1893 issue of *Forum*, now *Current History*. (See *Population and Development Review* Vol. 2, no. 2, June 1976, pp. 281–282, for source of reference). His remarkable prophecy eventually proved correct (although he could not anticipate a few not so minor intervening changes, most notably the post-World War II baby boom). Its simple logic has proven basically sound, and in large measure for precisely the reasons he cited.

Judging from current fertility expectations and the experience of young cohorts up till now, a transition to stability, or zero population growth (ZPG), appears to be under way. This objective has long been championed by a sizable segment of Americans who regard population growth as one of the most worrisome threats to cultural and even human survival. It is now evident, however, that even approaching ZPG will not eliminate the impact of rapid growth in some places (e.g., Houston or Fort Lauderdale), and that certain other places (e.g., New York State) are destined to feel the effects of population decline well before the rest.

When population growth slows it does not slow uniformly everywhere and for every age group. This has profound implications for how the nation will experience the prolonged transition to stability. Nationally measured population shifts are abstractions far removed from the palpable experience of population change in specific regions and localities. Those experiences are proving diverse and sometimes painful. Inevitably, public opinion is aroused when people with strong bonds to any geographic area find their economic and political interests sharply modified.

My objective in this chapter is to explore some of these new concerns and how they are tied to the population's spatial redistribution. Analytically, one can approach this task either by building up from the bottom or by working down from the top. The first approach starts with an absence of babies and asks how and where that absence will make itself felt. Some answers are obvious (empty maternity wards and declining school enrollments); others are easily inferred (higher per capita family income, changes in the types of housing demanded). Second-order effects, of course, are more difficult to gauge. The contrasting "top down" approach is fundamentally different. Starting with ongoing demographic and migratory changes as the context, it asks how these changes will make themselves felt, and with what repercussions, in an era of slowing growth. This is the approach I shall use here.

Migration is a largely autonomous process and, at least in the United States, has always been an indication of opportunity-seeking. But as it rearranges population in space to answer the changing needs of the national economy, migration also restructures the political interests of a region. Its effects are not so evident when they are diluted by strong population growth, as in the 1950s and early 1960s. Then, growth and its demands monopolized political concerns, and places that did not grow were just as concerned with it as those that did.

But now, the declining birth rate has withdrawn the protective mantle of natural increase, and "shrinking pains" have become commonplace in many parts of the nation. Migration's selectivity—of individuals but especially of places—has become more clearly recognizable. We can now more clearly perceive that migratory gains in the Sunbelt-South occur at least partly at the expense of the Northern Industrial Tier states. This new "zero sum" framework, in part demographically engendered, has given rise to new regional alliances: the Coalition of Northeast Governors, the Northeast-Midwest Economic Advancement Coalition, the Southern Growth Policies Board. Although these groups have, in general, refrained from casting migratory and economic issues in the extreme terms of "regional conflict" and "sectionalism," the associated publicity has aroused sentiment in that direction (Breckenfeld, 1977; Jusenius and Ledebur, 1977). In the course of only a decade, recognition has grown that migration determines which areas of the nation grow and which do not. Accordingly, this demographic factor has taken on political and economic import.

Several features of current demographic and migratory change are shaping the issues that emerge and the form they are taking:

1. *The population's more gradual increase is being offset by its fragmentation into a larger number of separate households.* The proportion of adults who choose to live with relatives has fallen for several reasons. More young people are leaving home at an early age, fewer elderly persons are moving in with grown children, and fewer families of all ages are doubling up.
2. *Trends in migration at regional and local scales have changed significantly in the 1970s.* The effects of the national slowdown in growth have been intensified in, for example, the metropolitan sector and much of the Northeast and nullified in the nonmetropolitan sector and much of the South.
3. *Concern with undocumented aliens has intensified.* Alien Mexican workers are thought to compete with or displace disadvantaged native Americans (especially Blacks and Chicanos) and to take more in the form of social welfare services than they contribute in taxes.

The Contrasting Growth Trends in Population and Households

U.S. population growth has slowed considerably, but the growth in the number of households has not. The average annual rate of increase in households rose from 1.8% during 1955–1965 to 2.2% during 1970–1977. As Figure 9.1 shows, the dissimilarity in population and household growth trajectories is projected to persist in the foreseeable future (through the 1980s).

The current and impending surge of household formations is attributable largely to the massive cohorts of young adults born during the postwar baby boom, who are now passing through the prime household-forming ages (roughly speaking, 20–30). Other concurrent trends lend further impetus to this surge:

1. The tendency for unmarried young adults (whose ranks are increasing) to set up transitional, independent living arrangements after leaving their parental homes
2. The increase in the number of "survivor" households (mostly elderly widows) who choose to occupy separate living quarters after their children have formed their own families (see Morrison, 1977a).

Household changes over the last three decades furnish ample evidence that affluence encourages separate living arrangements, with young adults departing from the parental home at an earlier age and elderly persons living apart from their adult children. But budget constraints can foster new social inventions, as cohabitation and communal living in the inflationary 1970s have demonstrated. For at least two reasons, such adaptations are bound to be easier in the future than they were in the past: First, the younger age groups, having been exposed to a broad range of possible living arrangements, can be expected to retain a degree of flexibility in living arrangements throughout their lives; and, second, the rising incidence of marital dissolution will increase the "population at risk" for new kinds of arrangements.

The dissimilarity in the growth trajectories of population and households blurs the growth-slowing effects of lower fertility, for "population" can be said to be contracting or expanding, depending on whether people or households is the unit. That is why in many cities where the population is declining—South Bend, Indiana, for example—public institutions must nevertheless meet the needs of an expanding "population" of households.

Over the next decade, the sheer number of households will increase

Emerging Public Concerns over U.S. Population Movements

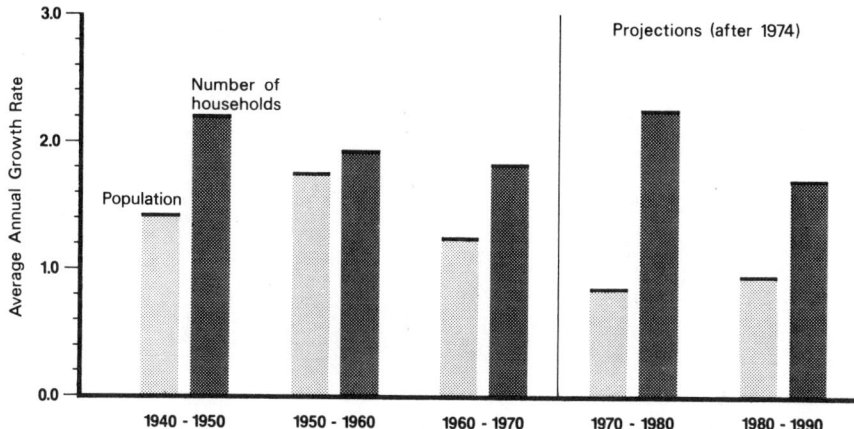

Figure 9.1. Annual growth rates in population and number of households, 1940–1970, and projections to 1990. Population series II (U.S. Bureau of the Census, 1975b) and household series B (U.S. Bureau of the Census, 1975c) are used.

substantially faster than the population, owing to the baby boom's compression effect. The calculus of future household formation, however, may change for several reasons (Frieden and Solomon, 1977):

1. Since large families will become far less common, individuals who in the past might have formed separate households will feel less compelled to do so in the future.
2. Growth in real per capita income, which spurred formation of separate households during most of the 1960s, is unlikely to continue as strong.
3. There may be growing mismatches between housing supply and demand, creating incentives to consolidate. The supply of large houses will become more abundant (because of fewer large families), but middle-sized houses will grow scarce (because of more small families and low housing production).

These and other considerations complicate our view of the future, and it is by no means clear what their net effect will be. Frieden and Solomon (1977) foresee a slight decline in the incidence of households in the population through 1985, a departure from the previous 15-year trend; because their assumptions are not yet fully documented, however, it is difficult to judge their plausibility. Census Bureau projections (which by way of contrast rely on extrapolations of the 1960–1974 trend) envision a continued rise in the proportion of adults who form separate households (U.S. Bureau of the Census, 1975c).

Whatever the case may be, living arrangements are sure to constitute an important mediating factor between slowed population growth and how it is experienced. Future residential energy, for example, can be expected to differ according to alternative rates of future household formation.[2]

New Migration Trends

Population change in any given locale is, by definition, the net effect of births, deaths, and the difference between arriving and departing migrants. Together, the recent sharp drop in fertility and changing migration patterns have made for surprising shifts in regional and local fortunes. Some former "boomtown" metropolitan areas—for example, Huntsville, Alabama and Melbourne-Titusville-Cocoa, Florida—have abruptly changed course. During the 1960s, both these areas experienced rapid inmigration associated with the flourishing defense and aerospace industry; since 1970, each has registered net outmigration, and population growth has virtually halted.[3] Conversely, the metropolitan area with the severest rate of outmigration during the 1960s—the Brownsville-Harlingen-San Benito, Texas SMSA—shifted from population decline (−.7% annually) during the 1960s to rapid growth (+3.6% annually) since 1970, despite the low birth rate.

Net migration trends surprise us because they seem to lie beyond our forecasting capabilities, particularly at the local scale. There are two reasons for this. First, the changing spatial distribution of economic opportunity, to which net migration flows respond, lies largely beyond our predictive reach. National development is twisted around accidents that achieve visible expression in specific places. The effects of the aero-

---

[2]How future residential energy use might differ according to alternative rates of future household formation is suggested by the results of a study by Hirst (1976). The study contrasts two boundary projections made by the Bureau of the Census: Series A (assuming a high future household formation rate) and Series C (assuming a low rate). These two necessarily arbitrary assumptions provide a useful contrast for purposes of assessing future energy use. A simulation of the two alternatives suggests that for the Series C pattern of household formation, residential energy use nationally in the year 2000 would be 7% less, and cumulative energy use between 1975 and 2000 would be 5% less. (Calculations based on Hirst, 1976, Table 1.)

[3]Metropolitan Huntsville's 3.9% average annual rate of population increase between 1960–1970 slumped to .2% between 1970–1975 (despite redefinition after 1970 to include rapidly increasing Marshall County). For Brevard County (subsequently the Melbourne-Titusville-Cocoa SMSA), the corresponding shift was from 7.2 to .2%.

space boom in Texas and California were foreseeable, but what about the effects of rising energy prices in Appalachia and the Northern Great Plains? Second, net migration figures offset inmigrants against outmigrants, showing only the resulting number following what amounts to a large exchange of individuals. Slight changes in rates of arrival or departure may abruptly alter or even reverse the net migration figure.

Although migration trends may be difficult to forecast, the public concerns they will engender can be foreseen. Today as never before, migration is serving as a catalyst for larger political issues, quick to mature in a period of economic depression and uncertain energy supply. As the American predilection to migrate fosters rearrangement of population in space in answer to the changing needs of the national economy, it also restructures regional political interests.

Several major shifts in migration that have appeared in the 1970s are shaping the particular manifestations of the population slowdown around the nation. For convenience I shall group these under three headings, regional (where reference is to Census regions and divisions, and states), sectoral (comparing metropolitan and nonmetropolitan areas), and local (with the focus on individual metropolitan areas).

Regional Migration Shifts

The 1970s have seen major shifts in migration among regions, shifts that at once signal and reinforce their changing economic fortunes. These shifts have sharply redirected population change at the regional scale (see Figure 9.2). The South's 5.1 million population increase in the first 5 years of this decade represents a sharp departure from the experience of other recent 5-year periods. The Northeast, in contrast, has entered an era of virtual population stasis, and the North Central region's population increase has slowed considerably.

The Northeast affords an excellent illustration of how a shift in net migration, in conjunction with a lower birth rate, can combine to halt population growth in a region and thus determine where the harbingers of national decline will first appear. As seen in Table 9.1, natural increase has diminished everywhere, but more so in the Northeast than in other regions since 1960. The Northeast's population gained 2.3 million through natural increase between 1960 and 1965, but only 1.0 million between 1970 and 1975. Net migration has gone down from nominal gains of several hundred thousand in preceding 5-year periods to a sizable loss of 700,000 between 1970 and 1975. This loss has intensified since 1972 and has affected the three Middle Atlantic states (New York,

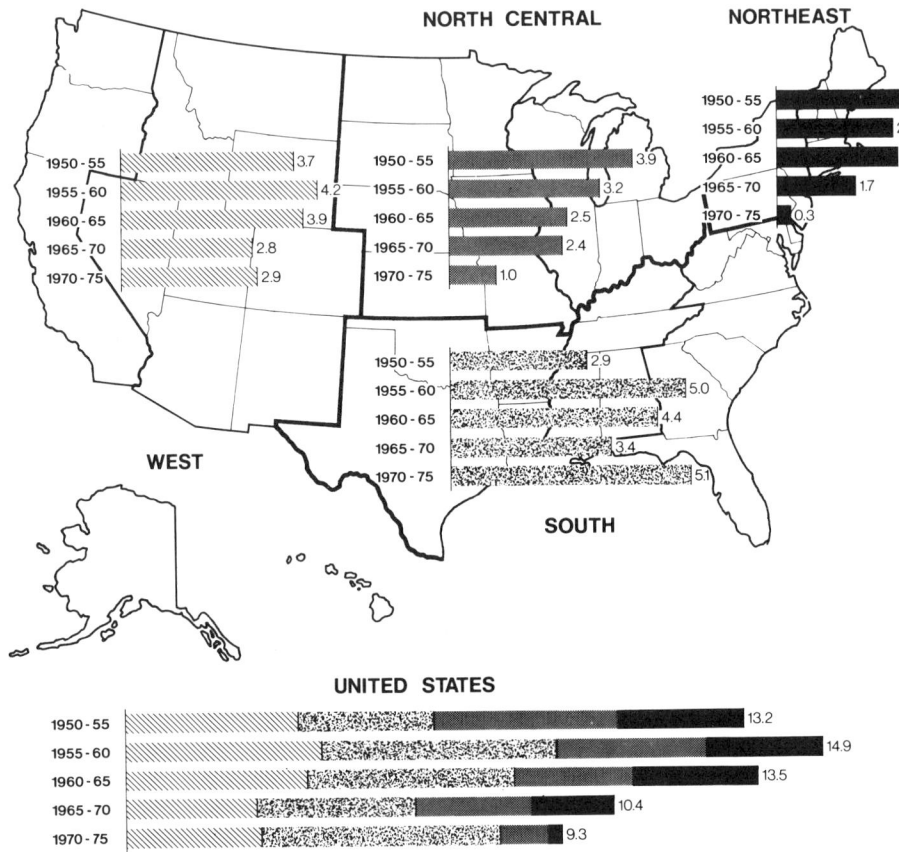

Figure 9.2. Population change for 5-year periods by region: 1950 to 1975. Redrawn from U.S. Bureau of the Census, 1976a.

New Jersey, and Pennsylvania) worse than those in New England (which comprise the remainder of the Northeast).[4]

The five East North Central states (which surround the Great Lakes) provide an interesting contrast. They have experienced migratory losses comparable in severity to those of the Middle Atlantic states, especially since 1972; however, somewhat higher rates of natural increase in the former have staved off a halt in population growth there.

[4]Between 1970 and 1976, for example, 851,000 more persons migrated away from these three states than migrated to them, resulting in a 2.3% loss of the Middle Atlantic states' 1970 population. In conjunction with comparatively low natural increase, this loss has virtually halted population growth.

TABLE 9.1
Population Change by Component for Each Region: 5-Year Periods, 1950-1975[a] (in millions. Periods begin July 1.)

	Natural increase					Net migration			
	United States	Region				United States	Region		
Period		Northeast	North Central	South	West		Northeast	North Central	South	West
1950-1955	12.1	2.3	3.5	4.5	1.9	1.0	.4	.4	-1.6	1.9
1955-1960	13.2	2.6	3.9	4.7	2.2	1.7	.0	-.7	.3	2.0
1960-1965	12.0	2.3	3.3	4.2	2.2	1.5	.3	-.8	.3	1.7
1965-1970	8.7	1.6	2.3	3.0	1.7	1.7	.1	.1	.4	1.1
1970-1975	6.8	1.0	1.8	2.5	1.5	2.5	-.7	-.8	2.6	1.4

[a]U.S. Bureau of the Census, 1976a.

The sharply increased streams of migrants out of some of the nation's colder regions have been gravitating south and west, especially into the South Atlantic and Mountain states. A massive influx of migrants into Florida has added 22% to its population between 1970 and 1976. More important, though, migratory growth appears to be diffusing throughout the South and West in this decade. Prior to 1970, the large numbers of inmigrants into Florida had offset what was in fact a migratory loss for the rest of the South (Table 9.2). Since 1970, Florida's ballooning net inmigration has been matched by an equally large inmigration to the rest of the region. This migration into the other Southern states is noteworthy, since it foreshadows a future wave of growth throughout the region.

The nation's other fast-growing region, the West, shows a comparable diffusion of migratory growth. California's migratory experience no longer dominates the West's regional migration growth as it did prior to 1965 (Table 9.2). Between 1970 and 1975, the other 12 states in the West gained 1.0 million through net inmigration (more than twice California's share), compared with only .2 million (less than one-seventh of California's share) between 1960 and 1965.

Overall, these regional trends are departures from the past, and low natural increase in no small part contributes to their manifestation at the local level. The course these migration trends will follow in the future is difficult to forecast, however, because the coincidence with an economic depression makes this an atypical period. Moreover, as noted earlier, net migration is a statistical fiction that masks the underlying dynamics of change. Migrants continue to move in considerable numbers *into* areas of net *out*flow and, conversely, *out of* areas with net *in*flow. For example, between 1973 and 1974 an estimated 359,000 workers migrated from the Northern Industrial Tier to the Sunbelt-South, but fully 267,000 migrated in the opposite direction (Jusenius and Ledebur, 1976, Table 2).[5] In all likelihood both regions have benefited from this exchange of workers, but it is the departing "net migrant" whose absence is felt when federal funds (e.g., revenue sharing) are allocated by population-based formulas. Being the net beneficiary of 92,000 workers makes the Sunbelt-South visible as a winner, and the Northern Industrial Tier a loser.

[5]Data refer to social-security-covered workers (about 9/10 of wage and salary workers nationally). The "Northern Industrial Tier" is composed of the East North Central and Middle Atlantic divisions plus the states of Connecticut, Massachusetts, and Rhode Island. The "Sunbelt-South" is composed of the West South Central, East South Central, and South Atlantic census divisions, excluding Maryland, Delaware, and the District of Columbia.

TABLE 9.2
Net Migration for Selected Areas: 5-Year Periods, 1950–1975[a]

Period	California	Rest of West	Florida	Rest of South
In millions				
1950–1955	1.6	.3	.7	−2.3
1955–1960	1.7	.4	.9	−.6
1960–1965	1.5	.2	.6	−.4
1965–1970	.5	.6	.7	−.3
1970–1975	.4	1.0	1.4	1.2
As percentage of beginning population				
1950–1955	14.7	3.0	24.8	−5.3
1955–1960	12.3	4.4	24.9	−1.3
1960–1965	9.7	1.8	12.8	−.8
1965–1970	2.7	4.1	11.7	−.5
1970–1975	2.1	6.7	19.9	2.1

[a] U.S. Bureau of the Census (1976a).

Shifts between Metropolitan and Nonmetropolitan Sectors

Migration is intensifying or nullifying the national fertility decline for sectors as well as for regions. The metropolitan sector is composed of all counties that are part of a Standard Metropolitan Statistical Area (SMSA); the nonmetropolitan sector, of all other counties. The distinction between the two sectors can be refined in various ways—for example, counties in the metropolitan sector can be classified by the population size of the SMSA they belong to, and those in the nonmetropolitan sector by the percentage of their work force that commutes to a job in a nearby SMSA.

As is now widely known, more Americans are moving away from the metropolitan sector than are moving to it, reversing a long-established urbanization trend (see Morrison, 1976b; Tucker, 1976). Each year between 1970 and 1975, for every 100 people who moved to the metropolitan sector, 131 moved out.[6] For the most recent period measured (1975

---

[6] This comparison is restricted to internal migration and excludes net immigration from abroad, which contributes newcomers to both metropolitan and nonmetropolitan sectors. For that reason, the metropolitan sector (like the nation as a whole) registers a slight net inmigration in the 1970s.

to 1977), this reversal continues.[7] As a result, nearly two-thirds of all nonmetropolitan counties are gaining migrants, compared with only one-quarter in the 1960s.

The underlying demographic structure of these shifts is suggested by the data shown in Table 9.3, which compares the direction of population change in the decade of the 1960s with that for 1970–1975. Notice in particular the reversal of net migration for the counties with little commuting and those that are entirely rural and not adjacent to an SMSA. Clearly, the migration reversal cannot be explained away semantically as just more metropolitan sprawl or "spillover," for it is affecting distinctly remote nonmetropolitan areas as well as those adjacent to metropolitan centers. For now, at least, nonmetropolitan areas have become more attractive, both to their residents and to outsiders, whereas metropolitan areas have become less so.[8]

If the nonmetropolitan sector has become known in the 1970s for the revival of population growth, the metropolitan sector has become notorious for population loss (see Alonso, 1977). Where only one of the nation's 25 largest Standard Metropolitan Statistical Areas (Pittsburgh) lost population during the 1960s, fully 9 were declining as of 1975: New York, Los-Angeles–Long Beach, Philadelphia, St. Louis, Pittsburgh, Newark, Cleveland, Seattle–Everett, and Cincinnati.

Approximately one-sixth of the nation's 259 metropolitan areas are losing population, and one-third of metropolitan residents live in areas of population decline. As with major regions, migration is what determines *where* the manifestations of slowdown in overall population growth first appear.

Population Decline in Individual Metropolitan Areas

The onset of population decline in the 1970s has caught most of the residents of affected SMSAs unaware, largely because during the 1960s the effects on metropolitan growth of two distinct demographic trends

[7]Nonmetropolitan areas have continued gaining migrants after the economic depression earlier in the decade. Between 1975 and 1977, migrants to the metropolitan sector were outnumbered by those moving out by a ratio of six to five (U.S. Bureau of the Census, *Current Population Reports*, Series P-20, No. 320, February 1978).

[8]Whether this reversal will be a temporary or a long-term phenomenon, though, is unclear, for the shift coincided with and may be due in part to the severe economic recession of the past several years. If so, a resumption of metropolitan growth would be expected with improvement in the economy. (Although the latter has occurred, the former has not.)

TABLE 9.3
Components of Population Change for Groups of Metropolitan and Nonmetropolitan Counties: 1960-1970 and 1970-1975[a]

Population category	Provisional 1975 population (1000s)	Annual population change rate		Annual natural increase rate		Annual net migration rate[b]	
		1960-1970	1970-1975	1960-1970	1970-1975	1960-1970	1970-1975
United States total	213,051	1.3	.9	1.1	.7	.2	.2
Metropolitan							
Total, all SMSAs[c]	156,098	1.6	.8	1.1	.7	.5	.1
>1.0 million	94,537	1.6	.5	1.1	.6	.6	-.2
.5-1.0 million	23,782	1.5	1.0	1.2	.8	.4	.3
.25-.5 million	19,554	1.4	1.3	1.2	.8	.2	.5
<.25 million	18,225	1.4	1.5	1.2	.8	.2	.7
Nonmetropolitan							
Total, all nonmetropolitan counties	56,954	.4	1.2	.9	.6	-.5	.6
In counties from which							
≥20% commute to SMSAs	4,407	.9	1.8	.8	.5	.1	1.3
10-19% commute to SMSAs	10,011	.7	1.3	.8	.5	-.1	.8
3-9% commute to SMSAs	14,338	.5	1.2	.9	.6	-.4	.6
<3% commute to SMSAs	28,197	.2	1.1	1.0	.6	-.8	.5
Entirely rural counties[d] not adjacent to an SMSA	4,661	-.4	1.3	.8	.4	-1.2	.9

[a] Unpublished preliminary statistics furnished by Richard L. Forstall, Population Division, U.S. Bureau of the Census and Calvin L. Beale, Economic Research Service, U.S. Department of Agriculture.
[b] Includes net immigration from abroad, which contributes newcomers to the United States as a whole and to the metropolitan sector, thereby producing positive net migration rates for both.
[c] Population inside Standard Metropolitan Statistical Areas (SMSAs) or, where defined, Standard Consolidated Statistical Areas (SCSAs). In New England, New England County Metropolitan Areas (NECMAs) are used.
[d] "Entirely rural" means the counties contain no town of 2500 or more inhabitants.

cancelled each other out. In 1973 William Alonso called attention to the fact that people have been leaving SMSAs for some time. During the 1960s about 40% of all metropolitan areas recorded net outmigration (compared with 44% for 1970-1975). At the same time, however, the birth rate was high and this net outflow was more than offset by natural increase; nearly all SMSAs continued to register population gains even though people were leaving. When birth rates dropped in the 1970s, natural increase was no longer sufficient to offset net outmigration, and the previously unnoticed trend became apparent in many places where population statistics revealed an abrupt halt in growth.

The lower rate of natural increase in the 1970s has slowed growth everywhere, but where there is actual population decline it cannot be attributed to low natural increase alone. In fact, outmigration appears to have been the decisive factor in bringing about local ZPG. As Table 9.4 shows, SMSAs that have registered population declines since 1970 share another feature: In all but a few cases the direction of net migration has shifted toward outmigration. That is, SMSAs that had net inmigration now have net outmigration; those with no change through migration in the 1960s are now net losers; and those that were net losers are now losing even faster.

To elucidate this point, I have assembled data (shown in Figures 9.3-9.5) on the demographic components of change since 1970 for a selection of metropolitan areas. The SMSAs shown (each of which is numbered as shown beneath each figure) have been sampled randomly from the list of all SMSAs, ordered by their 1970-1975 rate of population change. The SMSAs shown in Figure 9.3 were sampled from the second and third quartiles of the list; those in Figure 9.4, from the bottom quartile; and those in Figure 9.5, from the top quartile.

The SMSAs shown in Figure 9.3, which are neither declining nor growing extremely rapidly, reflect the broad middle range of local experience in the 1970s. Ignoring the arrows for the moment, note that each metropolitan area is positioned on three axes. The vertical axis shows its annual rate of natural increase. (Compare SMSA 43 at the top, which has increased at an annual rate of 2.2%, with bottom-ranked SMSA 20, with a rate of only .3.) The horizontal axis shows its annual rate of net migration. (Compare SMSA 48 on the right, registering a 1.1% rate of net *in*migration, with SMSA 43 on the left, registering a 1.0% rate of net *out*migration.) These components of change together determine an SMSA's overall annual rate of population change, shown on the diagonal lines. Thus, we see that SMSAs 43 and 33 are alike in that each is growing at a rate of 1.2% annually, but this similarity can be

TABLE 9.4
Components of Population Change for 36 SMSAs with Declining Population, 1970–1975[a]

SMSA[b]	Annual rate 1960–1970			Annual rate 1970–1975		
	Natural increase	Net migration	Population change	Natural increase	Net migration	Population change
Akron, Ohio	1.1	.0	1.2	.7	-1.0	-.3
Altoona, Pa.	.5	-.7	-.2	.2	-.5	-.3
Anderson, Ind.	1.1	-.2	1.0	.8	-.9	-.1
Buffalo, N.Y.	.9	-.6	.3	.4	-.7	-.3
Cincinnati, Ohio-Ky.-Ind.	1.1	-.3	.9	.7	-.7	-.0
Cleveland, Ohio	1.0	-.2	.8	.6	-1.4	-.8
Columbus, Ga.-Ala.	1.8	-1.1	.9	1.3	-2.6	-1.3
Dayton, Ohio	1.3	.3	1.6	.9	-1.2	-.3
Duluth-Superior, Minn.-Wis.	.7	-1.0	-.4	.3	-.7	-.4
Elmira, N.Y.	1.0	-.7	.3	.4	-.7	-.3
Jersey City, N.J.	.7	-.8	-.1	.4	-1.2	-.8
Kankakee, Ill.	1.2	-.7	.5	.9	-1.2	-.3
Lawton, Okla.	2.2	-.5	1.7	2.0	-2.9	-.9
Los Angeles-Long Beach, Calif.	1.2	.4	1.5	.7	-1.0	-.3
New York, N.Y.-N.J.	.8	-.1	.8	.4	-1.1	-.7
Newark, N.J.	.9	.0	.9	.5	-1.1	-.6
Paterson-Clifton-Passaic, N.J.	.9	.5	1.3	.7	-1.0	-.3
Petersburg-Colonial Heights-Hopewell, Va.	1.5	.4	1.9	.8	-1.5	-.7
Philadelphia, Pa.-N.J.	.9	.0	1.0	.5	-.6	-.1
Pine Bluff, Ark.	1.4	-1.0	.5	.8	-1.2	-.4
Pittsburgh, Pa.	.7	-.7	-.0	.2	-.9	-.7
Pittsfield, Mass.	.8	-.3	.5	.2	-.3	-.1

	Annual rate 1960–1970			Annual rate 1970–1975		
SMSA[b]	Natural increase	Net migration	Population change	Natural increase	Net migration	Population change
Providence–Warwick–Pawtucket, R.I.	.7	–.0	.7	.4	–.5	–.1
Rockford, Ill.	1.4	.3	1.7	.9	–1.0	–.1
St. Louis, Mo.–Ill.	1.1	.0	1.2	.7	–1.0	–.3
Savannah, Ga.	1.2	–1.3	–.0	.8	–1.3	–.5
Seattle–Everett, Wash.	1.1	1.5	2.5	.5	–.7	–.2
Sherman–Denison, Tex.	.8	.6	1.3	.3	–1.3	–1.0
South Bend, Ind.	.9	–.6	.3	.6	–.7	–.1
Springfield, Ohio	1.1	.8	1.8	.7	–.7	–.0
Steubenville–Weirton, Ohio–W. Va.	.7	–.9	–.2	.4	–.5	–.1
Tacoma, Wash.	1.3	1.3	2.5	.9	–1.0	–.1
Terre Haute, Ind.	.4	–.2	.2	.2	–.7	–.5
Topeka, Kans.	1.4	–.5	.9	.8	–1.0	–.2
Utica–Rome, N.Y.	.9	–.6	.3	.5	–.8	–.3
Wichita, Kans.	1.3	–1.2	.2	.9	–1.2	–.3

[a]U.S. Bureau of the Census, 1977a.
[b]SMSAs have not been adjusted for redefinition since 1970; in some cases, therefore, data for 1960–1970 are not strictly comparable with data for 1970–1975.

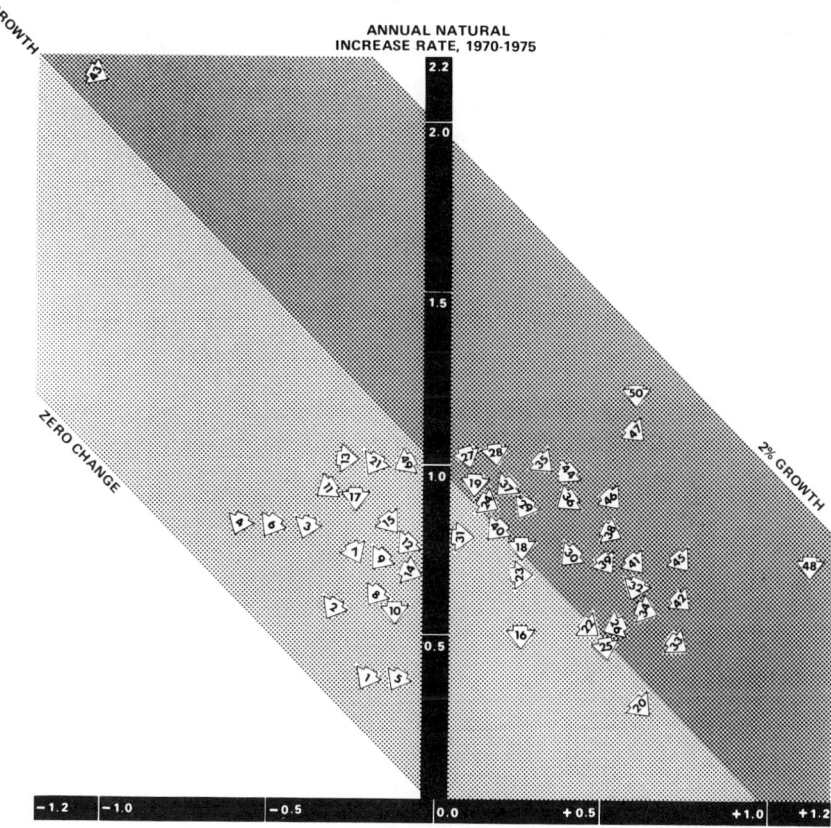

Figure 9.3. Components of change for SMSAs with moderate (quartiles 2 and 3) growth rates, 1970–1975. All rates are based on SMSAs defined with reference to constant geography (OMB's December 31, 1975 definition) for both 1960–1970 and 1970–1975 periods.

1. Worcester–Fitchburg–Leominster, Mass.
2. Syracuse, N.Y.
3. Cedar Rapids, Iowa
4. Bay City, Mich.
5. New Haven–West Haven–Waterbury–Meriden, Conn.
6. Owensboro, Ky.
7. Peoria, Ill.
8. Parkersburg–Marietta, W. Va.–Ohio
9. Louisville, Ky.–Ind.
10. Burlington, N.C.
11. Indianapolis, Ind.
12. Wilmington, Del.–N.J.–Md.
13. Lake Charles, La.
14. Sioux City, Iowa–Nebr.
15. Dubuque, Iowa
16. Harrisburg, Pa.
17. Bakersfield, Calif.
18. Kenosha, Wis.
19. New Orleans, La.
20. Allentown–Bethlehem–Easton, Pa.–N.J.
21. Lorain–Elyria, Ohio
22. Springfield, Ill.
23. Abilene, Tex.
24. Amarillo, Tex.
25. Trenton, N.J.
26. Long Branch–Asbury Park, N.J.
27. Norfolk–Virginia Beach–Portsmouth, Va.–N.C.
28. Omaha, Nebr.–Iowa
29. Columbus, Ohio
30. Santa Barbara–Santa Maria–Lompoc, Calif.
31. Pueblo, Col.
32. Richmond, Va.
33. Waco, Tex.
34. Knoxville, Tenn.
35. Mobile, Ala.
36. Bloomington, Ind.
37. Charlotte–Gastonia, N.C.
38. Fargo–Moorhead, N.Dak.–Minn.
39. Lancaster, Pa.
40. Madison, Wisc.
41. Johnson City–Kingsport, Bristol, Tenn.–Va.
42. Lynchburg, Va.
43. Laredo, Tex.
44. Dallas–Fort Worth, Tex.
45. Nashville–Davidson, Tenn.
46. Fresno, Calif.
47. Monroe, La.
48. Sacramento, Calif.
49. Ann Arbor, Mich.
50. Baton Rouge, La.

seen to arise out of quite different circumstances. The population of SMSA 43 (Laredo) has generated an extraordinarily high rate of natural increase, but a sizable portion of this growth has been offset by net outmigration. The population of SMSA 33 (Waco) generated natural increase at less than one-quarter Laredo's rate, but because Waco is gaining through net migration, it registers the same 1.2% population growth rate.

The final aspect of this figure is shown by the direction of each SMSA's arrow. It indicates the direction in which an SMSA's position on these three dimensions has changed between 1960–1970 and 1970–1975. One might think of this as the demographic path it is following in a three-dimensional space, with the diagonals representing different "altitudes." In this fanciful view, Cedar Rapids (No. 3) is "diving" directly toward zero change: Since the 1960s it has been losing "altitude" on both the natural increase and the net migration dimensions. It would plunge through the zero-change diagonal if its path continued. Springfield (No. 22), on the other hand, has been "gliding" along the 1% growth diagonal. Its loss on the natural increase dimension has been offset by its improving position on the net migration dimension.

More generally, the arrows indicate that metropolitan areas occupying the same demographic "altitude" may be moving in quite different directions. Furthermore, the national slowdown will *hasten the descent of some areas more than that of others.*

The SMSAs shown in Figures 9.4 and 9.5 show the extremes on either side of the preceding figure. Thus, we can inspect SMSAs that are already beneath the zero-change diagonal as well as those with uncommonly high rates of population growth.

The most apparent difference between these two groups is the consistency with which their arrows point in opposite directions. Although these arrows must be regarded as unreliable in the case of any individual SMSA, there is an overall pattern: The SMSAs that are now below zero change (Figure 9.4) are pointing both to the left and vertically down. Thus, *the onset of decline in these SMSAs is not generally attributable to the national fertility decline alone.* Consistent with the data shown earlier in Table 9.4, they seem to have arrived at their present locations because their declining natural increase has been exacerbated by increasing rates of net outmigration.

The SMSAs in Figure 9.5, growing rapidly for the most part, are pointing to the right and downward. They, too, are showing the effect of lower fertility, but in this case net inmigration is compensating for reduced natural increase.

Emerging Public Concerns over U.S. Population Movements

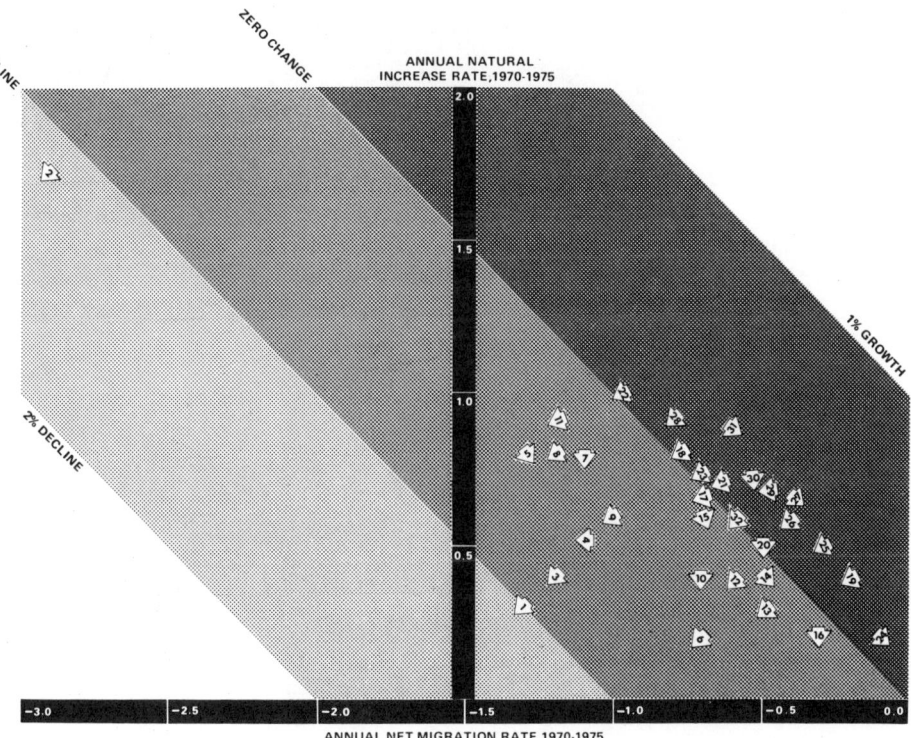

Figure 9.4. Components of change for SMSAs with low or negative (bottom quartile) growth rates, 1970-1975. All rates are based on SMSAs defined with reference to constant geography (OMB's December 31, 1975 definition) for both 1960-1970 and 1970-1975 periods.

1. Sherman-Denison, Texas
2. Lawton, Okla.
3. Jersey City, N.J.
4. Newark, N.J.
5. Savannah, Ga.
6. Terre Haute, Ind.
7. Pine Bluff, Ark.
8. Dayton, Ohio
9. Paterson-Clifton-Passaic, N.J.
10. Elmira, N.Y.
11. Kankakee, Ill.
12. Philadelphia, Pa.-N.J.
13. Providence-Warwick-Pawtucket, R.I.
14. Steubenville-Weirton, Ohio-W.Va.
15. South Bend, Ind.
16. Pittsfield, Mass.
17. Springfield, Ohio
18. Muncie, Ind.
19. Bridgeport-Stamford-Norwalk-Danbury, Conn.
20. Binghamton, N.Y.-Pa.
21. Chicago, Ill.
22. Augusta, Ga.-S.C.
23. Mansfield, Ohio
24. Wheeling, W.Va.-Ohio
25. San Francisco-Oakland, Calif.
26. Rochester, N.Y.
27. Huntington-Ashland, W.Va.-Ky.-Ohio
28. Gary-Hammond-East Chicago, Ind.
29. Melbourne-Titusville-Cocoa, Fla.
30. Waterloo-Cedar Falls, Iowa
31. Wichita Falls, Tex.
32. Milwaukee, Wis.

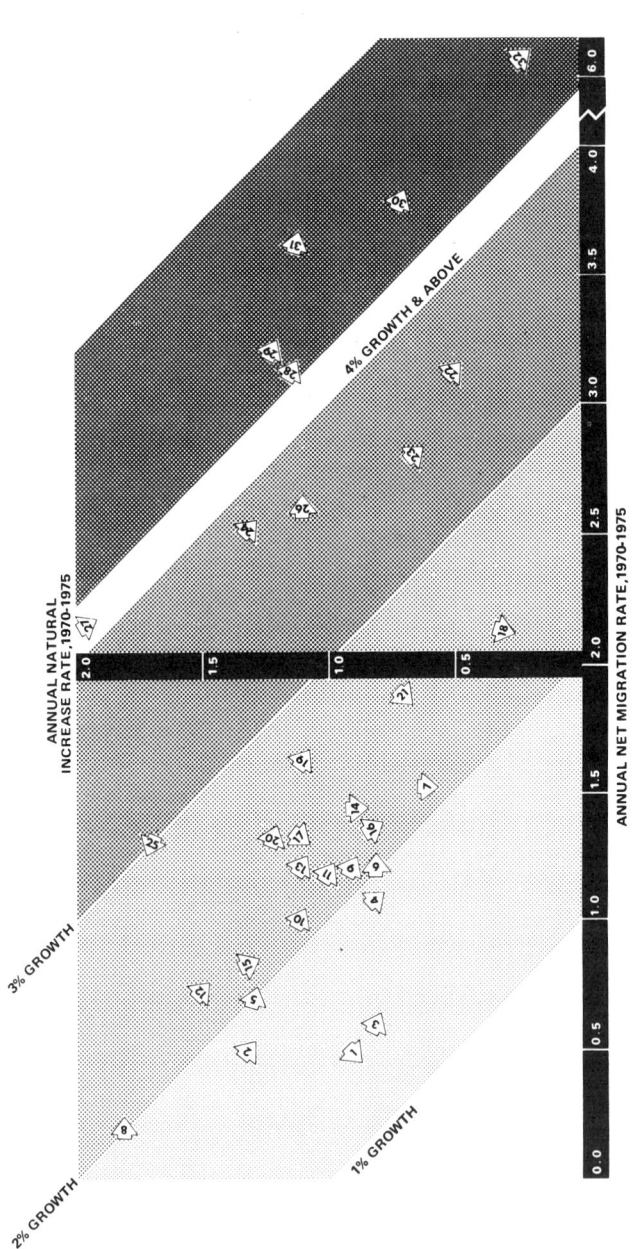

Figure 9.5. Components of change for SMSAs with high (top quartile) growth rates, 1970–1975. All rates are based on SMSAs defined with reference to constant geography (OMB's December 31, 1975 definition) for both 1960–1970 and 1970–1975 periods.

1. Lexington-Fayette, Ky.
2. San Antonio, Tex.
3. Lincoln, Nebr.
4. Vallejo-Fairfield-Napa, Cal.
5. Charleston–North Charleston, S.C.
6. Tyler, Tex.
7. Salem, Ore.
8. Salt Lake City–Ogden, Utah

9. Greenville-Spartenburg, S.C.
10. Jackson, Miss.
11. Billings, Mont.
12. Honolulu, Hawaii
13. St. Cloud, Minn.
14. Eugene-Springfield, Ore.
15. Lafayette, La.
16. Raleigh-Durham, N.C.
17. Atlanta, Ga.

18. Miami, Fla.
19. Columbia, S.C.
20. Albuquerque, N.M.
21. Fayetteville-Springdale, Ark.
22. Santa Rosa, Cal.
23. Reno, Nev.
24. Clarksville-Hopkinsville, Ky.–Tenn.
25. Colorado Springs, Col.

26. Boise City, Idaho
27. Anchorage, Alaska
28. Gainesville, Fla.
29. Bryan–College Station, Tex.
30. Fort Smith, Ark.–Okla.
31. Tallahassee, Fla.
32. Fort Lauderdale–Hollywood, Fla.

Emerging Concerns

Decline is not a graceful process. It has a certain internal logic that can be disclosed through demographic analysis. But logic is cold comfort for an area afflicted with the socially contentious, sometimes ugly, political moods and problems that evolve in the absence of growth. In the past, local and regional slowdown was regarded as the prelude to economic stagnation, and, even today, it smacks of things gone wrong. We have much to learn about the institutional arrangements to manage shrinkage. One common truth has emerged in hundreds of places around the country: Contraction cannot be accomplished simply by reversing the process of expansion within an existing organizational setting (Berman and McLaughlin, 1977).

The local school district, where enrollment decline is imposing the need to contract, is a case in point. The local severity of this problem, of course, varies widely, with migration a pivotal factor in determining which areas need to contract how much. (Since migrants largely consist of young adults and their offspring, a modest outflow of migrants from a locality may subtract disproportionate numbers of children.)

The experience of New York's suburban Westchester County may be typical here. Between 1960 and 1970, its population increased 10%, of which 2% represented net migration gain. Between 1970 and 1975, however, its population decreased 2%, owing to net outmigration of better than 3%. Because of this noticeable (although not extraordinary) change of migratory fortunes, the local manifestation of the national enrollment decline has become salient. The Westchester County Planning Department foresees an overall decline of nearly 30% between 1977 and 1990 in that county's public school enrollment (Westchester, N.Y., County Planning Department, 1977). (That figure is far in excess of the projected decline of the public school population nationally, other qualifications notwithstanding.) During this 13-year period, dwindling enrollments will render unnecessary the equivalent of about 50 neighborhood schools, whose closing about 50 local constituencies will oppose.

More generally, old ways of financing prove awkward in newly stable areas. The formulas whereby federal largesse—for example, revenue sharing, LEAA funding to states, and the like—is distributed among localities and regions typically give weight to the number of people the area claims as its inhabitants. Regions unable to boast more bodies (or, worse, to establish even as many as they had last year) will lose funds even though—perhaps for that very reason—they may merit more federal assistance.

There is another and very different side to this coin. Some areas may resent the problems migrants leave behind them, but other areas equally resent the problems that arriving migrants cause—to the point that territorial issues concerning access have cropped up (see Morrison, 1977b). Migrants are often unwelcome in destination areas. This issue of access is arousing concern at the local level, where officials have felt frustrated over their inability to affect the external forces that attract migrants or to regulate directly the numbers and types of arriving newcomers. The results differ from place to place; they include:

1. High rates of growth, which have provoked population ceiling ordinances in Boulder, Colorado, Petaluma, California, and elsewhere
2. A heavy burden on the pocketbooks of local residents, which prompted wholesale religious ordination to gain property tax exemption in Hardenburg, New York, and unilateral withdrawal from federal welfare in Plumas County, California
3. Statewide opposition to migratory influx, exemplified by the governor of Hawaii's recent proposal for federal legislation to control the influx of migrants to his state

Submerged beneath the contemporary concerns with migration and the often unwelcome access it confers on destination areas are important but unresolved legal and political questions. From their review of these questions, Evans and Vestal (1977) conclude that "the law affecting migration is in a very uncertain state [p. 448]." Given this uncertainty, the new sensitivity to the costs of migration can only intensify with the new pattern of migration away from large centers to small places, and the arithmetic asymmetry whereby sheer numbers inevitably destroy "smallness."

10

Policy Implications and Future Research Needs

ROBERT L. CLARK

Introduction

The preceding chapters have examined the economic consequences of slowing population growth by employing different methodological techniques and by focusing on alternative aspects of the interaction between population growth and economic factors. A recurring theme is how little we know concerning the long-run implications of changes in the rate of population growth. This concluding chapter will highlight the findings of the previous chapters, review potential population policy options they raise, and outline the principal areas that require additional research.

The chapter by Serow and Espenshade (S–E) provides a detailed review of the economic and demographic literature concerning the influence of population changes on economic variables. Their discussion acquaints the potential analyst with relevant research in this field and also reveals critical gaps in our knowledge of the interdependent relationship between economic factors and population characteristics. Other chapters in this volume represent efforts to respond to research needs outlined by Serow and Espenshade.

Investigators often are tempted to examine effects of alternative rates of population growth within the framework of stable populations and the assumed continuation of a specified fertility rate. Serow and Espenshade note that previous research has shown that the time required to reach a stationary population after replacement-level fertility is achieved and maintained is a function of past fertility patterns and the existing age structure. This time lag may involve a significant number of years as well as dramatic shifts in the age composition of the population. It is during this transition phase that stress is placed on economic institutions.

The seemingly large variations in population age structure between alternative fertility assumptions may not cause serious economic disruptions if the population transition occurs slowly, thus providing sufficient time for economic agents to adjust. The nation's capital stock can be transformed through depreciation and reinvestment, and new labor force entrants can be trained for alternative occupations in response to the shifting needs of the economy as population growth slows. However, large fluctuations over short periods of time may leave physical facilities idle and create relatively high rates of unemployment in selected industries. Therefore, the interaction between population and economic variables must be examined during these transition phases.

Wander makes the important observation that it is doubtful that any fertility rate will be maintained continuously. Instead she argues that "There is nothing to suggest that birth rates eventually will stop fluctuating...[p. 44]." Therefore, it is more realistic to assume that countries will follow the European experience, with fertility fluctuating around certain rates. Wander calls a nation in which the birth rate is oscillating around the replacement level a pseudostationary population and notes that such a country can undergo substantial changes in age structure even if the population size stays constant. The existence of a pseudostationary population raises the question of whether the demographic impact on economic variables may be more significant when there is oscillation around one fertility rate than when a shift to a permanently higher or lower level of fertility is involved.

Perhaps the most important relationship on which researchers have focused is the impact of fertility decline on individual well-being. Per capita income is frequently adopted as a proxy for well-being, and several of the papers in this volume follow this tradition. Some environmentalists may object to this measure because national income usually does not capture the negative effects of the additional pollution and congestion generated by larger populations. Ridker attempts to measure these environmental effects of population change by simulating the cost of pollution control with alternative fertility assumptions.

The relationship between fertility patterns and per capita income is both complex and simultaneous in nature. Wachter and Wachter, and Neal review the literature concerning the demographic response to economic conditions. Neal finds that, contrary to past behavior, American society apparently "has entered a period when an increase in the flow of real output is associated with a decrease in the flow of newborn babies, whereas a decrease in output means an increase in births [p. 121]."

The direction of correlation between changes in the fertility rate and economic well-being is a much debated topic. After reviewing the literature, S–E conclude that "the overall consensus... thus far would appear to be that the net impact of a decline in population growth would be positive, in terms of a per capita measure of economic well-being [p. 18]." This, however, may not be the final verdict concerning this complex relationship, since little is known about how the rate of growth and the age structure of the population influence a variety of economic variables that in turn determine the national income.

Slowing population growth may be expected to increase per capita income due to the increase in the proportion of the population that is of working age. The relative decline in the dependency ratio should permit output to expand, increase investment per capita, and stimulate the labor-force participation of females. Factors tending to offset the positive contribution of lower rates of fertility include the decreased mobility of the labor force and the change in type of the nation's stock of human capital. In addition, it is sometimes asserted that an aging population is less responsive to technological innovation and thus reduces investment opportunities. The age structure of the population also may influence aggregate measures of labor productivity positively through increased experience but negatively due to slowed introduction of human capital and reduced responsiveness of the economy. The impact of slowing population growth and the accompanying age structure changes on these economic factors is frequently theoretically ambiguous, and empirical studies have been severely limited by inadequate data. As a result, many hypotheses concerning the demographic influence on economic variables remain unverified. Other factors that might be expected to respond to population changes include consumption patterns, health requirements, and residential location. Ridker, Wander, and Morrison attempt to assess the nature of these influences.

In a nation undergoing a demographic transition from high rates of growth to lower birth rates, the total dependency ratio will be falling. Simultaneously, the composition of the dependent population will be shifting to include a higher proportion of the aged. Therefore, the increased cost of maintaining the elderly will be moderated by cost reductions associated with having relatively fewer children to support. The nature of this trade-off depends on the relative cost of the two dependent groups, and these costs must be known if we are to be able to project trends in future dependency costs. Wander states that in West Germany the total cost of raising a child to age 20 is greater than that of providing for a person aged 60 for the duration of life, whereas Clark and Spengler (1977) estimate that in the United States the public cost of financing transfers to the aged is three times greater than is such financing for children. A related question concerns how society would be able to reallocate resources now being spent on children in order to provide benefits for the elderly, given that the expenditures are made by different governmental units and that some are public, whereas others are private.

Summary Findings

Wander's chapter documents the Western European pattern of fertility rates fluctuating around the replacement level. She argues that the actual experience of the fertility rates of most countries illustrates the lack of realism inherent in analyses using stationary population models. The pseudostable populations that Wander describes can undergo significant age structure changes. These fluctuations are what cause economic dislocation by influencing the utilization of educational institutions, employment, and many transfer programs.

One aspect of the pseudostable state that concerns Wander is its tendency to degenerate into population decline. The longer the fertility rate remains below the replacement rate, the more likely it is that momentum will be created that may carry the country toward progressive decline. Wander worries whether momentum in favor of decline can be reversed once it has been produced. This argument is analogous to the more traditional observation of population momentum favoring continued growth and merits additional investigation. Wander suggests that conditions in Western Europe currently favor continued population decline, rather than a return to steady growth. She then argues for a public policy aimed at supporting zero population growth, with one option being the immigration of young families. Thus, immigration policy may increase in importance for developed countries facing the dangers of population decline.

Wander concludes that the influence of fertility changes on business fluctuations depends on the prevalent social and economic behavior patterns, general social and economic conditions, and the existing standard of living. She believes that these circumstances are largely governed by social and economic policy. Therefore, the impact of alternative fertility patterns is determined simultaneously with these policy actions. In summary, she states that the demographic influences are "indeterminate, hard to identify, and unfit for easy generalizations, especially with regard to the future [p. 53]." While concurring with this assessment, I would interpret this statement as a call for further, more sophisticated investigation into the relationship between demographic and economic variables.

The impact of changing age structure on product demand is also considered by Wander. She notes that products with low income elasticities and those specifically related to the needs of young people are likely to suffer. The smaller households of the future are likely to demand more consumer durables and services. If increased per capita income follows, it will accentuate these trends. Such influences are likely, however, to be "too slow and too small to have any immediate strong effect of the aforementioned kind [p. 61]." However, the empirical studies in this area have yet to uncover any significant impact of declining population growth on the distribution of household consumption by broad expenditure group.

Wachter and Wachter (W-W) examine the relationship between population characteristics and aggregate unemployment. Their model indicates that the recent high unemployment rates are due in part to bottlenecks and supply-side constraints. Wachter and Wachter estimate a noninflationary rate of unemployment (U_{NI}) and illustrate how it has risen in response to supply constraints. They conclude that the demographic influence "is likely to be the single most important factor causing U_{NI} to change over the past two decades [p. 82, Footnote 17]."

Wachter and Wachter employ a Leontief fixed-coefficient production function that allows no substitution in the production process and thus exaggerates the ensuing supply bottlenecks. One wonders how the use of a more traditional production function would influence the results obtained by W-W. The existence of substitutability of inputs would imply that the estimates obtained by using a fixed-coefficient model are biased upward.

Despite this limitation, the research of W-W provides a very useful and interesting investigation of the influence of population factors on the aggregate unemployment rate. They estimate that U_{NI} rose from 4% in 1955 to 5.5% in 1976 because of demographic changes in conjunction with the expansion of minimum wage restrictions, increased income transfers, and the mismatching of labor and capital. The principal changes in the characteristics of the population affecting the labor force have been the increased numbers of youths and the continuing high rates of growth in the female labor force.

Simulating the course of unemployment, W–W project a slight decline in U_{NI} between 1977 and 1980 and a more rapid decline after 1980 until it reaches 4.5% in 1985–1987. The downward trend is the lagged result of the low fertility rates of the past decade and the related population aging. They find that "the aging of the population, ceteris paribus, should translate into a significant reduction in the nonaccelerating-inflation rate of unemployment [p. 73]."

The authors note that continued increases in female labor-force participation could offset this projected decline. Wachter and Wachter note that the tendency for increased female participation to raise U_{NI} is reduced by the fact that most of the likely rise in the market work effort of women will come from older women who historically have had rates of unemployment below the aggregate level. The increased supply of older women may, however, adversely affect their job prospects, thus raising the unemployment rate for this cohort. Wachter and Wachter have provided us with a provocative paper that dramatically illustrates the influence of supply constraints, especially demographic variables, on the unemployment rate. They note that U_{NI} is not a single number but a variable that responds to changes in other factors. Thus, the policymaker is confronted with an uncertain target. Their model demonstrates that an effective fiscal policy is one that increases aggregate supply or potential output as it increases aggregate demand. They observe further that only supply policy has the potential of significantly lowering the nonaccelerating inflationary rate of unemployment. It is shown that population aging and age structure shifts are one of the primary determinants of U_{NI} and that "the demographics . . . are favorable for a significant decline in U_{NI} over the next decade [p. 93]."

Neal examines the relationship between slowing population growth and investment demand. He states that the reduction in births in the 1960s and early 1970s has been "primarily responsible for the current slowdown [p. 102]," but Neal does not foresee secular stagnation as a necessary by-product of slowing population growth. This paper looks to past experience for help in analyzing the future relationship between demographic and economic variables.

Alvin Hansen (1939), among others, felt that reduced population growth in the 1930s would decrease investment opportunities on the extensive margin, where 60% of American investment occurred during the nineteenth century, and would likely discourage investment to increase the capital–labor ratio. Factors which forestalled stagnation included continued immigration, increased female labor-force participation, the rise in the government sector, and the postwar baby boom. Despite reversals in these trends, Neal does not envision a period of stagnation, but he does anticipate "a new era of economic–demographic interactions [p. 104]." He believes that the labor force will continue to grow from either continued increases in female participation rates or a new wave of immigration.

Neal's review of the literature includes papers that relate to short-run interactions (2 or 3 years), long-run relationships, and the transition period. He finds that models of short-run economic activity indicate that investment demand wanes in response to slower population growth. This relationship operates through the influence of population change on the size of the labor force; thus, population declines may be partially offset by increased participation. Growth models predict that, in the long run, slowing population growth reduces investment demand but does not necessarily imply lower per capita income.

Neal's earlier empirical work using spectral analysis has indicated that swings in population growth drive the economic variables. This contradicts work by Richard Easterlin (1968), who stated that the causal influence flowed in the opposite direction. This paper also finds evidence of significant economic–demographic interaction. Neal argues that the nature of this interaction may have undergone a recent structural change. He finds that there is now an inverse relationship between the birth rate and the flow of real output. This unprecedented correlation may be attributable to women with increased labor force attachment who have children when they are unemployed.

The possibility that future booms will be choked off by a lack of available workers and by the tendency for reduced investment is outlined. He notes that there are a variety of possibilities to ameliorate the dampening effects of slowing population growth. They include a fall in individual savings and increased investment in human capital. In addition, policies aimed at encouraging immigration could forestall or retard the decline in population growth. Neal's paper is a combination of historical analysis and projections for future behavior. His methodology and conclusions represent an important contribution to our understanding of the demographic–economic relationships. But gaps in our knowledge are once again illustrated by the lack of a theoretical basis for many of the mechanisms mediating the transition from demographic variables to economic characteristics.

Ridker generates 50-year scenarios in his applications of alternative fertility rates in an attempt to assess the importance of population in the determination of well-being. He uses a system of interlinked models of the U.S. economy designated in the Resources for the Future/Strategic Environmental Assessment System (RFF/SEAS). Assumptions concerning technology, tastes, availability of raw materials, patterns of labor supply, etc. are made in order to project economic characteristics over the period.

The fertility assumptions used in the simulation process are 2.5, 2.1, and 1.8 births per woman. These population series are from Bureau of Census data. The predictions of this model are that if fertility is set at 2.5 births per woman, per capita consumption will grow at an annual rate of approximately 2.0% per year, whereas a fertility rate of 1.8 would produce a growth rate of 2.2%. Noting the small difference, Ridker concludes that "our best guess is that the kind of slowdown in population growth that the United States is likely to experience during the next 50 years is unlikely to have a significant effect on this country's long-term economic growth [p. 155]."

To be able to assess the value of Ridker's contribution and conclusions, we must understand how population factors influence the model. Although it is impossible without examining the entire model to know every instance of interaction between demographic and economic variables, one can review the relationships outlined in the chapter. For example, the future course of labor productivity is determined by trends in hours of work and output per man-hour. Ridker does not permit changes in weekly hours of work to vary between the fertility assumptions. The unemployment rate is assumed to be insensitive to population aging, contrary to the analysis of Wachter and Wachter. Output per man-hour is allowed to fluctuate with changes in the age-sex composition; however, wage rates are the proxies for productivity, and the wage structure is assumed to remain constant over time. Thus, the wage rates are not affected by changes in the supply of workers of different ages and skills.

Ridker also assumed that "It seems safest to conclude that the rate of innovation is not likely to be affected by probable demographic changes during the next 50 years [p. 137]" and that "we should not attempt to make the savings rate a direct function of changes in population growth rates over time and between runs [p. 138]." Savings are indirectly related to population size through investment requirements that are influenced by population growth.

This series of assumptions that relevant economic variables are not a function of population growth rates and the related age structure changes helps to generate the conclusion that economic well-being is not a function of population growth. Ridker is, of course, correct in his assertion that the influences of demographic variables on economic characteristics are the subject of continued debate and that no consensus has been reached. Therefore, an interesting experiment with this simulation model would be to alter the magnitudes of the demographic-economic interactions and to observe the sensitivity of the measure of economic well-being to these assumptions.

Morrison examines the impact of slowing population growth on communities. In a period of declining fertility and decreased population growth at the national level, some areas continue to experience rapid population growth when others are declining in size. With a stable national population, migration exerts a dominant influence on the size of local populations, an influence that is not so evident when accompanied by the "protective mantle of natural increase [p. 227]."

This chapter documents local patterns of growth and separates the influences of fertility and migration. Areas may swing quickly from a state of net in-migration to one of out-migration. These fluctuations are difficult to forecast because slight changes in gross flows can produce large swings in net migration rates. Stressing the importance of migration, Morrison states that "out-migration appears to have been the decisive factor in bringing about local ZPG [p. 238]."

The declining attraction of the large metropolitan areas is graphically depicted in the data. The metropolitan areas as a group are experiencing net out-migration, with approximately one in six areas actually losing population. The net flow of people from the metropolitan areas has been occurring for some time but was previously disguised by high birth rates. Morrison observes that some of the economic effects of slowing population growth have been offset by the continuing high rate of household formation. Household formation rates have risen in recent years due to the baby boom cohorts reaching household-forming years, to unmarried young adults leaving the home of their parents, and to the elderly's not moving in with their children. He concludes that "living arrangements are sure to constitute an important mediating factor between slowed population growth and how it is experienced [pp. 229–230]."

The diversity of population growth patterns within a country necessitates that future researchers explore the relationship between economic and demographic factors at both local and national levels. Morrison seems to imply that for cities population decline is concomitant with economic deterioration. Yet, are not some areas resorting to legislation to slow or eliminate population growth? Can decreased population growth be good for the country but bad for a particular area? I would tend to believe that migration is first of all a response to changing economic conditions, with such migratory flows aggravating the local economy. Whether population growth is beneficial to local areas will probably depend on many of the same factors that would answer the question at the national level.

Pitts examines the current status of the social security system and explores the impact of population aging on this income transfer program. The obvious result of a ceteris paribus increase in the beneficiary–worker ratio is higher taxes. With a constant replacement ratio, the projected increase in the aged population (assuming replacement-level fertility) will require an increase of approximately 50% in the tax rate by the middle of the next century. Lower fertility rates would require still greater increases in the per-worker cost of financing future benefits.

Mean elasticities of per-worker costs with shifts in relevant demographic and economic variables are reported. The mean elasticity represents the average percentage change in annual Old Age, Survivors, Disability, and Health Insurance (OASDI) per-worker costs corresponding to a 1% change in the value of the independent variable. Assuming intergenerationally constant replacement ratios, changes in prices and real wages should have little impact on the portion of earnings needed to finance retirement benefits. Because nominal wages adjust more quickly than benefits to increases in prices and real wages, increases in these variables slightly reduce the per-worker costs.

Rising labor-force participation of women offers the potential of reducing future tax rates, whereas mortality reductions will tend to increase costs. Noting that the old age dependency ratio among new immigrants is only 3.8 per hundred persons aged 20–64 whereas the rate for the resident U.S. population is 19.1 per hundred workers, Pitts states that "immigration should serve as a slight brake on any likely future rise in real per-worker OASDI costs [p. 177]." An additional offset to increasing tax rates would be raising the age of eligibility for benefits. The 1975 Advisory Council on Social Security estimated that future costs might be reduced 1.5 percentage points if the pensionable age were raised to 68. Broadening the base of support to include federal civil servants is another possibility.

Pitts' paper represents an informative review of a series of policy issues that must be addressed in the next 25 years. Action taken by Congress in 1977 decoupled the benefit system and increased the legislated future tax rates. Social security will not, however, slip silently from public scrutiny, and many of the issues outlined in this paper will continue to demand attention.

Wertheimer and Zedlewski (W–Z) employ the Urban Institute Dynamic Simulation of Income Model (DYNASIM) to project the impact of alternative birth, marriage, and divorce rates on the number of low-income families. The model estimates that the number of families will grow more rapidly in proportion to the population as a whole over the period 1975-1985, a result that is consistent with the findings of Morrison. Wertheimer and Zedlewski also note that the number of female-headed families will increase at a faster rate in proportion to the total population. Their experiments indicate that the number of families, the size of families, and the marital status of the population are sensitive to the demographic assumptions.

An important finding of W-Z concerns the effect of family stability on the distribution of income. Low marriage rates and high divorce rates increase the number of families at lower income levels. A curious result is the response of family income to alternative birth rates. High birth rates increase the number of families due to a related rise in illegitimate births. Yet examination of the income distribution data reveals that higher birth rates slightly increase the percentage of families in the higher income brackets. The authors conclude that the birth rate experiments point to inconclusive changes in the distribution of income.

The base line projections of Aid to Families with Dependent Children (AFDC) caseloads reveal an upward trend in the number of welfare families. These estimates, which hold the birth, marriage, and divorce rates at their 1977 levels, indicate an increase of 10.6% in the number of AFDC families in 1985 as compared to 1975. This is approximately the same rate of growth as the population over the 11-year period, but lower than the increase in the number of families receiving social security benefits. The AFDC caseload grows considerably more slowly than the 20% rise in the number of families during the period. The impact of fertility changes on the AFDC caseload is clearly illustrated by a series of simulations. On the average, a fertility rate of 1.7 children per woman decreases the caseload by 5% each year, whereas the high fertility assumption of 2.7 children per woman increased the number of welfare families by over 6% as compared to the baseline projections.

An argument frequently employed in examinations of future transfer payments is that higher costs of income transfers to the elderly will be offset by decreased expenditures on children. The baseline projections indicate that a 10% rise in the caseload will imply a 10% increase in expenditures if benefits are indexed to the rate of inflation. With real Gross National Product (GNP) projected to rise by over 40%, the proportion of national income needed to support this welfare program declines. If, however, benefits are adjusted for growth in GNP, welfare costs escalate more significantly. The average AFDC family payment in 1958 dollars rises from $1470 to $1936, and the number of families receiving benefits is raised by 17.8%. As a result of adjusting benefits to reflect real growth, total costs of the program would rise by 70%, and an increased proportion of GNP would be required to fund the AFDC program. Therefore, welfare payments for children would rise in conjunction with increased social security benefits.

Policy Implications

A careful analysis of these papers requires the thoughtful reader to consider the public policy questions associated with demographic change. Perhaps the most important issue is whether the government should intervene in family fertility decisions in order to influence the birth rate. This could be accomplished through economic incentives such as demogrants or taxes, as well as through direct birth control policies. Explicit population policies have been adopted by some nations; however, the United States has yet to adopt population goals. There are, of course, many government programs that alter the cost of supporting children and the probability of childbirth. These programs include educational and child care subsidies, health and welfare programs, abortion policy, and the dissemination of birth control information. Typically, these programs have the stated objective of improving the welfare of the mother and child and are not aimed at achieving an aggregate population target. Since these papers do not reach a consensus on the relationship between population growth and per capita well-being, they do not provide the policymaker with a clear guide for government initiatives to influence the fertility rate. Several of the papers do, however, argue for positive government action to prevent population decline.

For individual countries or regions, immigration offers an alternative to fertility increases. Neal and Wander suggest that the low-fertility, developed countries may be required to reconsider their immigration policies in order to maintain their domestic population and labor force. The desirability of increased migratory flows hinges on many of the same factors that influence fertility policy; however, new migrants are able to enter the labor force immediately in order to offset labor shortages (Neal) and increase the worker-dependent ratio (Pitts). Thus, with the continuation of low fertility, the developed countries may be required to reassess their immigration policies.[1]

[1] Faced with a tightening labor market, however, several of the Western European nations are reconsidering their heretofore liberal immigration policies. France, for example, has been offering $2000 bonuses to immigrant workers who will return home.

Morrison notes that migration exerts a dominant influence on local population growth in the presence of low fertility. The depletion of local labor forces through out-migration will adversely affect the economy of the declining cities. In order to influence the direction of internal population flows so as to prevent or retard regional deterioration, national governments may be required to reconsider the allocation of federal funds. Current debate in the United States has centered on the demands of the Northeast and Midwest states (areas of net out-migration) to receive increased federal funds relative to the South and West. A continued decline in the birthrate will probably intensify this debate.

The chapters by Pitts and by Wertheimer and Zedlewski illustrate the policy considerations associated with the primary income transfer systems for the aged and for young dependents. Questions are raised in relation to the appropriate benefit levels and tax rates necessary to finance these programs. Of considerable interest is change in the cost of these programs in relation to population growth. Low fertility should reduce the relative cost of child support programs as it increases the relative cost of old age transfers.

Policy considerations in providing income security for the aged have clearly been at the forefront of recent Congressional debates. Pension reform, mandatory retirement, and social security revision have all been important items on the Congressional agenda. Population aging increases the importance and impact of these decisions. Future costs and economic consequences of policy initiatives concerning the elderly will increase in importance over the next half century.

To the extent that Wander is correct in her anticipation of pseudostable populations, an important area for public policy may be to smooth the transition of economic institutions in conjunction with the continuing age structure changes that are inherent with such populations. Governments must be prepared to cope with the changes that are required in an economy that shifts from relatively large cohorts of youths to increases in the number of older consumers.

Further Research Needs

The papers contained in this volume provide a theoretical framework that permits the examination of the relationship between economic and demographic variables. Several of the authors estimate the interaction of economic and population characteristics on the basis of existing data, whereas other concentrate on forecasting future fluctuations. As a group, these research efforts have increased our understanding of the potential economic consequences of slowing population growth. An equally important outcome of these discussions has been to identify the limits of our knowledge and to outline avenues for future research.

A reading of these chapters reveals the importance of including transitional phases of demographic change in any analysis of population effects on the economy. The possible existence of a pseudostable population in which fertility rates continue to fluctuate around a near-replacement level is a significant factor that must be considered in future research. Fertility rates that differ widely among cities and regions (or nations) imply that localities will have different experiences even as the nation approaches zero population growth. Economic differences may explain net migration rates that, combined with the rate of natural increase, determine population changes. Thus, the potential for migration to offset or exacerbate fertility shifts should be examined. Such analysis would include the feasibility and desirability of using economic incentives to influence migration rates.

Considerable research is needed to focus on the transition mechanism between population shifts and economic factors. Qualitative results remain theoretically ambiguous, and existing studies have been unable to test competing hypotheses satisfactorily. Of crucial importance to the determination of the demographic influence on economic well-being is the relationship between investment-savings and shifts in the rate of population growth. Labor-force mobility, introduction of technology, age-specific consumption, and rates of labor-force participation may all be influenced by demographic characteristics, yet their qualitative as well as quantitative impacts remain a source of controversy.

There is a dearth of information concerning the consequences of age structure changes on the productivity of the work force. To examine this area of demographic influence, additional knowledge of individual productivity over the life cycle must be acquired. Age structure changes produce shifts in dependency ratios and in the composition of the dependent groups. Further research is needed to ascertain the relative costs of young and old dependents. Special attention should be focused on social programs that provide benefits to these groups and on the ability of social institutions to adjust to the changing population age structure. The consequences of slowing population growth will be determined in part by the willingness and ability of older individuals to remain in the labor force. Therefore, analysis of retirement patterns and their causes should receive high research priority.

In sum, the interested reader will find these papers replete with topics for further research. Those who are responsible for policy formulation will find the papers helpful in assessing the possible impact of demographic change upon alternative governmental policies.

Acknowledgment

I wish to thank Joseph J. Spengler for his useful comments.

References

Aaron, Henry. "The Social Insurance Paradox." *Canadian Journal of Economics and Political Science* 32 (August 1966): 371–374.
———. "Social Security: International Comparisons." In *Studies in the Economics of Income Maintenance*, edited by Otto Eckstein. Washington: The Brookings Institution, 1967.
Abramovitz, Moses. "Resources and Output Trends in the United States Since 1870." *American Economic Review* 46 (May 1956): 5–24.
———. "The Passing of the Kuznets Cycle." *Economica* 35 (November 1968): 349–367.
Almon, Clopper, Jr.; Buckley, Margaret B.; Horowitz, Lawrence M.; and Reimbold, Thomas C. *1985: Interindustry Forecasts of the American Economy.* Lexington: D. C. Heath, 1974.
Alonso, William. "Urban Zero Population Growth." In *The No-Growth Society*, edited by Mancur Olson and Hans H. Landsberg. New York: Norton, 1973.
———. "The Current Halt in the Metropolitan Phenomenon." Paper presented at the Symposium on Challenges and Opportunities in the Mature Metropolis, St. Louis, June 1977.
Alterman, Jack. "Projections of Labor Force, Labor Productivity, Gross National Product, and Households: Methodology and Data." Working Paper no. 1. Washington: Resources for the Future, RFF/NIH Project, 1976.
Altmeyer, Arthur. *The Formative Years of Social Security.* Madison: University of Wisconsin Press, 1966.
Appleman, Jack; Butz, William P.; Greenberg, David H.; Jordan, Paul L.; and Pascal, Anthony H. "Population Change and Public Resource Requirements: The Impact of Future United States Demographic Trends on Education, Welfare and Health Costs." In *Economic Aspects of Population Change*, edited by Elliott R. Morss and Ritchie H. Reed. Washington: Government Printing Office, 1972.

Archibald, G. C. "The Structure of Excess Demand for Labor." In *Micro-Economic Foundations of Employment and Inflation Theory*, edited by Edmund Phelps *et al*. New York: Norton, 1970.
Arthur, W. Brian, and McNicoll, Geoffrey. "Large Scale Simulation Models in Population and Development: What Use to Planners?" *Population and Development Review* 1 (December 1975): 251–265.
Baily, Martin N., and Tobin, James. "Direct Job Creation, Inflation, and Unemployment." Paper presented at the Brookings Conference on Direct Job Creation, Washington, April 1977.
Barber, C. L. *Some Implications of the Move Towards Zero Population Growth in Developed Countries Upon the Level of Capital Expenditures*. Ottawa: Economic Council of Canada, 1975.
Bayo, Francisco, and McKay, Steven. "United States Population Prediction for OASDHI Cost Estimates." Actuarial Study no. 72. Washington: Social Security Administration, July 1974.
Becker, Gary S. "An Economic Analysis of Fertility." In *Demographic and Economic Change in Developed Countries*. New York: National Bureau of Economic Research, 1960.
Berelson, Bernard, ed. *Population Policy in Developed Countries*. New York: McGraw-Hill, 1974.
Berman, P., and McLaughlin, M. W. "The Management of Decline: Problems, Opportunities, and Research Questions." Paper no. P-5984. Santa Monica: The Rand Corporation, August 1977.
Bixby, Lenore. "Income of People Aged 65 and Over: Overview from the 1968 Survey of the Aged." *Social Security Bulletin* 34 (April 1970): 3–34.
Blackburn, John. "The Macroeconomics of Pension Funds." In *Old Age Income Assistance*. Washington: Joint Economic Committee, U. S. Congress, 1967.
Blake, Judith. "The Microfamily and Zero Population Growth." In *Families of the Future*. Ames: Iowa State University, College of Home Economics, 1972.
Bourgeois-Pichat, Jean, and Taleb, Si-Ahmed. "Un Taux d'Accroisement Nul pour les Pays en Voie de Développement en l'An 2000: Rêve ou Réalité?" *Population* 25 (September–October 1970): 957–974.
Bowen, William; Davis, Richard; and Kopf, David. "The Public Debt: A Burden on Future Generations?" *American Economic Review* 50 (September 1960): 701–706.
Breckenfeld, G. "Business Loves the Sunbelt (and vice versa)." *Fortune* 95 (June 1977): 132–146.
Brems, Hans. *Labor, Capital, and Growth*. Lexington: D. C. Heath, 1973.
Brinkman, George L. "The Effects of Zero Population Growth on the Spatial Distribution of Economic Activity." *American Journal of Agricultural Economics* 54 (December 1972): 964–971.
Browning, Edgar K. "Social Insurance and Intergenerational Transfers." *Journal of Law and Economics* 16 (October 1973): 215–237.
Browning, Harley L. "Speculations on Labor Mobility in a Stationary Population." In *Zero Population Growth: Implications*, edited by J. J. Spengler. Chapel Hill: University of North Carolina, Carolina Population Center, 1975.

Buchanan, James. "Social Insurance in a Growing Economy." *National Tax Journal* 21 (December 1968): 376–394.
Burns, Arthur F. *Production Trends in the United States Since 1870.* New York: National Bureau of Economic Research, 1934.
Butz, William P., and Ward, Michael P. "The Emergence of Countercyclical U.S. Fertility." Report no. R-1605-NIH. Santa Monica: The Rand Corporation, June 1977.
Cagan, Philip. *The Effect of Pension Plans on Aggregate Saving.* New York: National Bureau of Economic Research, 1965.
Calot, Gerard, and Hecht, Jacqueline. "Long-Term Population Policies." Paper presented at the Council of Europe Seminar on the Implications of a Stationary or Declining Population in Europe, Strasbourg, September 1976.
Campbell, Arthur A. "Baby Boom to Birth Dearth and Beyond." *Annals of the American Academy of Political and Social Science* 435 (January 1978): 40–60.
Campbell, Colin. "Social Insurance in the United States: A Program in Search of an Explanation." *Journal of Law and Economics* 12 (October 1969): 249–266.
Clark, Peter. "A New Estimate of Potential GNP." Washington: Council of Economic Advisors, January 1977.
Clark, Robert L. "Age Structure Changes and Intergenerational Transfers of Income." Durham: Duke University, Center for the Study of Aging and Human Development, 1976. (a).
———. "The Impact of Zero Population Growth on the OASDHI Program: Further Comment." *Journal of Risk and Insurance* 43 (June 1976): 322–324. (b).
———. "The Influence of Low Fertility Rates and Retirement Policy on Dependency Costs." Raleigh: North Carolina State University, Department of Economics and Business, 1976. (c).
———. "Increasing Income Transfers to the Elderly Implied by Zero Population Growth." *Review of Social Economy* 35 (April 1977): 37–54.
———, and Spengler, J. J. "Changing Demography and Dependency Costs: The Implications of Future Dependency Ratios." In *Income and Aging: Essays on Policy Prospects,* edited by Barbara R. Herzog. New York: Human Sciences Press, 1977.
Coale, Ansley J. "Should the United States Start a Campaign for Fewer Births?" *Population Index* 34 (October 1968): 468–474.
———. "Population Growth and Dependency Burden." In *Economic Development and Population Growth: A Conflict?,* edited by H. Peter Gray and Shanti S. Tangri. Lexington: D. C. Heath, 1970.
———. "Alternative Paths to a Stationary Population." In *Demographic and Social Aspects of Population Growth,* edited by Charles F. Westoff and Robert Parke, Jr. Washington: Government Printing Office, 1972.
———, and Hoover, Edgar M. *Population Growth and Economic Development in Low-Income Countries.* Princeton: Princeton University Press, 1958.
———, and Zelnick, Melvin. *New Estimates of Fertility and Population in the U.S.* Princeton: Princeton University Press, 1963.
Cohen, Wilbur, and Friedman, Milton. *Social Security: Universal or Selective?* Washington: American Enterprise Institute for Public Policy Research, 1972.
Cooper, Ronald L., and Jorgenson, Dale W. "The Predictive Performance of

Quarterly Econometric Models of the U.S." Paper presented at the Conference on Econometric Models of Cyclical Behavior, Harvard University, November 1969.
Cornelius, Wayne A. "Progress Report for NIH Grant HD PO1 09272-03." Bethesda: National Institute of Child Health and Human Development, Center for Population Research, 1977.
Davis, Kingsley. "Zero Population Growth: The Goal and the Means." In *The No-Growth Society*, edited by Mancur Olson and Hans H. Lansberg. New York: Norton, 1973.
Day, Lincoln H. "The Social Consequences of a Zero Population Growth Rate in the United States." In *Demographic and Social Aspects of Population Growth*, edited by Charles F. Westoff and Robert Parke, Jr. Washington: Government Printing Office, 1972.
DeKerpel, A.; Wijewickrema, S.; Lesthaeghe, R.; and Despontin, M. "Will Low Fertility Generate Economic Stagnation in the Industrialized West?" Brussels: Vrije Universiteit, Centrum voor Sociologie, 1976.
Denison, Edward F. *Accounting for U.S. Economic Growth, 1929-1969*. Washington: The Brookings Institution, 1974.
Denton, F. T., and Spencer, B. G. "A Simulation Analysis of the Effects of Population Change on a Neoclassical Economy." *Journal of Political Economy* 81 (March-April 1973): 356-375.
―――, and ―――. "The Demographic Element in the Burden of Government Old Age Pensions." Hamilton: McMaster University, Department of Economics, 1975. (a).
―――, and ―――. "Health Care Costs When the Population Changes." *Canadian Journal of Economics* 8 (February 1975): 34-48. (b).
―――, and ―――. "Household and Population Effects on Aggregate Consumption." *Review of Economics and Statistics* 58 (February 1976): 86-95.
de Sandre, Paolo. "Critical Study of Population Policies in Europe." Paper presented at the Council of Europe Seminar on the Implications of a Stationary or Declining Population in Europe, Strasbourg, September 1976.
Dorfman, Robert. "Comment." In *Economic Aspects of Population Change*, edited by Elliott R. Morss and Ritchie H. Reed. Washington: Government Printing Office, 1972.
Dresch, Stephen P. "Demography, Technology, and Higher Education: Toward a Formal Model of Educational Adaptation." *Journal of Political Economy* 83 (June 1975): 535-569.
Duncan, Greg J., and Morgan, James N. eds. *Five Thousand American Families— Patterns of Economic Progress*, vol. 4. Ann Arbor: University of Michigan, Institute for Social Research, 1975.
Easterlin, Richard A. "Long Swings in U.S. Demographic and Economic Growth: Some Findings on the Historical Pattern." *Demography* 2 (1965): 490-507.
―――. *Population, Labor Force, and Long Swings in Economic Growth: The American Experience*. New York: Columbia University Press (for National Bureau of Economic Research), 1968.

———. "Relative Economic Status and the American Fertility Swing." In *Social Structure, Family Life Styles, and Economic Behavior*, edited by Eleanor B. Sheldon. Philadelphia: Lippincott, 1973.

Eilenstine, Donald L., and Cunningham, James P. "Projected Consumption Demands for a Stationary Population." *Population Studies* 26 (June 1972): 223–231.

Eisner, Robert. "A Distributed Lag Investment Function." *Econometrica* 28 (January 1960): 1–29.

———. "Capital Expenditures, Profits, and the Acceleration Principle." In *Models of Income Determination*. Princeton: Princeton University Press (for National Bureau of Economic Research), 1964.

———, and Nadiri, M. I. "Investment Behavior and the Neo-Classical Theory." *Review of Economics and Statistics* 50 (August 1968): 369–382.

———, and Strotz, R. H. "Determinants of Business Investment." In *Impacts of Monetary Policy*. Englewood Cliffs: Prentice-Hall (for Commission on Money and Credit), 1968.

Enke, Steven. "Population Growth and Economic Growth." *The Public Interest* 32 (Summer 1973): 86–96.

Espenshade, Thomas J. "How the Trend Toward a Stationary Population Affects Consumer Demand." *Population Studies* 32 (March 1978): 147–158.

Evans, V. Jeffery. "Higher Education in the Stationary Population: A Comment on North Carolina's System." In *Zero Population Growth: Implications*, edited by J. J. Spengler. Chapel Hill: University of North Carolina, Carolina Population Center, 1975.

———, and Vestal, B. "Local Growth Management: A Demographic Perspective." *North Carolina Law Review* 55 (March 1977): 421–460.

Eversley, David. "Demographic Aspects of Welfare Policies." Paper presented at the Council of Europe Seminar on the Implications of a Stationary or Declining Population in Europe, Strasbourg, September 1976.

———; Ermisch, J.; and Overton, E. "The Revision of Regional Plans and Regional Policy in Light of the Recent Stabilisation or of Possible Decrease in Population with Special Reference to the Demand for Housing." Paper presented at the IUSSP General Conference, Mexico City, August 1977.

Feldstein, Martin. "Social Security, Induced Retirement and Aggregate Capital Accumulation." *Journal of Political Economy* 82 (September–October 1974): 905–926.

———. "Toward a Reform of Social Security." *The Public Interest* 40 (Summer 1975): 75–95.

———. "Social Security and Saving: The Extended Life Cycle Theory." *American Economic Review* 66 (May 1976): 77–86.

———. "Facing the Social Security Crisis." *The Public Interest* 47 (Spring 1977): 88–100.

———, and Summers, Lawrence. "Is the Rate of Profit Falling?" *Brookings Papers on Economic Activity* (1: 1977): 211–227.

Finifter, Ada W. "American Emigration." *Society* 13 (July–August 1976): 30–36.

Foust, James D. "ZPG? Hansen, Myrdal, and Keynes Revisited." *Mississippi Valley Journal of Business and Economics* 10 (Fall 1974): 24-42.
Frejka, Tomas. "Reflections on the Demographic Conditions Needed to Establish a U.S. Stationary Population Growth." *Population Studies* 22 (November 1968): 379-397.
———. *The Future of Population Growth.* New York: Wiley, 1973.
Frieden, B. J., and Solomon, A. P. *The Nation's Housing: 1975 to 1985.* Cambridge: Joint Center for Urban Studies of MIT and Harvard, 1977.
Friedman, Judith J. "Some Implications of a Stationary Population for the Environment." Paper presented at the IUSSP General Conference, Mexico City, August 1977.
Friedman, Milton. *A Theory of the Consumption Function.* Princeton: Princeton University Press (for National Bureau of Economic Research), 1957.
———, and Kuznets, Simon. *Income from Independent Professional Practice.* New York: National Bureau of Economic Research, 1945.
Germany, Federal Republic. *Statistiches Jahrbuch 1976 für die Bundesrepublik Deutschland.* Stuttgart-Mainz: Statistiches Bundesamt, 1976.
———. *Arbeits—und Sozialstatistik.* Bonn: Bundesarbeitsministerium, 1977.
Gibson, Campbell. "The Elusive Rise in the American Birthrate." *Science* 196 (29 April 1977): 500-503.
Gordon, Robert A. *The Goal of Full Employment.* New York: Wiley, 1967.
Gordon, Robert J. "Structural Unemployment and the Productivity of Women." In *Stabilization of the Domestic and International Economy,* edited by K. Brunner and A. H. Meltzer. Amsterdam: North-Holland, 1977.
Graf, Hans-Georg. "Zusammenhänge und Wechselbeziehungen zwischen Bevölkerungs-und Wirtschaftswachstum." In *Bevölkerungsbewegung zwischen Quantität und Qualität: Beitrage zum Problem einer Bevölkerungspolitik in Industriellen Gesellschaften,* edited by Franz-Xavier Kaufman. Stuttgart: Enke Verlag, 1975.
Greenough, William C., and King, Francis P. *Pension Plans and Public Policy.* New York: Columbia University Press, 1976.
Guilmot, Pierre, assisted by Monique Renaerts. "Demographic Introduction." Paper presented at the Council of Europe Seminar on the Implications of a Stationary or Declining Population in Europe, Strasbourg, September 1976.
Hall, Robert E. "The Process of Inflation in the Labor Market." *Brookings Papers on Economic Activity* (2: 1974): 343-393.
Hansen, Alvin H. "Economic Progress and Declining Population Growth." *American Economic Review* 29 (March 1939): 1-15.
———. *Fiscal Policies and Business Cycles.* New York: Norton, 1941.
Heber, B. P. *Modern Public Finance.* Homewood: Irwin, 1967.
Heeren, H. J. "Declining Population Growth and Population Policy." *International Social Science Journal* 26 (2: 1974): 244-254.
Heeren, R. Stanley. "The Relationships between Age Structure and Income Distribution." Durham: Duke University, Center for the Study of Aging and Human Development, 1976.

Hendershot, Gerry E. "Population Size, Military Power, and Antinatalist Policy." *Demography* 10 (November 1973): 517-524.
Henle, Peter. "Recent Trends in Retirement Benefits Related to Earnings." *Monthly Labor Review* 95 (June 1972): 12-20.
Hickman, Bert F., and Coen, Robert M. *An Annual Growth Model of the U.S. Economy.* Amsterdam: North-Holland, 1976.
Hicks, J. R. *A Contribution to the Theory of the Trade Cycle.* Oxford: Oxford University Press, 1950.
Hieser, R. O. "The Economic Consequences of Zero Population Growth." *Economic Record* 49 (June 1973): 241-262.
Higgins, Benjamin. "Public Work and Our Post War Economy." In *Postwar Goals and Economic Reconstruction,* edited by Arnold J. Zurcher and Richmond Page. New York: New York University, Institute of Postwar Reconstruction, 1944.
Hirst, E. "Residential Energy Use Alternatives: 1976 to 2000." *Science* 194 (17 December 1976): 1247-1252.
Hogan, Timothy D. "Implications of Zero Population Growth." *Arizona Business* 19 (December 1972): 3-11.
———. "The Implications of Population Stationarity for the Social Security System." *Social Science Quarterly* 55 (June 1974): 151-158.
———. "The Impact of Zero Population Growth on the OASDHI Program: Comment." *Journal of Risk and Insurance* 43 (June 1976): 317-321.
Hoover, Edgar M. "Reduced Population Growth and the Problems of Urban Areas." In *Population Distribution and Policy,* edited by Sarah Mills Mazie. Washington: Government Printing Office, 1972.
Howard, John A., and Lehmann, Donald R. "The Effect of Different Populations on Selected Industries in the Year 2000." In *Economic Aspects of Population Change,* edited by Elliott R. Morss and Ritchie H. Reed. Washington: Government Printing Office, 1972.
Institut National d'Études Démographiques (INED). "Sixième rapport sur la situation démographique de la France." *Population* 32 (March-April 1972): 254-338.
Johnston, Denis F. "Illustrative Projections of the Labor Force of the United States to 2040." In *Economic Aspects of Population Change,* edited by Elliott R. Morss and Ritchie H. Reed. Washington: Government Printing Office, 1972.
Johnston, J. *Econometric Methods.* New York: McGraw-Hill, 1972.
Jones, David. "Projections of Housing Demand to the Year 2000, Using Two Population Projections." In *Economic Aspects of Population Change,* edited by Elliott R. Morss and Ritchie H. Reed. Washington: Government Printing Office, 1972.
Jorgenson, Dale W. "Investment Behavior in U.S. Manufacturing, 1947-1960." *Econometrica* 35 (April 1967): 169-220.
———. "Optimal Capital Accumulation and Corporate Investment Behavior." *Journal of Political Economy* 76 (November 1968): 1123-1151.
———. "Econometric Studies of Investment Behavior." *Journal of Economic Literature* 9 (December 1971): 1111-1148.

Jupp, Kathleen M. "The Borrie Report: Background, Findings, Recommendations." *Population and Development Review* 2 (March 1976): 65–77.
Jürgens, Hans W. "Sociopsychological Implications of a Population Decrease." Paper presented at IUSSP General Conference, Mexico City, August 1977.
Jusenius, C. L., and Ledebur, L. C. "A Myth in the Making: The Southern Economic Challenge and Northern Economic Decline." Washington: U.S. Department of Commerce, Economic Development Administration, November 1976.
———, and ———. "Federal and Regional Responses to the Economic Decline of the Northern Industrial Tier." Washington: U.S. Department of Commerce, Economic Development Administration, March 1977.
Katona, George. "Private Pensions and Individual Saving." Monograph no. 40. Ann Arbor: University of Michigan, Institute for Social Research, 1965.
Kelley, Allen C. "Demographic Changes and American Economic Development." In *Economic Aspects of Population Change*, edited by Elliott R. Morss and Ritchie H. Reed. Washington: Government Printing Office, 1972.
———. "Demographic Change and the Size of the Government Sector." *Southern Economic Journal* 43 (October 1976): 1056–1066. (a).
———. "Savings, Demographic Change, and Economic Development." *Economic Development and Cultural Change* 24 (July 1976): 683–693. (b)
Kelly, William J. "Economic and Demographic Determinants of the Viability of Nations." *Journal of Peace Studies* 2 (Spring 1976): 57–75.
Keyfitz, Nathan. "Models of Population Dynamics: The Partial Fraction Components of Population Change." *Journal of the American Statistical Association* 60 (June 1965): 655.
———. "Changing Vital Rates and Age Distribution." *Population Studies* 22 (July 1968): 235–252.
———. "On the Momentum of Population Growth." *Demography* 8 (February 1971): 71–80.
———. "Individual Mobility in a Stationary Population." *Population Studies* 27 (July 1973): 335–352.
———. "Demographic Changes and Funding for Pension Plans." Paper presented at the Bald Peak Conference, Federal Reserve Bank of Boston, October 1976.
Keynes, John M. "Some Economic Consequences of a Declining Population." *Eugenics Review* 29 (March 1937): 13–17.
Klotz, Benjamin P. "Oscillatory Growth in Three Nations." *Journal of the American Statistical Association* 68 (September 1973): 562–567.
———, and Neal, Larry. "Spectral and Cross-Spectral Analysis of the Long-Swing Hypothesis." *Review of Economics and Statistics* 55 (August 1973): 291–298.
Kreps, Juanita M. "Economics of a Stationary Population: Implications for the Elderly." Durham: Duke University, Center for the Study of Aging and Human Development, 1976.
———; Ferguson, Charles; and Folsom, James. "Employment of Older Work-

ers." In *Employment, Income and Retirement Problems of the Aged*, edited by Juanita M. Kreps et al. Durham: Duke University Press, 1963.

Kuznets, Simon. *Secular Movements in Production and Prices*. New York: Houghton-Mifflin, 1934.

———. "Population Change and Aggregate Output." In *Demographic and Economic Change in Developed Countries*. New York: National Bureau of Economic Research, 1960.

Lancaster, Clarise, and Scheuren, Frederick J. "Counting the Uncountable Illegals: Some Initial Statistical Speculations Employing Capture-Recapture Techniques." Paper presented at the annual meeting of the American Statistical Association, Chicago, 1977.

Lauriat, Patience, and Rabin, William. "Men Who Claim Benefits Before Age 65: Findings from the Survey of New Beneficiaries, 1968." *Social Security Bulletin* 33 (November 1970): 2–26.

Lee, Ronald D. *Fluctuations in U.S. Fertility, Age Structure and Income*. Final report on Contract NO1-HD-42857 submitted to the National Institute for Child Health and Human Development, July 1977.

Leibenstein, Harvey. "The Impact of Population Growth on the American Economy." In *Economic Aspects of Population Change*, edited by Elliott R. Morss and Ritchie H. Reed. Washington: Government Printing Office, 1972.

Leibling, H. I., and Russel, J. M. "Forecasting Business Investment by Anticipation Surveys and Econometric Models in 1968–1969." *Proceedings of the American Statistical Association, Business and Economics Statistics Section* (1969): 250–260.

Leuchtenburg, William. *Franklin Roosevelt and the New Deal, 1932–1940*. New York: Harper and Row, 1963.

Leyhausen, Paul. "Bevölkerungsdichte und Ökologie." In *Sterbendes Volk? Fakton, Ursachen, Konsequenzen des Geburtenrückgangs in der BRD*, edited by Johannes Gründel. Dusseldorf: Patmos Verlag, 1973.

Lösch, August. *Bevölkerungswellen und Wechsellagen*. Jena: G. Fischer, 1936.

Lucas, Robert E., Jr. "Optimal Investment Policy and the Flexible Accelerator." *International Economic Review* 8 (February 1967): 78–85.

Maillat, Denis. "Population Growth and Economic Growth." Paper presented at the Council of Europe Seminar on the Implications of a Stationary or Declining Population in Europe, Strasbourg, September 1976.

Marcin, Thomas E. *The Effects of Declining Population Growth on the Demand for Housing*. St. Paul: North Central Forest Experiment Station, 1974.

Markides, Kyriakos S., and Tracy, George S. "The Effect of the Age Structure of a Stationary Population on Crime Rates." *Journal of Criminal Law and Criminology* 67 (September 1976): 351–355.

Matthiessen, Poul C. "Short, Medium and Long Term Implications of a Stationary or Declining Population on Population Distribution, on Urbanization, on Migratory Movements, on the Development of Households and Families, on the Life Cycle of the Family and on the Reaction of the People to a Declining Population." Paper presented at the IUSSP General Conference, Mexico City, August 1977.

Mayer, Lawrence A. "It's a Bear Market for Babies, Too." *Fortune* 90 (December 1974): 134–137, 206, 210, 212.
Mazek, Warren F., and Chang, John. "The Chicken or Egg Fowl-Up in Migration: A Comment." *Southern Economic Journal* 39 (July 1972): 133–139.
Mazie, Sarah Mills, ed. *Population Distribution and Policy*, vol. 5. Research Reports, Commission on Population Growth and the American Future. Washington: Government Printing Office, 1972.
McKinley, Charles, and Frase, Robert. *Launching Social Security*. Madison: University of Wisconsin Press, 1970.
McMahon, Walter W. *Investment in Higher Education*. Lexington: D. C. Heath, 1974.
———. "Economic and Demographic Effects on Investment in Higher Education." *Southern Economic Journal* 41 (January 1975): 506–514.
McNicoll, Geoffrey. "The Borrie Report: Issues of Population Policy in Australia." *Population and Development Review* 2 (March 1976): 79–89.
Michael, Robert. "Education and the Derived Demand for Children." *Journal of Political Economy* 81 (March–April 1973): 128–164 (supplement).
Miller, Herman P. "Population, Pollution, and Affluence." *Business Horizons* 14 (April 1971): 5–16.
Mincer, Jacob. "Market Prices, Opportunity Costs, and Income Effects." In *Measurement in Economics*, edited by Carl Christ et al. Stanford: Stanford University Press, 1963.
———. "Unemployment Effect of Minimum Wages." *Journal of Political Economy* 84 (August 1976): 87–104 (supplement).
Modigliani, Franco. "The Monetarist Controversy or Should We Forsake Stabilization Policy?" *American Economic Review* 67 (March 1977): 1–19.
———, and Ando, Albert. "The 'Life Cycle' Hypothesis of Savings." *American Economic Review* 53 (March 1963): 55–84.
———, and Papademos, Lucas. "Targets for Monetary Policy in the Coming Year." *Brookings Papers on Economic Activity* (1: 1975): 141–163.
Morrison, Peter A. "The Impact of Population Stabilization on Migration and Redistribution." In *Population Distribution and Policy*, edited by Sarah Mills Mazie. Washington: Government Printing Office, 1972.
———. "The Demographic Context of Educational Policy Planning." Paper no. P-5592. Santa Monica: The Rand Corporation, 1976. (a).
———. "Rural Renaissance in America? The Revival of Population Growth in Remote Areas." *Population Bulletin* 31 (October 1976): 1–26. (b).
———. "Demographic Trends That Will Shape Future Housing Demand." *Policy Sciences* 8 (1977): 203–215. (a).
———. "Migration and Rights of Access: New Public Concerns of the 1970s." Paper no. P-5785. Santa Monica: The Rand Corporation, 1977. (b).
Munnell, Alicia H. *The Effects of Social Security on Personal Savings*. Cambridge: Ballinger, 1974. (a).
———. "The Impact of Social Security on Personal Savings." *National Tax Journal* 27 (December 1974): 553–567. (b).

———. "The Future of Social Security." *New England Economic Review* 40 (July-August 1976): 3–28.

Muth, Richard F. "Migration: Chicken or Egg." *Southern Economic Journal* 38 (January 1971): 295–306.

———. "The Chicken or Egg Fowl-Up in Migration: Reply." *Southern Economic Journal* 39 (July 1972): 139–141.

Myrdal, Gunnar. *Population: A Problem for Democracy.* Cambridge: Harvard University Press, 1940.

Nadiri, M. I., and Rosen, Sherwin. "Interrelated Factor Demand Functions." *American Economic Review* 59 (September 1969): 457–471.

———, and ———. *A Disequilibrium Model of Demand for Factors of Production.* New York: National Bureau of Economic Research, 1974.

National Center for Health Statistics. *Fertility Tables for Birth Cohorts by Color: United States, 1917–73.* Washington: Government Printing Office, 1976.

Neal, Larry. "Structural Breaks, Shifting Harmonics or Random Effects?" *Proceedings of the American Statistical Association, Business and Economics Statistics Section* (1974): 34–43.

———. "Cross-Spectral Analysis of Long Swings in Atlantic Migration." *Research in Economic History* 1 (1976): 260–297.

———, and Uselding, Paul. "Immigration—A Neglected Source of American Economic Growth, 1790–1914." *Oxford Economic Papers* 24 (March 1972): 68–88.

Notestein, Frank W. "Zero Population Growth." *Population Index* 36 (October 1970): 444–452.

———. "Negative Population Growth: How to Go About It?" *Population Index* 41 (October 1975): 567–569.

O'Neill, C. J. "Fertility Trends and Implications in New Zealand—Transition to a Stationary Population." Paper presented at the IUSSP General Conference, Mexico City, August 1977.

Orcutt, Guy; Caldwell, Steven; and Wertheimer, Richard II. *Policy Exploration Through Microanalytic Simulation.* Washington: The Urban Institute, 1976.

Organisation for Economic Cooperation and Development. *Expenditure Trends in OECD Countries, 1960–1980.* Paris: OECD, 1972.

———. *Quarterly National Accounts Bulletin.* Paris: OECD, December 1975.

———. *Quarterly National Accounts Bulletin.* Paris: OECD, March 1977.

Organski, Katherine, and Organski, A. F. K. *Population and World Power.* New York: Knopf, 1961.

Pechman, Joseph; Aaron, Henry; and Taussig, Michael. "The Objectives of Social Security." In *Old Age Income Assistance.* Washington: U.S. Congress, Joint Economic Committee, 1967.

"Pension Reform—A 'Boon' that's Backfiring for Many." *U. S. News and World Report* 78 (16 June 1975): 73–74.

Perry, Charles; Anderson, Bernard; Rowan, Richard; and Northrup, Herbert. *The Impact of Government Manpower Programs.* Philadelphia: University of Pennsylvania, Industrial Research Unit, 1975.

Perry, George L. "Potential Output and Productivity." *Brookings Papers on Economic Activity* (1: 1977): 11–47.
Phelps, Edmund S. "Some Macroeconomics of Population Levelling." In *Economic Aspects of Population Change*, edited by Elliott R. Morss and Ritchie H. Reed. Washington: Government Printing Office, 1972.
Pitchford, J. D. *Population in Economic Growth*. Amsterdam: North-Holland, 1974.
Pool, D. Ian, and Bracher, Michael. "A Note on Implications of Canadian Family Formation in the Near Future." *Canadian Studies in Population* 1 (1974): 117–122.
Reddaway, W. B. *The Economics of a Declining Population*. New York: Macmillan, 1939.
———. "The Economic Consequences of Zero Population Growth." *Lloyds Bank Review* 124 (April 1977): 14–30.
Rejda, George E. "Social Security and the Paradox of the Welfare State." *Journal of Risk and Insurance* 37 (March 1970): 17–39.
———, and Shepler, Richard J. "The Impact of Zero Population Growth on the OASDHI Program." *Journal of Risk and Insurance* 40 (September 1973): 313–325.
Reno, Virginia. "Women Newly Entitled to Social Security Benefits." In *Preliminary Findings from the Survey of New Beneficiaries*. Report no. 4. Washington: Social Security Administration, 1973.
Resek, Robert W., and Siegel, Frederick. "Consumption Demand and Population Growth Rates." *Eastern Economic Journal* 1 (October 1974): 282–290.
Resources for the Future. *RFF/NIH Project Reports*. Washington: Resources for the Future, 1978.
Ridker, Ronald G., and Watson, William D. *Energy and the Environment in the United States, 1975–2025*. Washington: Resources for the Future, 1978.
———; ———; and Shapanka, A. "Economic, Energy, and Environmental Consequences of Alternative Energy Regimes, An Application of the RFF/SEAS Modeling System." Discussion paper no. D-6. Washington: Resources for the Future, 1977.
Rogers, Andrei. "The Mathematics of Multiregional Demographic Growth." *Environment and Planning* 5 (January–February 1973): 3–29.
———, and Willekens, Frans. "Spatial Zero Population Growth." Paper no. RM-76-25. Laxenburg: International Institute for Applied Systems Analysis, 1976.
Rowen, Hobart. "Illegal Alien Dilemma." *The Washington Post* (21 July 1977): A-19.
Rückert, G. R. "The Employment of Women as a Cause of a Declining Number of Births." Paper presented at the IUSSP General Conference, Mexico City, August 1977.
Ryder, Norman B. "A Demographic Optimum Population for the United States." In *Demographic and Social Aspects of Population Growth*, edited by Charles F. Westoff and Robert Parke, Jr. Washington: Government Printing Office, 1972.

---. "Two Cheers for ZPG." In *The No-Growth Society*, edited by Mancur Olson and Hans H. Lansberg. New York: Norton, 1973.

---. "Notes on Stationary Populations." *Population Index* 41 (January 1975): 3-28.

Samuelson, Paul. "An Exact Consumption-Loan Model of Interest With or Without the Social Contrivance of Money." *Journal of Political Economy* 66 (October 1958): 467-482.

Sauvy, Alfred. *Croissance Zéro?* Paris: Calmann-Lévy, 1973.

Schmookler, Jacob. *Invention and Economic Growth*. Cambridge: Harvard University Press, 1966.

Schramm, R. "The Influence of Relative Prices, Production Conditions, and Adjustment Costs on Investment Behavior." *Review of Economic Studies* 37 (July 1970): 361-376.

Schubnell, Hermann. "Probleme des Null-Wachtums einer Bevölkerung." *Mitteilungsblatt der Österreichischen Gesellschaft für Statistik und Informatik* 4 (June 1974): 43-60. (a).

---. "Volkstad oder Neue Chancen: Ursachen und Auswirkungen des Geburtenrückgang." *Saarlandische Arbeitnehmer* 22 (4: 1974): 153-160. (b).

Schulz, James H. "The Economic Impact of an Aging Population." *The Gerontologist* 13 (Spring 1973): 111-118.

Schwarz, Karl. "Regional Differences in Natality and Consequences of the Decline in the Birth Rate for Problems of Regional Planning." Paper presented at the IUSSP General Conference, Mexico City, August 1977.

Serow, William J. "The Implications of Zero Growth for Agricultural Commodity Demand." *American Journal of Agricultural Economics* 54 (December 1972): 955-963.

---. "The Economics of Stationary and Declining Populations: Some Views from the First Half of the Twentieth Century." In *Zero Population Growth: Implications*, edited by J. J. Spengler. Chapel Hill: University of North Carolina, Carolina Population Center, 1975.

---. "Slow Population Growth and the Relative Size and Productivity of the Male Labor Force." *Atlantic Economic Journal* 4 (Spring 1976): 61-68.

Sica, Mario. "Advantages and Disadvantages of Recourse to Immigration in a Situation of Population Decline." Paper presented at the Council of Europe Seminar on the Implications of a Stationary or Declining Population in Europe, Strasbourg, September 1976.

Silver, Morris. "Births, Marriages, and Business Cycles in the United States." *Journal of Political Economy* 73 (June 1965): 237-255.

Simon, Julian L. "The Influence of Population Growth on per Worker Income in Developed Countries." Urbana: University of Illinois, Department of Economics, 1971.

---. *The Economics of Population Growth*. Princeton: Princeton University Press, 1977.

Simons, John. "The Interpretation of Survey Data on Attitudes to Family Size." Paper presented at the Council of Europe Seminar on the Implications of a Stationary or Declining Population in Europe, Strasbourg, September 1976.

Sklar, June, and Berkov, Beth. "The American Birth Rate: Evidence of a Coming Rise." *Science* 189 (29 August 1975): 693–700.
Smith, Ralph E. "A Simulation Model of the Demographic Composition of Employment, Unemployment, and Labor Force Participation: Status Report." Working Paper 350-65. Washington: The Urban Institute, 1974.
Spengler, Joseph J. "Aging Populations: Mechanics, Historical Emergence, Impact." In *Employment, Income, and Retirement Problems of the Aged*, edited by Juanita M. Kreps, *et al.* Durham: Duke University Press, 1963.
———. *Declining Population Growth Revisited*. Chapel Hill: University of North Carolina, Carolina Population Center, 1971.
———. "Declining Population Growth: Economic Effects." In *Economic Aspects of Population Change*, edited by Elliott R. Morss and Ritchie H. Reed. Washington: Government Printing Office, 1972. (a).
———. "Prospective Population Change and Price Level Tendencies." *Southern Economic Journal* 38 (April 1972): 459–467. (b).
———. *Population and America's Future*. San Francisco: W. H. Freeman, 1975. (a).
———. "Stationary Populations: Economic and Educational Implications." *Canadian Studies in Population* 2 (1975): 1–14. (b).
———. "Stationary Populations and Changes in Age Structure: Implications for the Economic Security of the Aged." Durham: Duke University, Center for the Study of Aging and Human Development, 1976.
———. "Economic Implications of Low Fertility." Paper presented at NIH/WHO Conference on Social, Economic, and Health Aspects of Low Fertility, Washington, March 1977.
Stassart, Joseph. *Les Avantages et les Inconvénients Economique d'une Population Stationnaire*. The Hague: Martinus Nijhoff (for Faculté de Droit, Liège), 1965.
Stekler, H. O. "Forecasting with Econometric Models: An Evaluation." *Econometrica* 36 (July–October 1968): 437–463.
Sundquist, James L. *Dispersing Population*. Washington: The Brookings Institution, 1975.
Sweezy, Alan R. "The Natural History of the Stagnation Thesis." In *Zero Population Growth: Implications*, edited by J. J. Spengler. Chapel Hill: University of North Carolina, Carolina Population Center, 1975.
———, and Owens, Aaron. "The Impact of Population Growth on Employment." *American Economic Review* 64 (May 1974): 45–50.
Terborgh, George. *The Bogey of Economic Maturity*. Chicago: Machinery and Allied Products Institute, 1945.
Thompson, Gayle. "Income of the Aged Population: 1971 Money Income and Changes for 1967." Research and Statistical Note no. 14. Washington: Social Security Administration, 1973.
Thompson, Lawrence H. "An Analysis of the Factors Currently Determining Benefit Level Adjustments in the Social Security Retirement Program." Technical Analysis Paper no. 1. Washington: U. S. Department of Health, Education and Welfare, Office of Income Security Policy, September 1974.
———. "An Analysis of the Issues Involved in Securing Constant Replacement

Rates in the Social Security OASDHI Program." Technical Analysis Paper no. 5. Washington: U. S. Department of Health, Education and Welfare, Office of Income Security Policy, May 1975.

Tobin, James. "The Wage–Price Mechanism: Overview of the Conference." In *The Econometrics of Price Determination*. Washington: Conference of the Board of Governors of the Federal Reserve System, October 1970.

Tucker, C. J. "Changing Patterns of Migration between Metropolitan and Non-Metropolitan Areas in the United States: Recent Evidence." *Demography* 13 (November 1976): 435–443.

Turchi, Boone A. "Stationary Populations: Pensions and Social Security." In *Zero Population Growth: Implications*, edited by J. J. Spengler. Chapel Hill: University of North Carolina, Carolina Population Center, 1975.

United Nations, Department of Economic and Social Affairs. *The Determinants and Consequences of Population Trends: New Summary of Findings on Interaction of Demographic, Economic and Social Factors*. Population Studies no. 50. New York: United Nations, 1973.

United States, Advisory Council on Social Security—1971. *Reports of the Quadrennial Advisory Council on Social Security*. Washington: Government Printing Office, 1971.

———, Advisory Council on Social Security—1975. *Reports of the Quadrennial Advisory Council on Social Security*. Washington: Government Printing Office, 1975.

———, Board of Trustees of the Federal Old-Age and Survivors Insurance and Disability Insurance Trust Funds. *Annual Report*. Washington: Government Printing Office, various years.

———, Bureau of the Census. *The Two-Child Family and Population Growth: An International View*. Washington: Government Printing Office, 1971.

———, ———. "Illustrative Population Projections for the United States: The Demographic Effects of Alternate Paths to Zero Growth." *Current Population Reports*, Series P-25, no. 480. April 1972. (a).

———, ———. "Projections of the Population of the United States, by Age and Sex: 1972 to 2020." *Current Population Reports*, Series P-25, no. 493, December 1972. (b).

———, ———. "Marital Status and Living Arrangements: March 1974." *Current Population Reports*, Series P-20, no. 271, October 1974.

———, ———. *Historical Statistics of the U. S., Colonial Times to 1970*. Washington: Government Printing Office, 1975. (a).

———, ———. "Projections of the Population of the United States: 1975 to 2050." *Current Population Reports*, Series P-25, no. 601, October 1975. (b).

———, ———. "Projections of the Number of Households and Families: 1975 to 1990." *Current Population Reports*, Series P-25, no. 607, August 1975. (c).

———, ———. "Estimates of the Population of States with Components of Change: 1970 to 1975." *Current Population Reports*, Series P-25, no. 640, November 1976. (a).

———, ———. *Statistical Abstract of the U.S., 1976*. Washington: Government Printing Office, 1976. (b).

———, ———. "Estimates of the Population of Counties and Metropolitan Areas: July 1, 1974 and 1975." *Current Population Reports*, Series P-25, no. 709, September 1977. (a).
———, ———. "Geographic Mobility: March 1975 to March 1976." *Current Population Reports*, Series P-20, no. 305, January 1977. (b).
———, ———. "Projections of the Population of the United States: 1977 to 2050." *Current Population Reports*, Series P-25, no. 704, July 1977. (c).
———, ———. "Fertility of American Women: June 1977 (Advance Report)." *Current Population Reports*, Series P-20, no. 316, December 1977. (d).
———, Bureau of Economic Analysis. *Long-Term Economic Growth: 1860–1970*. Washington: Government Printing Office, 1973.
———, Bureau of Labor Statistics. *Population and Labor Force Projections*. Bulletin no. 1809. Washington: Government Printing Office, 1974.
———, ———. *Employment and Earnings*. Washington: Government Printing Office, 1975.
———, Congress. *Studies in Public Welfare*. Paper no. 6, Joint Economic Committee. Washington: Government Printing Office, 1974.
———, Immigration and Naturalization Service. *1974 Annual Report*. Washington: Government Printing Office, 1975.
———, Office of Management and Budget. "Mid-Session Review of the 1976 Budget." Washington: Office of Management and Budget, May 1975.
van de Kaa, D. J. "Long-Term Population Policies in Western Europe." Paper presented at the Council of Europe Seminar on the Implications of a Stationary or Declining Population in Europe, Strasbourg, September 1976.
Van Gorkom, J. W. *Social Security—The Long Term Deficit*. Washington: American Enterprise Institute for Public Policy Research, 1976.
Wachter, Michael L. "A Labor Supply Model for Secondary Workers." *Review of Economics and Statistics* 54 (May 1972): 141–151.
———. "A Time-Series Fertility Equation: The Potential for a Baby Boom in the 1980's." *International Economic Review* 32 (October 1975): 609–623.
———. "The Changing Cyclical Responsiveness of Wage Inflation." *Brookings Papers on Economic Activity* (1: 1976): 115–159.
Wachter, Susan M. *Latin American Inflation*. Lexington: Lexington Heath, 1976.
Wander, Hilde. "Der Geburtenrückgang in Westeuropa Wirtschaftlich Gesehen." Kiel: Universität Kiel, Institut für Weltwirtschaft, 1971.
———. "The Decline of the Birth Rate in Western Europe: Economic Implications." Bloomington: Indiana University, International Development Research Center, 1972.
———. "Demographic Aspects of the Active Population." Paper presented at the Council of Europe Seminar on the Implications of a Stationary or Declining Population in Europe, Strasbourg, September 1976.
———. "Short, Medium, and Long Term Implications of a Stationary or Declining Population on Education, Labour Force, Housing Needs, Social Security and Economic Development." Paper presented at the IUSSP General Conference, Mexico City, August 1977.

Warren, Robert and Peck, Jennifer. "Emigration from the United States: 1960 to 1970." Paper presented at the annual meeting of the Population Association of America, Seattle, 1975.
Westchester (N.Y.) County Planning Department. "The Empty Classroom, What's Next." As reported in *The New York Times* (13 May 1977): B-8.
Westoff, Charles F. "The Populations of the Developed Countries." *Scientific American* 231 (September 1974): 108-120.
———, and Parke, Robert, Jr. eds. *Demographic and Social Aspects of Population Growth*, vol. I. Research Reports, Commission on Population Growth and the American Future. Washington: Government Printing Office, 1972.
———, and Ryder, Norman B. "The Predictive Validity of Reproductive Intentions." *Demography* 14 (November 1977): 431-453.
Wetrogan, Signe. "Birth Expectations and Subsequent Fertility." Paper presented at the Annual Meeting of the Population Association of America, New Orleans, 1973.
Whelpton, Pascal K.; Campbell, Arthur A.; and Patterson, John E. *Fertility and Family Planning in the United States*. Princeton: Princeton University Press, 1966.
"When Pension Liabilities Dampen Profits." *Business Week* 2385 (16 June 1975): 80.
Wijewickrema, S.; DeKerpel, A.; Despontin, M.; and Lesthaeghe, R. "Alternative Demographic Evolutions for Belgium and their Impact on Macro-Economic Growth: A Quantitative Approach." Brussels: Vrije Universiteit, Centrum voor Sociologie, n.d.
Williamson, Jeffrey G. "Public Expenditures and Revenue: An International Comparison." *Manchester School of Economics and Social Studies* 29 (January 1961): 43-56.
Wilson, Thomas. "Pensions, Inflation, and Growth." *Lloyds Bank Review* 108 (April 1973): 1-17.
Winger, Max. "Demographic Aspects of Sociology and Family Micro-Economics." Paper presented at the Council of Europe Seminar on the Implications of a Stationary or Declining Population in Europe, Strasbourg, September 1976.
Zellner, A. and Palme, F. "Time Series Analysis and Simultaneous Equations Econometric Models." *Journal of Econometrics* 2 (May 1974): 17-54.
Zinam, Oleg. "Optimum Population Concept and the Zero Population Growth Thesis." *Economia Internazionale* 27 (May 1974): 320-338.
Zollinger, R. "The Economic Position of Young Couples." Paper presented at the NIH/WHO Conference on Social, Economic, and Health Aspects of Low Fertility, Washington, March 1977.
zu Castell Rüdenhausen, A. G.; Marschalck, Peter; and Tennagels, Peter. "Implications of the Development of Population Structure and Distribution for Regional Social and Economic Policies under Conditions of Long-Term Stagnation." Paper presented at the IUSSP General Conference, Mexico City, August 1977.

Index

A
Aaron, Henry, 184, 187
Abortion, effects on fertility, 11
Abramovitz, Moses, 75, 115
Age composition, *see also* Dependency
  changes as a result of fertility change, 15, 43–48, 66–68
  economic consequences of changes, 16–17, 60
  and labor productivity, 18, 29–30, 134–135, 143, 254, 260
  in Sweden, 43–45
  in the United States, 5–8, 133, 169–171
  in West Germany, 43–48, 55, 65–66
Agriculture
  as a bottleneck, 73
  demand for, 36
  and population redistribution, 27
Aid to Families with Dependent Children (AFDC), *see* Transfer payments
Almon, Clopper Jr., 128, 141
Alonso, William, 27–28, 236, 238
Alterman, Jack, 134n
Altmeyer, Arthur, 190, 192, 195n
Ando, Albert, 123n
Appleman, Jack, 25, 32–35, 146n
Archibald, G. C., 79n
Arthur, W. Brian, 40
Australia, National Population Inquiry, 14, *see also* Oceania

Austria
  natural increase, 43
  net reproduction rate, 42

B
Baily, Martin N., 96n
Barber, Clarence L., 19, 38–40
Bayo, Francisco, 177
Beale, Calvin L., 237n
Belgium
  natural increase, 43
  net reproduction rate, 42
Berelson, Bernard, 14
Berkov, Beth, 11
Berman, P., 245
Billings, John S., 225–226
Bixby, Lenore, 159
Blackburn, John, 190
Blake, Judith, 15
Bourgeois-Pichat, Jean, 14
Bowen, William, 189
Bracher, Michael, 15
Breckenfeld, G., 227
Brems, Hans, 108n, 109
Brinkman, George L., 26–27
Browning, Edgar K., 23, 188–189
Browning, Harley L., 31
Buchanan, James, 188
Burns, Arthur F., 75
Butz, William P., 12

C

Cagan, Philip, 186
Calot, Gerard, 39–40
Campbell, Arthur A., 11
Campbell, Colin, 188
Canada, *see also* North America
  consumption patterns, 33–34
  health care, 36
  social security, 23
Capital, *see also* Human capital; Savings
  accumulation, 72, 97, 101–102
  and aggregate demand, 74
  and dependency, 143, 249
  and economic change, 104–105
  effects of education and, 25–26, 64–65, 125
  net investment, 19
  and nonaccelerating rate of inflation, 89–91
  and productivity, 19, 38–39
  surplus, 18
  and technological change, 21, 124
Capital–labor ratio, 17–18, 85–86, 102–103, 109–110, 252
Capital–output ratio, 19
Chang, John, 31
Clark, Robert L., 19, 22–23, 31, 180, 186, 250
Coale, Ansley J., 2n, 15, 17, 37, 104n, 168
Coen, Robert M., 86n
Cohen, Wilbur, 187
Consumption, *see also* Consumption patterns; Savings
  absolute level of, 32, 144
  and economic conditions, 52–53
  and education, 25–26, 52
  per capita, 17, 20, 32, 143, 153–154, 254
Consumption patterns, *see also* Education; Health services; Housing; Savings; Transportation
  effects of demographic change on, 32–34, 58–61, 133, 140–141, 145–148, 251, 260
  role of government, 35–36, 141–142
  role of industry, 35
Cooper, Ronald L., 107n
Cornelius, Wayne A., 5n
Council of Europe, 14
Cunningham, James P., 33, 148n

D

Davis, Kingsley, 38

Day, Lincoln H., 29–30
De Kerpel, A., 43n, 49n
Denison, Edward F., 134n
Denmark
  natural increase, 43
  net reproduction rate, 42
Denton, Frank T., 20, 23, 33–34, 36
Dependency, *see also* Age composition; Social security and pensions
  adult versus child, 16–17, 19, 57–58, 60, 65–66, 131, 169–171, 249–250, 259–260
  effects of changes in the retirement age on, 31
  effects on capital formation, 143, 249
  in Europe, 48, 57
de Sandre, Paolo, 40
Domar, Evsey D., 19–20, 108–109
Dorfman, Robert, 18, 30
Dresch, Stephen P., 25
Duncan, Greg J., 212

E

Easterlin fertility hypothesis, 11–12, 93
Easterlin, Richard A., 11, 12n, 76n, 93n, 112, 121n, 253
East Germany, *see* Germany, Democratic Republic
Economic conditions, effect on demographic behavior, 11–12, 40, 51–53, 93, 108, 110–113, 121–122, 249, *see also* Income; Inflation; Labor Force; Wages
Economic cycles
  induced by demographic change, 21, 38, 49, 53, 71, 102–103, 112–114, 117–120, 248, 250–253, 259
  Kuznets-type, 73, 75–76, 114, 120
Economic growth models
  accelerator, 105–107
  Harrod–Domar, 19–20, 108–109
  neoclassical, 20, 105–107, 109–110
  supply imbalance, 76–80
Economic policy
  fiscal, 71–73, 77, 79, 95–99, 103, 107, 252–253
  monetary, 17–18, 77, 79
Economic simulation models
  DYNASIM, 198–203
  RFF/SEAS, 128–142
Economies of scale, 32, 135, 155

Education, *see also* Human capital
  and age composition, 61–62
  and capital formation, 25–26, 64–65, 125
  and consumption, 25–26, 52
  elementary and secondary, 24–25, 54–55, 61, 145–146, 226, 245
  in Europe, 54–55
Eilenstine, Donald L., 33, 148n
Eisner, Robert, 105n
Energy
  as a bottleneck, 73
  effects of demographic change on, 154–155, 230
  and inflation, 139–140
  prices and population redistribution, 231
England, *see* United Kingdom
Enke, Steven, 16, 32
Environment, effects of demographic change on, 15, 150–153, 248
Espenshade, Thomas J., 33, 148n, 247–249
Europe, *see also* Austria; Belgium; Denmark; France; Germany, Democratic Republic; Germany, Federal Republic; Greece; Ireland; Italy; Netherlands; Portugal; Spain; Sweden; Switzerland; United Kingdom
  economic changes, 49–51
  fertility trends, 41–43, 68
  immigration, 39–40, 55, 69
  natural increase, 45
  population policy, 39–40, 69
  productivity, 39
Evans, V. Jeffery, 25–26, 30, 246
Eversley, David, 15, 24, 34

F

Feldstein, Martin, 91n, 157, 165n, 187–188
Fertility, *see also* Easterlin fertility hypothesis; Economic conditions, effect on demographic behavior; Natural increase; Population decline; Population growth
  and abortion, 11
  birth expectations and goals, 10–11
  in Europe, 41–43, 68
  fluctuations, 38, 43–44, 67, 248
  illegitimate, 11
  in the United States, 2–3, 5n, 10–12, 102, 168–169, 203–204, 225–226
  in West Germany, 41–43, 51, 59, 68

Finifter, Ada W., 5n
Forstall, Richard L., 237n
Foust, James D., 13
France
  fertility, 51
  immigration, 55
  natural increase, 42–43
  net reproduction rate, 42, 44
Frase, Robert, 181
Frejka, Tomas, 15
Frieden, B. J., 229
Friedman, Judith J., 15
Friedman, Milton, 123n, 187

G

Germany, Democratic Republic, natural increase, 41n
Germany, Federal Republic (as author), 57n
Germany, Federal Republic
  age composition, 43–48, 55, 65–66
  fertility, 41–43, 51, 59, 68
  immigration, 47, 55
  natural increase, 43, 48–49
  net reproduction rate, 42, 44
  pension plans, 55–57
  transfer payments, 57–58
Gibson, Campbell, 11
Gordon, Robert A., 96n
Gordon, Robert J., 96n
Graf, Hans-Georg, 65n
Greece
  natural increase, 43
  net reproduction rate, 42, 44
Greenough, William C., 164n, 165
Guilmot, Pierre, 15

H

Hall, Robert E., 95n
Hansen, Alvin H., 74, 102–104, 107, 252
Harrod, Roy F., 19–20, 108–109
Health services, effects of demographic change, 35–36, 57, 137, 145–146, 226, 249
Heber, B. P., 145
Hecht, Jacqueline, 39–40
Heeren, H. J., 38
Heeren, R. Stanley, 34–35
Hendershot, Gerry E., 39
Henle, Peter, 165
Hickman, Bert F., 86n

Hicks, J. R., 109
Hieser, R. O., 16, 18–19, 24, 28
Higgins, Benjamin, 102
Hirst, E., 230n
Hogan, Timothy D., 16, 22–23, 185–186
Hoover, Edgar M., 17, 26–27
Households
    female-headed, 210–211, 257
    formation, 112–114, 204, 227–229, 255, 257
    and marital status, 211–212
    size, 208–210
Housing
    effects of demographic change on, 36, 112, 124, 141, 226, 229
    and income elasticity, 19
Howard, John A., 32–34, 146
Human capital, *see also* Capital; Education
    and education, 26, 61–62, 125
    effects of demographic change on, 21, 66–67, 253
    effect of wage changes on, 35, 254
    and supply constraints, 97–98
    per worker, 18, 125

I
Income
    distribution and population change, 34–35, 198, 212–214, 257
    effects of demographic change on, 16, 60, 104, 143, 226, 229, 248–249
Inflation, *see also* Nonaccelerating inflation rate of unemployment
    effects of population change on, 21, 61–62, 72, 93, 252
    and employment, 95–97
    and energy production, 139–140
    and social security costs, 166, 174–175, 186, 256
    and supply constraints, 71, 78–79
    and transfer payments, 205
Infrastructure, effects of demographic change on, 53–55, 66, 112, 141, 226, 250–251
Innovation, *see also* Technical progress
    and age composition, 29–30
    and population growth, 18, 136–137, 155, 254
    and population size, 136

Institut National d'Etudes Démographique (INED), 51n
Internal migration, *see* Population redistribution
International migration
    and demand for labor, 69, 75, 94–95, 99, 123, 253, 258
    to Europe, 55
    illegal, 4n–5n, 227
    and social security costs, 176–177
    as stimulus to population growth, 40, 69, 258
    to the United States, past, 4–5, 103–104, 112
    to West Germany, 47, 55
International trade
    and economic interdependency, 13, 49–50, 94, 124
    effects of demographic change on, 38
Investment, *see* Capital
Ireland
    fertility, 41
    natural increase, 43
    net reproduction rate, 42
Italy
    natural increase, 43
    net reproduction rate, 42

J
Japan, productivity, 39
Johnston, Denis F., 28–30
Johnston, J., 222n
Jones, David, 32–33, 36, 146
Jorgenson, Dale W., 105n, 107n
Jupp, Kathleen, M., 14
Jürgens, Hans W., 15
Jusenius, C. L., 227

K
Katona, George, 186
Kelley, Allen C., 18–20, 24, 28, 32, 123n, 136n, 138n, 145
Kelly, William J., 39
Keyfitz, Nathan, 15, 31, 171n, 177n, 183
Keynes, John M., 18, 71, 74, 102n
King, Francis P., 164n, 165
Klotz, Benjamin P., 112–113, 115
Kreps, Juanita M., 16, 180–181

Kuznets, Simon, 73, 75–76, 114, 120, 123n, 136

L
Labor force
  demographic composition of, 30, 58, 64, 72–73, 77–78, 82–85, 91–95, 134–135, 252, 254, 260
  and employment, 54, 64, 72, 76, 80–85, 87–91, 96–97, 133–134, 155, 204–205, 251–252, 254
  industrial and occupational composition of, 28–29, 64
  participation, 17, 20–21, 29–30, 63–64, 74–75, 77–78, 92–93, 103–104, 107, 122, 131, 178–180, 204–205, 252–253, 260
  size, 16, 49–50, 63–64, 76, 103, 110, 129–130, 132
Labor mobility
  geographic, 17, 30, 153
  occupational, 17, 62, 64–65, 97
  promotion opportunities, 31, 93–94
Labor productivity, *see also* Capital–labor ratio; Education; Human capital
  and age composition, 18, 29–30, 134–135, 143, 254, 260
  and capital–labor ratio, 17, 63
  and demand structure, 143
  determinants, 131
  and human capital, 21
  and occupational composition, 64, 134, 143
Lancaster, Clarise, 4n
Lauriat, Patience, 165n
Ledebur, L. C., 227
Lee, Ronald D., 12
Lehmann, Donald R., 32–34, 146
Leibenstein, Harvey, 16, 18, 26, 28
Leibling, H. I., 107n
Leuchtenburg, William, 190
Lewis, Sinclair, 32
Leyhausen, Paul, 66n
Long, John, 10n
Losch, August, 51n
Lucas, Robert E. Jr., 105

M
Maillat, Denis, 24–25
Marcin, Thomas E., 33, 36
Markides, Kyriakos S., 15
Marriage and divorce, *see* Households
Matthiessen, Poul C., 15
Mayer, Lawrence A., 16
Mazek, Warren F., 31
Mazie, Sarah Mills, 15
McKay, Steven, 177
McKinley, Charles, 181
McLaughlin, M. W., 245
McMahon, Walter W., 25, 125
McNicoll, Geoffrey, 14, 40
Michael, Robert, 186
Miller, Herman P., 16
Mincer, Jacob, 78n, 111n
Modigliani, Franco, 75n, 95n, 123n
Morgan, James N., 212
Morrison, Peter A., 25–27, 36, 228, 235, 236n, 246, 249, 255–256, 259
Morss, Elliott R., 102n
Mortality
  and social security costs, 176, 256
  in the United States, 3–4
Munnell, Alicia H., 23–24, 165n, 180, 186–187
Muth, Richard F., 31
Myrdal, Gunnar, 102n

N
Nadiri, M. I., 105–107
Natural increase
  in Europe, 42–43, 48–49
  and internal migration, 227, 231–232, 236–243
Neal, Larry, 98n, 112–113, 117n, 123n, 249, 253, 258
Netherlands
  fertility, 43
  natural increase, 43
  net reproduction rate, 42, 44
Niehans, Jurg, 16
Nonaccelerating inflation rate of unemployment
  and the capital bottleneck, 89–91
  determinants of, 72, 96, 251–252
  and fiscal policy, 96–98, 252
  future levels, 91–93, 252
  model, 80–81
  normalized value, 82–85

North America, productivity, 39, *see also* Canada; United States
Notestein, Frank W., 15–16

O

Oceania, productivity, 39, *see also* Australia
O'Neill, C. J., 14
Orcutt, Guy, 198n, 207n
Organisation for Economic Cooperation and Development (OECD), 101, 102n, 123n
Organski, A. F. K., 39
Organski, Katherine, 39
Owens, Aaron, 29, 136

P

Palme, F., 107n
Papademos, Lucas, 95n
Parke, Robert Jr., 15
Pechman, Joseph, 186
Peck, Jennifer M., 5n
Perry, Charles, 97n
Perry, George L., 76n
Phelps, Edmund S., 17–18, 24, 35
Pitchford, J. D., 16
Pitts, Alfred M., 256, 258–259
Pool, D. Ian, 15
Population decline, *see also* Natural increase
  economic effects of, 62–63, 65–68
  in Europe, 42, 44, 249
  in the United States, 231–232, 236–238, 242, 245
  in West Germany, 48–49
Population growth, *see also* Stable population theory
  demographic consequences of, 15–16, 26–28, 37, 47–49
  population momentum, 15–16
  social consequences of, 14–15
  in the United States, future, 4–7, 129–130
  in the United States, past, 2–4, 6–7, 129
Population policy
  and fertility, 39–40, 258
  and the growth rate, 20–21, 37
  and immigration, 40, 69, 94–95, 99, 123, 258
  and internal redistribution, 153n, 246, 255–256, 259–260
  and size, 37, 39

Population redistribution, *see also* Labor mobility
  and age composition, 27, 30–31
  effects of fertility change on, 26–27, 153, 236–243, 255, 259–260
  in the United States, 8–10, 27, 230–236
Portugal
  fertility, 41
  natural increase, 43
  net reproduction rate, 42
Production function
  Cobb–Douglas, 20
  Leontief fixed coefficient, 77, 251

R

Rabin, William, 165n
Reddaway, W. B., 50n, 57n, 102n
Reed, Ritchie H., 102n
Rejda, George E., 22–23, 180, 185, 187
Renaerts, Monique, 15
Reno, Virginia, 178
Resek, Robert W., 32–33, 148n
Resources for the Future, 128, 140, 153, 254
Retirement age
  and demographic change, 64
  and dependency costs, 31, 180–181
  and employment, 74
  in Europe, 55n
Ricardo, David, 108
Ridker, Ronald G., 140n, 150, 248–249, 253–255
Rodgers, Andrei, 15, 177n
Rosen, Sherwin, 105–107
Rowen, Hobart, 4n
Rückert, G. R., 14
Russel, J. M., 107n
Ryder, Norman B., 11, 15, 29–31, 37–38

S

Samuelson, Paul A., 184, 194
Sauvy, Alfred, 14
Savings, *see also* Capital; Consumption
  effects of demographic change on, 24, 32, 123–124, 138–139, 143, 154, 253–254, 260
  effects of social security on, 157, 186–187, 189–190
  of firms, 24, 124, 138
Scheuren, Frederick J., 4n

Index

287

Schmookler, Jacob, 136
Schramm, R., 105, 107
Schubnell, Hermann, 14
Schulz, James H., 24, 31
Schwarz, Karl, 15
Secular stagnation thesis, 74–76, 102–103, 107, 252
Serow, William J., 13, 30, 32–33, 36, 247–249
Shepler, Richard J., 22–23, 180, 185, 187
Sica, Mario, 40
Siegel, Frederick, 32–33, 148n
Silver, Morris, 121n
Simon, Julian L., 123n, 138
Simons, John, 14
Sklar, June, 11
Smith, Ralph E., 204n
Social security and pensions, see also Dependency; Retirement age
  characteristics of the systems, 161–166
  costs, 22, 94, 163, 165–168, 172–174, 256, 259
  finances, 23–24, 183–184, 187–189, 193–196, 256
  goals, 65, 160, 165, 190–192
  and immigration, 176–177, 256
  and inflation, 166, 174–175, 186, 256
  intergenerational aspects of, 184–186, 192, 194–196
  and labor force participation, 74, 178–180
  and mortality change, 186, 256
  non-old-age components, 160, 182
  private plans, 23
  and retirement, 180–181
  and savings, 157, 186–187, 189–190
  in West Germany, 55–57
Solomon, A. P., 229
Solow, Robert M., 16
Spain
  fertility, 41
  natural increase, 43
  net reproduction rate, 42
Spencer, Byron G., 20, 23, 33–34, 36
Spengler, Joseph J., 16–17, 19, 21–22, 26–28, 30–32, 177n, 182, 250, 261n
Stable population, theory, 15–16, 42–45, 171, 248, 250–251, 260
Stassart, Joseph, 14
Stekler, H. O., 107n

Strotz, R. H., 105n
Summers, Lawrence, 91n
Sundquist, James L., 153n
Swan, Trevor W., 16
Sweden
  age composition, 43–45
  economic cycles, 117
  fertility, 51
  immigration, 55
  natural increase, 43
  net reproduction rate, 42–44
Sweezy, Alan R., 13, 18, 29, 136
Switzerland
  immigration, 55
  natural increase, 43
  net reproduction rate, 42

T

Taleb, Si-Ahmed, 14
Technical progress, 17–19, 20–21, 75, 124–125, 135–138, 260, see also Innovation
Terborgh, George, 102n, 123
Thompson, Gayle, 159
Thompson, Lawrence H., 166n
Tobin, James, 80n, 96n
Tracy, George S., 15
Transfer payments, see also Social security and pensions
  effects of demographic change on, 34, 198, 216–223, 245, 257, 259
  and government policy, 205–206
  effects of inflation on, 205
  and labor force participation, 84–85, 96, 98, 251
  and wages, 78–79
  in West Germany, 57–58
Transportation, effects of demographic change on demand for, 27–28, 137
Tucker, C. J., 235
Turchi, Boone A., 22–24, 185–186, 190

U

United Kingdom
  economic cycles, 117
  fertility, 51
  immigration, 55
  natural increase, 43
  net reproduction rate, 42, 44
United Nations, 15

United States (as author)
  Advisory Council on Social Security (1971), 163
  Advisory Council on Social Security (1975), 159, 161, 163, 165n, 178, 179n, 180, 185
  Board of Trustees of the Federal Old Age and Survivors Insurance and Disability Trust Funds, 163, 164n, 165n, 167n, 170, 172–173, 175, 177–179, 182
  Bureau of Economic Analysis, 178, 185
  Bureau of Labor Statistics, 133–134, 178
  Bureau of Mines, 149
  Bureau of the Census, 2n, 3–4, 7, 9, 11, 15, 25, 102, 113n, 129n, 130, 204, 229, 230n, 232–233, 240n, 254
  Commission on Population Growth and the American Future, 14, 32, 102
  Congress: Joint Economic Committee, 159, 160n
  Immigration and Naturalization Service, 4n–5n, 177
  National Center for Health Statistics, 2n
  Office of Management and Budget, 205n
United States
  age composition of, 5–8, 131, 169–171
  capital–labor ratio, 85–86
  economic conditions, 72–73, 143–148
  economic cycles, 75–76, 103–104, 114–121
  economic policy, 17–18, 95–99, 252–253
  fertility, 2–3, 5n, 10–12, 73, 168–169, 203–204
  households, 208–210, 228–229
  immigration levels, 4n–5n, 227
  immigration policy, 94–95, 99, 123, 253, 258
  income distribution, 212–214
  labor force and employment, 83–85, 89–92, 132–133
  mortality in, 2–4
  population decline, 231–232, 236–238, 242, 245
  population growth, 2–5, 129–130
  population redistribution, 8–10, 227, 230–236
  transfer payments, 22–24, 160, 163–164, 172–180, 259

Urban Institute, 198, 204
Uselding, Paul, 123n

V
van de Kaa, D. J., 40
van Gorkom, J. W., 23
Vestal, B., 246

W
Wachter, Michael L., 76n, 82n, 93n, 133n, 182, 249, 251–252, 254
Wachter, Susan M., 79n, 133n, 249, 251–252, 254
Wages
  differentials by demographic characteristics, 134–135
  effects of demographic change on, 21, 94, 98
  and human capital, 35, 354
  and social security costs, 174–175, 186, 256
  and transfer payments, 78–79
Wander, Hilde, 13, 17–18, 31, 34, 38, 50n, 248–251, 258–259
Ward, Michael P., 12
Warren, Robert, 5n
Watson, William D., 150
Wertheimer, Richard F. II, 256–257, 259
Westchester County (N. Y.) Planning Department, 245
West Germany, see Germany, Federal Republic
Westoff, Charles F., 11, 12n, 15
Wetrogan, Signe I., 11
Whelpton, Pascal K., 11
Wijewickrema, S., 38
Willekens, Frans, 15
Williamson, Jeffrey, G., 145
Wilson, Thomas, 188
Winger, Max, 15, 24

Z
Zedlewski, Sheila R., 256–257, 259
Zellner, A., 107n
Zelnick, Melvin, 2n, 168
Zinam, Oleg, 37
Zollinger, Richard, 28
zu Castell Rüdenhausen, A. G., 15